Shojo Beat

Story & Art by
Aya Nakahara

love★com

contents ④

The Story So Far...

Even though they're now in their second year of high school, "jumbo-gal" Risa Koizumi and shrimpy Atsushi Ôtani are still in the same class. The only difference is that now Risa has a crush on her former mortal enemy! Seiko, an adorable first-year girl, falls in love with Ôtani at first sight, and Ôtani eagerly laps up her attentions, which include a very public kiss! It looks like they'll start going out, but then it turns out that Seiko is actually a boy. That's a big shock for Ôtani and a big relief for Risa. But watching Seiko keep trying without letting her sex hold her back makes Risa want to cheer her on. Inspired by Seiko's example, Risa decides to stop worrying about her height and be more honest with herself. She loves Ôtani, and she's going to tell him!

T 251698

♥ To really get all the details, check out *Lovely Complex* vols. 1-3, available at bookstores everywhere!!

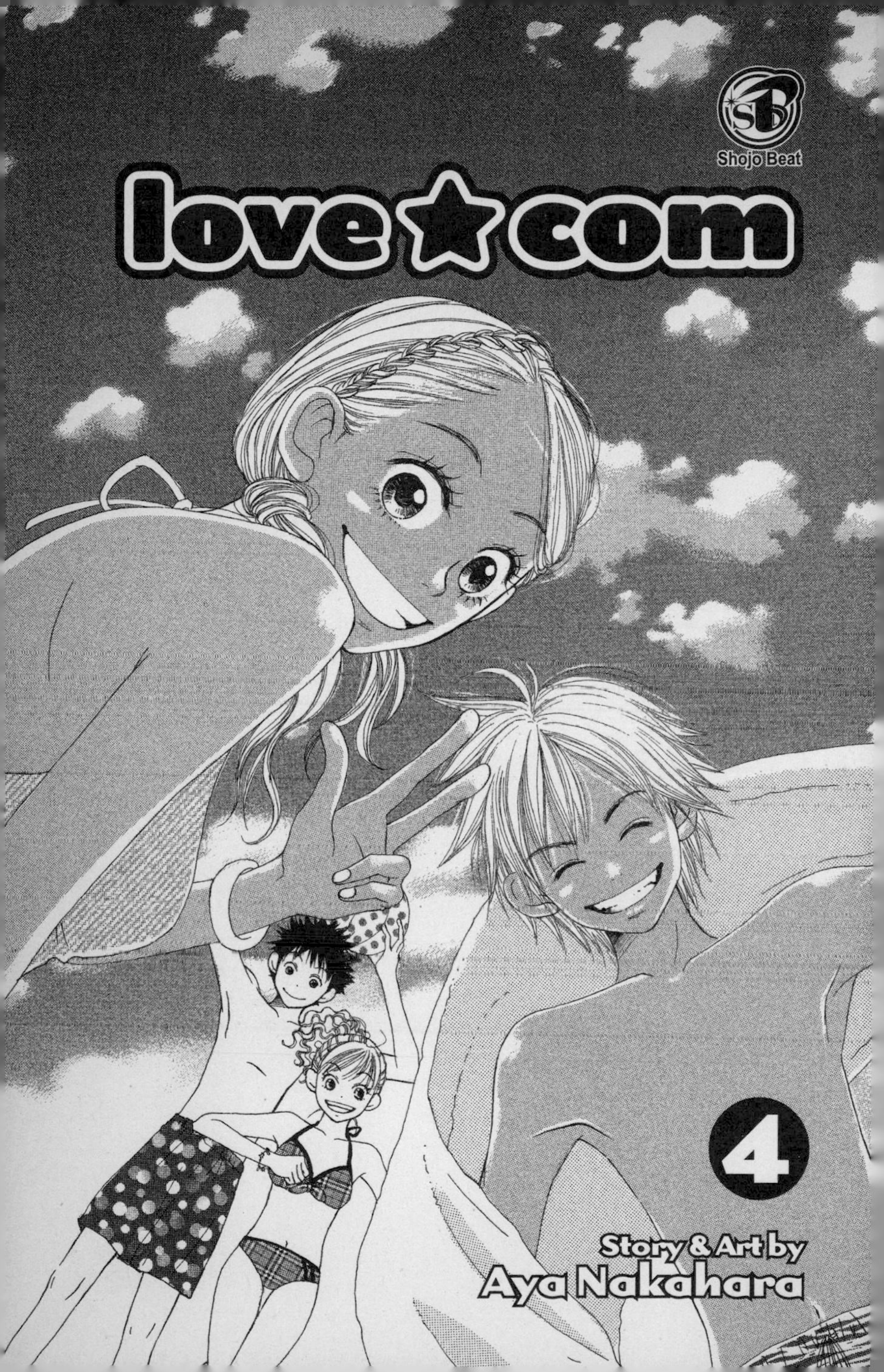
Shojo Beat
love☆com
4
Story & Art by
Aya Nakahara

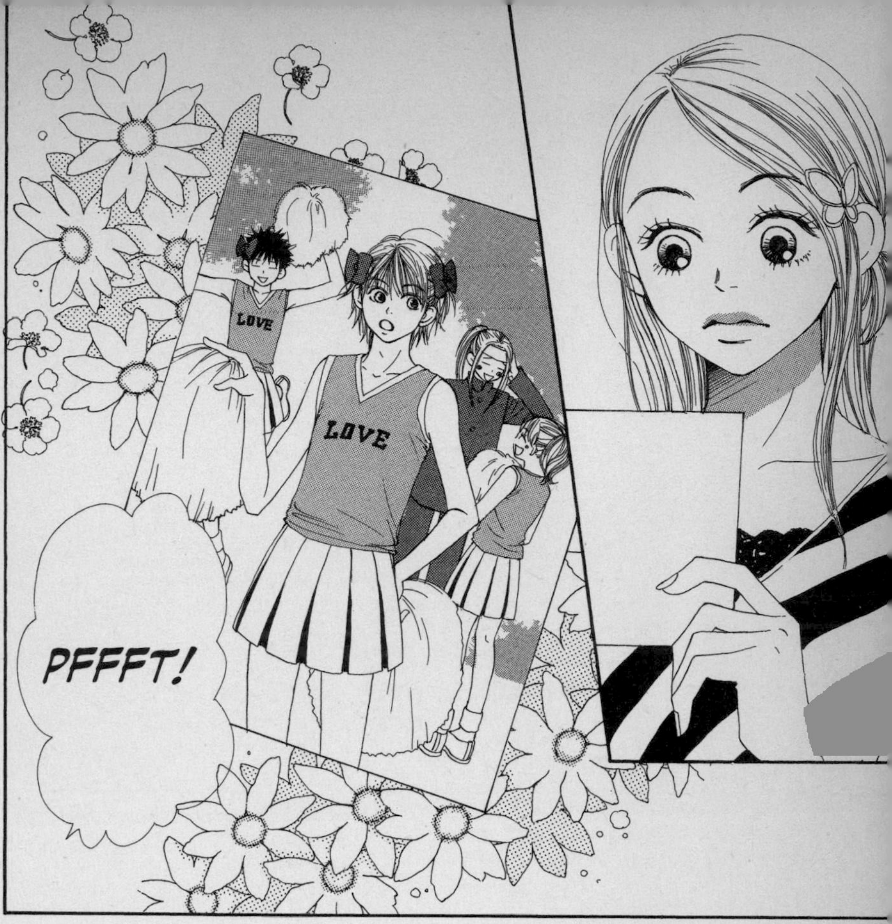
LOVE
LOVE
PFFFT!

CHAPTER 13

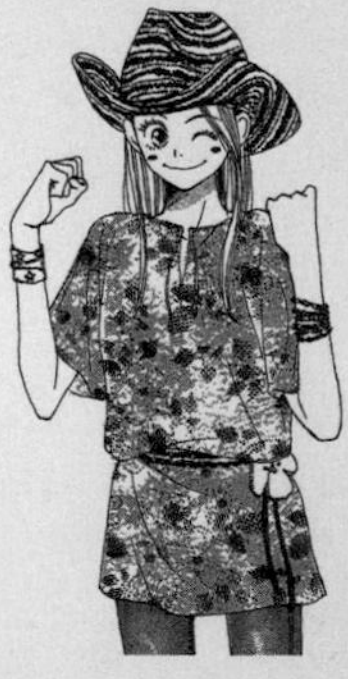

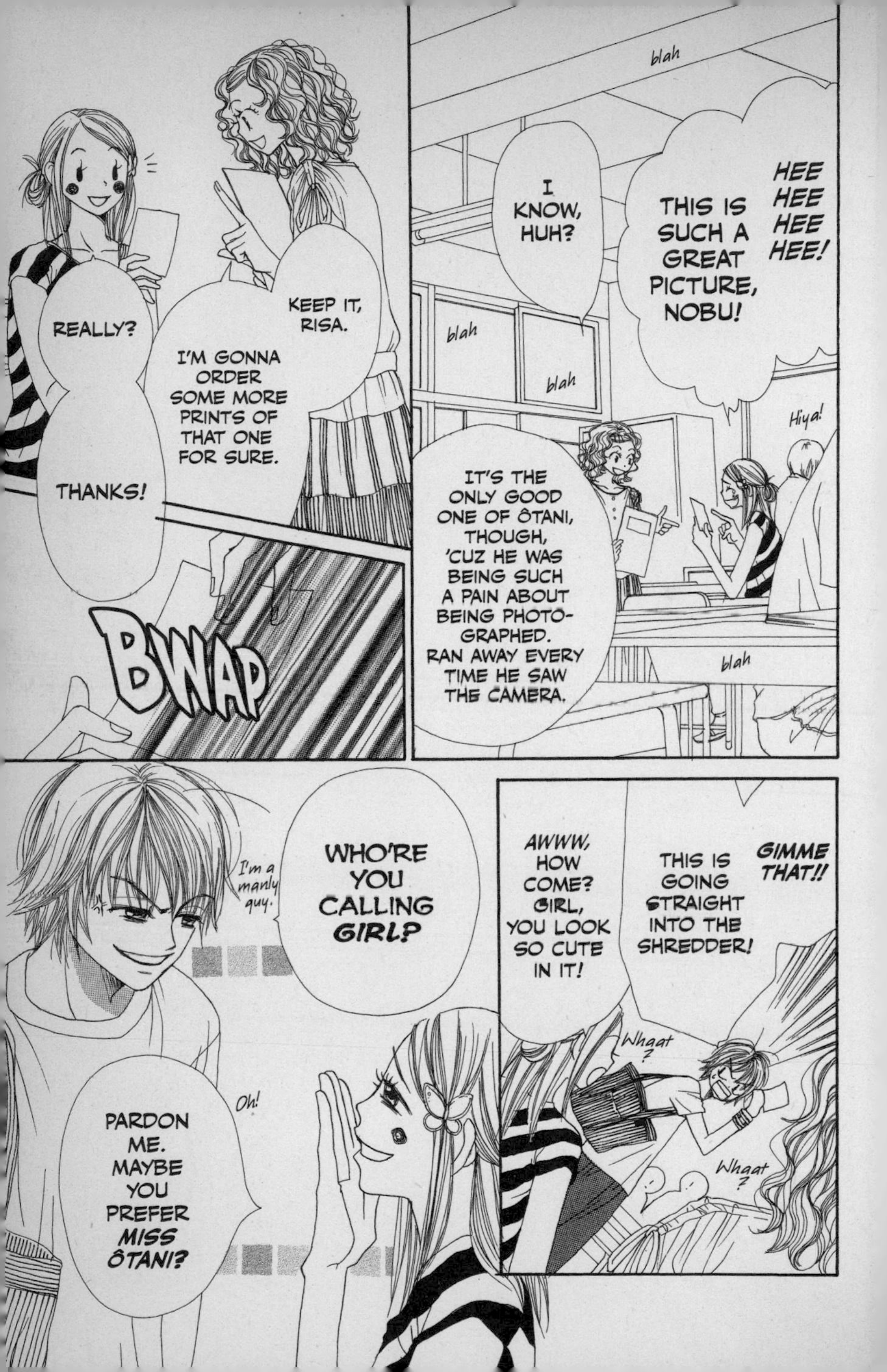
blah
HEE HEE HEE HEE!
THIS IS SUCH A GREAT PICTURE, NOBU!
I KNOW, HUH?
blah
blah
Hiya!
IT'S THE ONLY GOOD ONE OF ÔTANI, THOUGH, 'CUZ HE WAS BEING SUCH A PAIN ABOUT BEING PHOTO-GRAPHED. RAN AWAY EVERY TIME HE SAW THE CAMERA.
blah
KEEP IT, RISA.
I'M GONNA ORDER SOME MORE PRINTS OF THAT ONE FOR SURE.
REALLY?
THANKS!
BWAP
GIMME THAT!!
THIS IS GOING STRAIGHT INTO THE SHREDDER!
AWWW, HOW COME? GIRL, YOU LOOK SO CUTE IN IT!
Whaat?
Whaat?
WHO'RE YOU CALLING *GIRL*?
I'm a manly guy.
Oh!
PARDON ME. MAYBE YOU PREFER *MISS ÔTANI*?

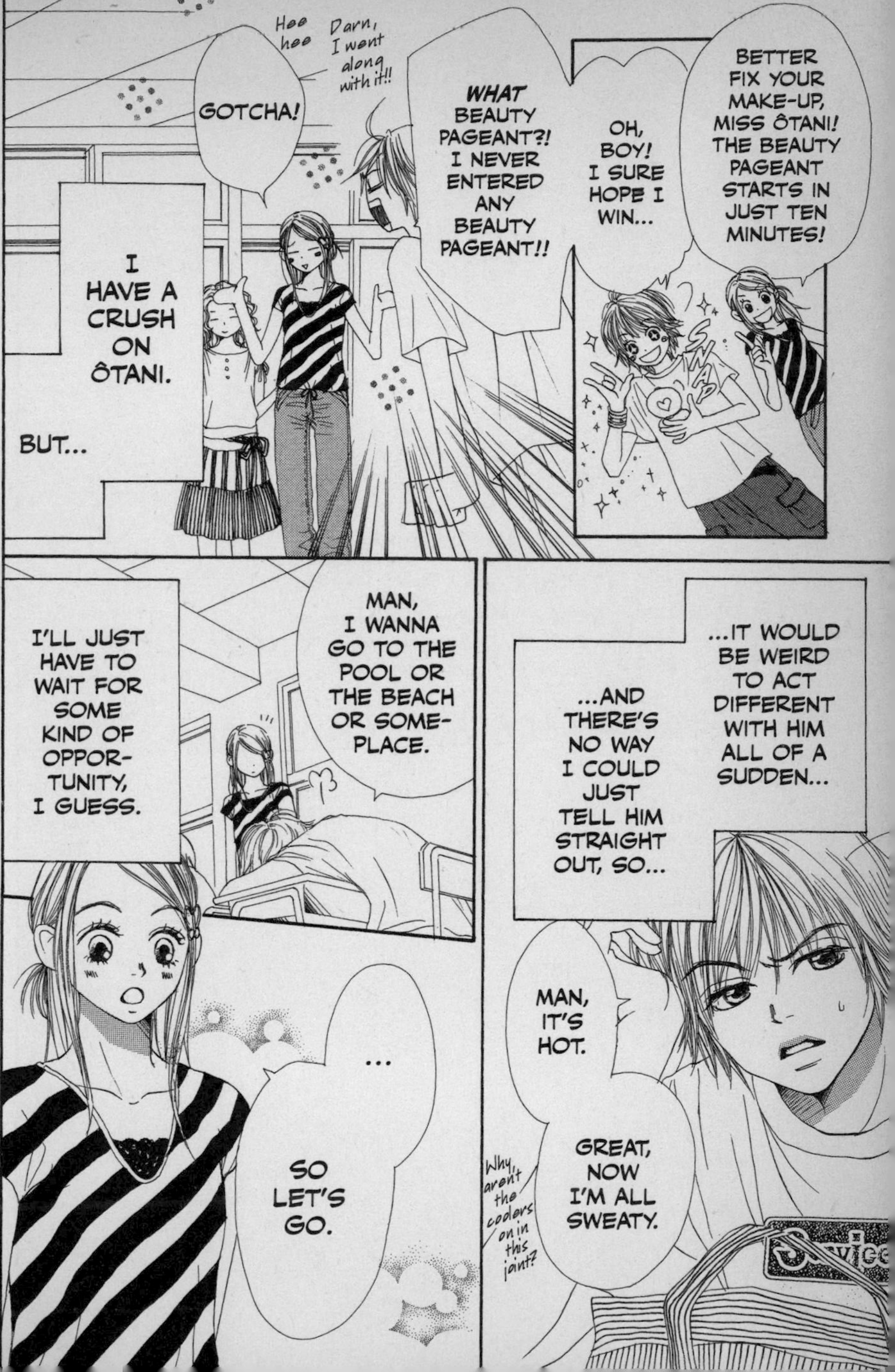
BETTER FIX YOUR MAKE-UP, MISS ÔTANI! THE BEAUTY PAGEANT STARTS IN JUST TEN MINUTES!
OH, BOY! I SURE HOPE I WIN...
WHAT BEAUTY PAGEANT?! I NEVER ENTERED ANY BEAUTY PAGEANT!!
Darn, I went along with it!!
Hee hee
GOTCHA!
I HAVE A CRUSH ON ÔTANI.
BUT...
...IT WOULD BE WEIRD TO ACT DIFFERENT WITH HIM ALL OF A SUDDEN...
...AND THERE'S NO WAY I COULD JUST TELL HIM STRAIGHT OUT, SO...
MAN, IT'S HOT.
GREAT, NOW I'M ALL SWEATY.
Why aren't the coolers on in this joint?
MAN, I WANNA GO TO THE POOL OR THE BEACH OR SOME-PLACE.
I'LL JUST HAVE TO WAIT FOR SOME KIND OF OPPOR-TUNITY, I GUESS.
...
SO LET'S GO.

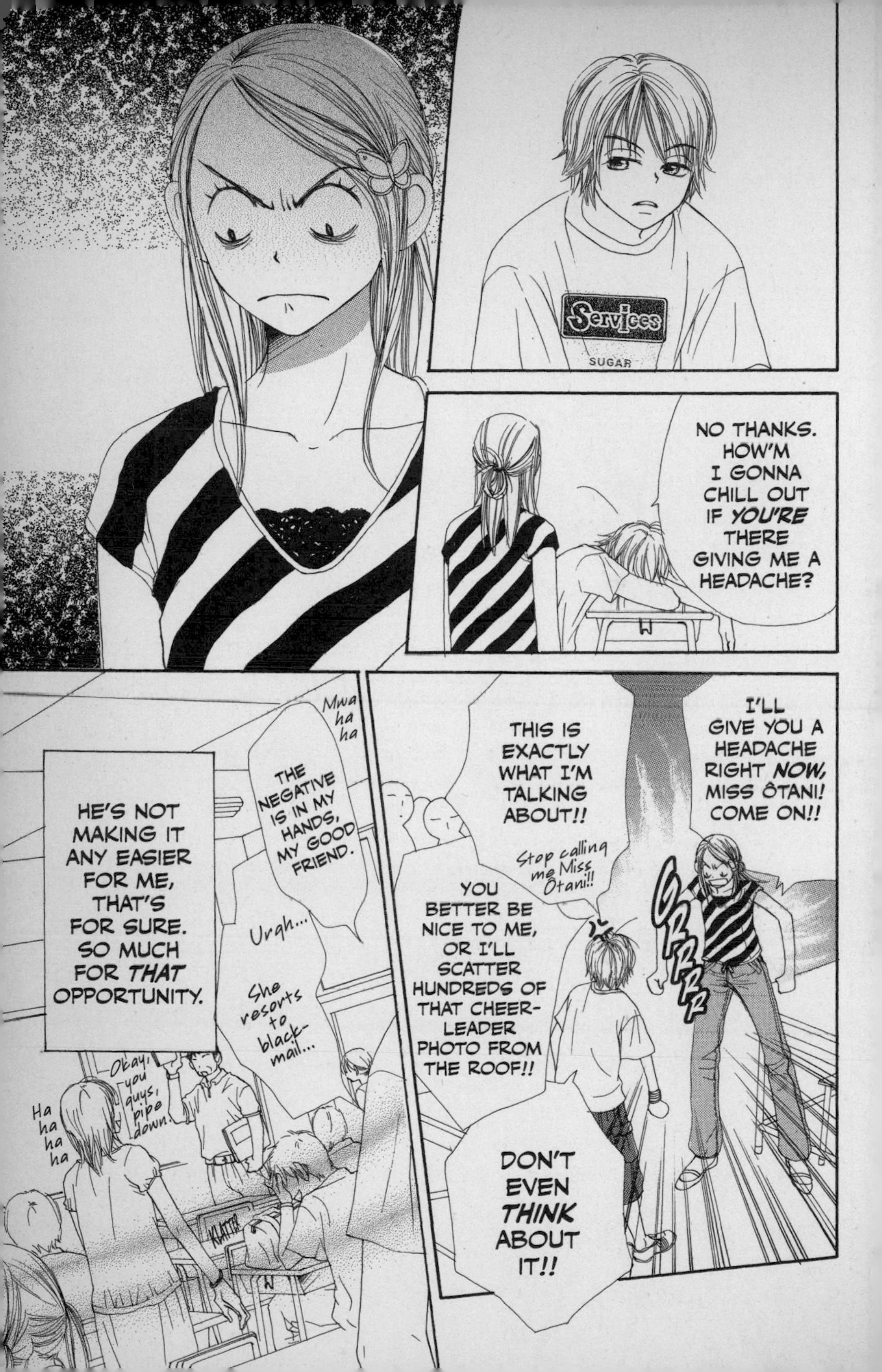
Services
SUGAR
NO THANKS. HOW'M I GONNA CHILL OUT IF *YOU'RE* THERE GIVING ME A HEADACHE?
I'LL GIVE YOU A HEADACHE RIGHT *NOW,* MISS ÔTANI! COME ON!!
GRRRR
THIS IS EXACTLY WHAT I'M TALKING ABOUT!!
Stop calling me Miss Ôtani!!
YOU BETTER BE NICE TO ME, OR I'LL SCATTER HUNDREDS OF THAT CHEER-LEADER PHOTO FROM THE ROOF!!
DON'T EVEN *THINK* ABOUT IT!!
Mwa ha ha
THE NEGATIVE IS IN MY HANDS, MY GOOD FRIEND.
HE'S NOT MAKING IT ANY EASIER FOR ME, THAT'S FOR SURE. SO MUCH FOR *THAT* OPPORTUNITY.
Urgh...
She resorts to blackmail...
Okay, you guys, pipe down.
Ha ha ha ha ha
KLATTER

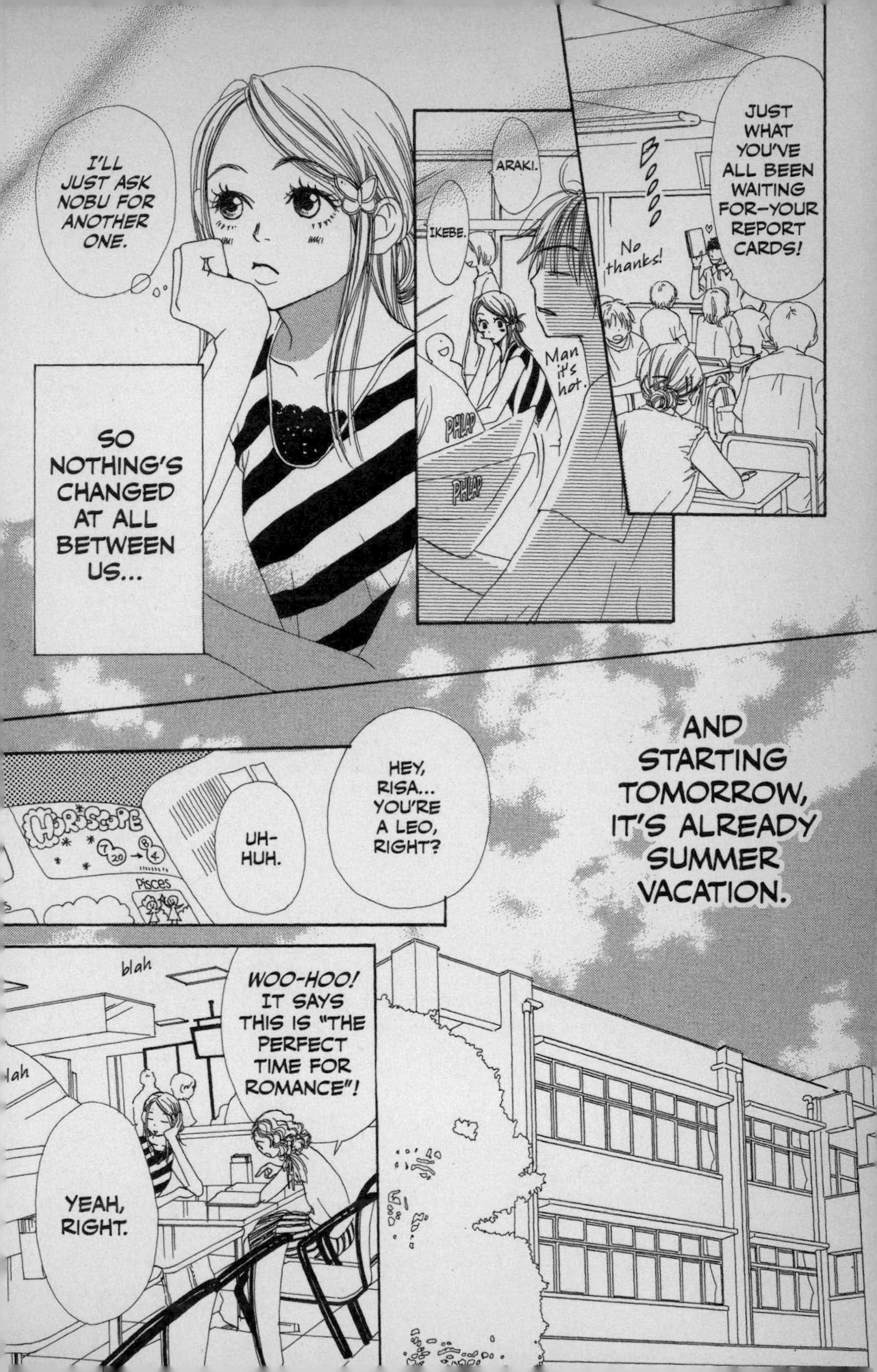
JUST WHAT YOU'VE ALL BEEN WAITING FOR—YOUR REPORT CARDS!
Boooo
No thanks!
ARAKI.
IKEBE.
Man it's hot.
PHLAP
PHLAP
I'LL JUST ASK NOBU FOR ANOTHER ONE.
SO NOTHING'S CHANGED AT ALL BETWEEN US...
AND STARTING TOMORROW, IT'S ALREADY SUMMER VACATION.
HEY, RISA... YOU'RE A LEO, RIGHT?
UH-HUH.
HOROSCOPE
Pisces
WOO-HOO! IT SAYS THIS IS "THE PERFECT TIME FOR ROMANCE"!
blah
blah
YEAH, RIGHT.

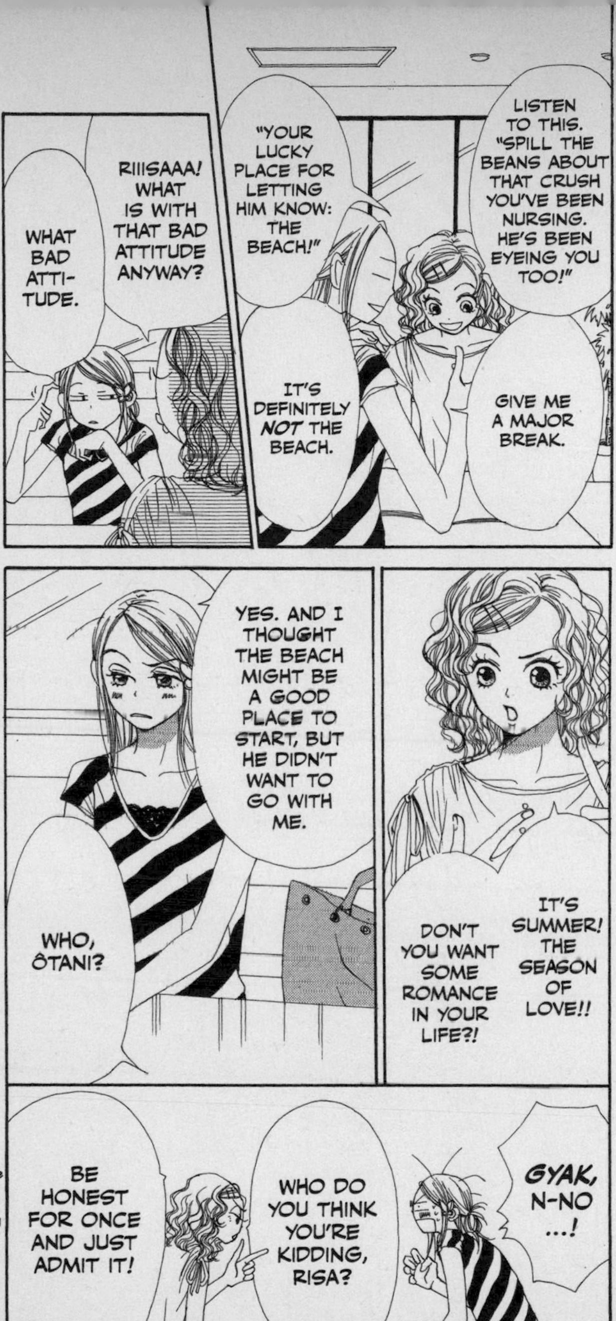
LISTEN TO THIS. "SPILL THE BEANS ABOUT THAT CRUSH YOU'VE BEEN NURSING. HE'S BEEN EYEING YOU TOO!"
"YOUR LUCKY PLACE FOR LETTING HIM KNOW: THE BEACH!"
GIVE ME A MAJOR BREAK.
IT'S DEFINITELY *NOT* THE BEACH.
RIIISAAA! WHAT IS WITH THAT BAD ATTITUDE ANYWAY?
WHAT BAD ATTI-TUDE.
IT'S SUMMER! THE SEASON OF LOVE!!
DON'T YOU WANT SOME ROMANCE IN YOUR LIFE?!
YES. AND I THOUGHT THE BEACH MIGHT BE A GOOD PLACE TO START, BUT HE DIDN'T WANT TO GO WITH ME.
WHO, ŌTANI?
GYAK, N-NO ...!
WHO DO YOU THINK YOU'RE KIDDING, RISA?
BE HONEST FOR ONCE AND JUST ADMIT IT!

1

Hello. Nakahara here. We're up to Vol. 4!

Ummmmmmmmm...

Let's see... What's new... Oh! I got to hold an autograph session in Osaka last fall (2002) when Vol. 3 came out. I was really happy to see so many people there. Thank you for coming! A few of the people asked me to draw a cat (neko) when it was their turn, and I wondered why... and decided they just wanted something easy, and I drew the rabbit I always draw instead. But then later, I found out that what they were really asking for was a poop (unko), not a cat... Ohhh, poop! Of course!! Very sorry, but I wasn't expecting requests of that nature, so I guess my ears just couldn't hear the word right.

Gosh, it's like I'm one of those people who don't get it when you tell a joke—so sorry!!

You want poop, I'll draw as many poops as you want. Here you go!

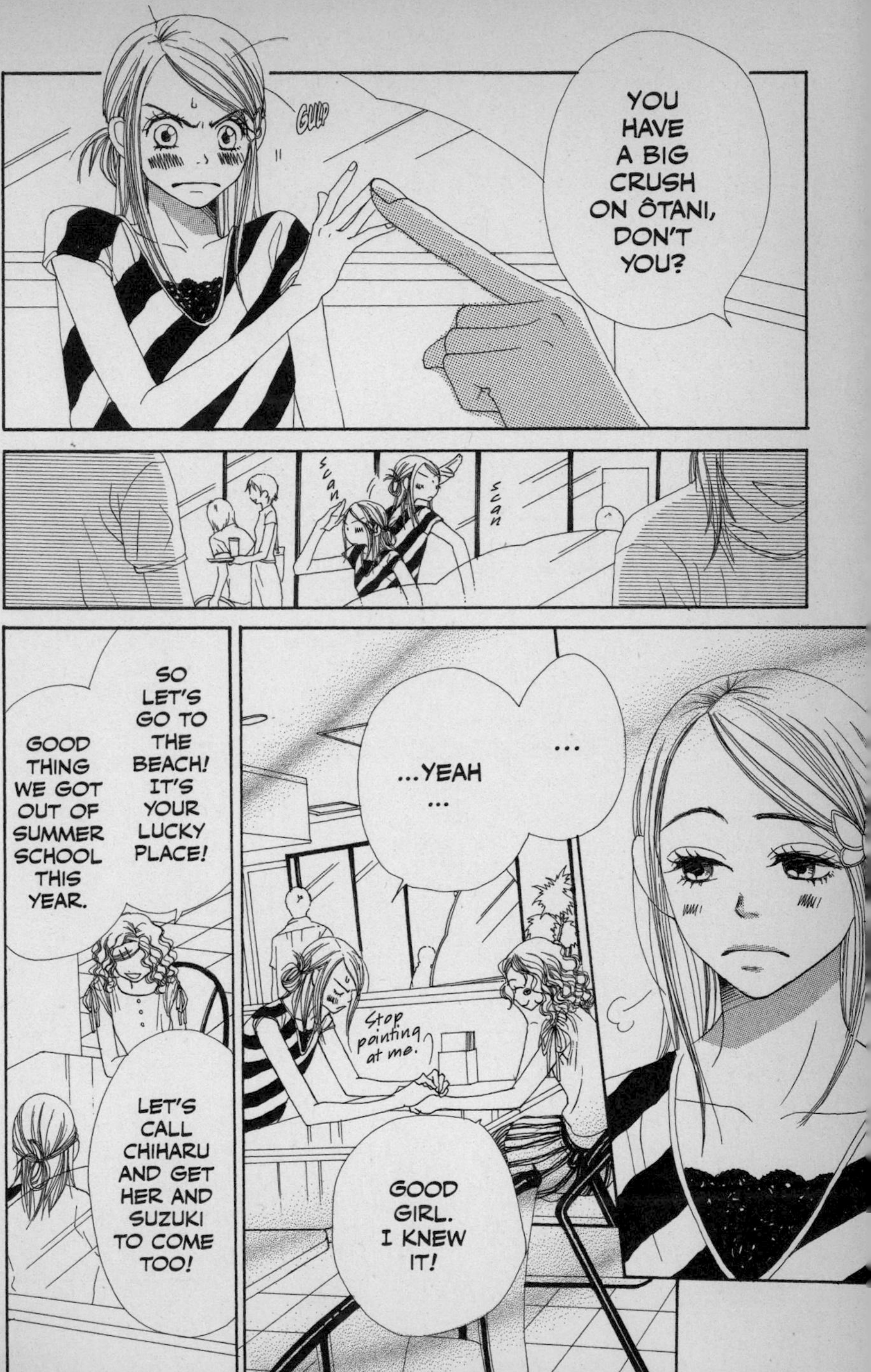
YOU HAVE A BIG CRUSH ON ÔTANI, DON'T YOU?
GULP
scan
scan
...
...YEAH ...
Stop pointing at me.
GOOD GIRL. I KNEW IT!
SO LET'S GO TO THE BEACH! IT'S YOUR LUCKY PLACE!
GOOD THING WE GOT OUT OF SUMMER SCHOOL THIS YEAR.
LET'S CALL CHIHARU AND GET HER AND SUZUKI TO COME TOO!

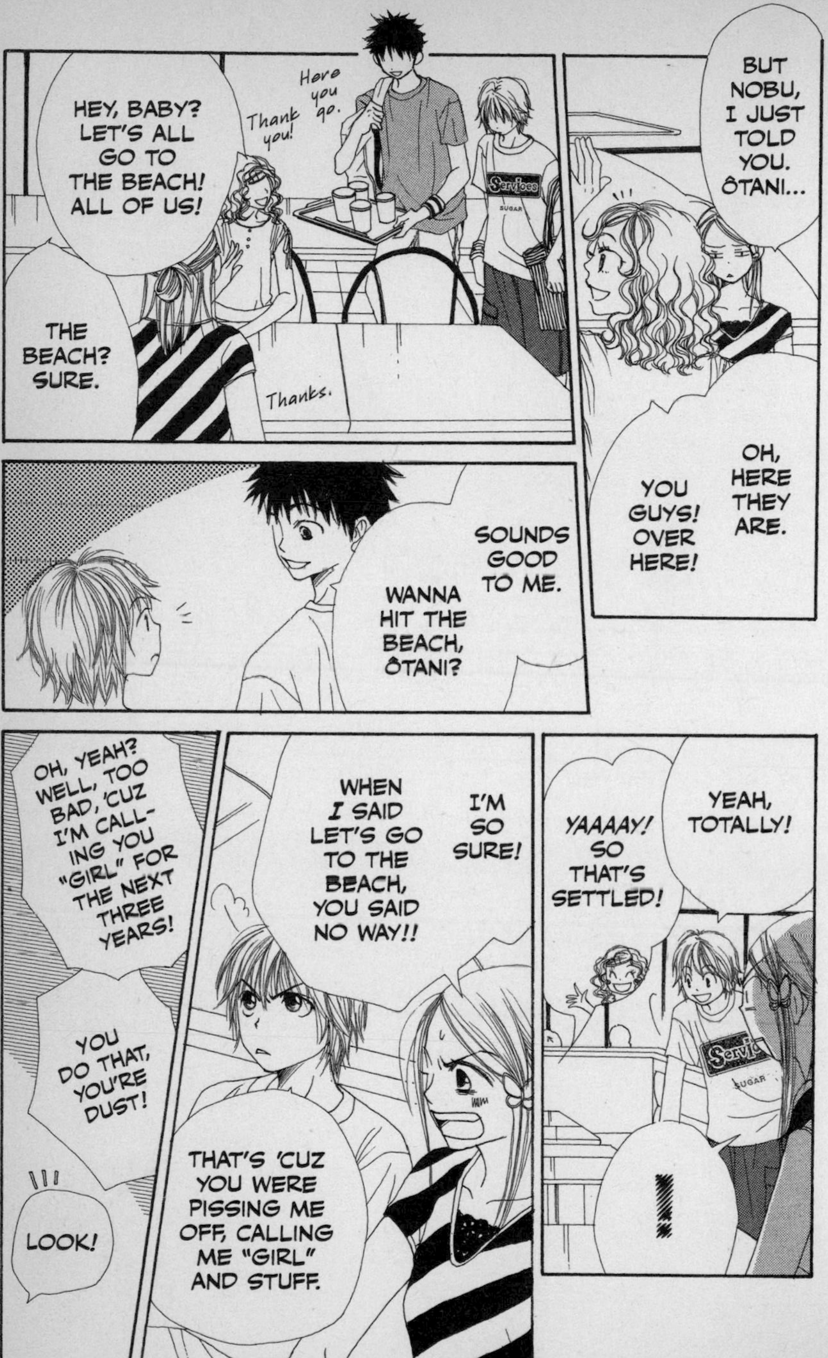
BUT NOBU, I JUST TOLD YOU. ŌTANI...
OH, HERE THEY ARE.
YOU GUYS! OVER HERE!
Here you go.
Thank you!
HEY, BABY? LET'S ALL GO TO THE BEACH! ALL OF US!
THE BEACH? SURE.
Thanks.
SOUNDS GOOD TO ME.
WANNA HIT THE BEACH, ŌTANI?
YEAH, TOTALLY!
YAAAAY! SO THAT'S SETTLED!
!
I'M SO SURE!
WHEN *I* SAID LET'S GO TO THE BEACH, YOU SAID NO WAY!!
THAT'S 'CUZ YOU WERE PISSING ME OFF, CALLING ME "GIRL" AND STUFF.
OH, YEAH? WELL, TOO BAD, 'CUZ I'M CALLING YOU "GIRL" FOR THE NEXT THREE YEARS!
YOU DO THAT, YOU'RE DUST!
LOOK!

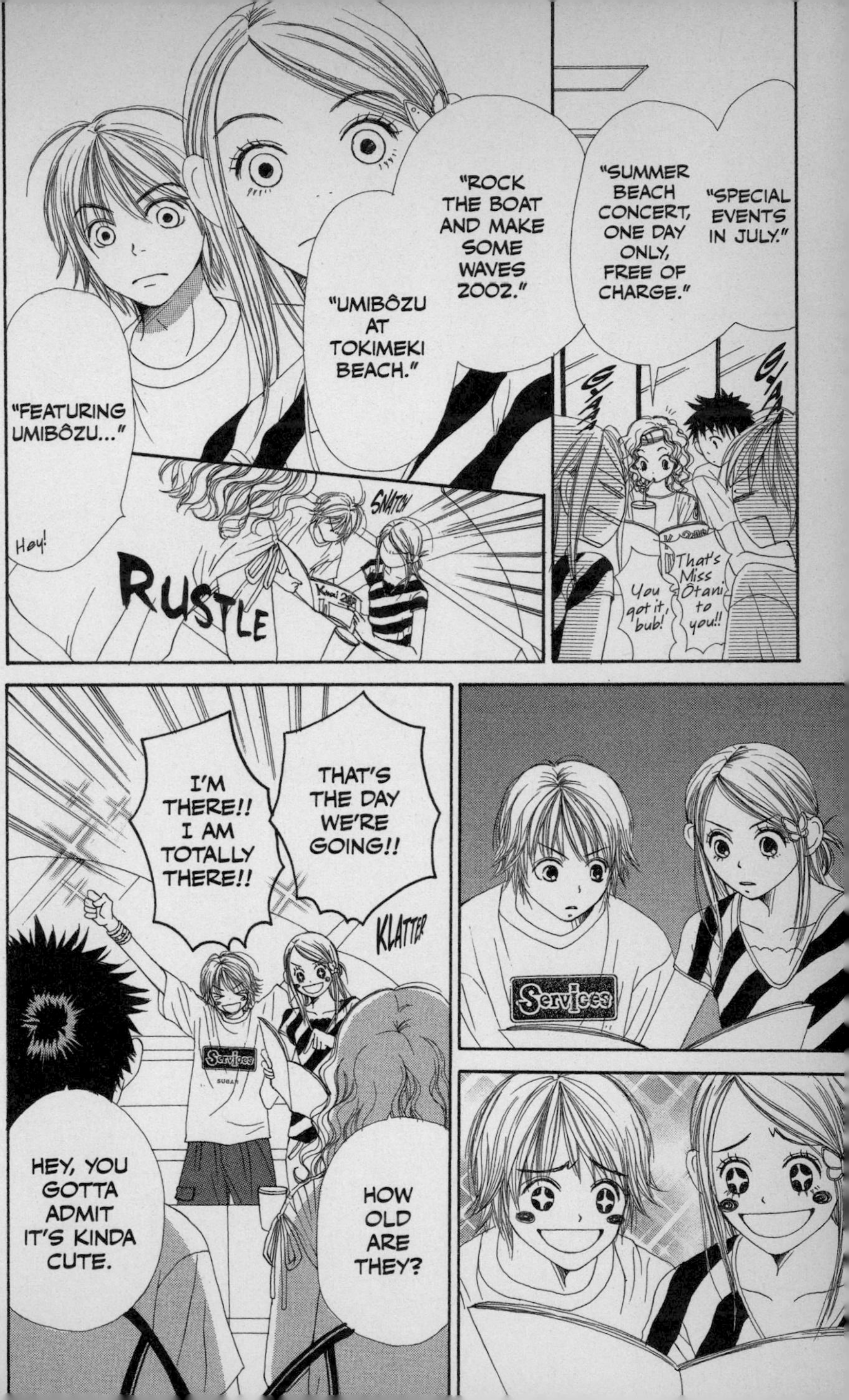
"SPECIAL EVENTS IN JULY."
"SUMMER BEACH CONCERT, ONE DAY ONLY, FREE OF CHARGE."
That's Miss Ōtani to you!!
You got it, bub!
"ROCK THE BOAT AND MAKE SOME WAVES 2002."
"UMIBÔZU AT TOKIMEKI BEACH."
"FEATURING UMIBÔZU..."
SNATCH
Hey!
RUSTLE
THAT'S THE DAY WE'RE GOING!!
I'M THERE!! I AM TOTALLY THERE!!
KLATTER
HOW OLD ARE THEY?
HEY, YOU GOTTA ADMIT IT'S KINDA CUTE.

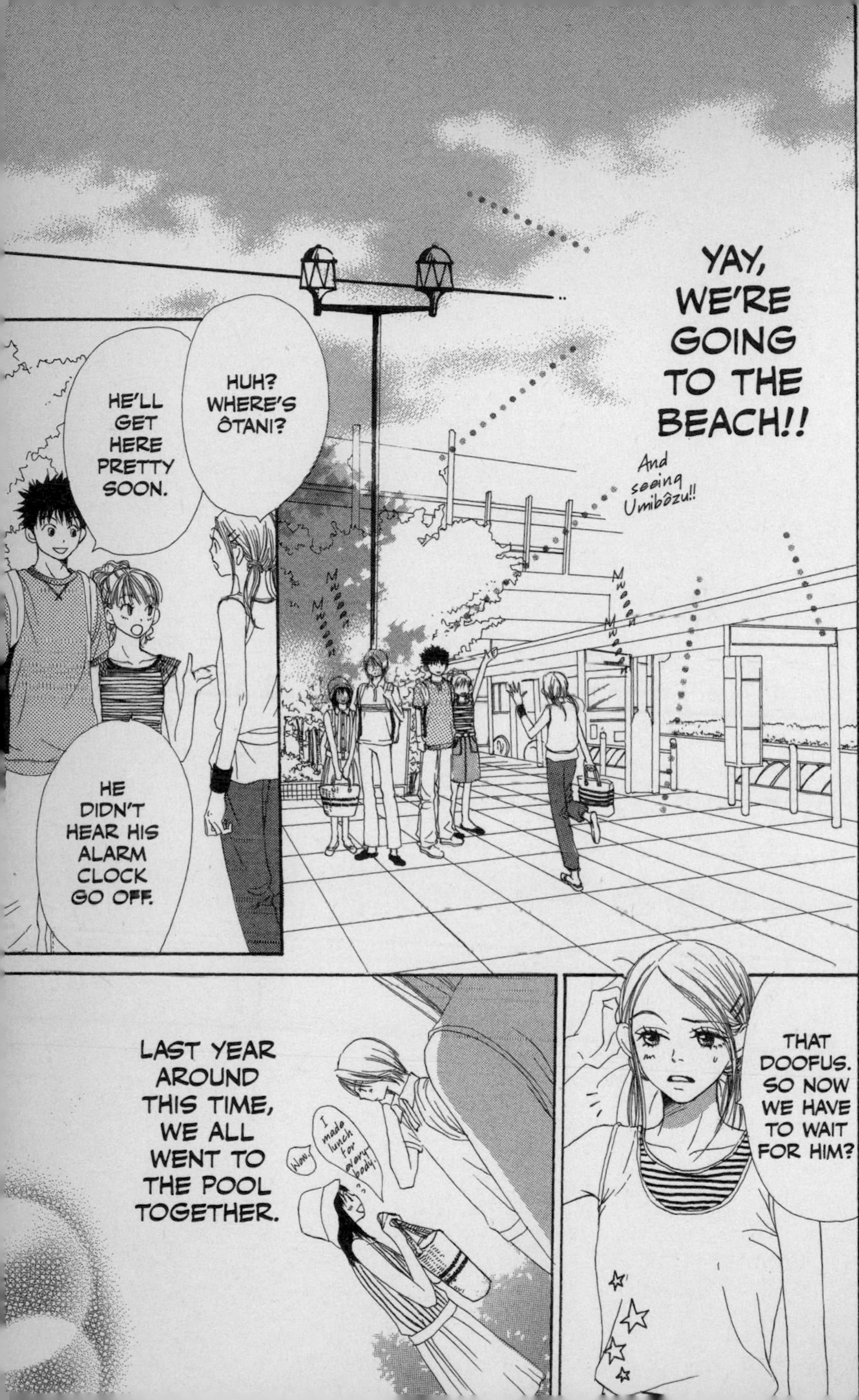

YAY, WE'RE GOING TO THE BEACH!!
And seeing Umibôzu!!
HUH? WHERE'S ÔTANI?
HE'LL GET HERE PRETTY SOON.
HE DIDN'T HEAR HIS ALARM CLOCK GO OFF.
THAT DOOFUS. SO NOW WE HAVE TO WAIT FOR HIM?
LAST YEAR AROUND THIS TIME, WE ALL WENT TO THE POOL TOGETHER.
I made lunch for everybody.
Wow.

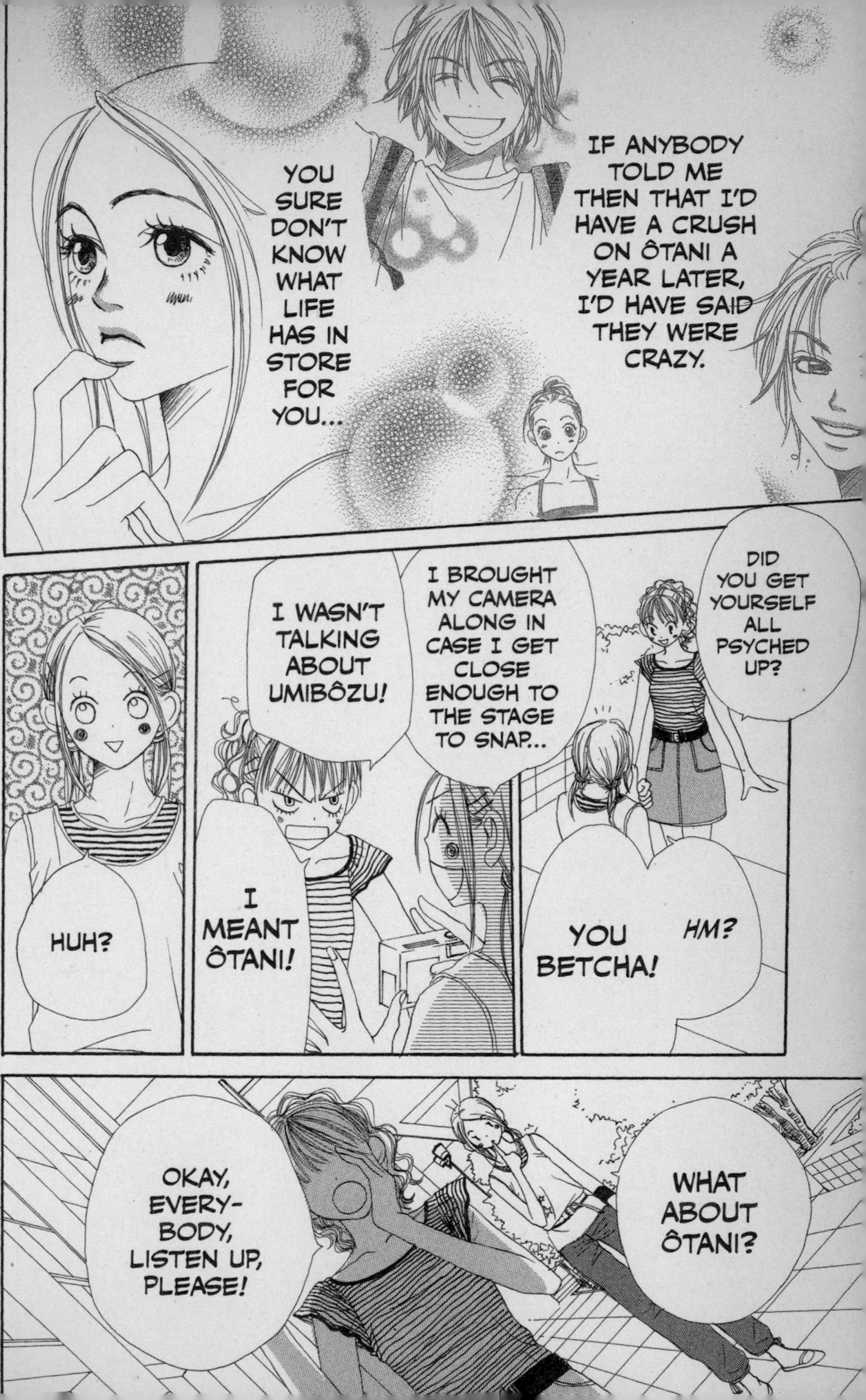
IF ANYBODY TOLD ME THEN THAT I'D HAVE A CRUSH ON ÔTANI A YEAR LATER, I'D HAVE SAID THEY WERE CRAZY.
YOU SURE DON'T KNOW WHAT LIFE HAS IN STORE FOR YOU...
DID YOU GET YOURSELF ALL PSYCHED UP?
HM?
YOU BETCHA!
I BROUGHT MY CAMERA ALONG IN CASE I GET CLOSE ENOUGH TO THE STAGE TO SNAP...
I WASN'T TALKING ABOUT UMIBÔZU!
I MEANT ÔTANI!
HUH?
WHAT ABOUT ÔTANI?
OKAY, EVERY-BODY, LISTEN UP, PLEASE!

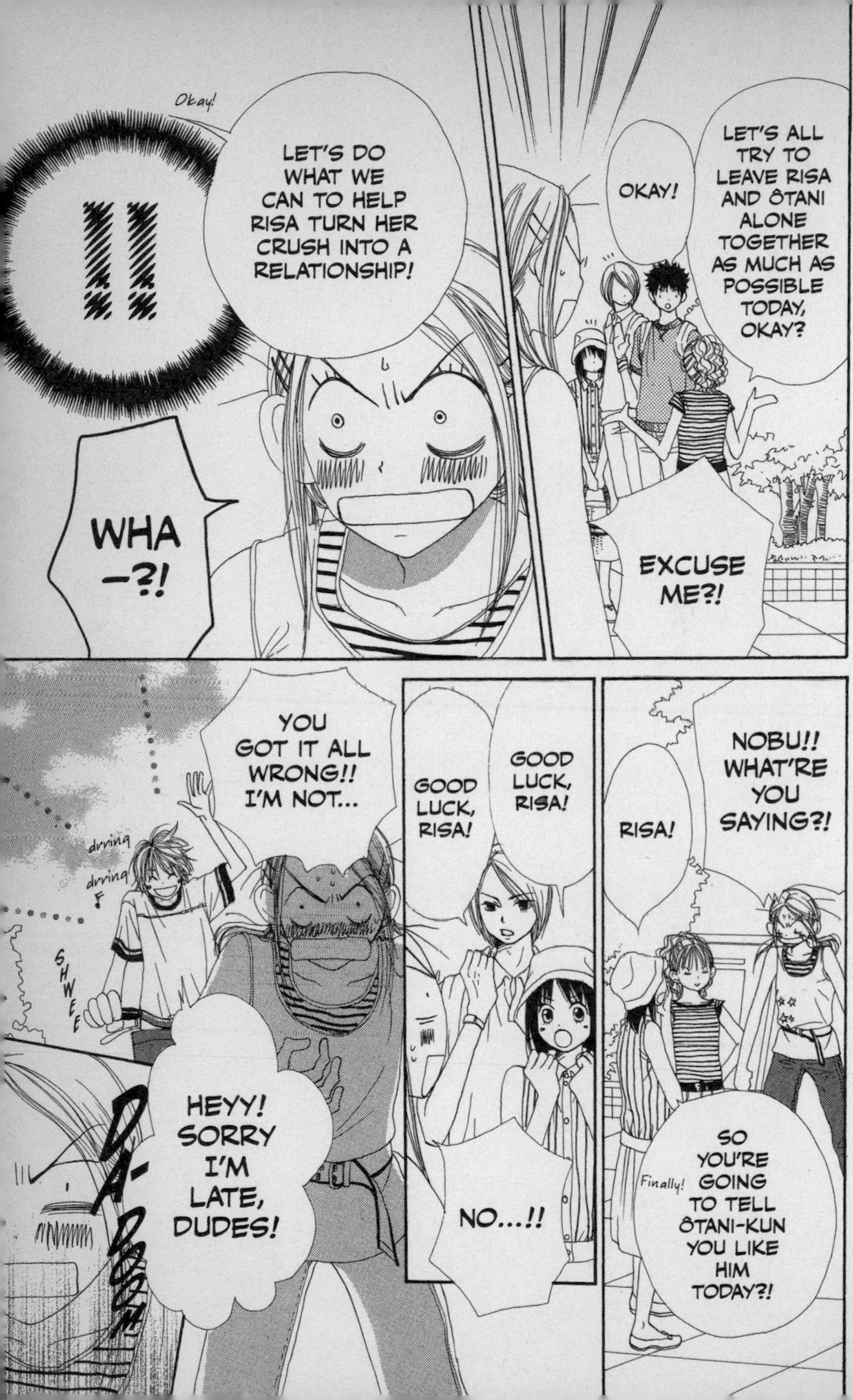

LET'S ALL TRY TO LEAVE RISA AND ŌTANI ALONE TOGETHER AS MUCH AS POSSIBLE TODAY, OKAY?
OKAY!
EXCUSE ME?!
LET'S DO WHAT WE CAN TO HELP RISA TURN HER CRUSH INTO A RELATIONSHIP!
Okay!
WHA—?!
NOBU!! WHAT'RE YOU SAYING?!
RISA!
SO YOU'RE GOING TO TELL ŌTANI-KUN YOU LIKE HIM TODAY?!
Finally!
GOOD LUCK, RISA!
GOOD LUCK, RISA!
NO...!!
YOU GOT IT ALL WRONG!! I'M NOT...
drring
drring
SHWEE
HEYY! SORRY I'M LATE, DUDES!

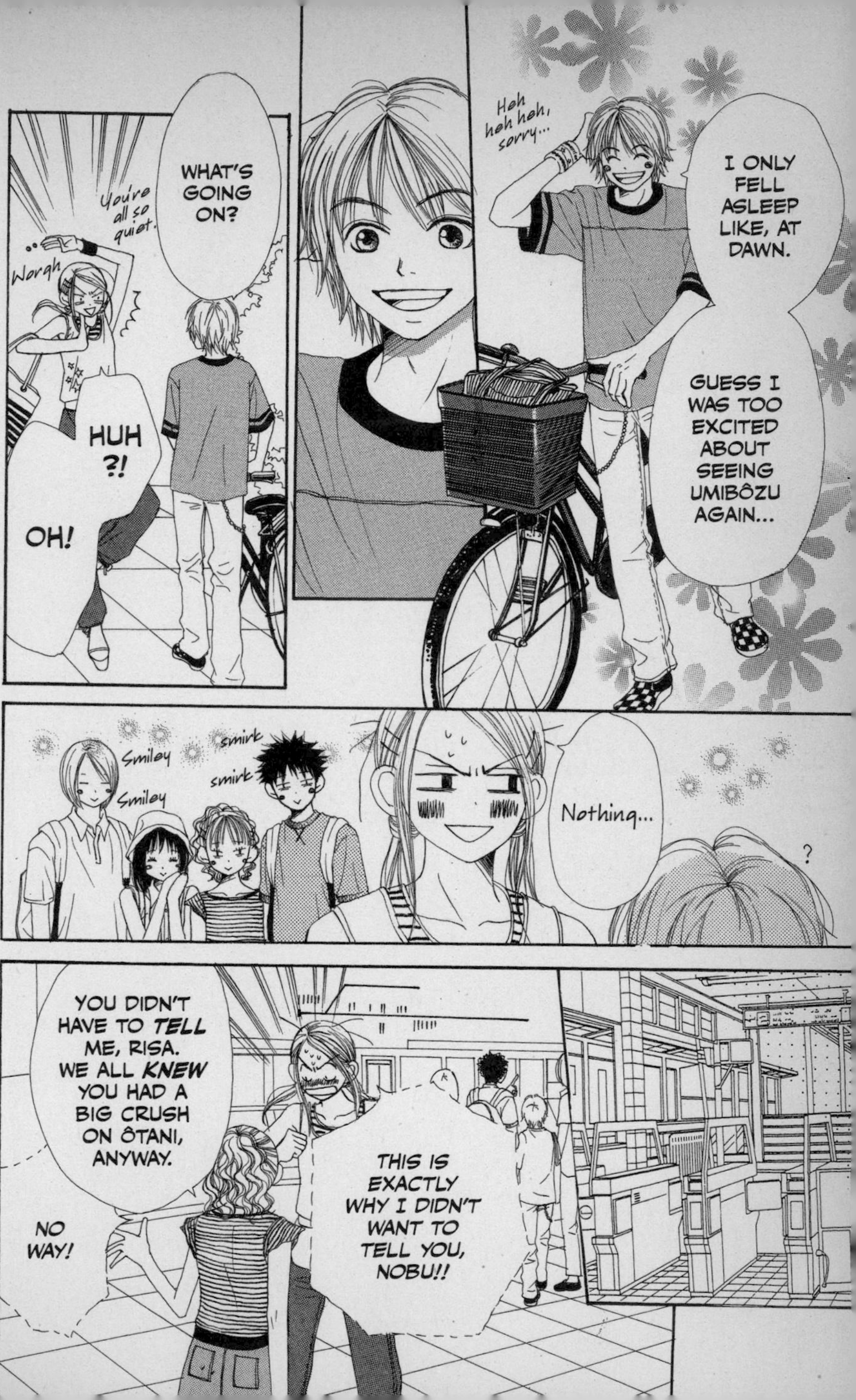
Heh heh heh, sorry...
I ONLY FELL ASLEEP LIKE, AT DAWN.
GUESS I WAS TOO EXCITED ABOUT SEEING UMIBÔZU AGAIN...
WHAT'S GOING ON?
You're all so quiet.
Worgh
HUH ?!
OH!
Nothing...
?
Smiley
smirk
smirk
Smiley
YOU DIDN'T HAVE TO *TELL* ME, RISA. WE ALL *KNEW* YOU HAD A BIG CRUSH ON ÔTANI, ANYWAY.
THIS IS EXACTLY WHY I DIDN'T WANT TO TELL YOU, NOBU!!
NO WAY!

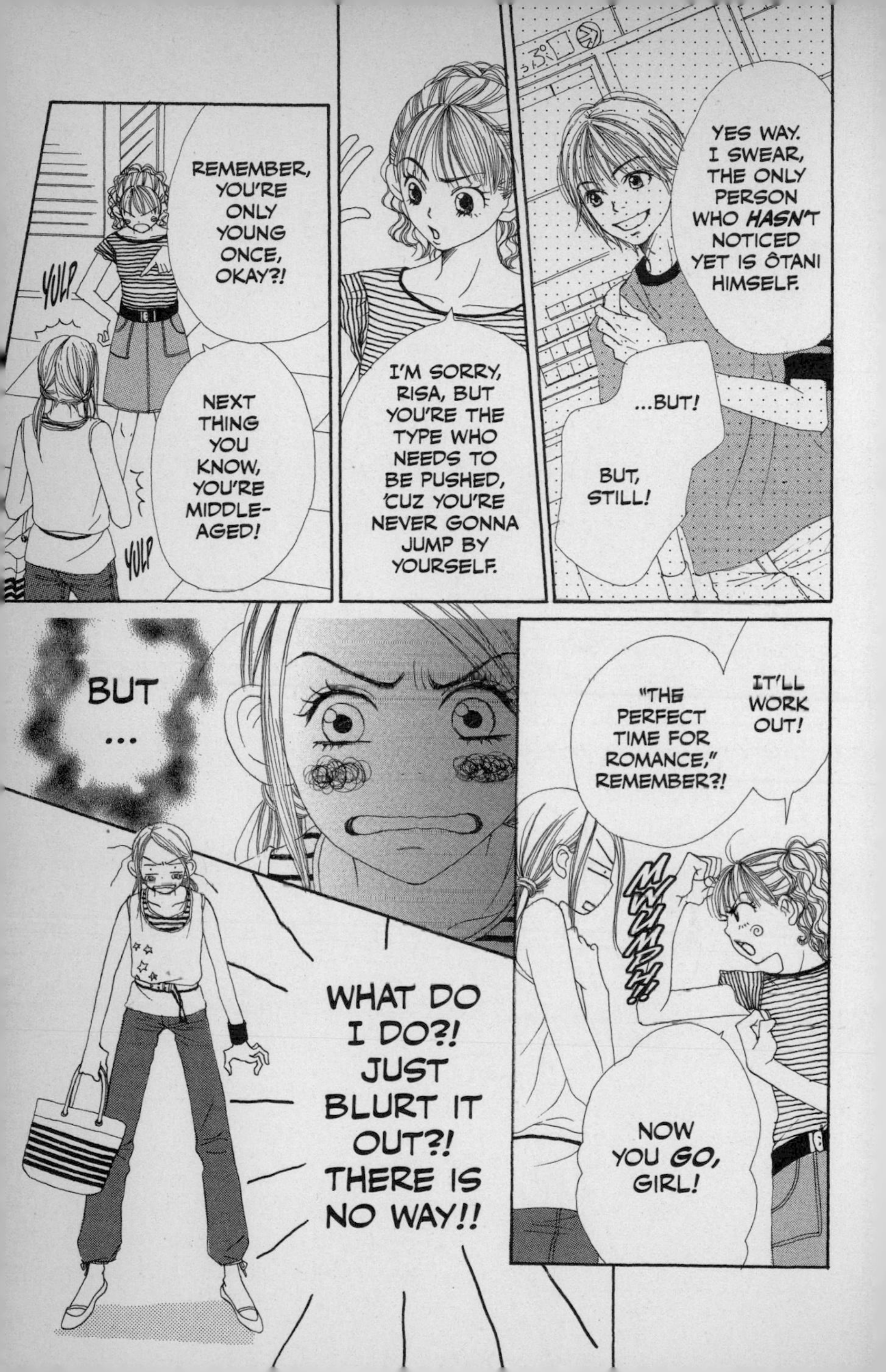
YES WAY. I SWEAR, THE ONLY PERSON WHO HASN'T NOTICED YET IS ÔTANI HIMSELF.
...BUT!
BUT, STILL!
I'M SORRY, RISA, BUT YOU'RE THE TYPE WHO NEEDS TO BE PUSHED, 'CUZ YOU'RE NEVER GONNA JUMP BY YOURSELF.
REMEMBER, YOU'RE ONLY YOUNG ONCE, OKAY?!
YULP
NEXT THING YOU KNOW, YOU'RE MIDDLE-AGED!
YULP
IT'LL WORK OUT!
"THE PERFECT TIME FOR ROMANCE," REMEMBER?!
MWUMPH!!
NOW YOU GO, GIRL!
BUT ...
WHAT DO I DO?! JUST BLURT IT OUT?! THERE IS NO WAY!!

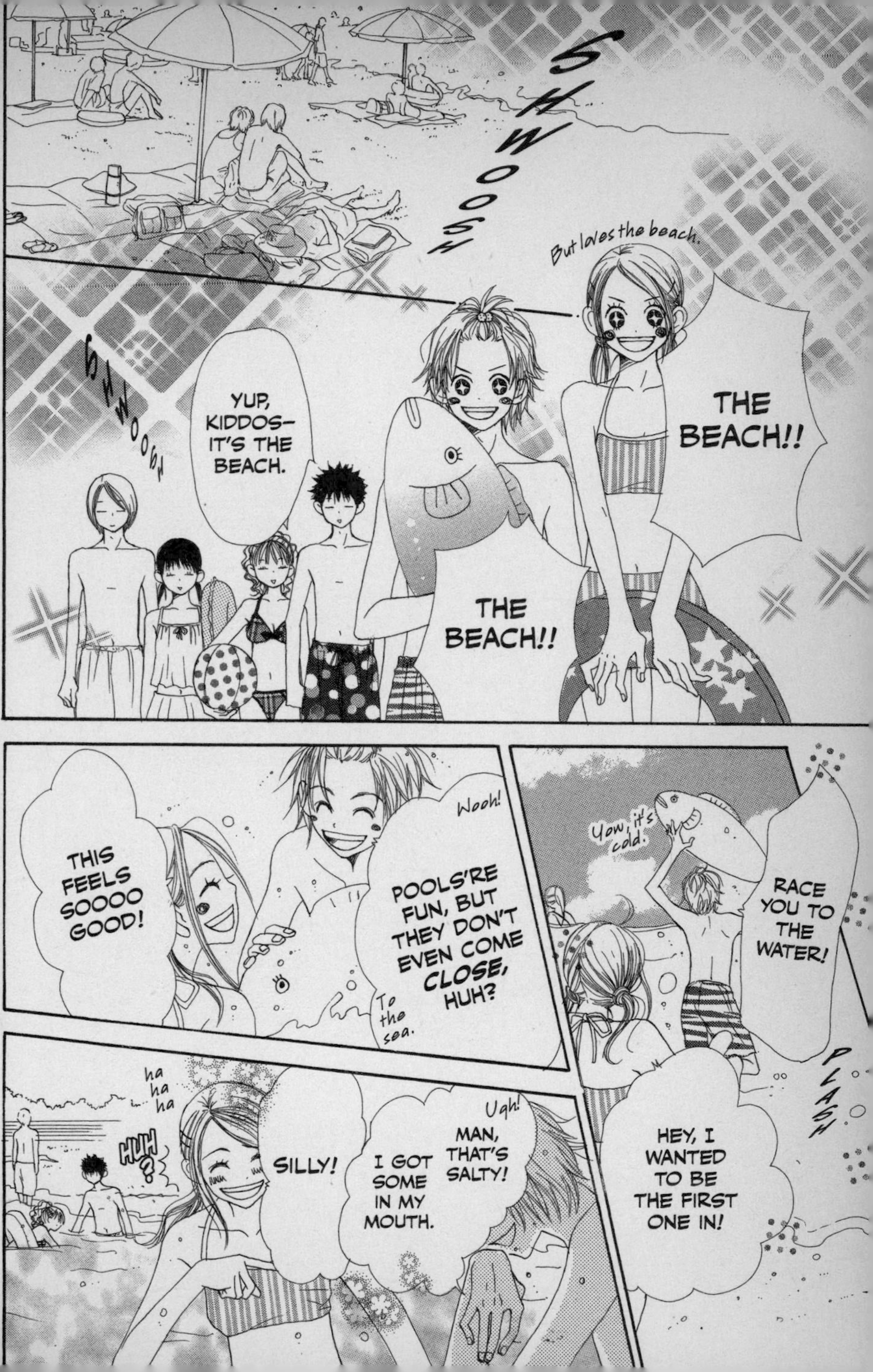
SHWOOOSH
But loves the beach.
THE BEACH!!
THE BEACH!!
YUP, KIDDOS— IT'S THE BEACH.
SHWOOSH
RACE YOU TO THE WATER!
Yow, it's cold.
Wooh!
POOLS'RE FUN, BUT THEY DON'T EVEN COME CLOSE, HUH?
To the sea.
THIS FEELS SOOOO GOOD!
PLASH
HEY, I WANTED TO BE THE FIRST ONE IN!
Ugh!
MAN, THAT'S SALTY!
I GOT SOME IN MY MOUTH.
SILLY!
HUH?
ha ha ha

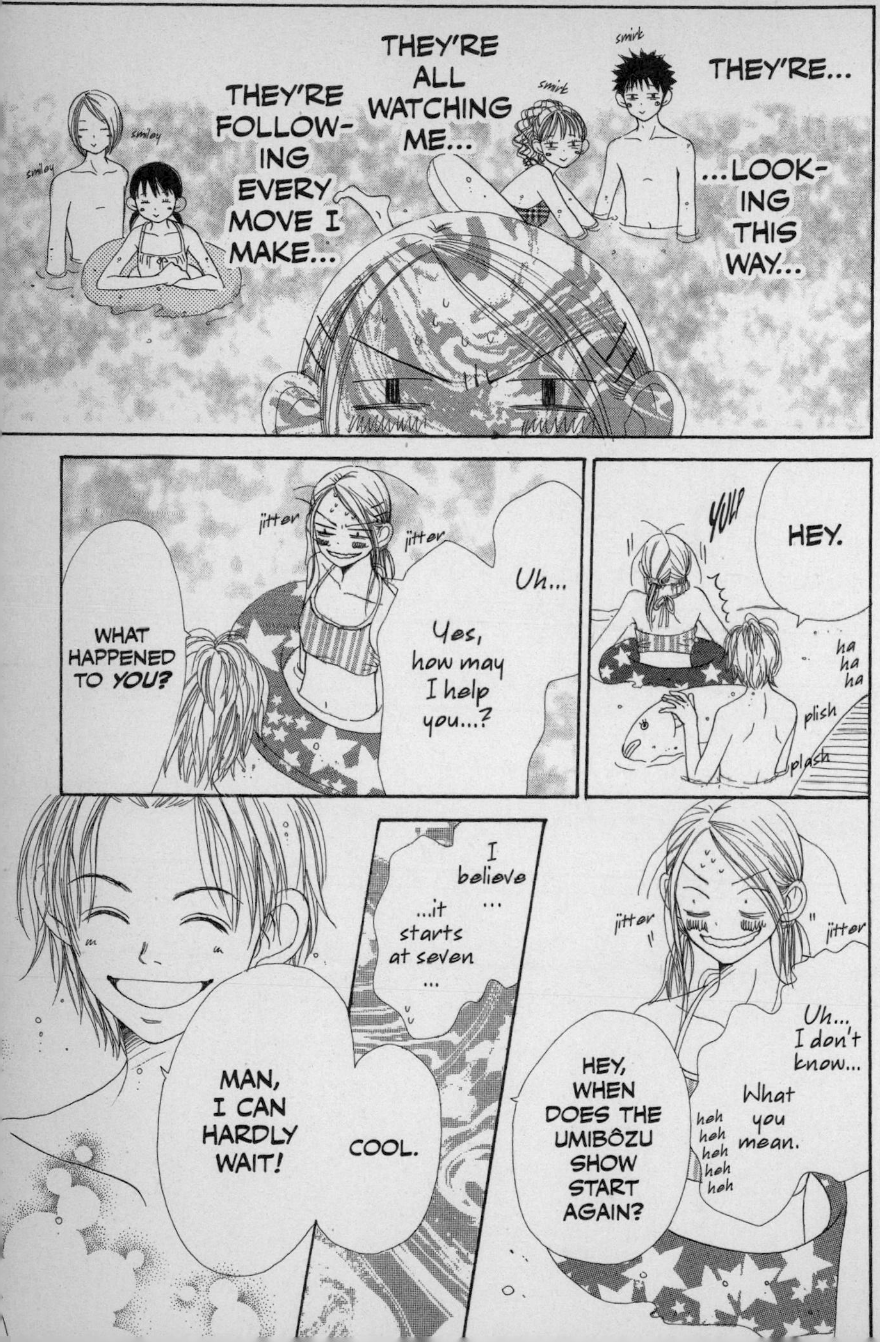
smirk
THEY'RE...
...LOOK-ING THIS WAY...
smirk
THEY'RE ALL WATCHING ME...
THEY'RE FOLLOW-ING EVERY MOVE I MAKE...
smiley
smiley
HEY.
ha ha ha
plish
plash
jitter
jitter
Uh...
Yes, how may I help you...?
WHAT HAPPENED TO *YOU*?
jitter
jitter
Uh... I don't know...
What you mean.
heh heh heh heh heh
HEY, WHEN DOES THE UMIBÔZU SHOW START AGAIN?
I believe...
...it starts at seven...
COOL.
MAN, I CAN HARDLY WAIT!

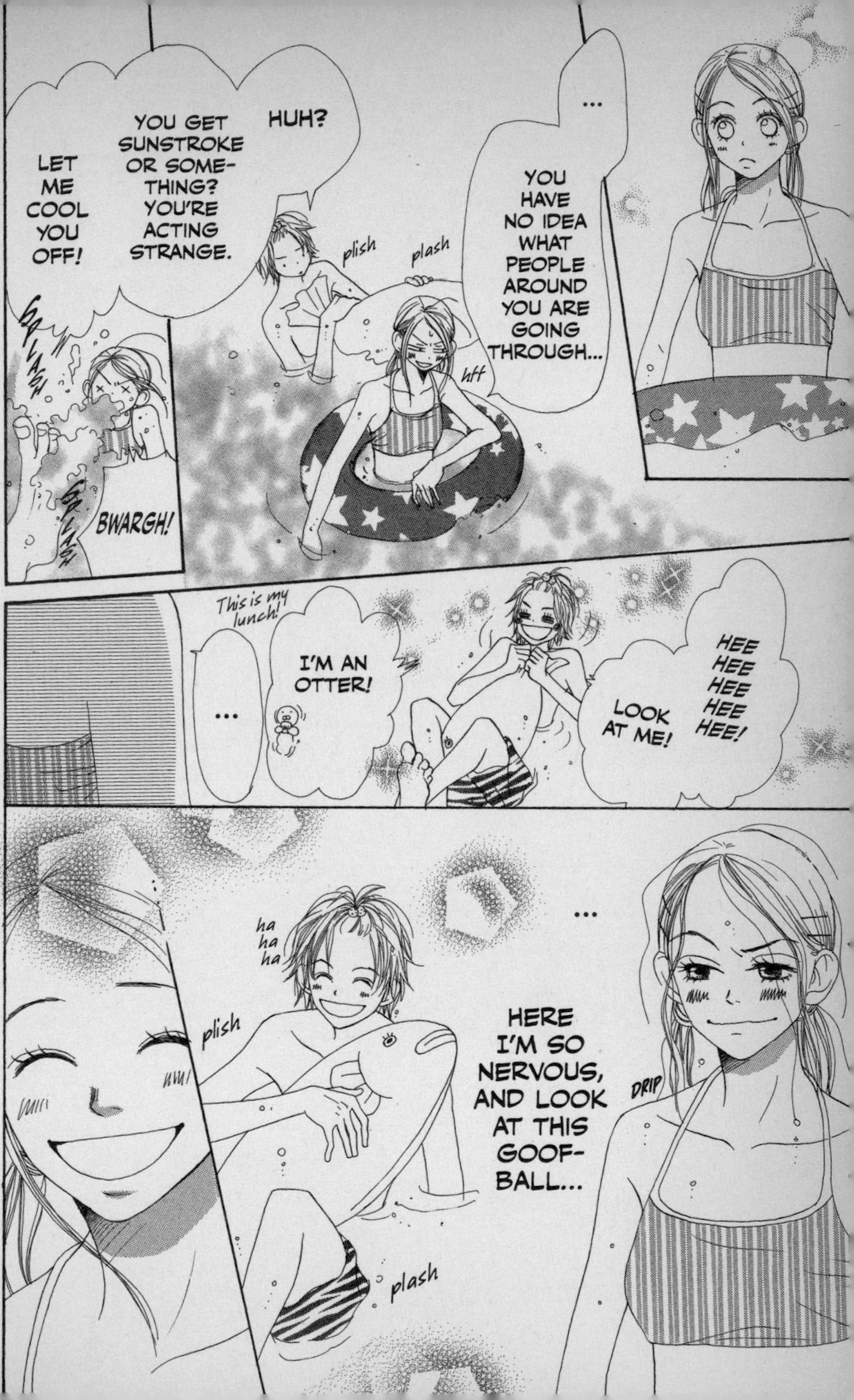
...
YOU HAVE NO IDEA WHAT PEOPLE AROUND YOU ARE GOING THROUGH...
HUH?
YOU GET SUNSTROKE OR SOME-THING? YOU'RE ACTING STRANGE.
plish
plash
hff
LET ME COOL YOU OFF!
SPLASH
BWARGH!
SPLASH
HEE HEE HEE HEE HEE!
LOOK AT ME!
I'M AN OTTER!
This is my lunch!
...
...
HERE I'M SO NERVOUS, AND LOOK AT THIS GOOF-BALL...
DRIP
ha ha ha
plish
plash

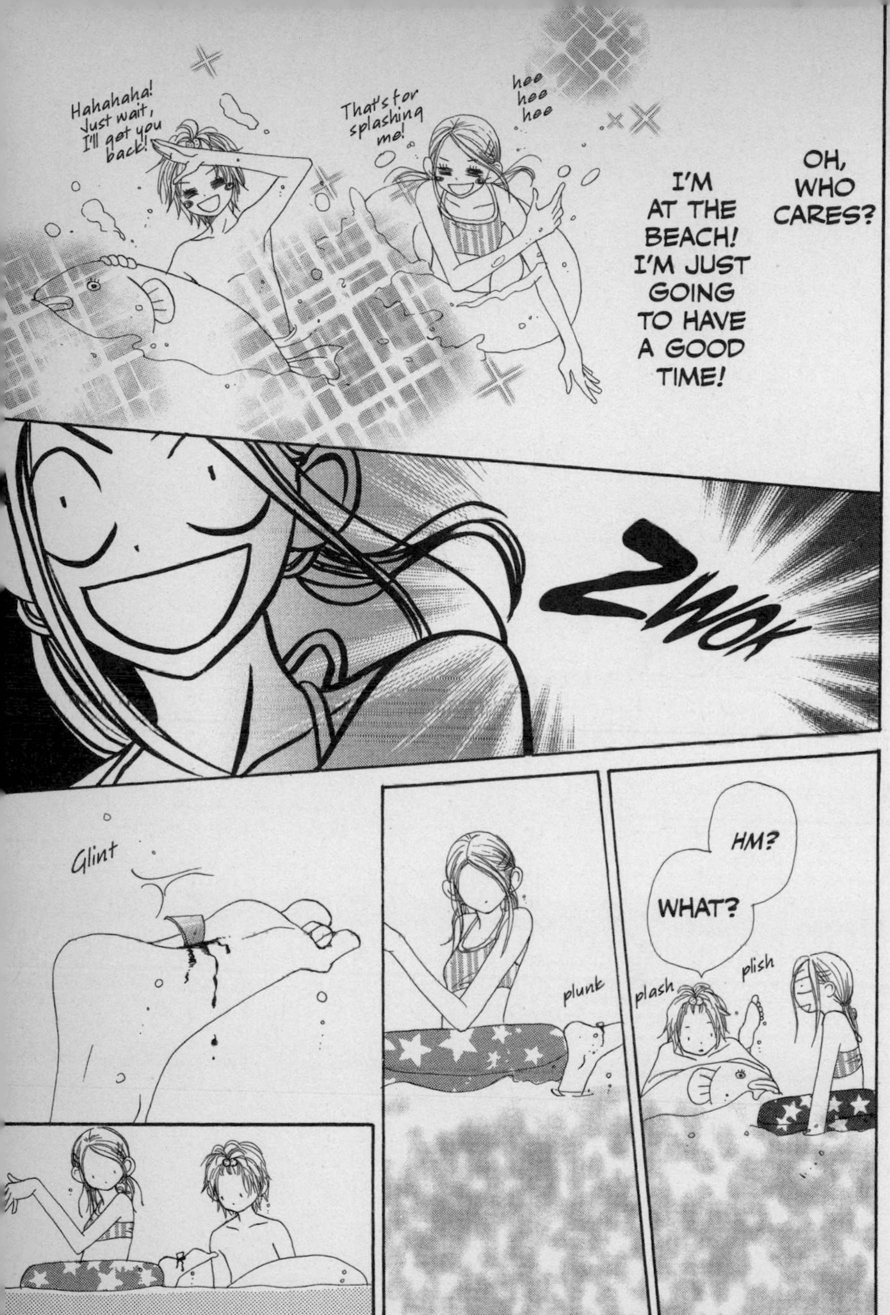
OH, WHO CARES?
I'M AT THE BEACH! I'M JUST GOING TO HAVE A GOOD TIME!
hee hee hee
That's for splashing me!
Hahahaha! Just wait, I'll get you back!
ZWOK
HM?
WHAT?
plish
plash
plunk
Glint

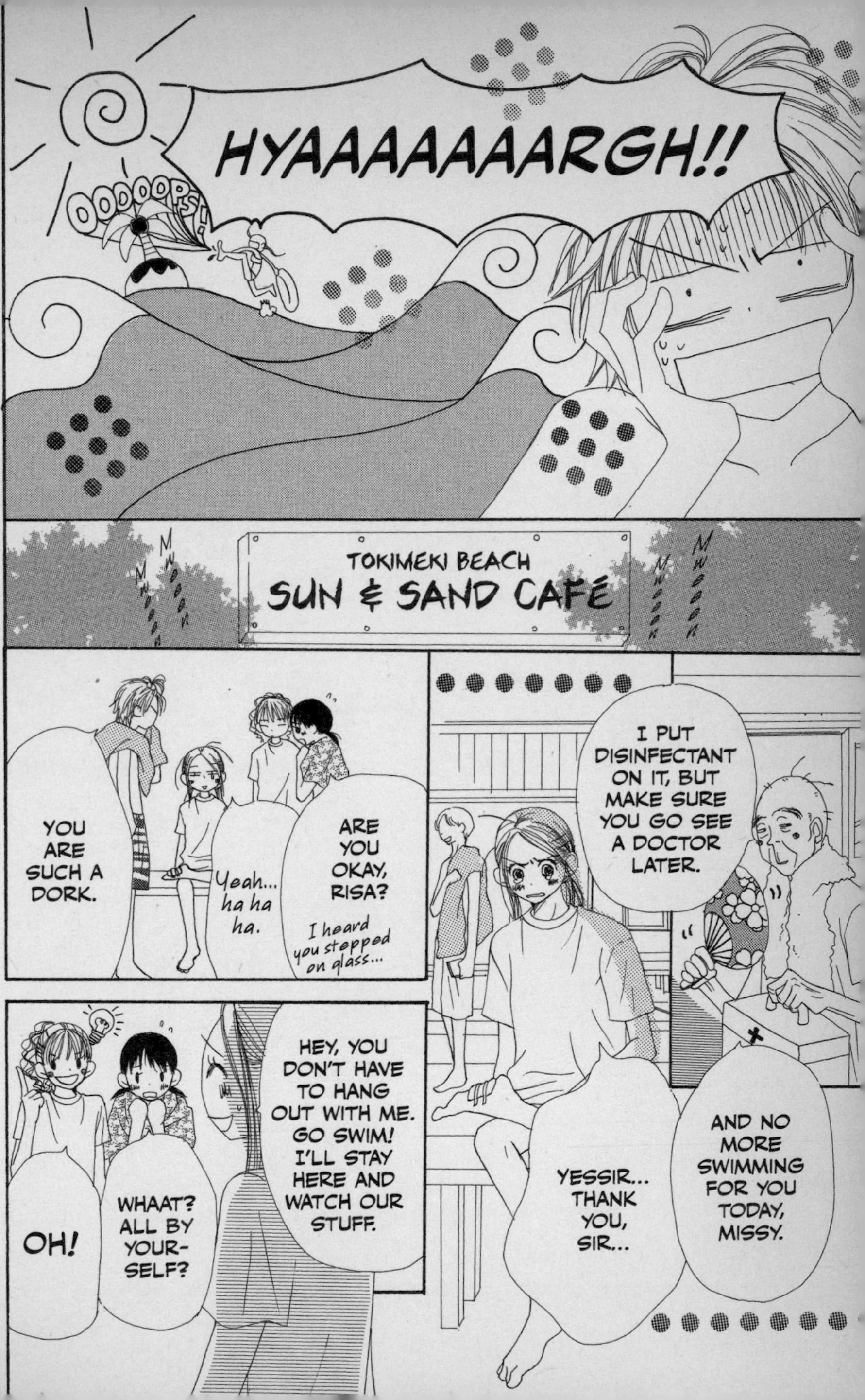
HYAAAAAAARGH!!
OODOOPS!
TOKIMEKI BEACH
SUN & SAND CAFÉ
I PUT DISINFECTANT ON IT, BUT MAKE SURE YOU GO SEE A DOCTOR LATER.
AND NO MORE SWIMMING FOR YOU TODAY, MISSY.
YESSIR... THANK YOU, SIR...
ARE YOU OKAY, RISA?
I heard you stepped on glass...
Yeah... ha ha ha.
YOU ARE SUCH A DORK.
HEY, YOU DON'T HAVE TO HANG OUT WITH ME. GO SWIM! I'LL STAY HERE AND WATCH OUR STUFF.
WHAAT? ALL BY YOUR-SELF?
OH!

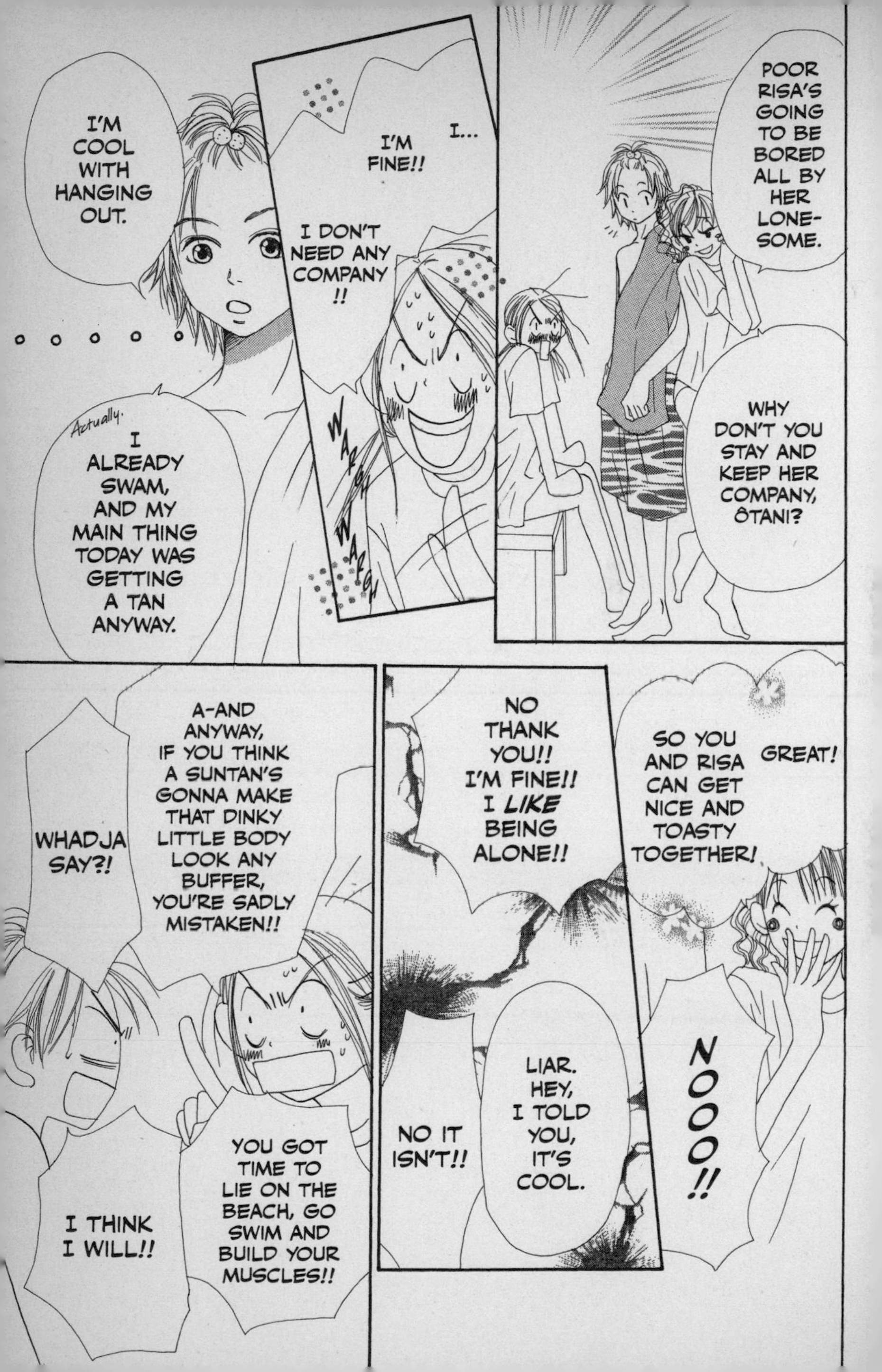
POOR RISA'S GOING TO BE BORED ALL BY HER LONESOME.
WHY DON'T YOU STAY AND KEEP HER COMPANY, ŌTANI?
I...
I'M FINE!!
I DON'T NEED ANY COMPANY!!
WARGH WARGH
I'M COOL WITH HANGING OUT.
......
Actually.
I ALREADY SWAM, AND MY MAIN THING TODAY WAS GETTING A TAN ANYWAY.
GREAT!
SO YOU AND RISA CAN GET NICE AND TOASTY TOGETHER!
NOOOO!!
NO THANK YOU!! I'M FINE!! I *LIKE* BEING ALONE!!
LIAR. HEY, I TOLD YOU, IT'S COOL.
NO IT ISN'T!!
A-AND ANYWAY, IF YOU THINK A SUNTAN'S GONNA MAKE THAT DINKY LITTLE BODY LOOK ANY BUFFER, YOU'RE SADLY MISTAKEN!!
WHADJA SAY?!
YOU GOT TIME TO LIE ON THE BEACH, GO SWIM AND BUILD YOUR MUSCLES!!
I THINK I WILL!!

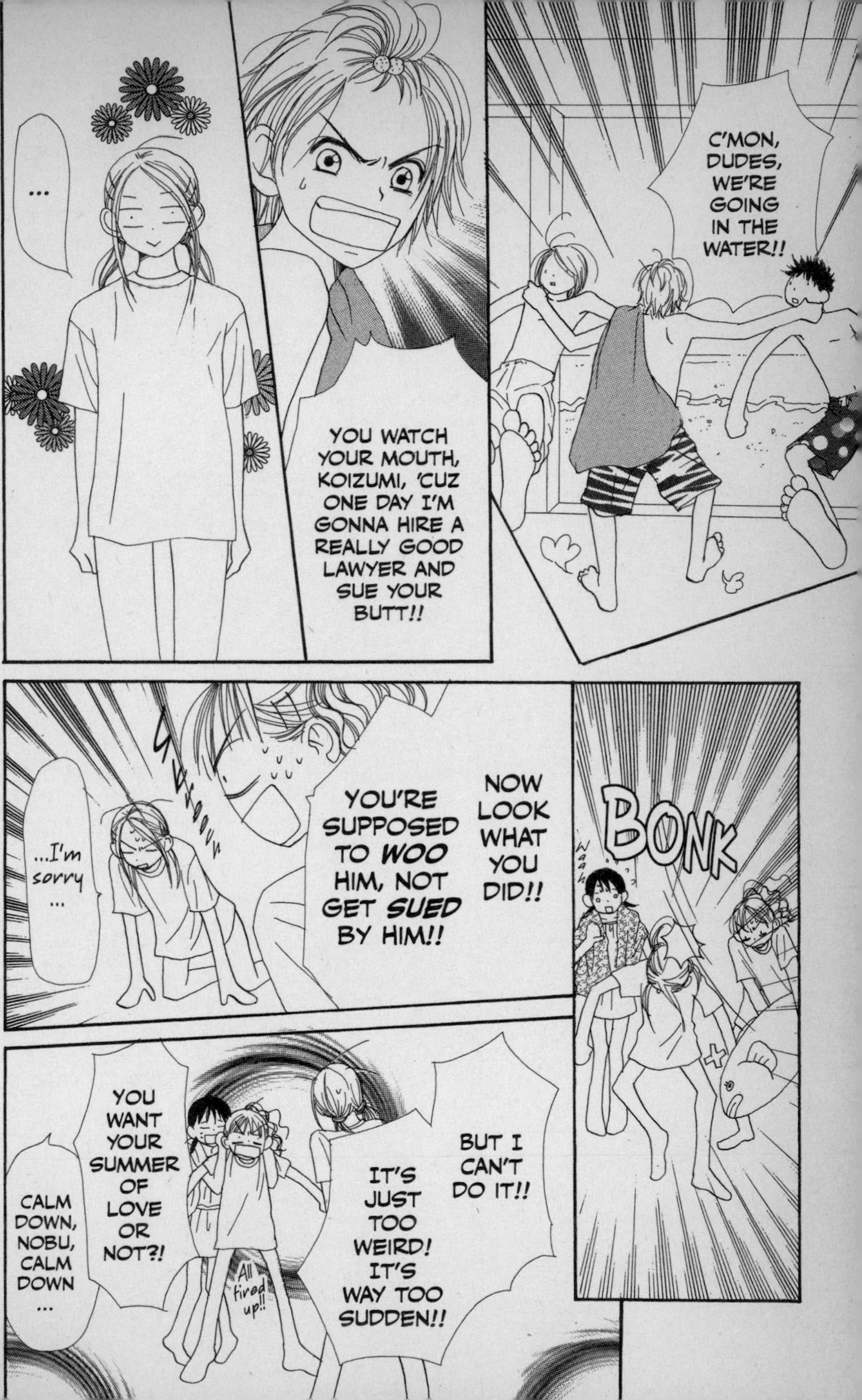
C'MON, DUDES, WE'RE GOING IN THE WATER!!
YOU WATCH YOUR MOUTH, KOIZUMI, 'CUZ ONE DAY I'M GONNA HIRE A REALLY GOOD LAWYER AND SUE YOUR BUTT!!
...
BONK
Waah
NOW LOOK WHAT YOU DID!!
YOU'RE SUPPOSED TO *WOO* HIM, NOT GET *SUED* BY HIM!!
...I'm sorry ...
BUT I CAN'T DO IT!!
IT'S JUST TOO WEIRD! IT'S WAY TOO SUDDEN!!
YOU WANT YOUR SUMMER OF LOVE OR NOT?!
All fired up!!
CALM DOWN, NOBU, CALM DOWN ...

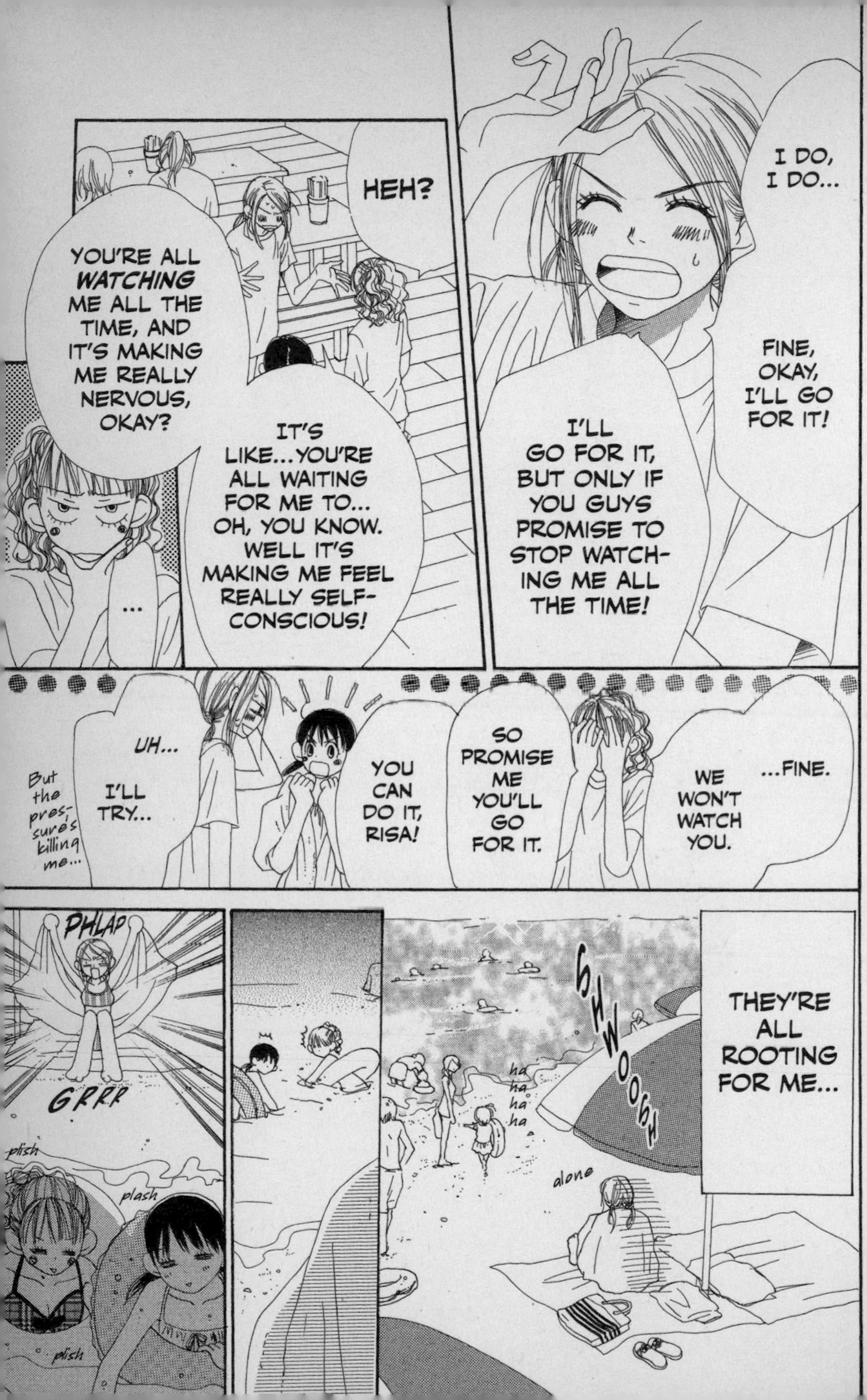
I DO, I DO...
FINE, OKAY, I'LL GO FOR IT!
I'LL GO FOR IT, BUT ONLY IF YOU GUYS PROMISE TO STOP WATCHING ME ALL THE TIME!
HEH?
YOU'RE ALL *WATCHING* ME ALL THE TIME, AND IT'S MAKING ME REALLY NERVOUS, OKAY?
IT'S LIKE...YOU'RE ALL WAITING FOR ME TO... OH, YOU KNOW. WELL IT'S MAKING ME FEEL REALLY SELF-CONSCIOUS!
...
...FINE.
WE WON'T WATCH YOU.
SO PROMISE ME YOU'LL GO FOR IT.
YOU CAN DO IT, RISA!
UH...
I'LL TRY...
But the pressure's killing me...
THEY'RE ALL ROOTING FOR ME...
SHWOOSH
alone
ha ha ha ha
PHLAP
GRRR
plish
plash
plish

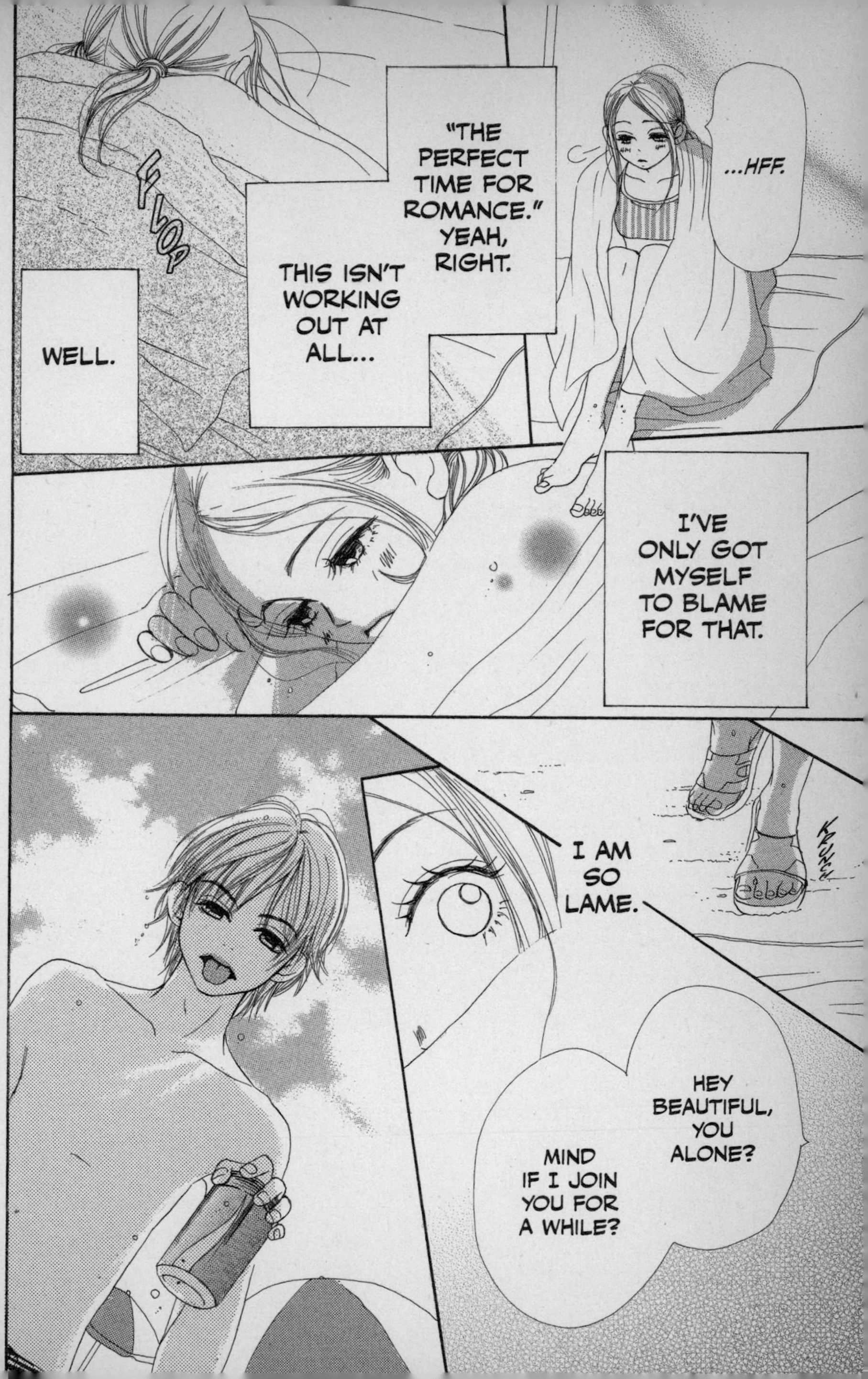
...HFF.
"THE PERFECT TIME FOR ROMANCE." YEAH, RIGHT.
THIS ISN'T WORKING OUT AT ALL...
FLOP
WELL.
I'VE ONLY GOT MYSELF TO BLAME FOR THAT.
KRUNCH
I AM SO LAME.
HEY BEAUTIFUL, YOU ALONE?
MIND IF I JOIN YOU FOR A WHILE?

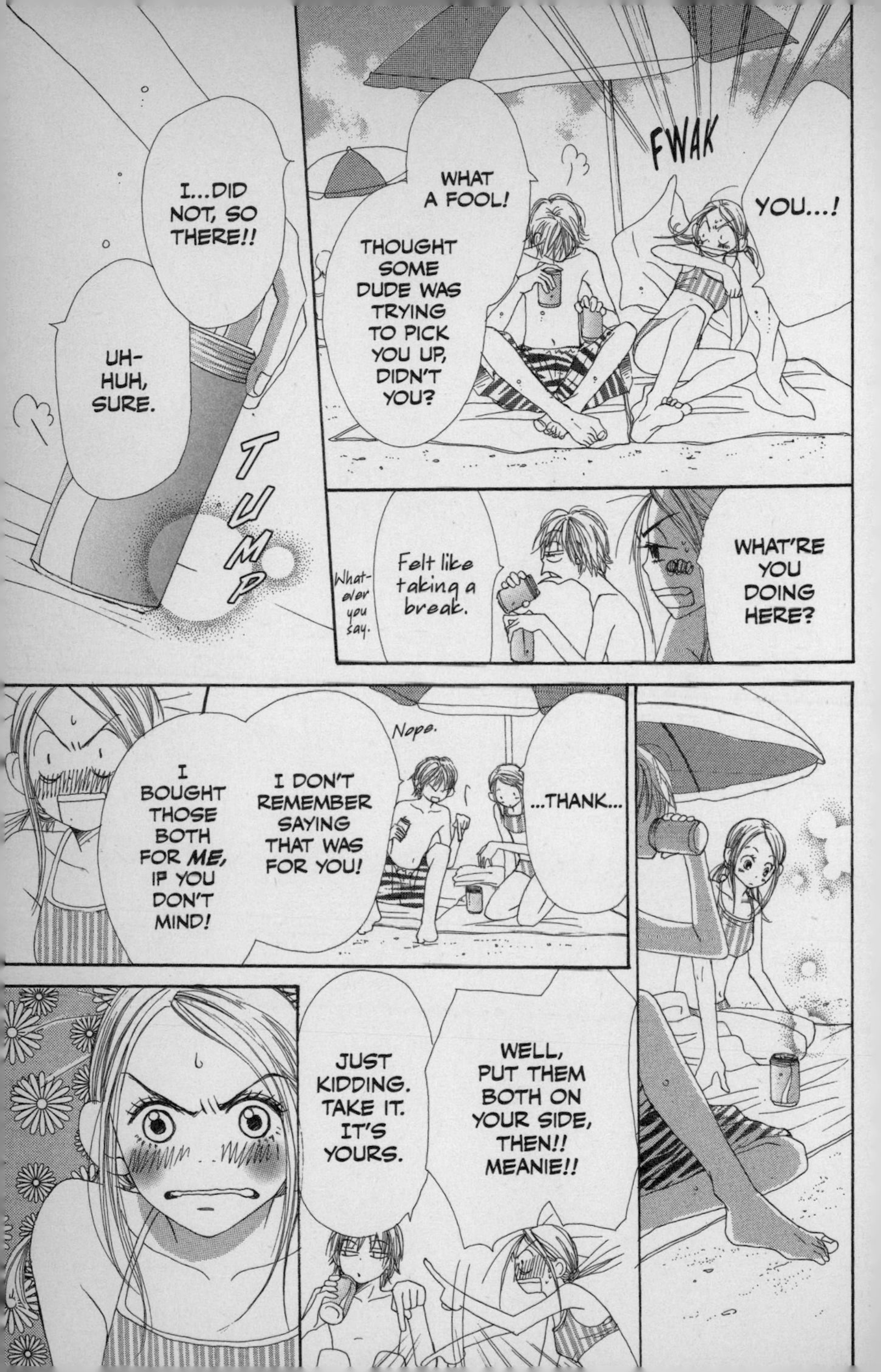
FWAK
YOU...!
WHAT A FOOL!
THOUGHT SOME DUDE WAS TRYING TO PICK YOU UP, DIDN'T YOU?
WHAT'RE YOU DOING HERE?
Felt like taking a break.
Whatever you say.
I...DID NOT, SO THERE!!
UH-HUH, SURE.
TUMP
...THANK...
Nope.
I DON'T REMEMBER SAYING THAT WAS FOR YOU!
I BOUGHT THOSE BOTH FOR *ME*, IF YOU DON'T MIND!
WELL, PUT THEM BOTH ON YOUR SIDE, THEN!! MEANIE!!
JUST KIDDING. TAKE IT. IT'S YOURS.

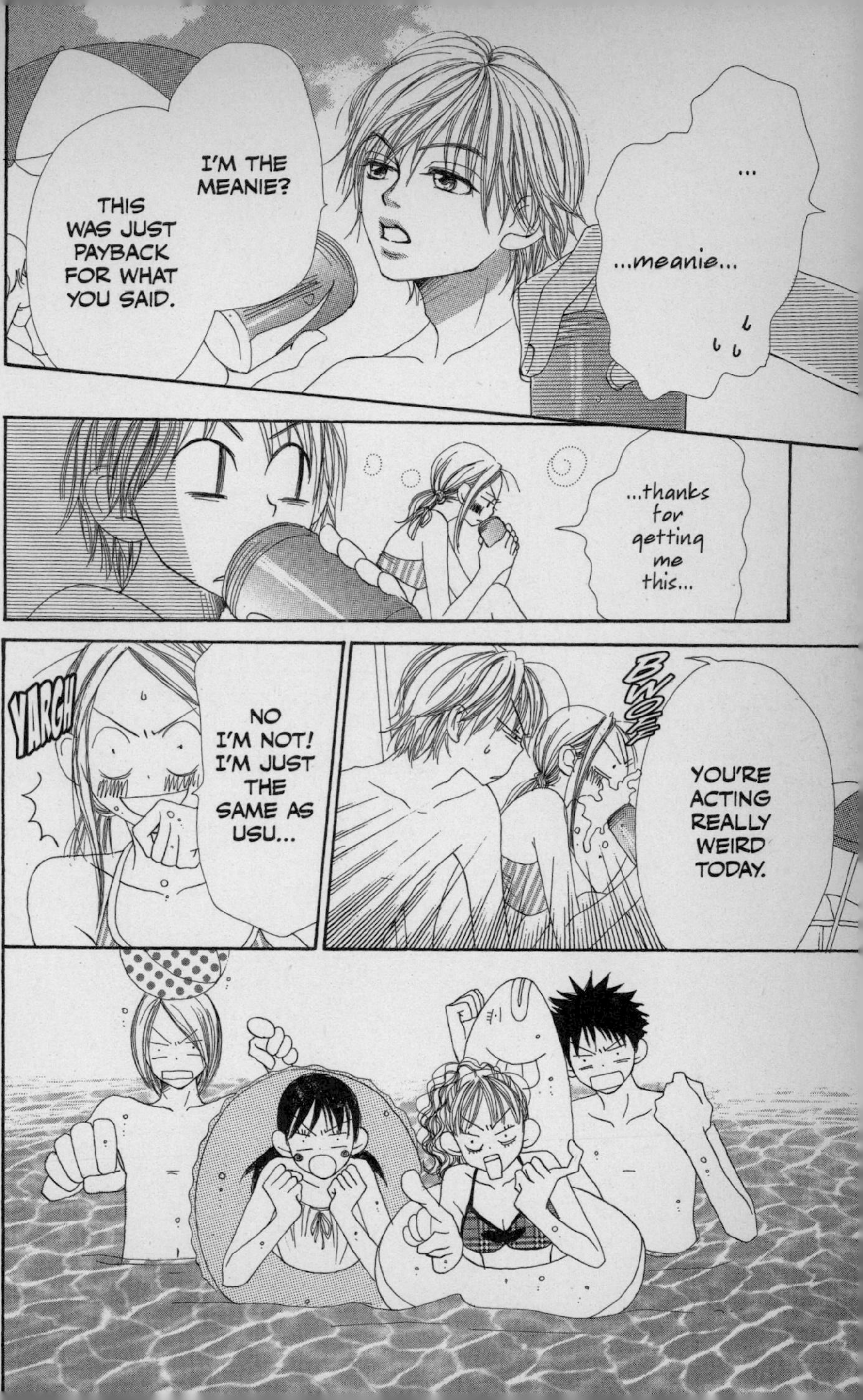
...
...meanie...
I'M THE MEANIE?
THIS WAS JUST PAYBACK FOR WHAT YOU SAID.
...thanks for getting me this...
BWOF
YOU'RE ACTING REALLY WEIRD TODAY.
YARGH
NO I'M NOT! I'M JUST THE SAME AS USU...

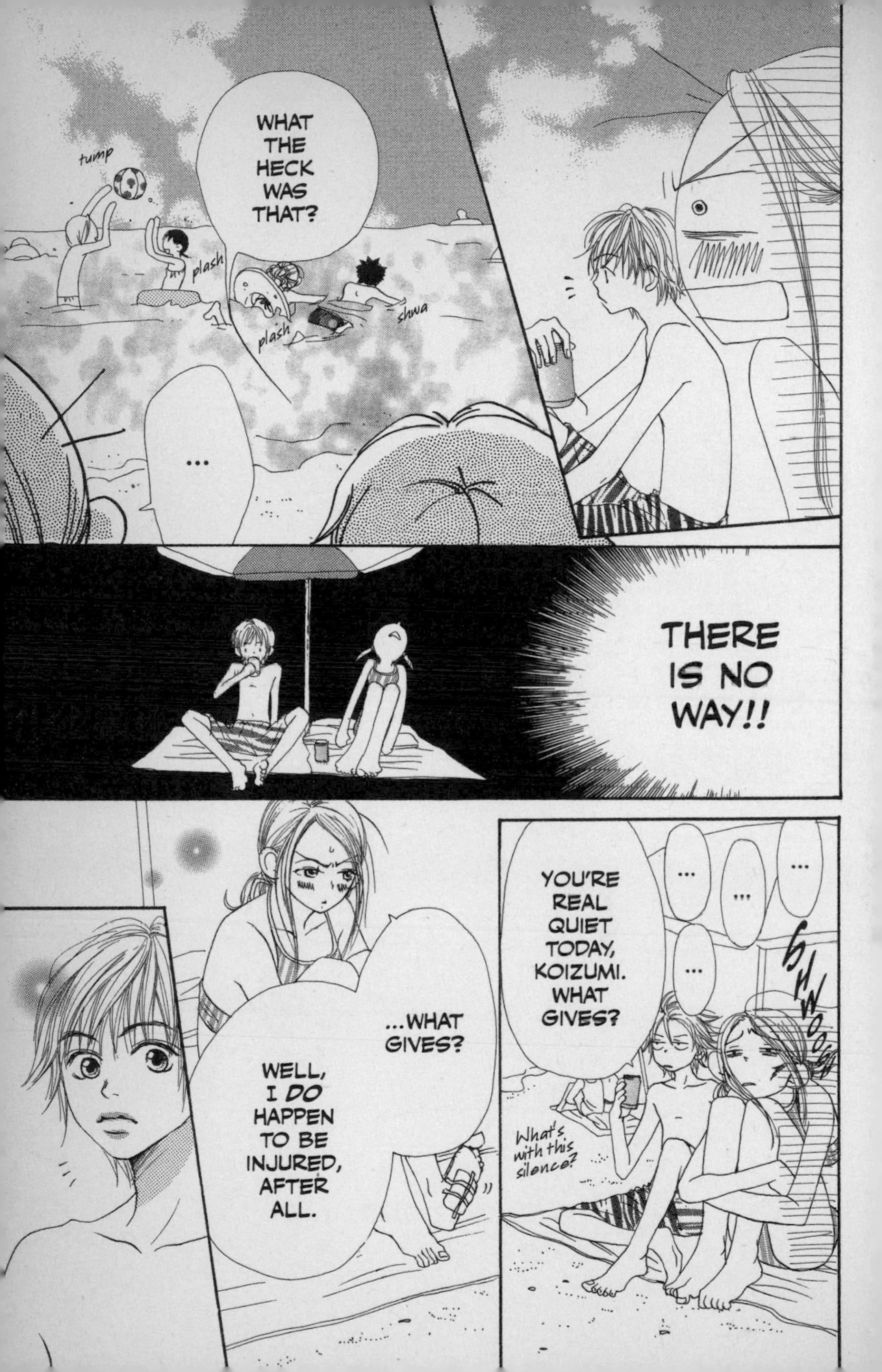
WHAT THE HECK WAS THAT?
tump
plash
plash
shwa
...
THERE IS NO WAY!!
...
...
...
...
YOU'RE REAL QUIET TODAY, KOIZUMI. WHAT GIVES?
SHWOOSH
What's with this silence?
...WHAT GIVES?
WELL, I *DO* HAPPEN TO BE INJURED, AFTER ALL.

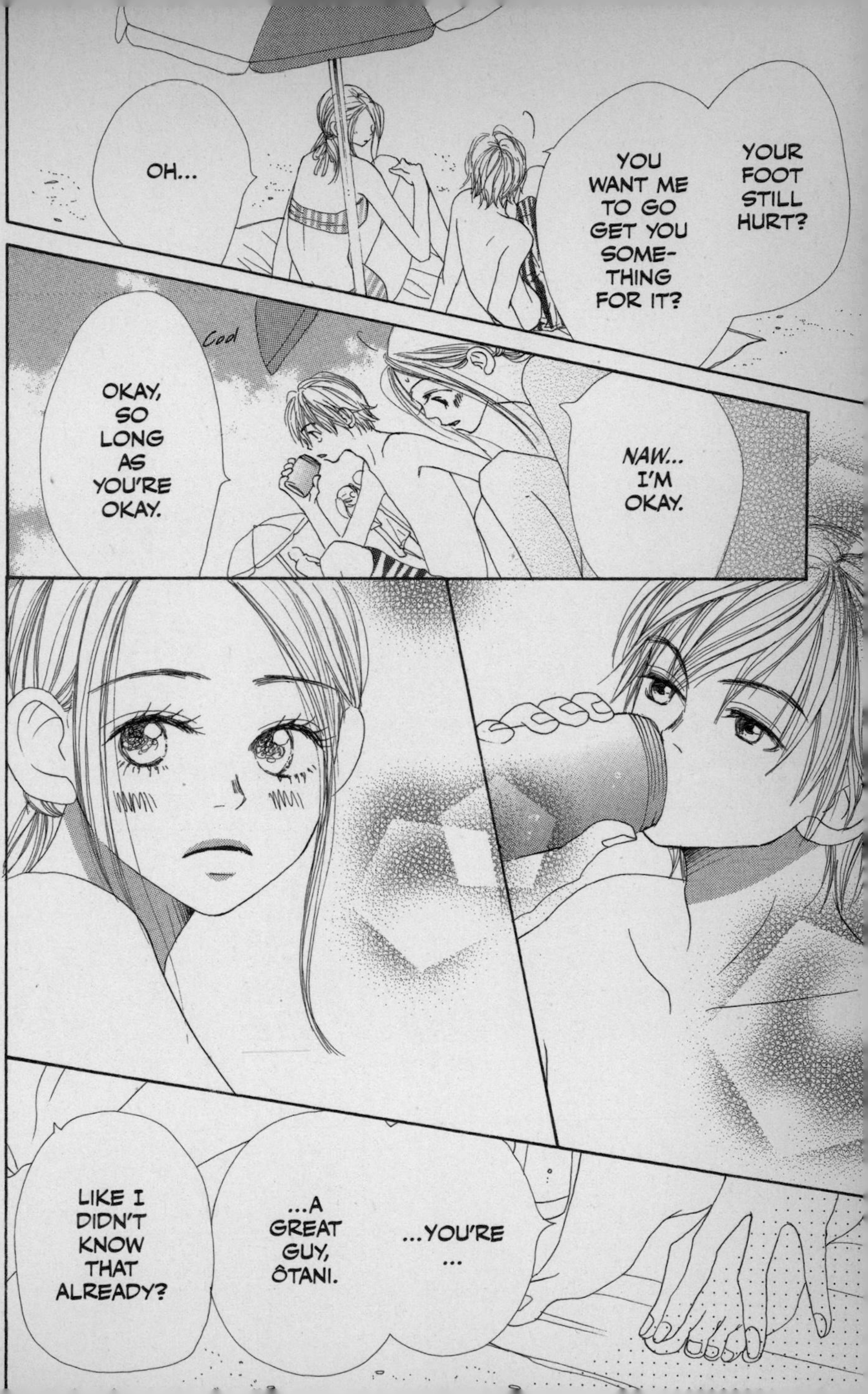
YOUR FOOT STILL HURT?
YOU WANT ME TO GO GET YOU SOME-THING FOR IT?
OH...
NAW... I'M OKAY.
OKAY, SO LONG AS YOU'RE OKAY.
...YOU'RE ...
...A GREAT GUY, ŌTANI.
LIKE I DIDN'T KNOW THAT ALREADY?

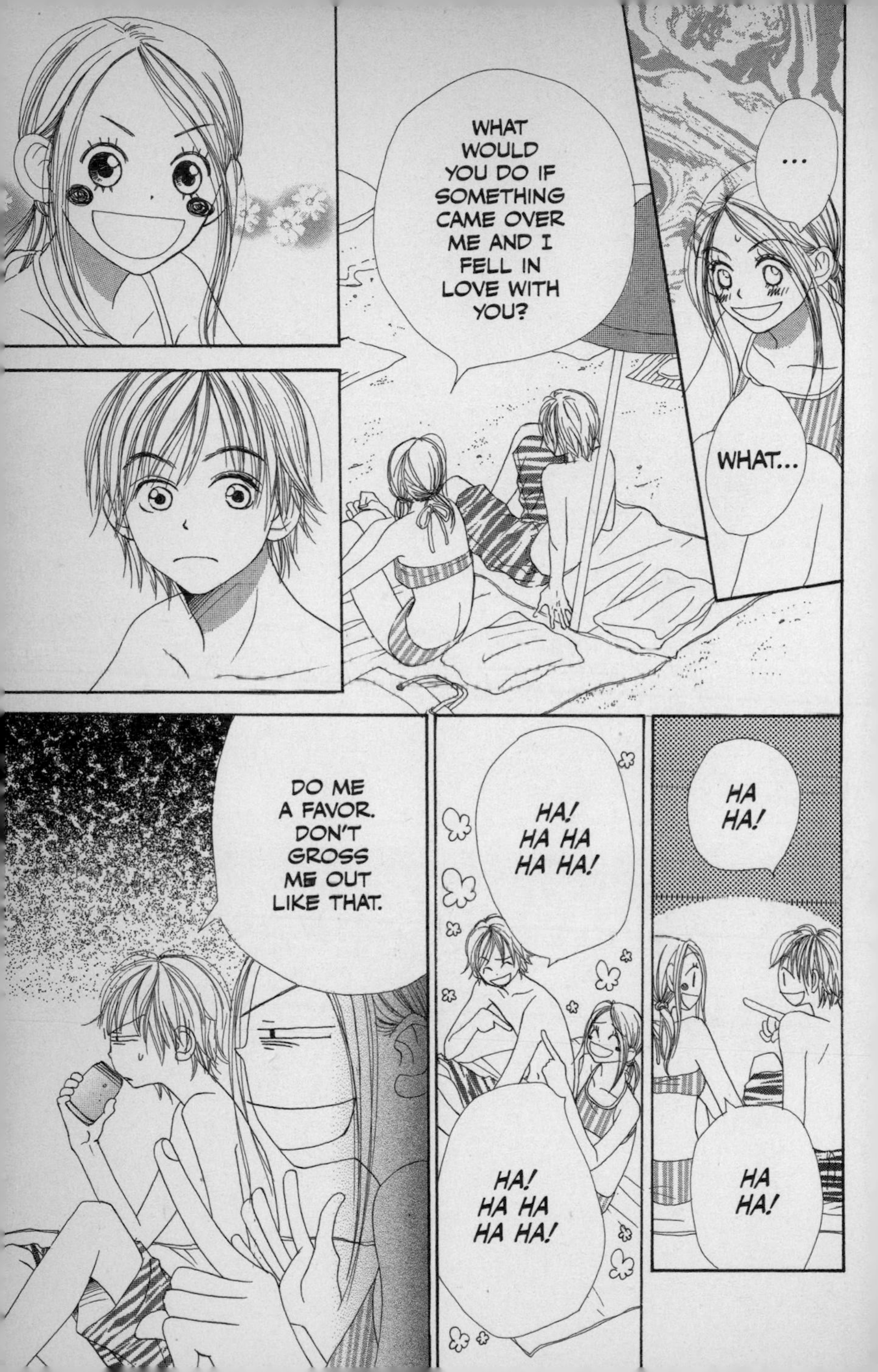
WHAT WOULD YOU DO IF SOMETHING CAME OVER ME AND I FELL IN LOVE WITH YOU?
...
WHAT...
HA HA!
HA HA!
HA! HA HA HA HA!
HA! HA HA HA HA!
DO ME A FAVOR. DON'T GROSS ME OUT LIKE THAT.

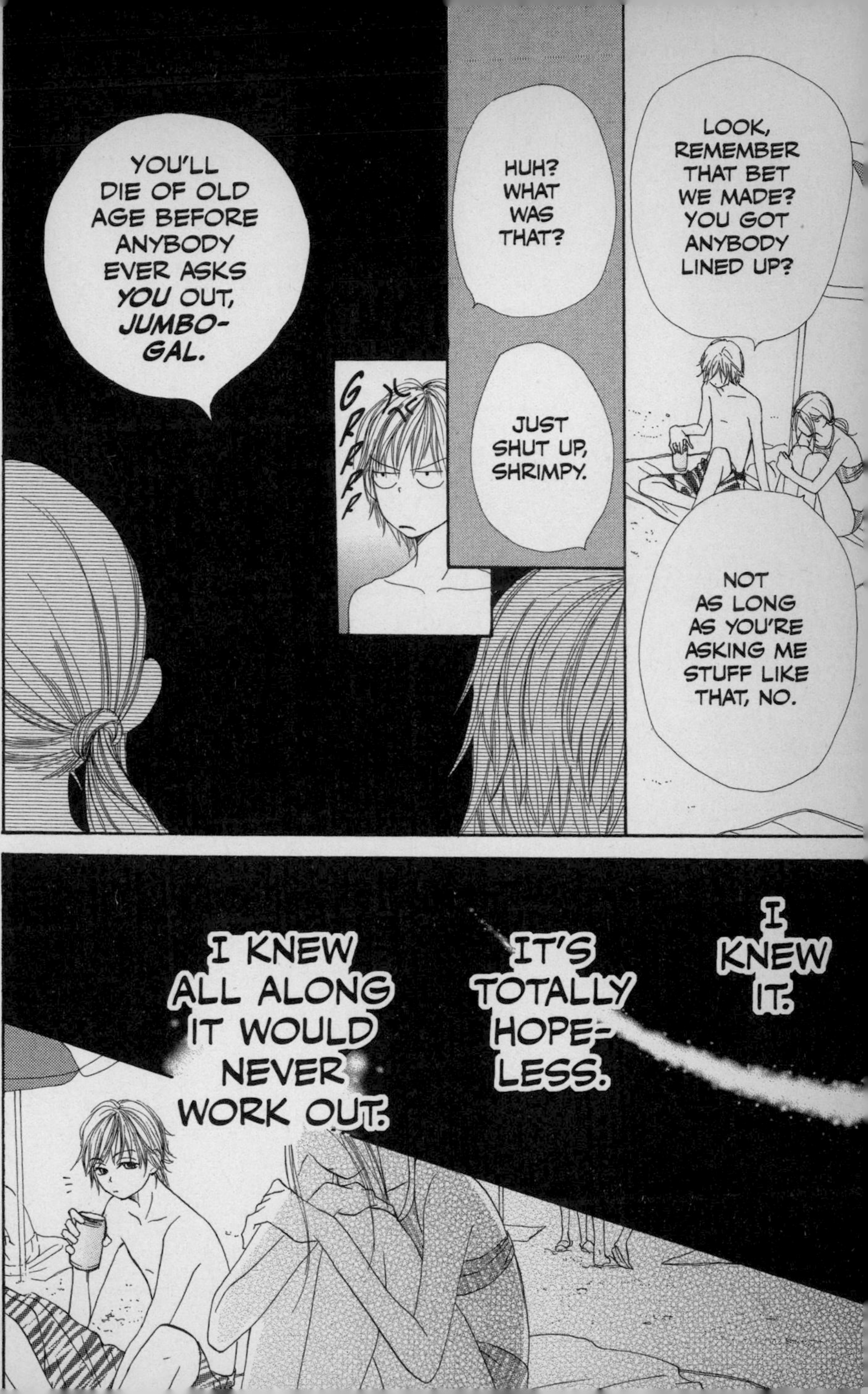
LOOK, REMEMBER THAT BET WE MADE? YOU GOT ANYBODY LINED UP?
NOT AS LONG AS YOU'RE ASKING ME STUFF LIKE THAT, NO.
HUH? WHAT WAS THAT?
JUST SHUT UP, SHRIMPY.
YOU'LL DIE OF OLD AGE BEFORE ANYBODY EVER ASKS *YOU* OUT, *JUMBO-GAL.*
I KNEW IT.
IT'S TOTALLY HOPELESS.
I KNEW ALL ALONG IT WOULD NEVER WORK OUT.

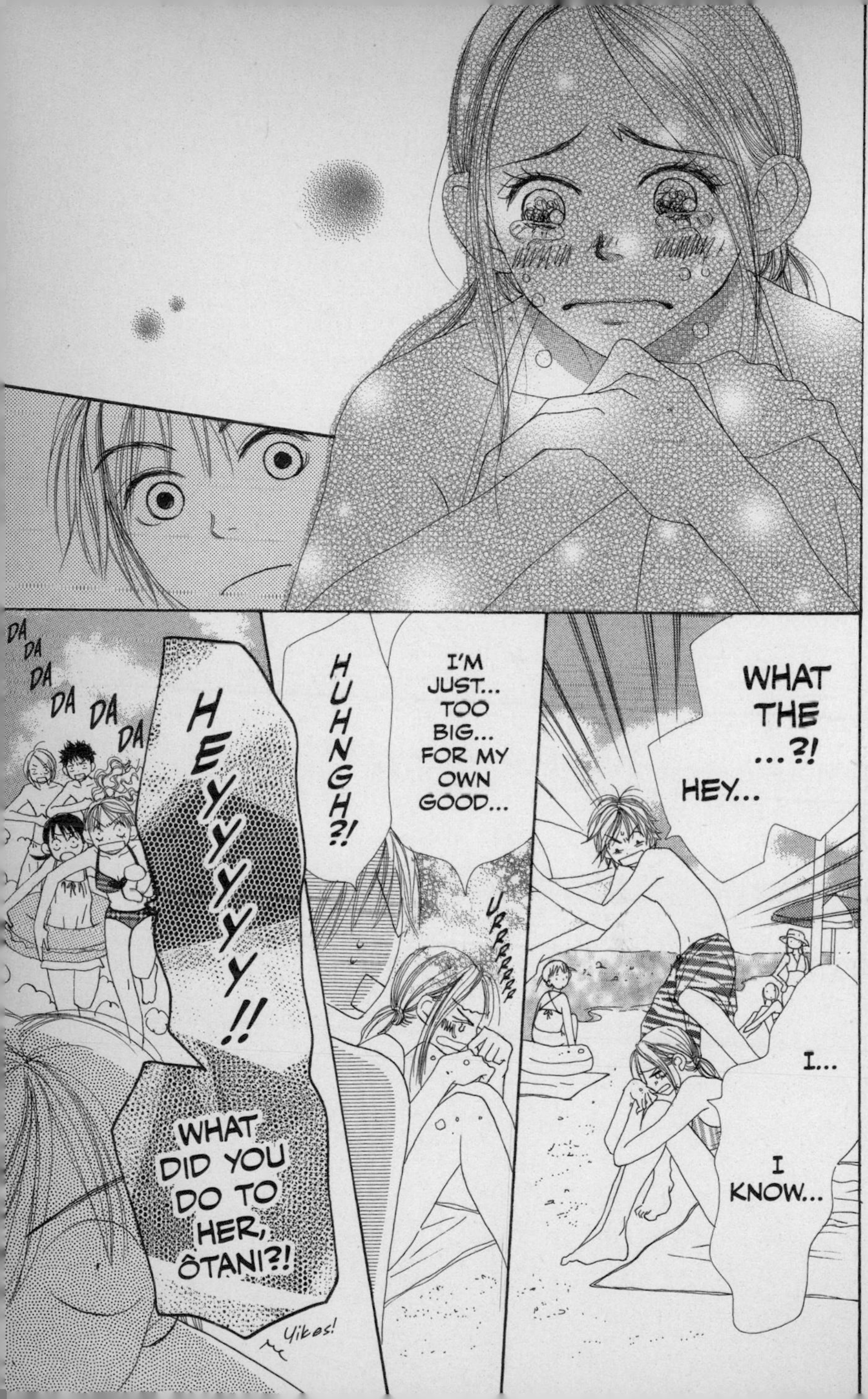
WHAT THE ...?!
HEY...
I...
I KNOW...
I'M JUST... TOO BIG... FOR MY OWN GOOD...
HUHNGH?!
HEYYYYY!!
WHAT DID YOU DO TO HER, ŌTANI?!
DA DA DA DA DA DA
Yikes!

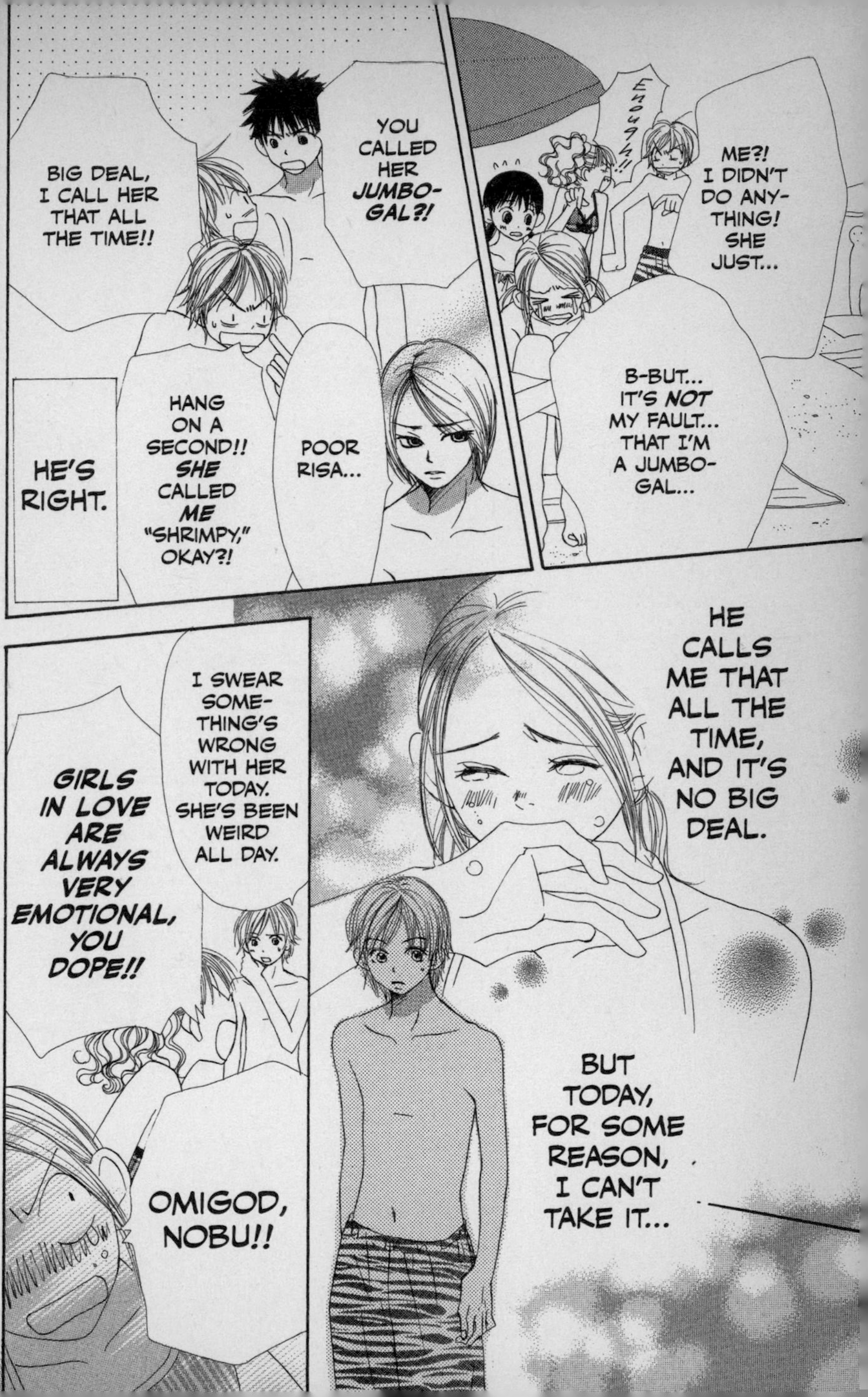
Enough!!
ME?! I DIDN'T DO ANYTHING! SHE JUST...
B-BUT... IT'S NOT MY FAULT... THAT I'M A JUMBO-GAL...
YOU CALLED HER JUMBO-GAL?!
BIG DEAL, I CALL HER THAT ALL THE TIME!!
POOR RISA...
HANG ON A SECOND!! SHE CALLED ME "SHRIMPY," OKAY?!
HE'S RIGHT.
HE CALLS ME THAT ALL THE TIME, AND IT'S NO BIG DEAL.
BUT TODAY, FOR SOME REASON, I CAN'T TAKE IT...
I SWEAR SOMETHING'S WRONG WITH HER TODAY. SHE'S BEEN WEIRD ALL DAY.
GIRLS IN LOVE ARE ALWAYS VERY EMOTIONAL, YOU DOPE!!
OMIGOD, NOBU!!

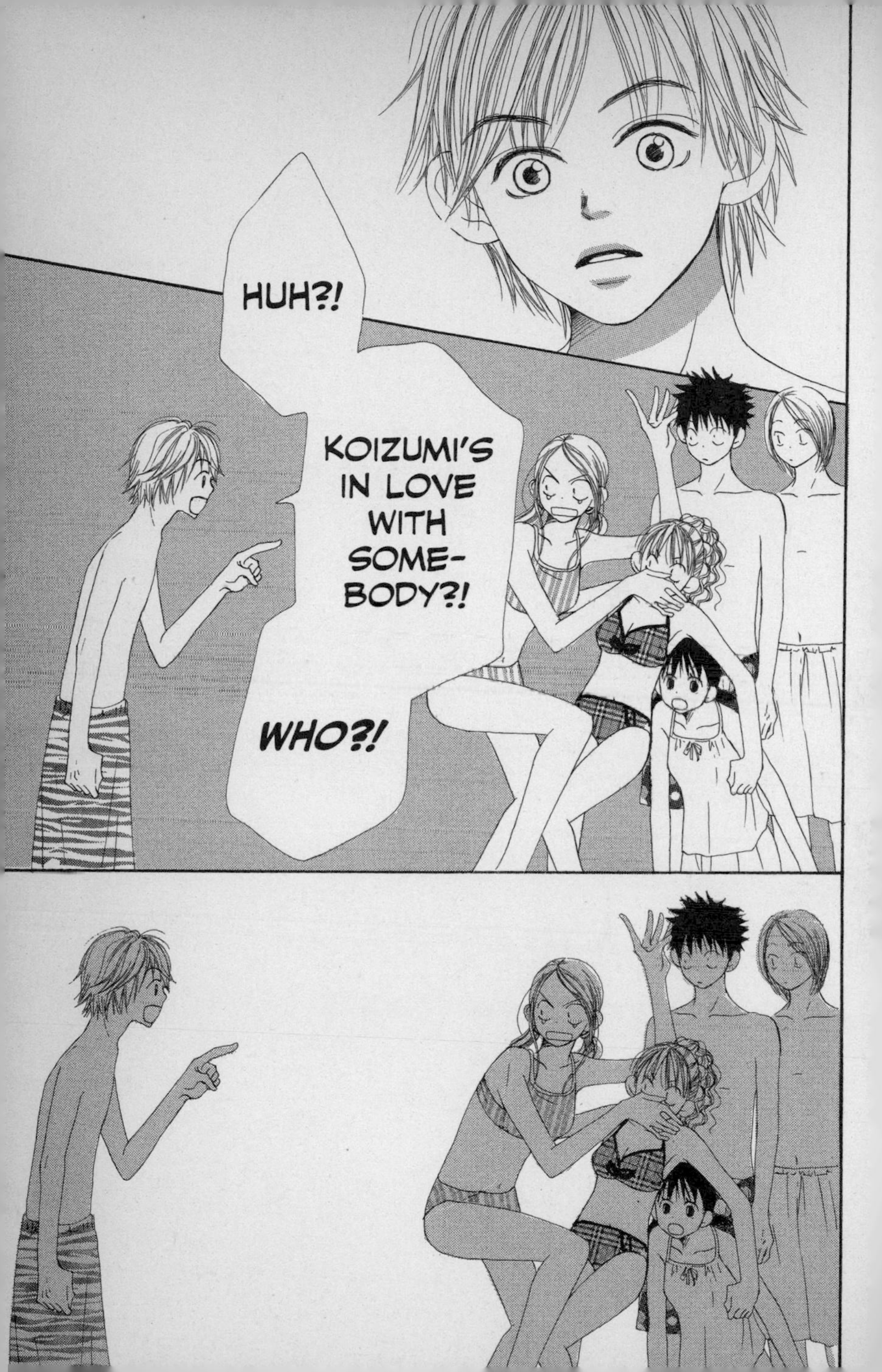
HUH?!
KOIZUMI'S IN LOVE WITH SOME-BODY?!
WHO?!

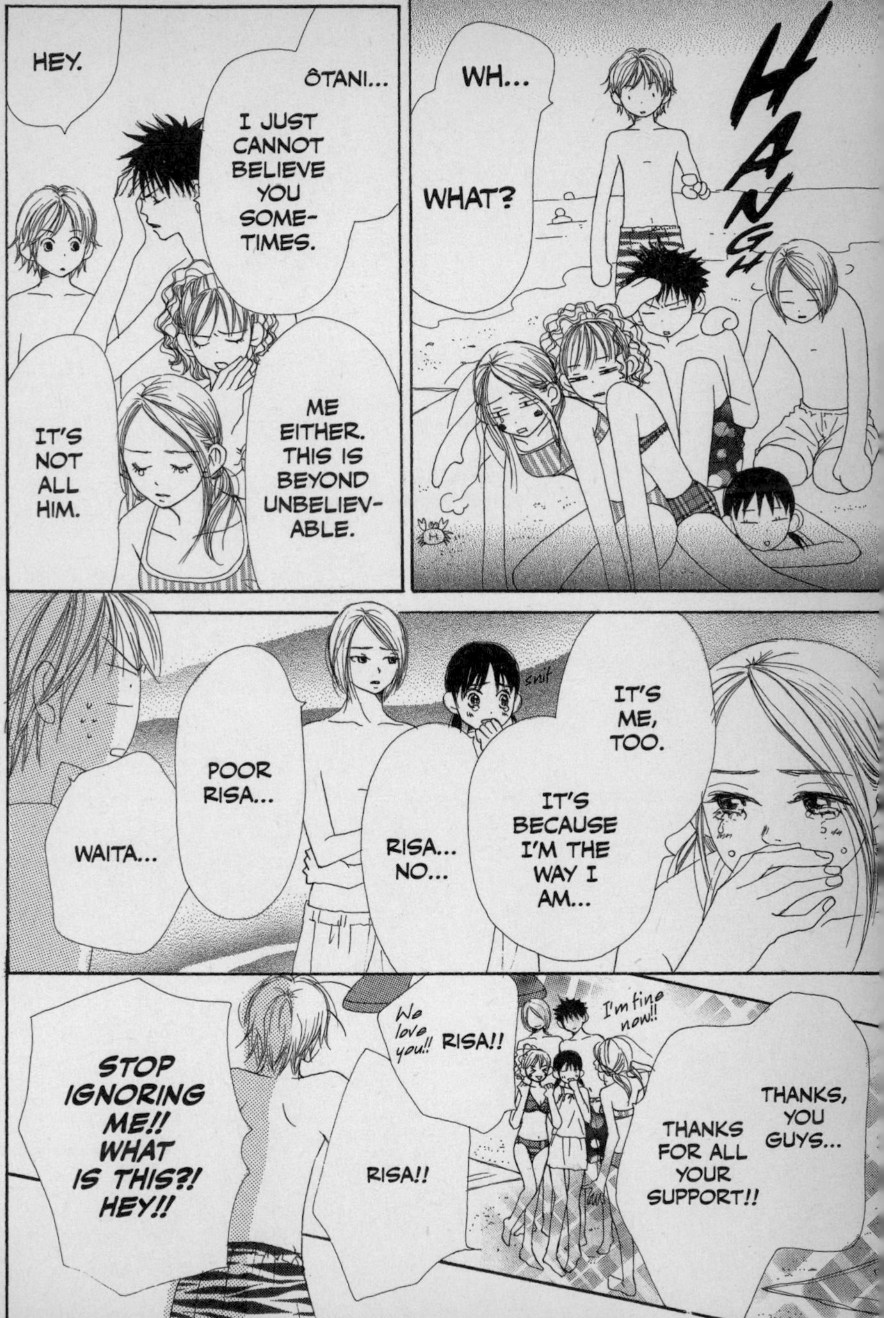
HANGH
WH...
WHAT?
ŌTANI...
I JUST CANNOT BELIEVE YOU SOMETIMES.
HEY.
ME EITHER. THIS IS BEYOND UNBELIEVABLE.
IT'S NOT ALL HIM.
IT'S ME, TOO.
IT'S BECAUSE I'M THE WAY I AM...
snif
RISA... NO...
POOR RISA...
WAITA...
I'm fine now!!
THANKS, YOU GUYS...
THANKS FOR ALL YOUR SUPPORT!!
We love you!! RISA!!
RISA!!
STOP IGNORING ME!! WHAT IS THIS?! HEY!!

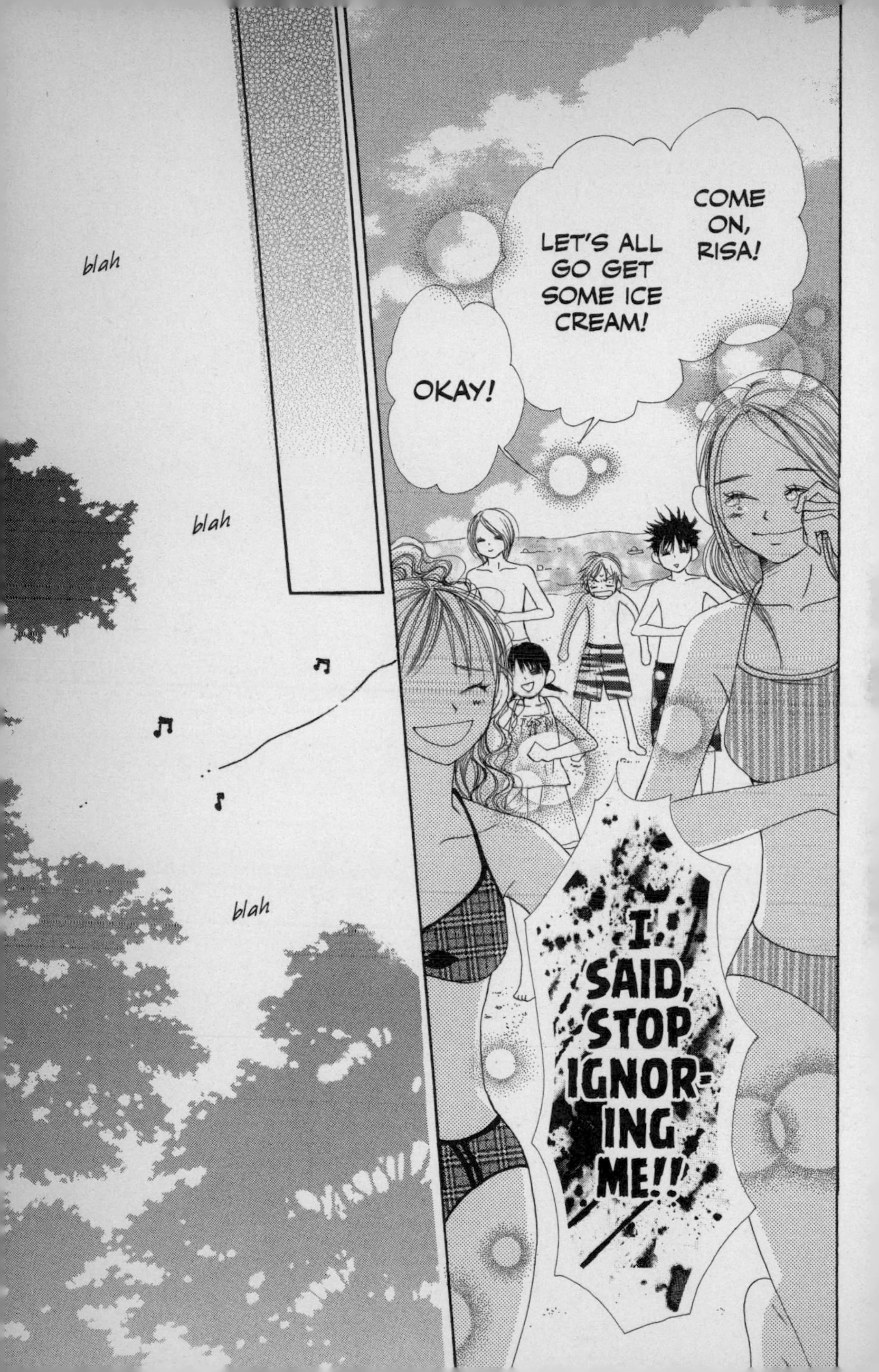
COME ON, RISA!
LET'S ALL GO GET SOME ICE CREAM!
OKAY!
I SAID, STOP IGNOR-ING ME!!
blah
blah
blah

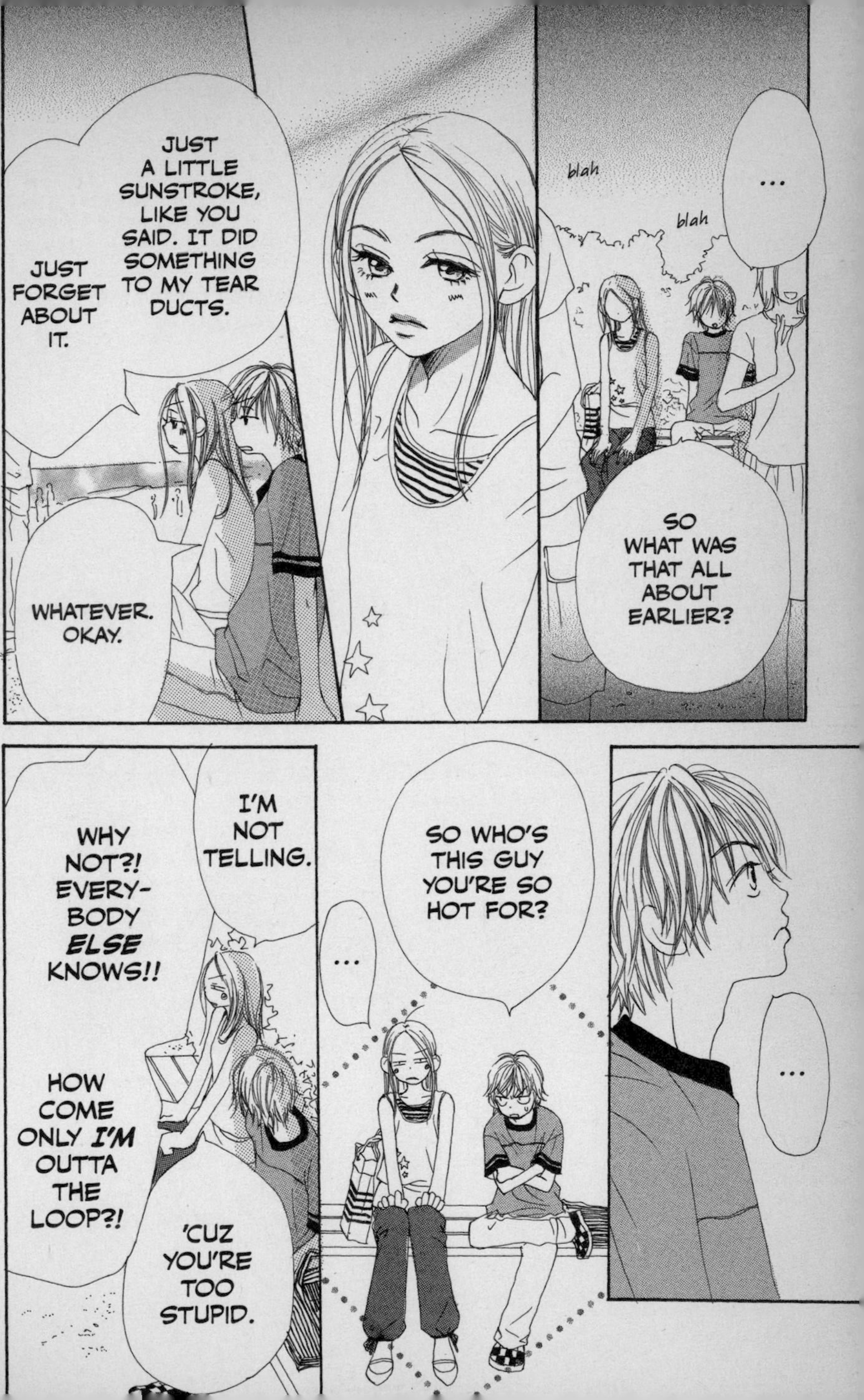
...
blah
blah
SO WHAT WAS THAT ALL ABOUT EARLIER?
JUST A LITTLE SUNSTROKE, LIKE YOU SAID. IT DID SOMETHING TO MY TEAR DUCTS.
JUST FORGET ABOUT IT.
WHATEVER. OKAY.
...
SO WHO'S THIS GUY YOU'RE SO HOT FOR?
...
I'M NOT TELLING.
WHY NOT?! EVERYBODY *ELSE* KNOWS!!
HOW COME ONLY *I'M* OUTTA THE LOOP?!
'CUZ YOU'RE TOO STUPID.

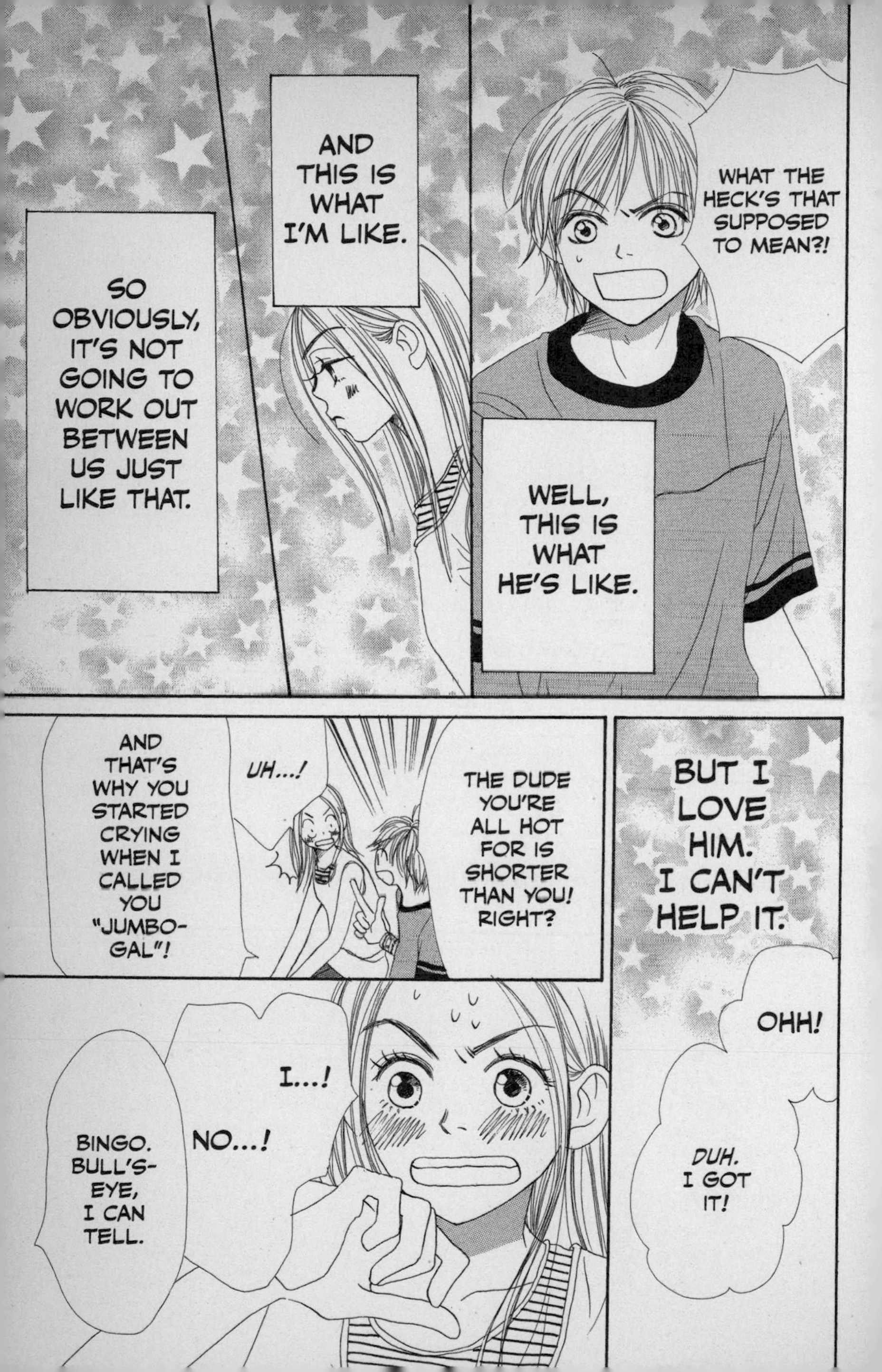
WHAT THE HECK'S THAT SUPPOSED TO MEAN?!
WELL, THIS IS WHAT HE'S LIKE.
AND THIS IS WHAT I'M LIKE.
SO OBVIOUSLY, IT'S NOT GOING TO WORK OUT BETWEEN US JUST LIKE THAT.
BUT I LOVE HIM. I CAN'T HELP IT.
THE DUDE YOU'RE ALL HOT FOR IS SHORTER THAN YOU! RIGHT?
UH...!
AND THAT'S WHY YOU STARTED CRYING WHEN I CALLED YOU "JUMBO-GAL"!
OHH!
DUH. I GOT IT!
I...!
NO...!
BINGO. BULL'S-EYE, I CAN TELL.

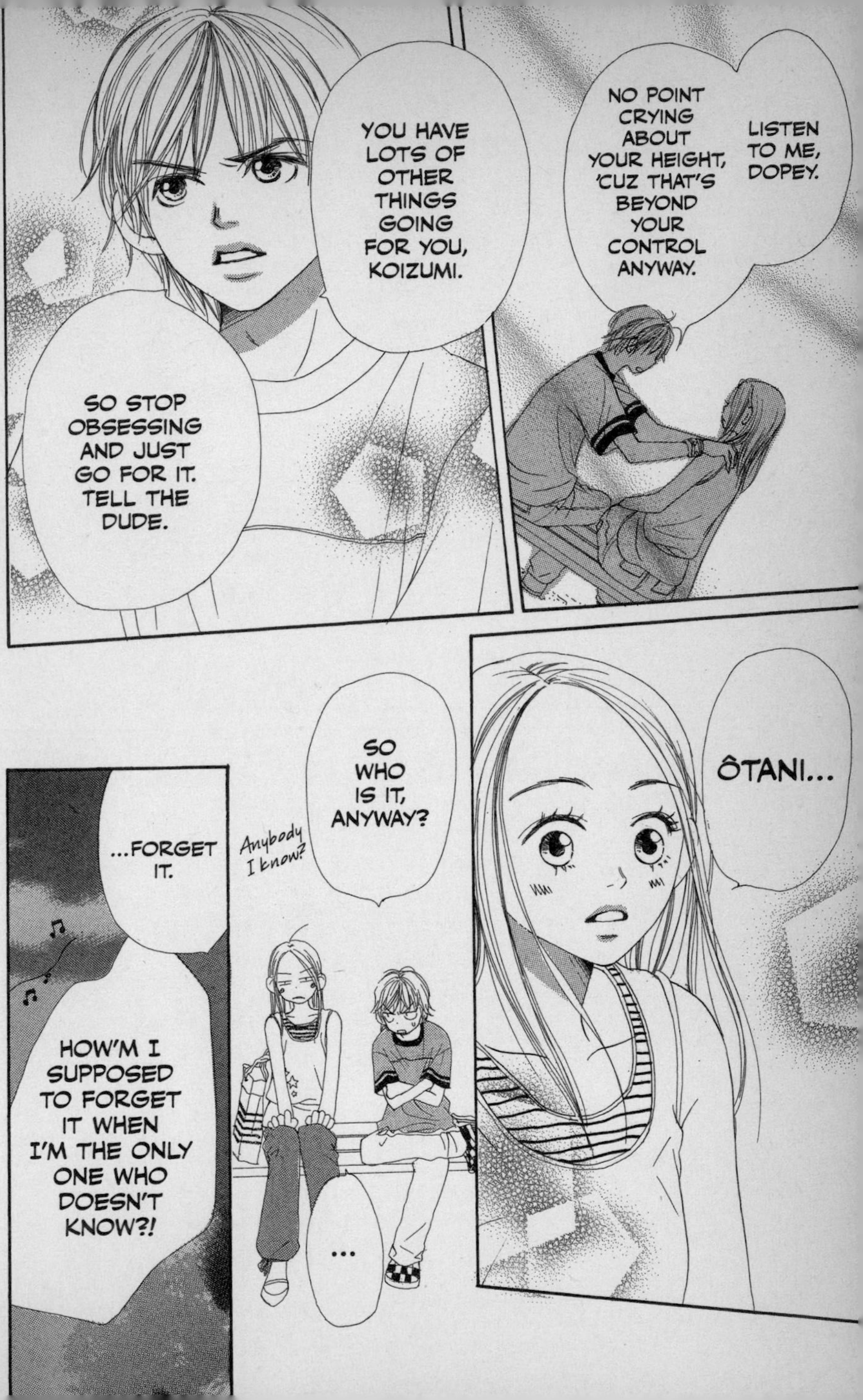
LISTEN TO ME, DOPEY.
NO POINT CRYING ABOUT YOUR HEIGHT, 'CUZ THAT'S BEYOND YOUR CONTROL ANYWAY.
YOU HAVE LOTS OF OTHER THINGS GOING FOR YOU, KOIZUMI.
SO STOP OBSESSING AND JUST GO FOR IT. TELL THE DUDE.
ÔTANI...
SO WHO IS IT, ANYWAY?
Anybody I know?
...
...FORGET IT.
HOW'M I SUPPOSED TO FORGET IT WHEN I'M THE ONLY ONE WHO DOESN'T KNOW?!

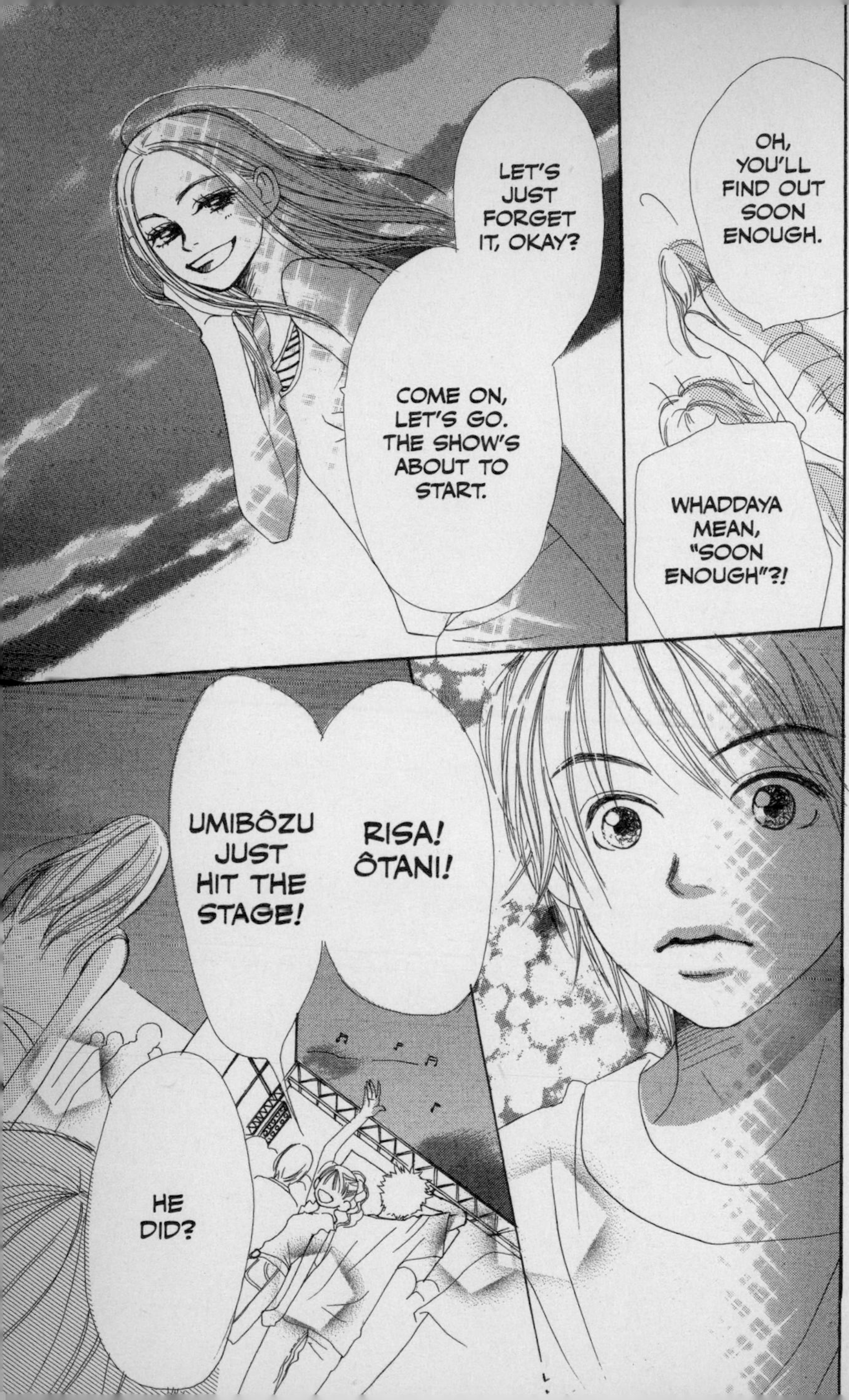
OH, YOU'LL FIND OUT SOON ENOUGH.
WHADDAYA MEAN, "SOON ENOUGH"?!
LET'S JUST FORGET IT, OKAY?
COME ON, LET'S GO. THE SHOW'S ABOUT TO START.
RISA! ÔTANI!
UMIBÔZU JUST HIT THE STAGE!
HE DID?

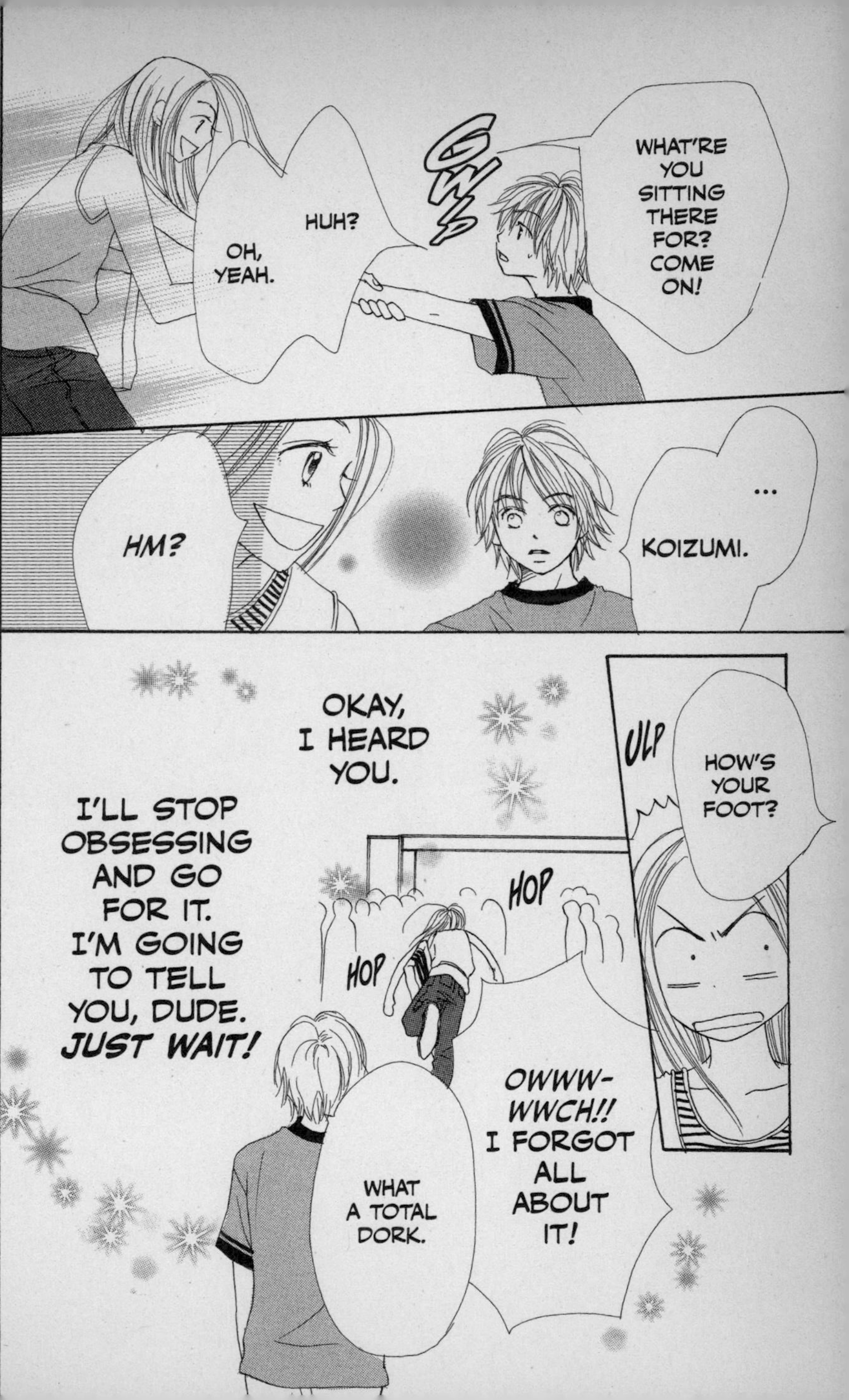
WHAT'RE YOU SITTING THERE FOR? COME ON!
HUH?
OH, YEAH.
... KOIZUMI.
HM?
ULP
HOW'S YOUR FOOT?
OKAY, I HEARD YOU.
I'LL STOP OBSESSING AND GO FOR IT. I'M GOING TO TELL YOU, DUDE. JUST WAIT!
HOP
HOP
OWWW-WWCH!! I FORGOT ALL ABOUT IT!
WHAT A TOTAL DORK.

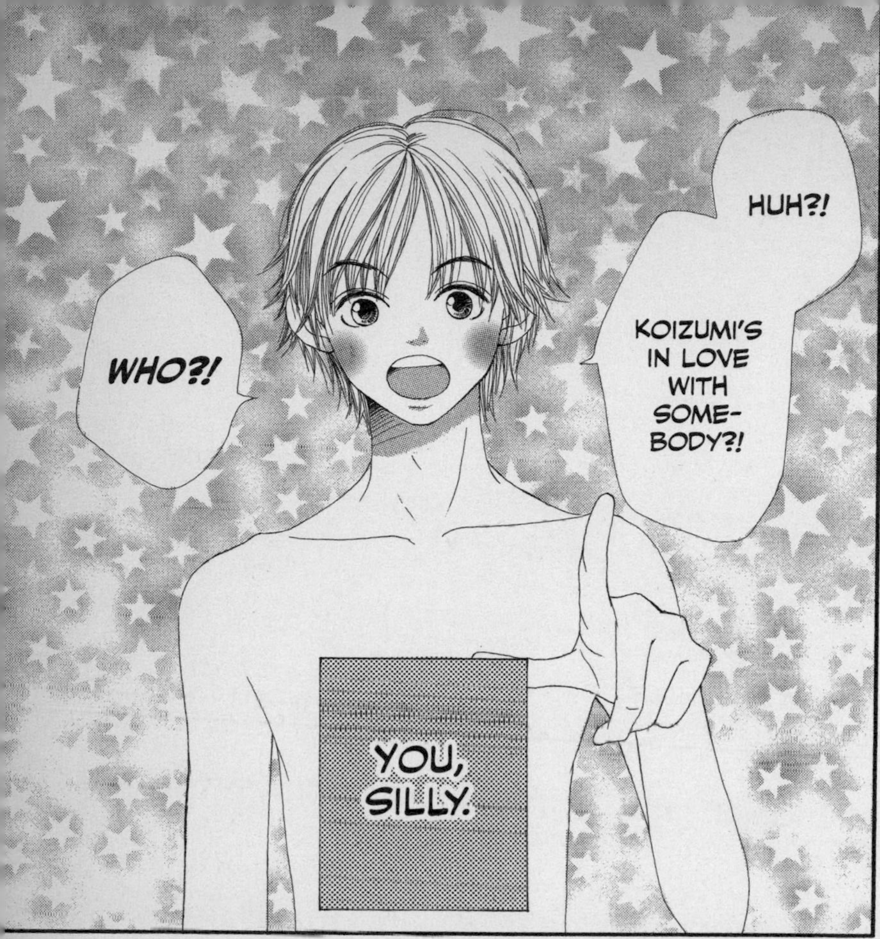
HUH?!
KOIZUMI'S IN LOVE WITH SOME-BODY?!
WHO?!
YOU, SILLY.

CHAPTER 14

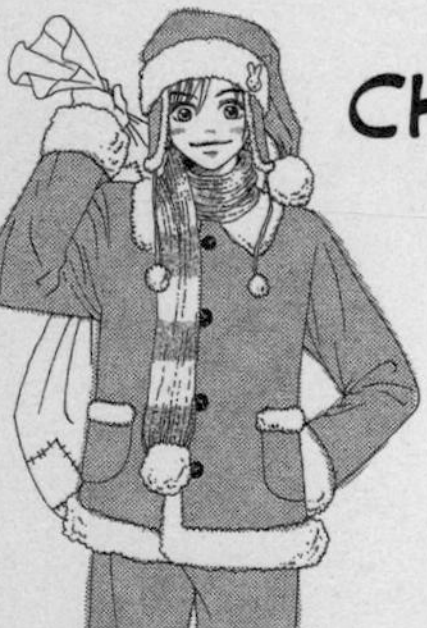

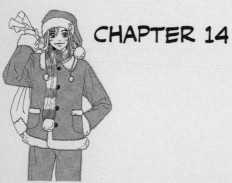

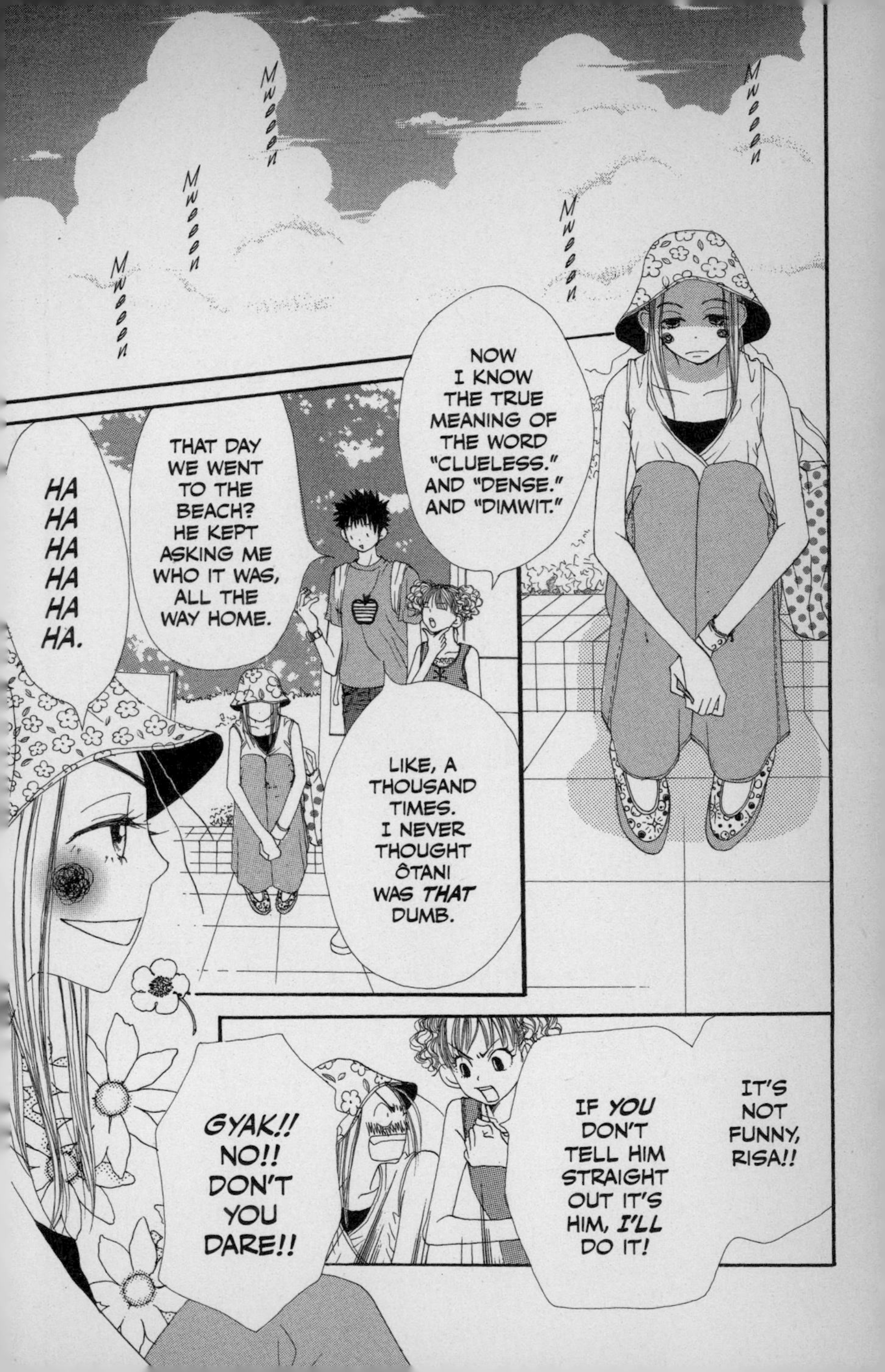
Mweeen
Mweeen
Mweeen
Mweeen
Mweeen
NOW I KNOW THE TRUE MEANING OF THE WORD "CLUELESS." AND "DENSE." AND "DIMWIT."
THAT DAY WE WENT TO THE BEACH? HE KEPT ASKING ME WHO IT WAS, ALL THE WAY HOME.
HA HA HA HA HA HA.
LIKE, A THOUSAND TIMES. I NEVER THOUGHT ÔTANI WAS *THAT* DUMB.
IT'S NOT FUNNY, RISA!!
IF *YOU* DON'T TELL HIM STRAIGHT OUT IT'S HIM, *I'LL* DO IT!
GYAK!! NO!! DON'T YOU DARE!!

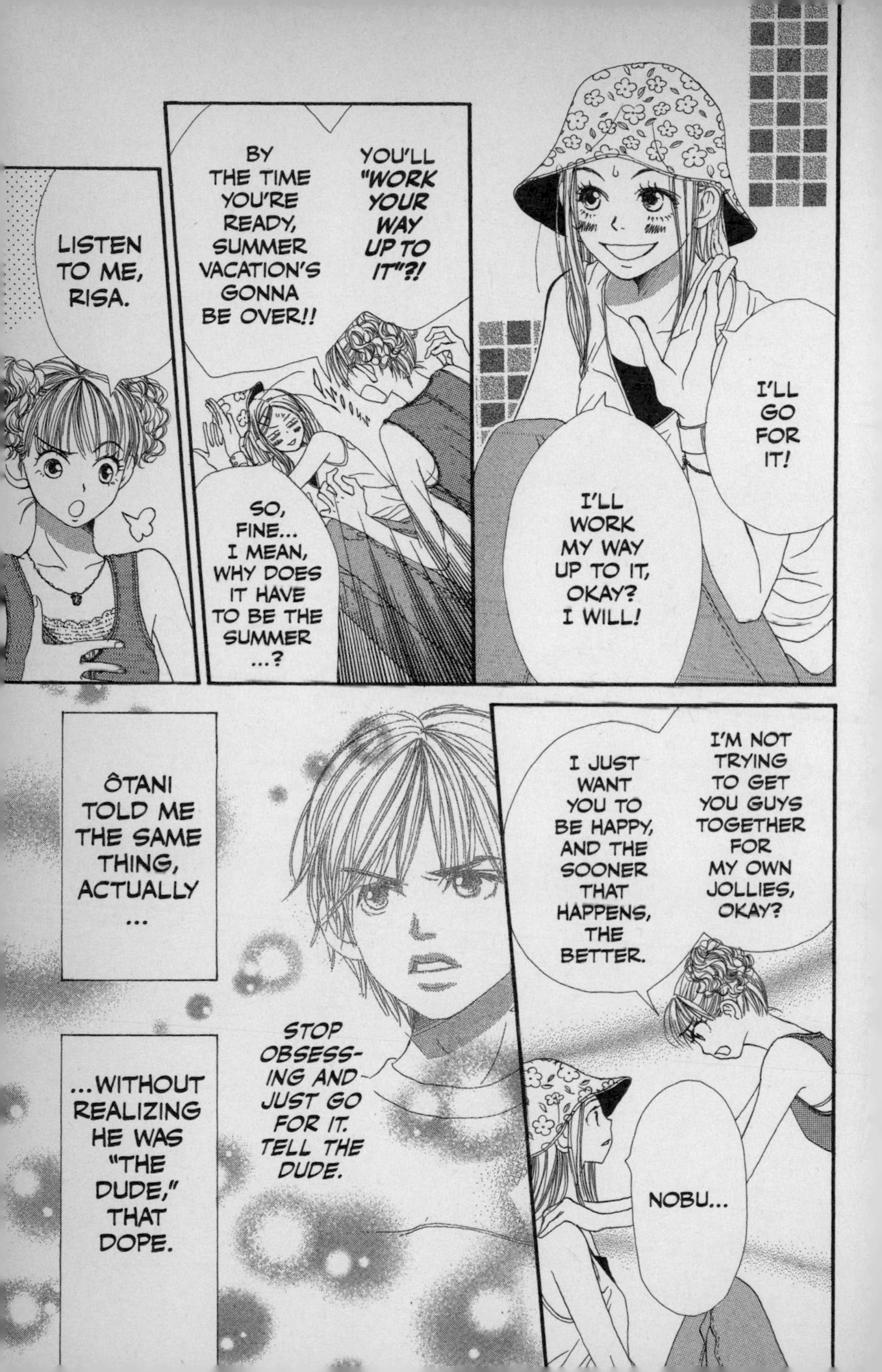
I'LL GO FOR IT!
I'LL WORK MY WAY UP TO IT, OKAY? I WILL!
YOU'LL "WORK YOUR WAY UP TO IT"?!
BY THE TIME YOU'RE READY, SUMMER VACATION'S GONNA BE OVER!!
SO, FINE... I MEAN, WHY DOES IT HAVE TO BE THE SUMMER ...?
LISTEN TO ME, RISA.
I'M NOT TRYING TO GET YOU GUYS TOGETHER FOR MY OWN JOLLIES, OKAY?
I JUST WANT YOU TO BE HAPPY, AND THE SOONER THAT HAPPENS, THE BETTER.
NOBU...
ÔTANI TOLD ME THE SAME THING, ACTUALLY ...
STOP OBSESSING AND JUST GO FOR IT. TELL THE DUDE.
...WITHOUT REALIZING HE WAS "THE DUDE," THAT DOPE.

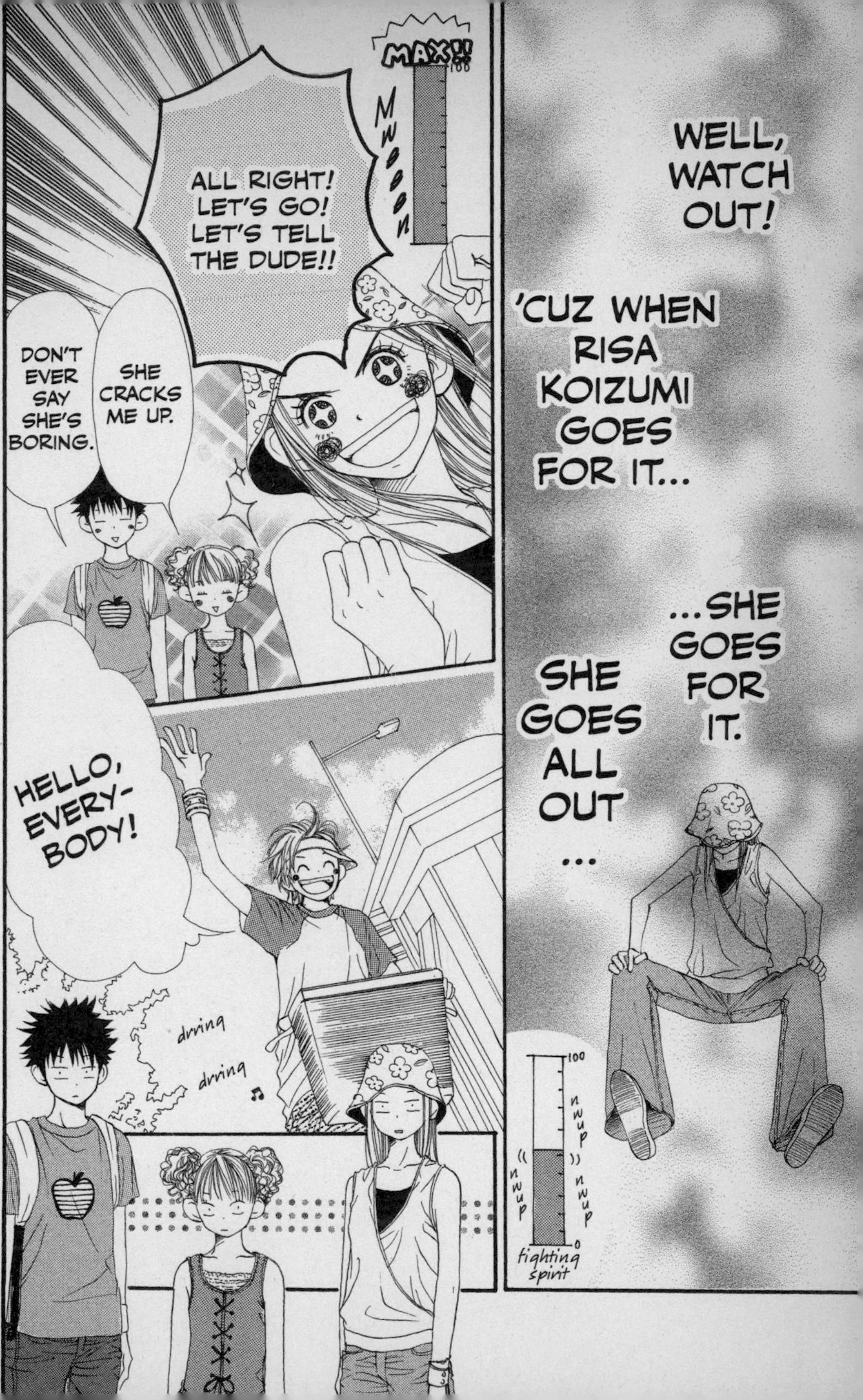
WELL, WATCH OUT!
'CUZ WHEN RISA KOIZUMI GOES FOR IT...
...SHE GOES FOR IT.
SHE GOES ALL OUT...
100
nwup
nwup
nwup
0
fighting spirit
MAX!!
100
MWOOOOn
ALL RIGHT! LET'S GO! LET'S TELL THE DUDE!!
SHE CRACKS ME UP.
DON'T EVER SAY SHE'S BORING.
HELLO, EVERY-BODY!
drring
drring

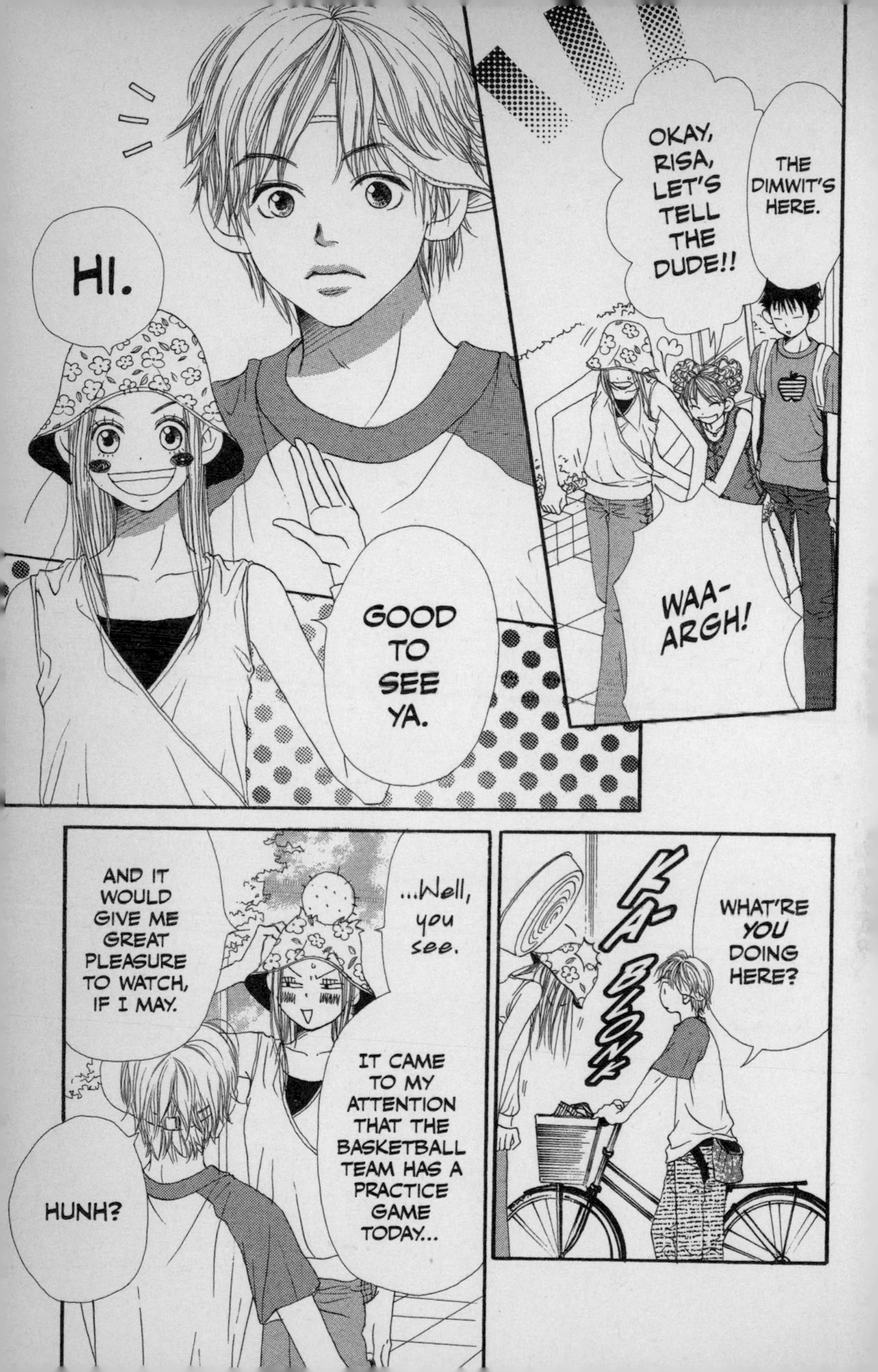
THE DIMWIT'S HERE.
OKAY, RISA, LET'S TELL THE DUDE!!
WAA-ARGH!
HI.
GOOD TO SEE YA.
WHAT'RE YOU DOING HERE?
KA-BLONK
...Well, you see.
IT CAME TO MY ATTENTION THAT THE BASKETBALL TEAM HAS A PRACTICE GAME TODAY...
AND IT WOULD GIVE ME GREAT PLEASURE TO WATCH, IF I MAY.
HUNH?

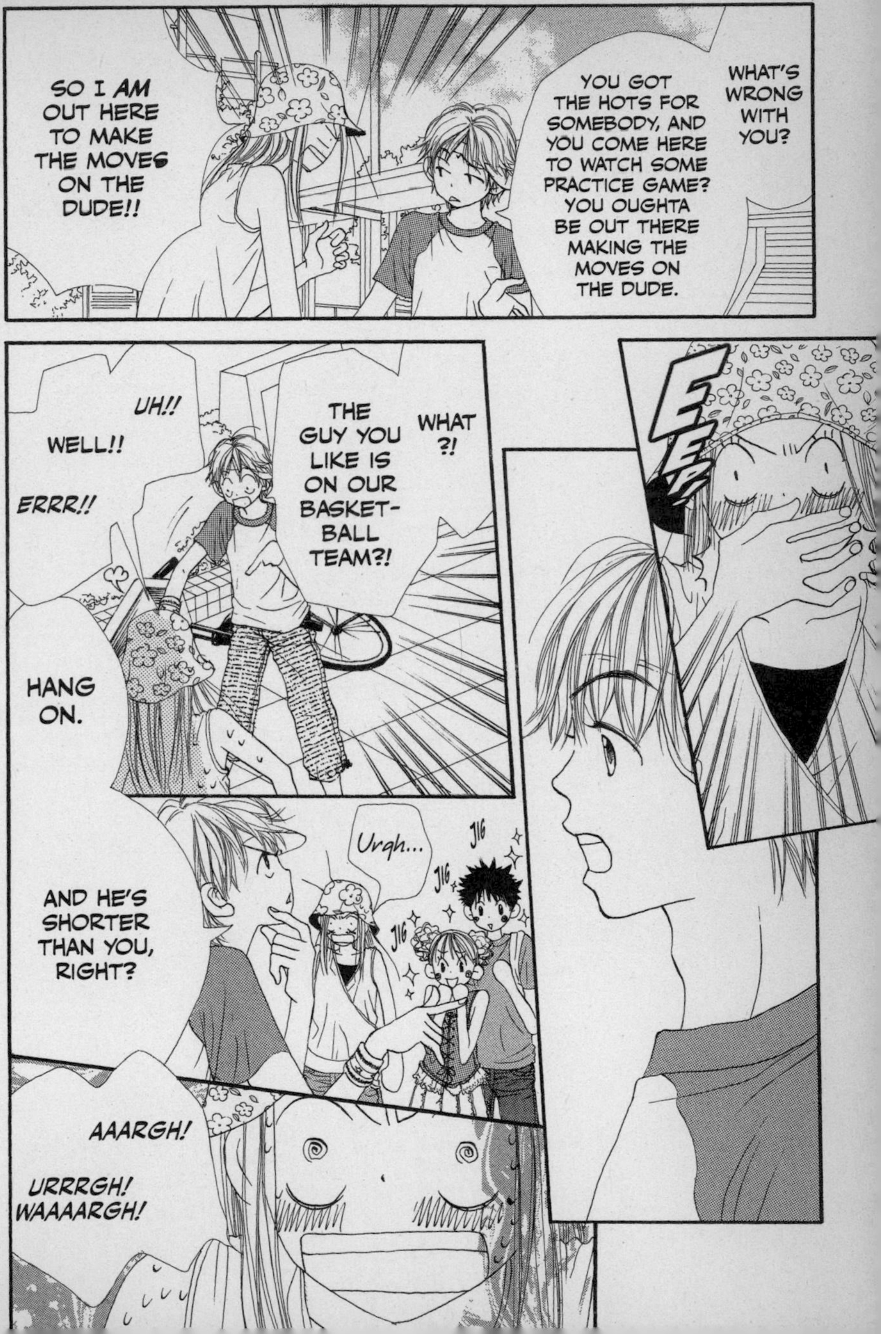

WHAT'S WRONG WITH YOU?
YOU GOT THE HOTS FOR SOMEBODY, AND YOU COME HERE TO WATCH SOME PRACTICE GAME? YOU OUGHTA BE OUT THERE MAKING THE MOVES ON THE DUDE.
SO I *AM* OUT HERE TO MAKE THE MOVES ON THE DUDE!!
EEP
WHAT?!
THE GUY YOU LIKE IS ON OUR BASKET-BALL TEAM?!
UH!!
WELL!!
ERRR!!
HANG ON.
Urgh...
JIG
JIG
JIG
AND HE'S SHORTER THAN YOU, RIGHT?
AAARGH!
URRRGH! WAAAARGH!

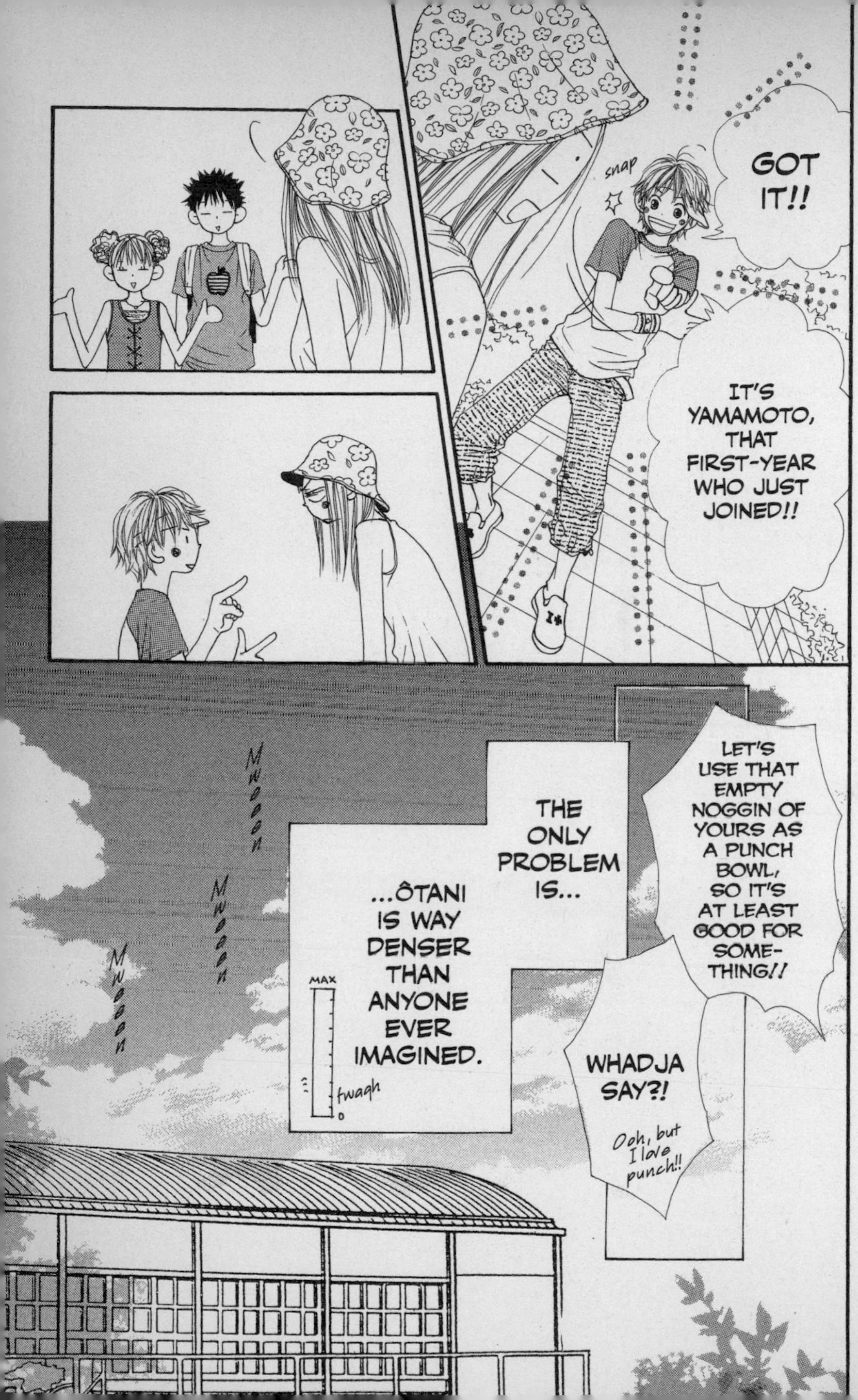
GOT IT!!
snap
IT'S YAMAMOTO, THAT FIRST-YEAR WHO JUST JOINED!!
LET'S USE THAT EMPTY NOGGIN OF YOURS AS A PUNCH BOWL, SO IT'S AT LEAST GOOD FOR SOME-THING!!
WHADJA SAY?!
Ooh, but I love punch!!
THE ONLY PROBLEM IS...
...ÔTANI IS WAY DENSER THAN ANYONE EVER IMAGINED.
MAX
fwagh
0
MWOOON
MWOOON
MWOOON

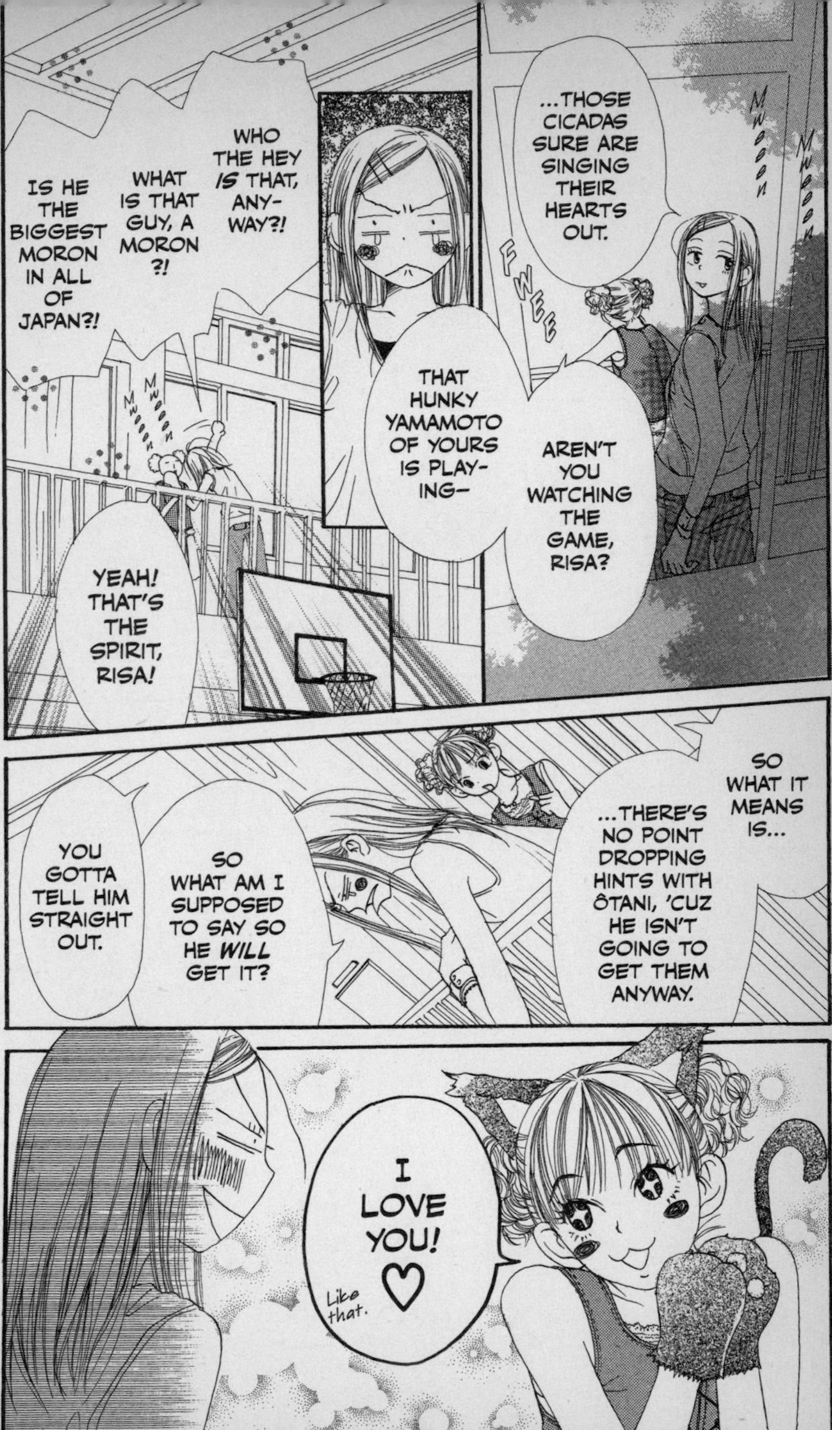
...THOSE CICADAS SURE ARE SINGING THEIR HEARTS OUT.
Mween
Mween
FWEE
AREN'T YOU WATCHING THE GAME, RISA?
THAT HUNKY YAMAMOTO OF YOURS IS PLAYING—
WHO THE HEY IS THAT, ANYWAY?!
WHAT IS THAT GUY, A MORON?!
IS HE THE BIGGEST MORON IN ALL OF JAPAN?!
Mween
Mween
YEAH! THAT'S THE SPIRIT, RISA!
SO WHAT IT MEANS IS...
...THERE'S NO POINT DROPPING HINTS WITH ŌTANI, 'CUZ HE ISN'T GOING TO GET THEM ANYWAY.
SO WHAT AM I SUPPOSED TO SAY SO HE WILL GET IT?
YOU GOTTA TELL HIM STRAIGHT OUT.
I LOVE YOU! ♡
Like that.

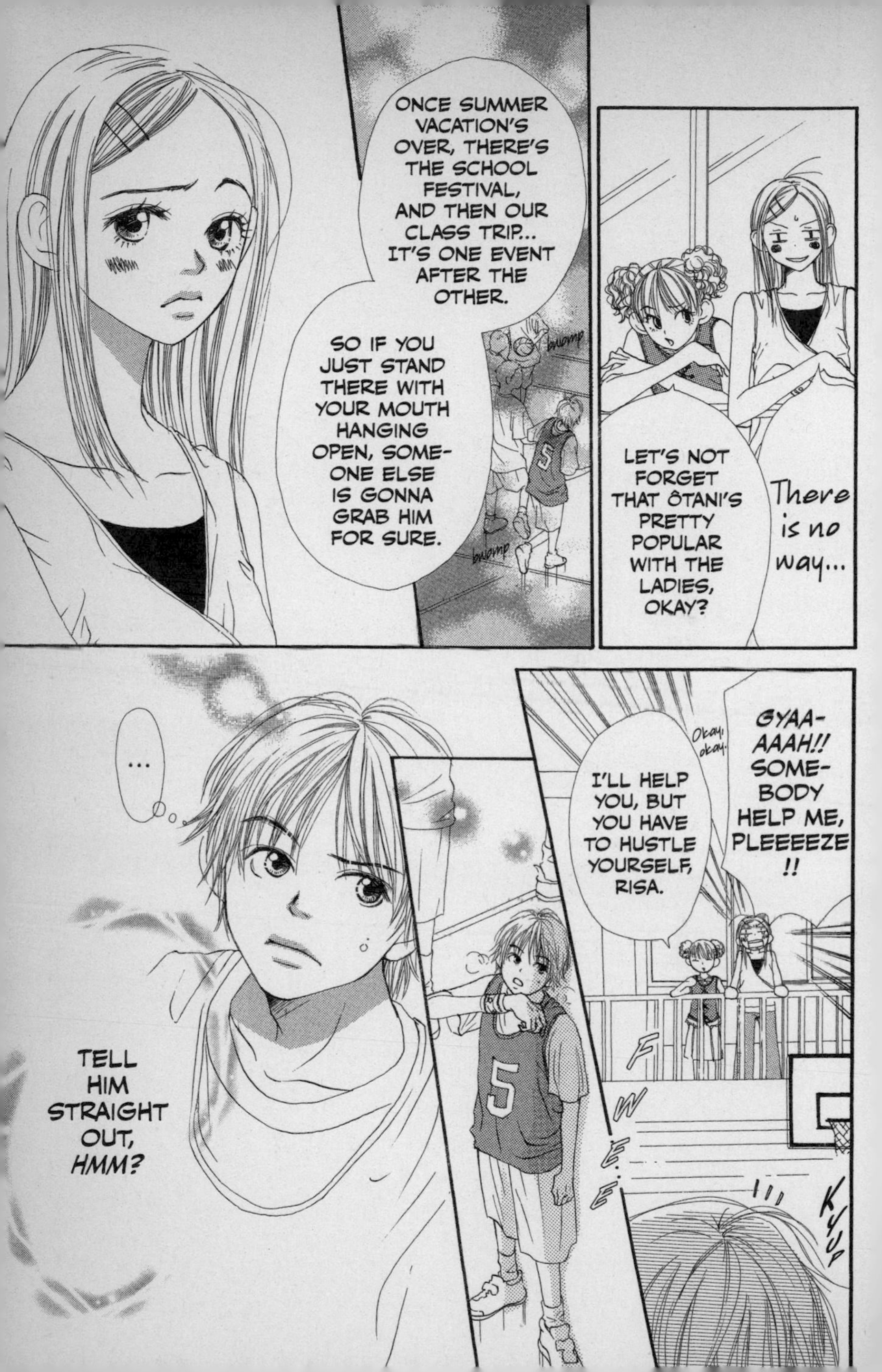
LET'S NOT FORGET THAT ŌTANI'S PRETTY POPULAR WITH THE LADIES, OKAY?
There is no way...
ONCE SUMMER VACATION'S OVER, THERE'S THE SCHOOL FESTIVAL, AND THEN OUR CLASS TRIP... IT'S ONE EVENT AFTER THE OTHER.
bwomp
SO IF YOU JUST STAND THERE WITH YOUR MOUTH HANGING OPEN, SOME-ONE ELSE IS GONNA GRAB HIM FOR SURE.
bwomp
GYAA-AAAH!! SOME-BODY HELP ME, PLEEEEZE!!
Okay, okay.
I'LL HELP YOU, BUT YOU HAVE TO HUSTLE YOURSELF, RISA.
FWEEE
KYUP
...
TELL HIM STRAIGHT OUT, HMM?

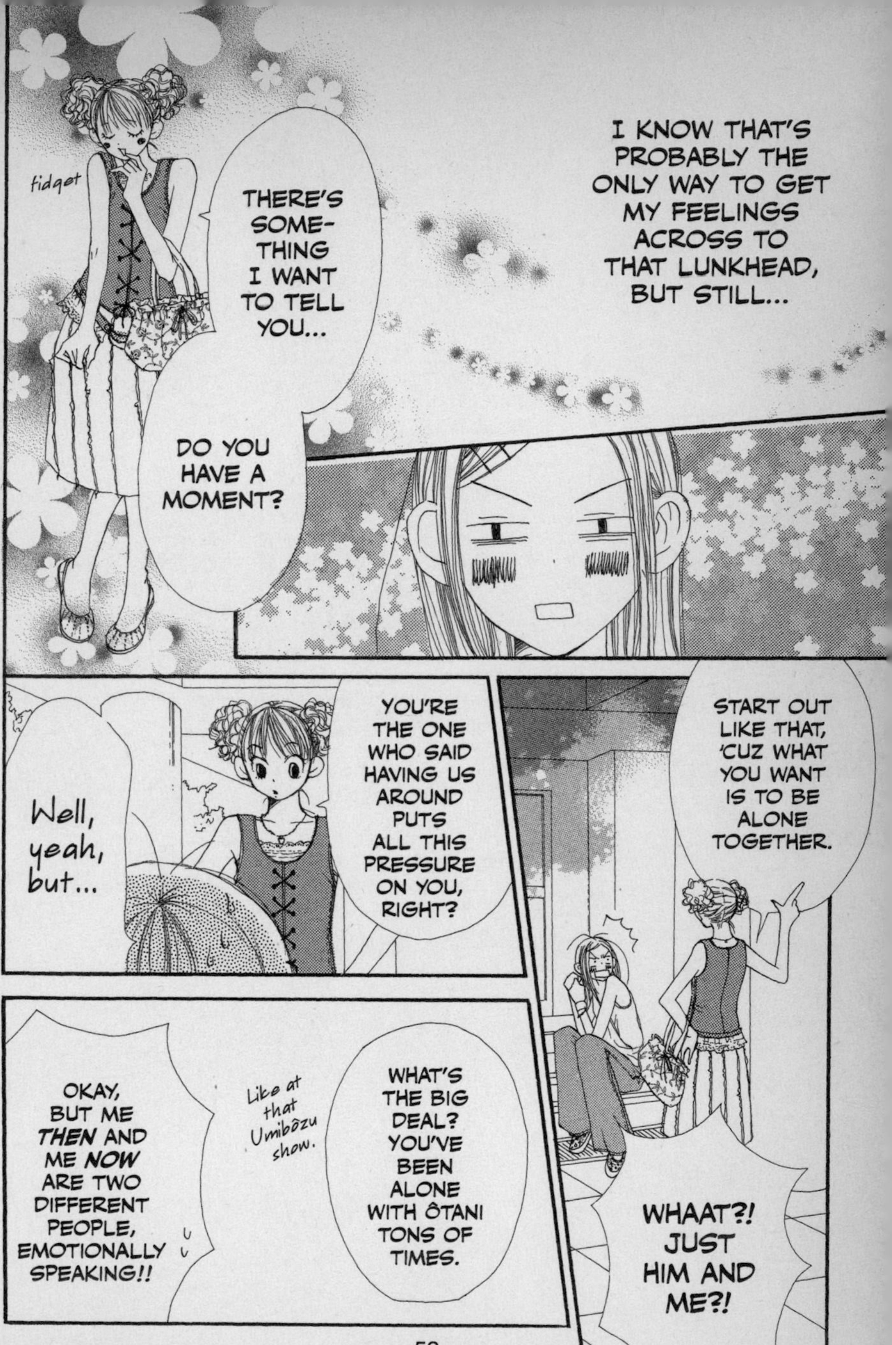
I KNOW THAT'S PROBABLY THE ONLY WAY TO GET MY FEELINGS ACROSS TO THAT LUNKHEAD, BUT STILL...
THERE'S SOME-THING I WANT TO TELL YOU...
DO YOU HAVE A MOMENT?
fidget
START OUT LIKE THAT, 'CUZ WHAT YOU WANT IS TO BE ALONE TOGETHER.
WHAAT?! JUST HIM AND ME?!
YOU'RE THE ONE WHO SAID HAVING US AROUND PUTS ALL THIS PRESSURE ON YOU, RIGHT?
Well, yeah, but...
WHAT'S THE BIG DEAL? YOU'VE BEEN ALONE WITH ÔTANI TONS OF TIMES.
Like at that Umibôzu show.
OKAY, BUT ME *THEN* AND ME *NOW* ARE TWO DIFFERENT PEOPLE, EMOTIONALLY SPEAKING!!

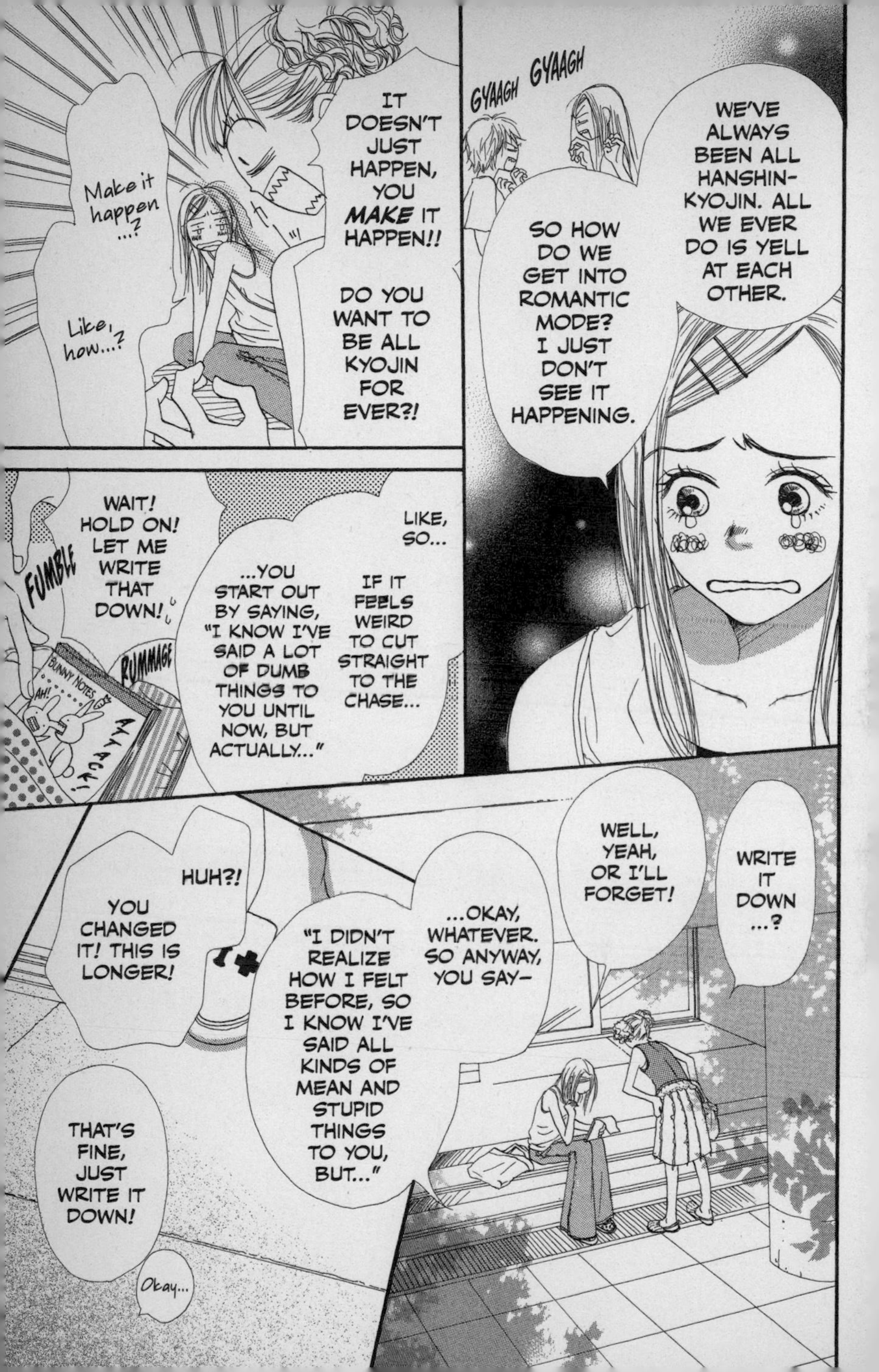
GYAAGH GYAAGH
WE'VE ALWAYS BEEN ALL HANSHIN-KYOJIN. ALL WE EVER DO IS YELL AT EACH OTHER.
SO HOW DO WE GET INTO ROMANTIC MODE? I JUST DON'T SEE IT HAPPENING.
IT DOESN'T JUST HAPPEN, YOU *MAKE* IT HAPPEN!!
Make it happen ...?
DO YOU WANT TO BE ALL KYOJIN FOR EVER?!
Like, how...?
LIKE, SO...
IF IT FEELS WEIRD TO CUT STRAIGHT TO THE CHASE...
...YOU START OUT BY SAYING, "I KNOW I'VE SAID A LOT OF DUMB THINGS TO YOU UNTIL NOW, BUT ACTUALLY..."
WAIT! HOLD ON! LET ME WRITE THAT DOWN!
FUMBLE
RUMMAGE
BUNNY NOTES
AH!
AAAACK!
WRITE IT DOWN ...?
WELL, YEAH, OR I'LL FORGET!
...OKAY, WHATEVER. SO ANYWAY, YOU SAY—
"I DIDN'T REALIZE HOW I FELT BEFORE, SO I KNOW I'VE SAID ALL KINDS OF MEAN AND STUPID THINGS TO YOU, BUT..."
HUH?!
YOU CHANGED IT! THIS IS LONGER!
THAT'S FINE, JUST WRITE IT DOWN!
Okay...

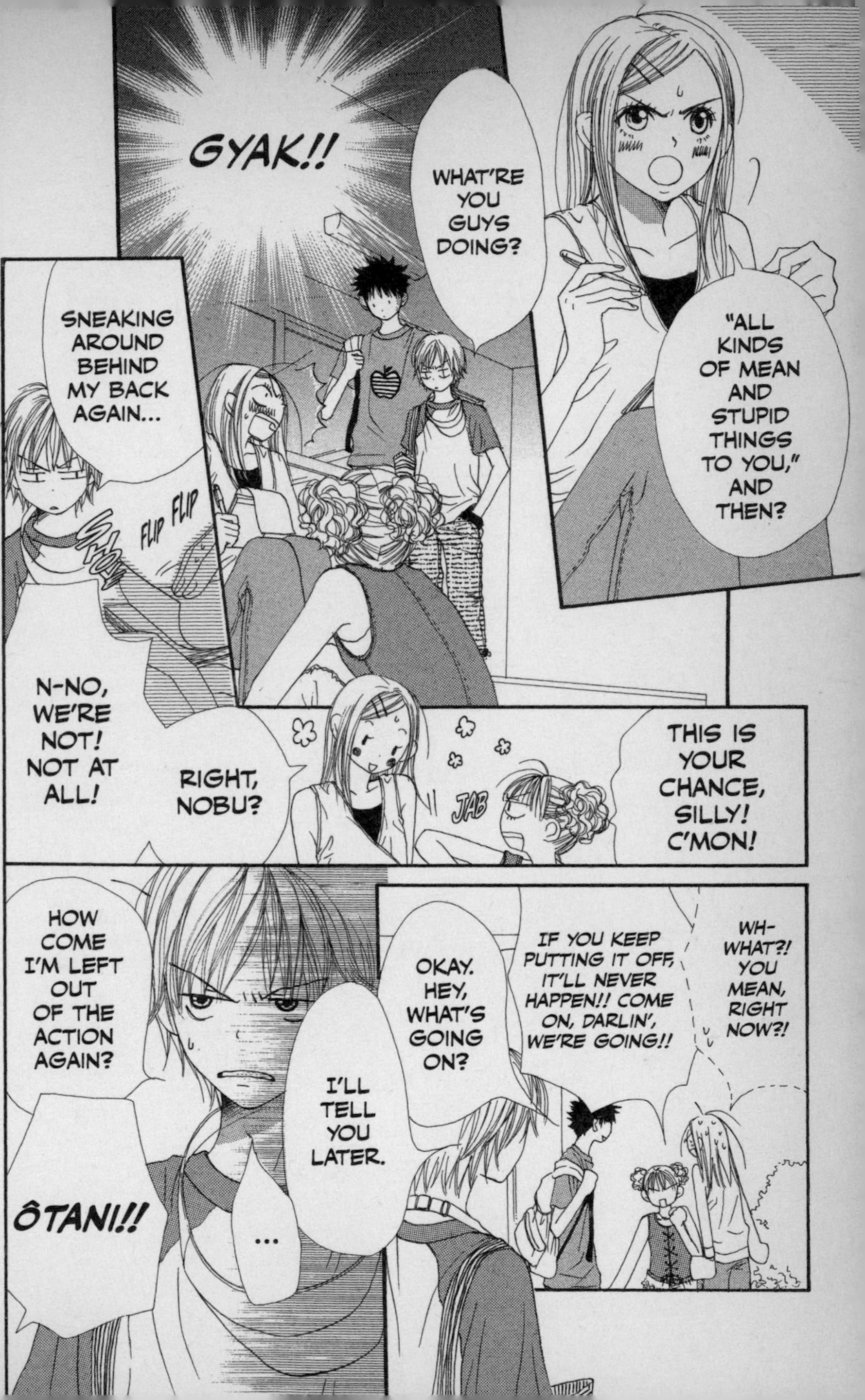
"ALL KINDS OF MEAN AND STUPID THINGS TO YOU," AND THEN?
GYAK!!
WHAT'RE YOU GUYS DOING?
SNEAKING AROUND BEHIND MY BACK AGAIN...
FLIP FLIP
THIS IS YOUR CHANCE, SILLY! C'MON!
JAB
RIGHT, NOBU?
N-NO, WE'RE NOT! NOT AT ALL!
WH-WHAT?! YOU MEAN, RIGHT NOW?!
IF YOU KEEP PUTTING IT OFF, IT'LL NEVER HAPPEN!! COME ON, DARLIN', WE'RE GOING!!
OKAY. HEY, WHAT'S GOING ON?
I'LL TELL YOU LATER.
HOW COME I'M LEFT OUT OF THE ACTION AGAIN?
ÔTANI!!
...

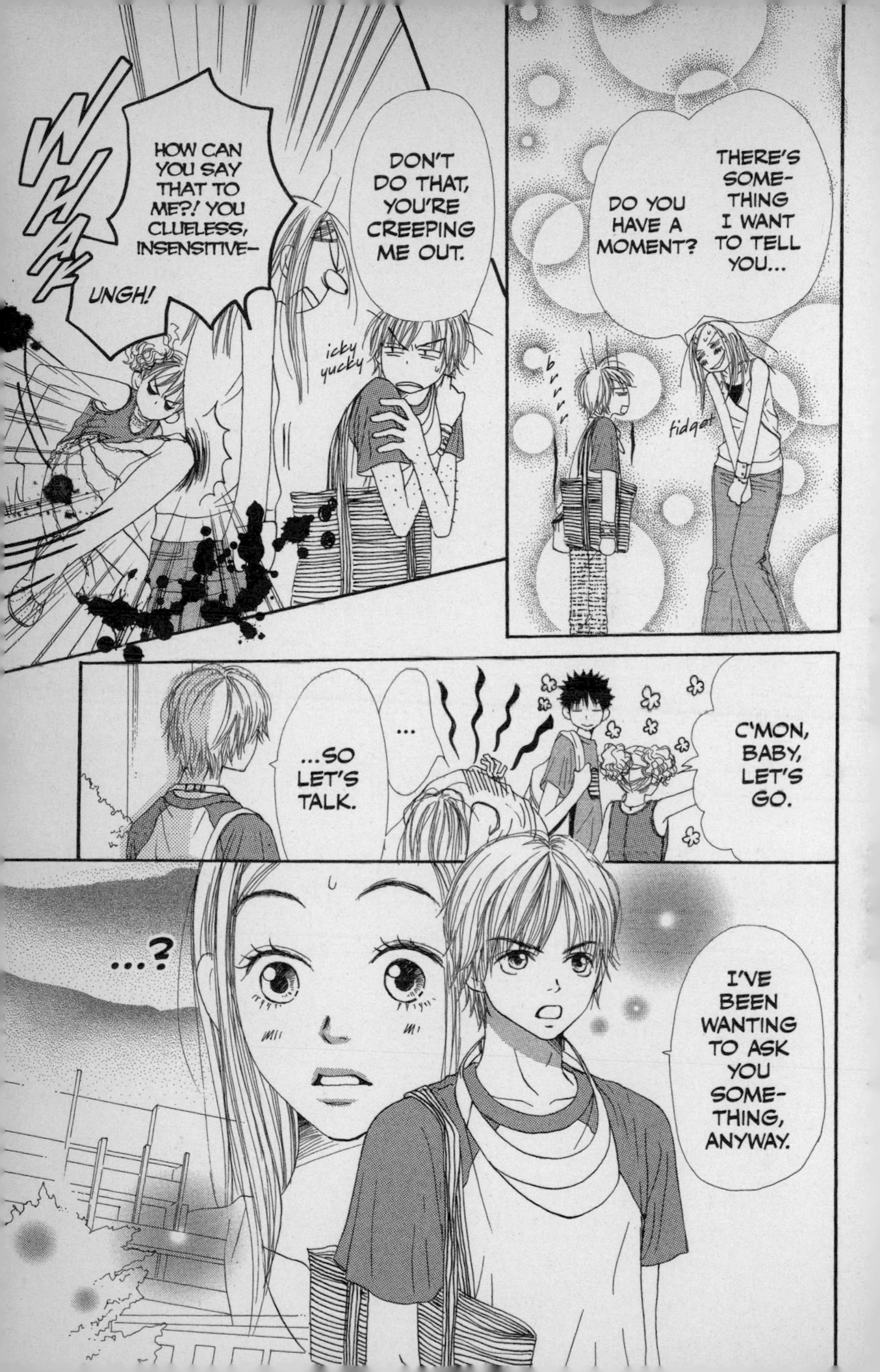
THERE'S SOMETHING I WANT TO TELL YOU...
DO YOU HAVE A MOMENT?
fidget
brrrr
DON'T DO THAT, YOU'RE CREEPING ME OUT.
icky yucky
HOW CAN YOU SAY THAT TO ME?! YOU CLUELESS, INSENSITIVE—
WHAK
UNGH!
C'MON, BABY, LET'S GO.
...
...SO LET'S TALK.
I'VE BEEN WANTING TO ASK YOU SOMETHING, ANYWAY.
...?

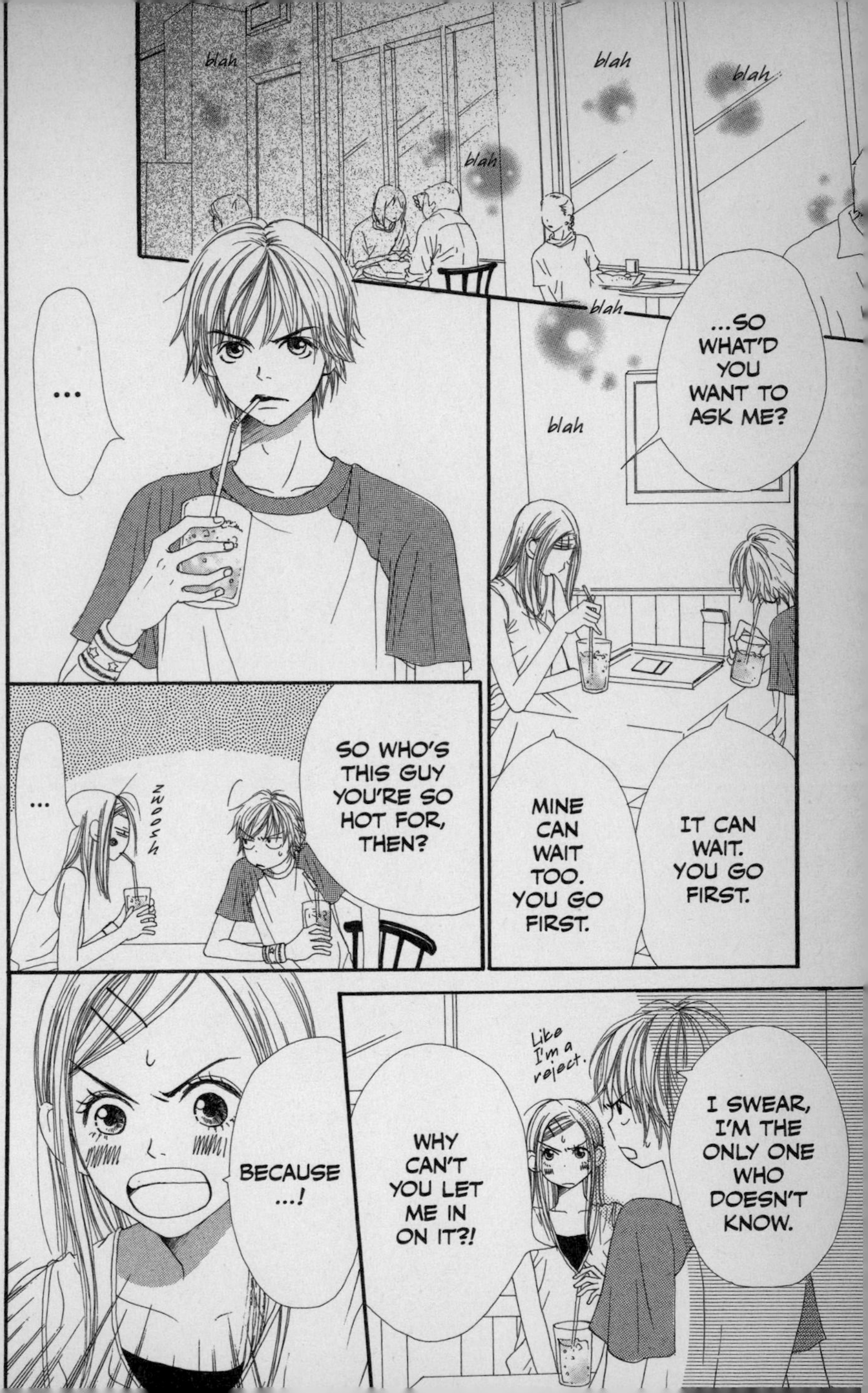
blah
blah
blah
blah
blah
blah
...SO WHAT'D YOU WANT TO ASK ME?
IT CAN WAIT. YOU GO FIRST.
MINE CAN WAIT TOO. YOU GO FIRST.
...
SO WHO'S THIS GUY YOU'RE SO HOT FOR, THEN?
ZWOOSH
...
I SWEAR, I'M THE ONLY ONE WHO DOESN'T KNOW.
Like I'm a reject.
WHY CAN'T YOU LET ME IN ON IT?!
BECAUSE ...!

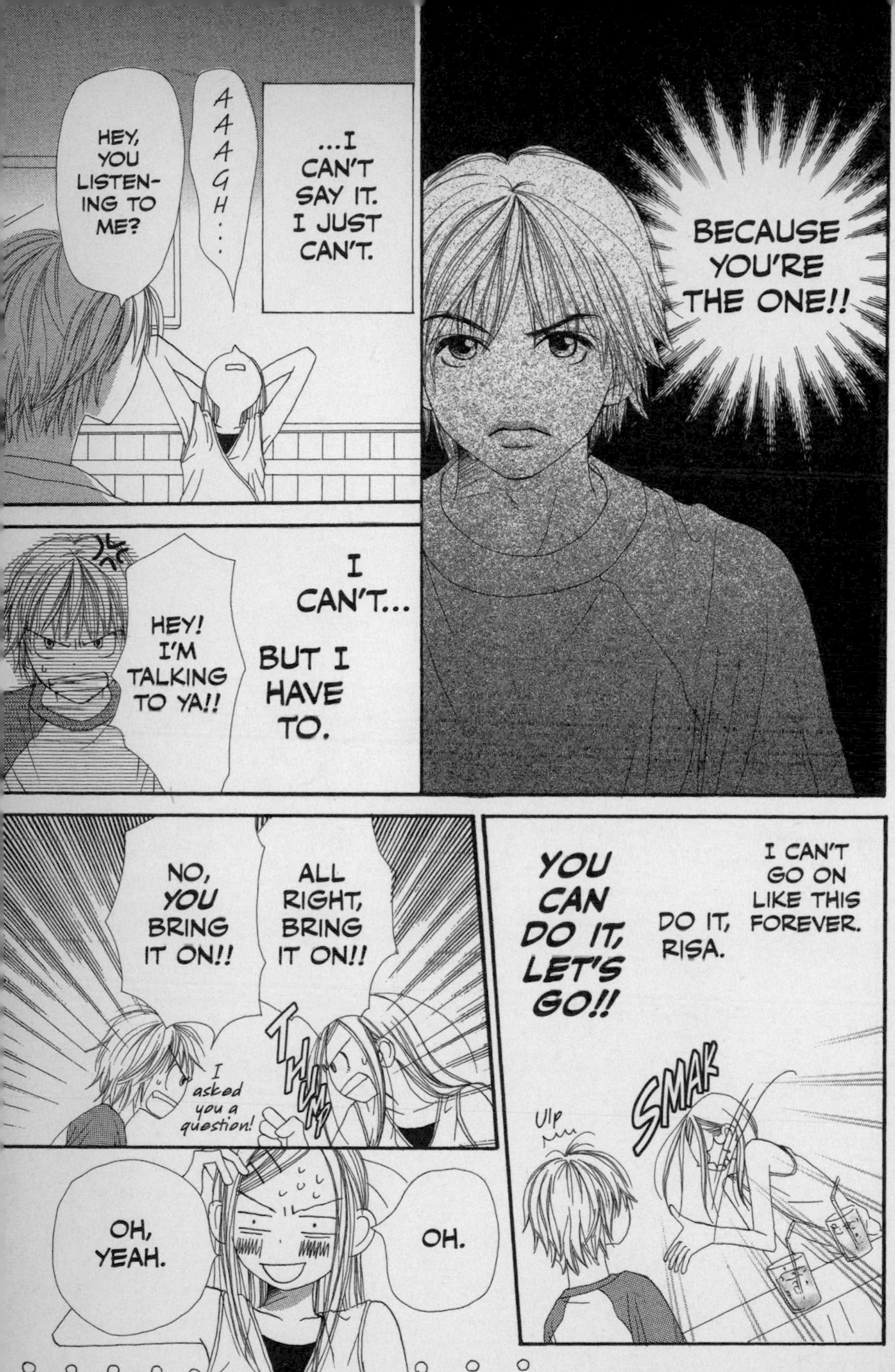
BECAUSE YOU'RE THE ONE!!
...I CAN'T SAY IT. I JUST CAN'T.
AAAGH...
HEY, YOU LISTENING TO ME?
I CAN'T...
BUT I HAVE TO.
HEY! I'M TALKING TO YA!!
I CAN'T GO ON LIKE THIS FOREVER.
DO IT, RISA.
YOU CAN DO IT, LET'S GO!!
SMAK
Ulp
ALL RIGHT, BRING IT ON!!
NO, YOU BRING IT ON!!
THUMP
I asked you a question!
OH.
OH, YEAH.

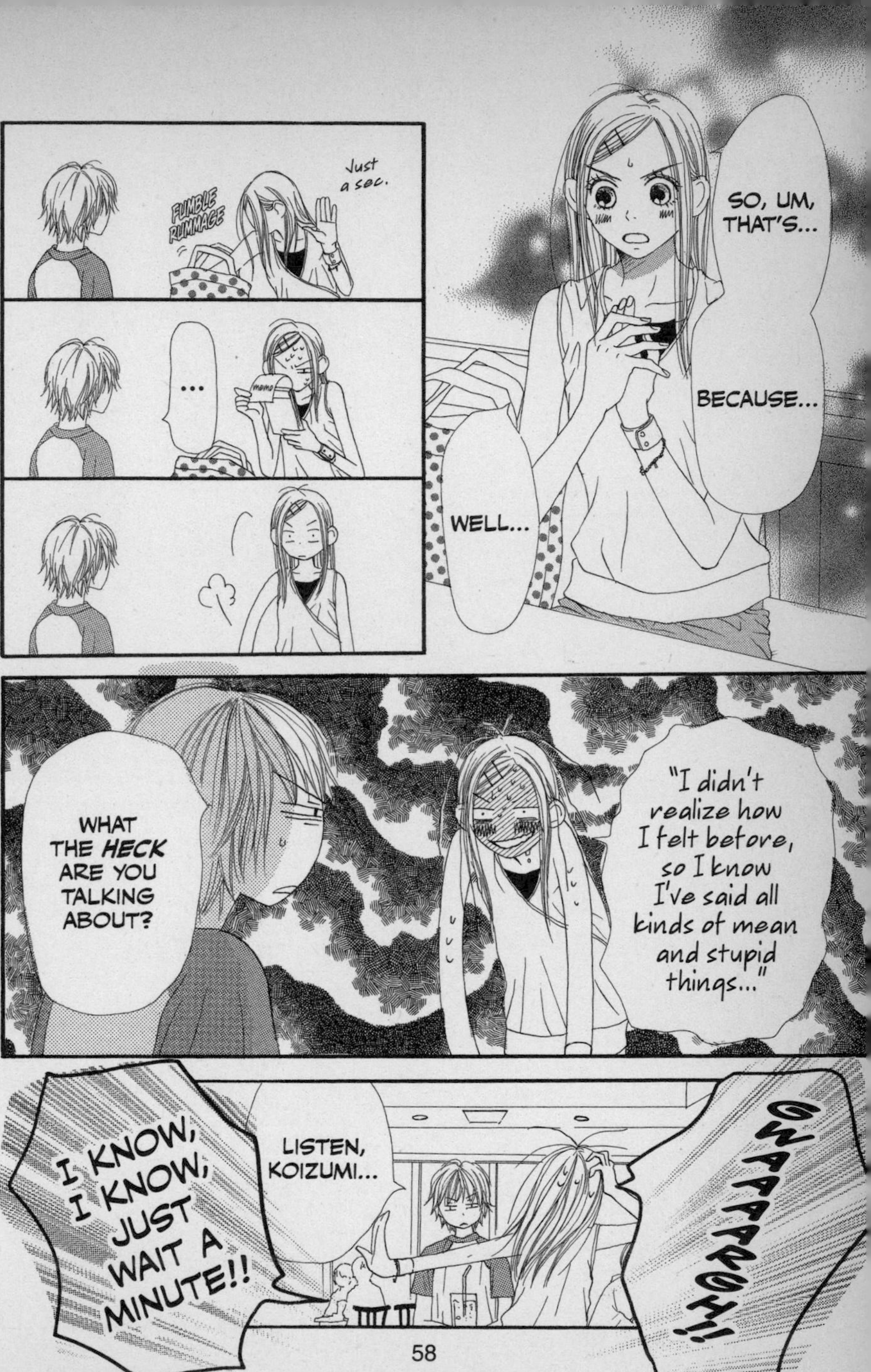
SO, UM, THAT'S...
BECAUSE...
WELL...
Just a sec.
FUMBLE RUMMAGE
...
"I didn't realize how I felt before, so I know I've said all kinds of mean and stupid things..."
WHAT THE HECK ARE YOU TALKING ABOUT?
GWAAAARGH!!
LISTEN, KOIZUMI...
I KNOW, I KNOW, JUST WAIT A MINUTE!!

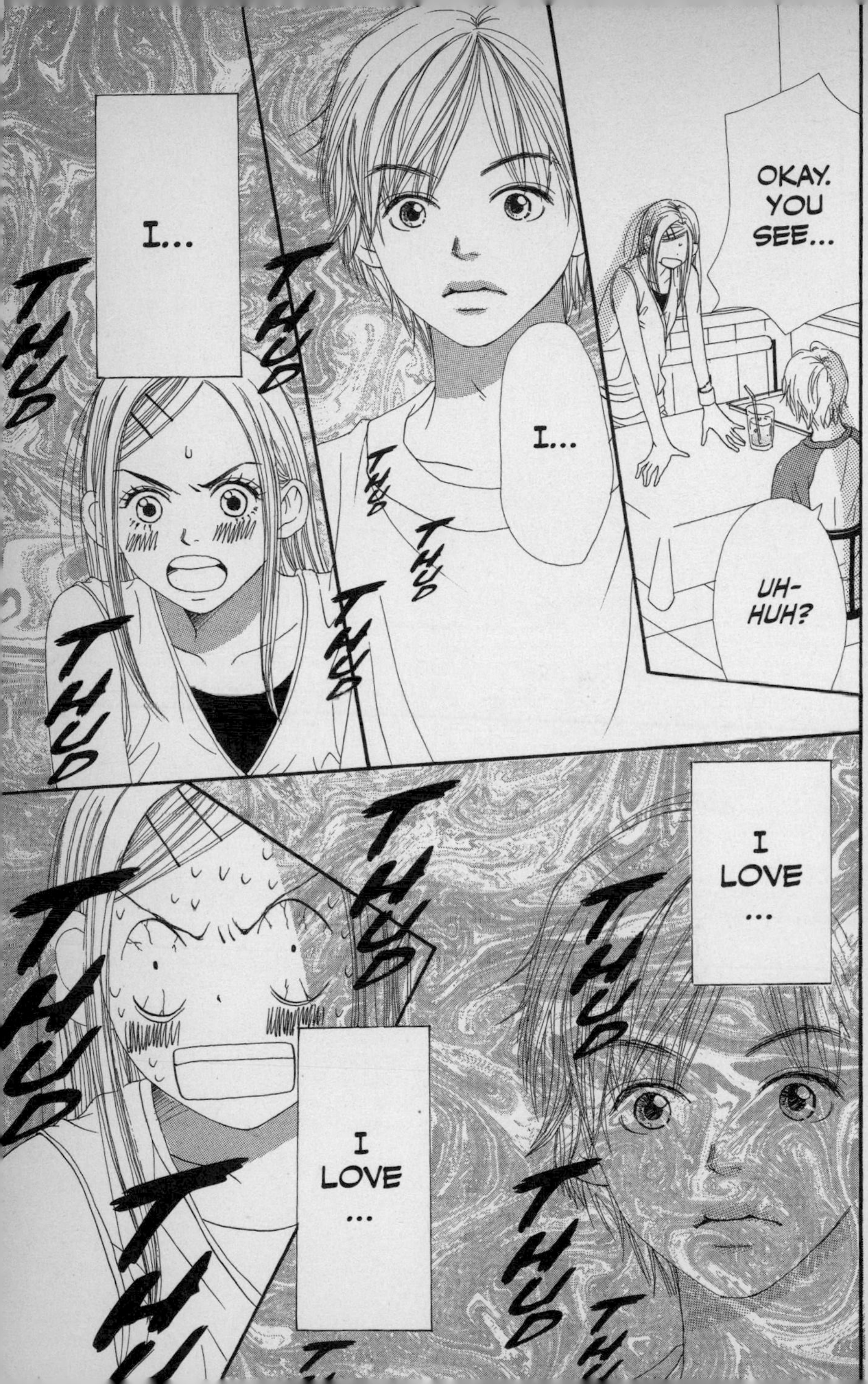
OKAY. YOU SEE...
UH-HUH?
THUD
I...
THUD THUD
THUD
I...
THUD
THUD
I LOVE ...
THUD
THUD
I LOVE ...
THUD
THUD

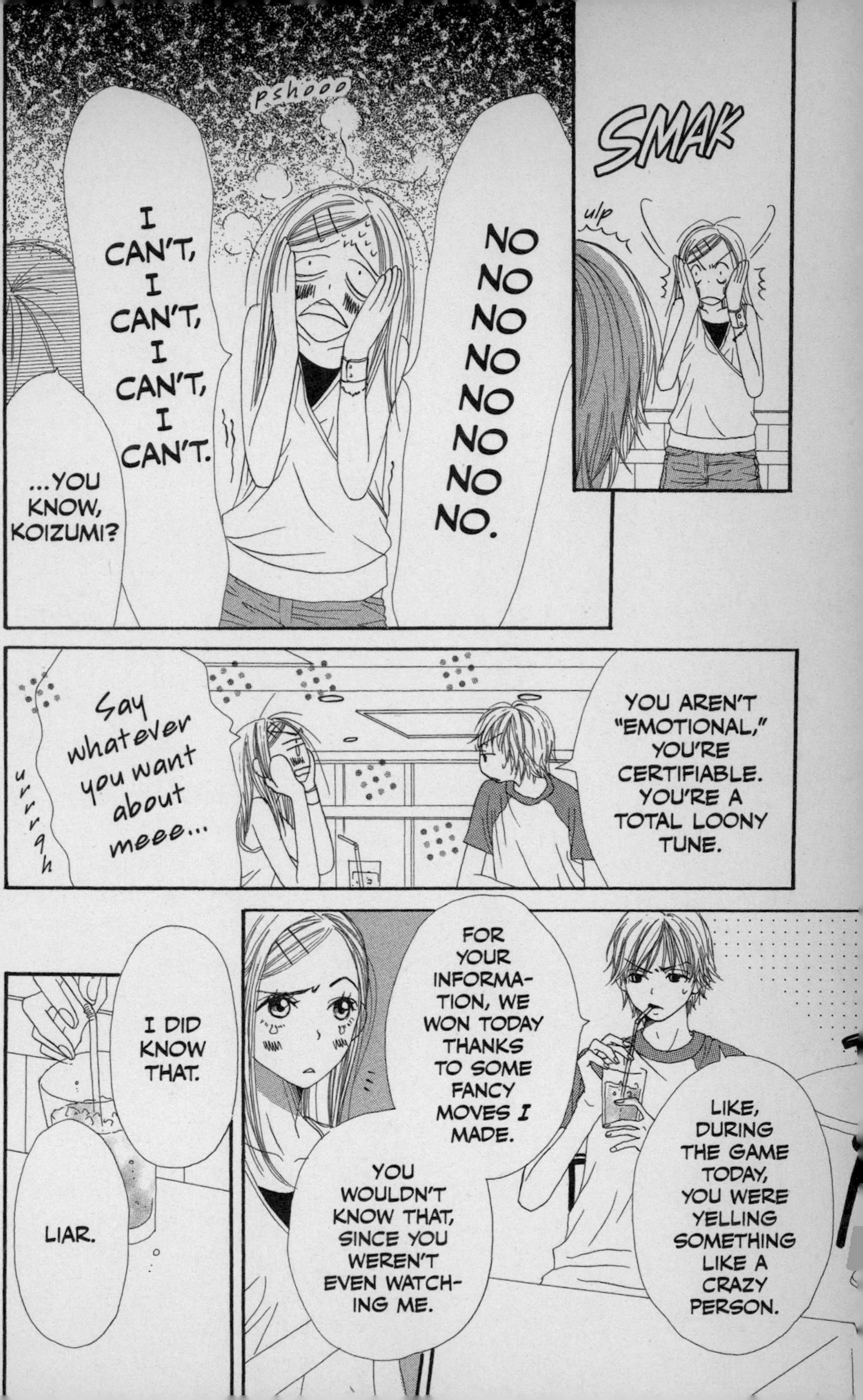
SMAK
ulp
pshooo
NO NO NO NO NO NO NO NO.
I CAN'T, I CAN'T, I CAN'T, I CAN'T.
...YOU KNOW, KOIZUMI?
YOU AREN'T "EMOTIONAL," YOU'RE CERTIFIABLE. YOU'RE A TOTAL LOONY TUNE.
Say whatever you want about meee...
urrrgh
FOR YOUR INFORMATION, WE WON TODAY THANKS TO SOME FANCY MOVES I MADE.
LIKE, DURING THE GAME TODAY, YOU WERE YELLING SOMETHING LIKE A CRAZY PERSON.
YOU WOULDN'T KNOW THAT, SINCE YOU WEREN'T EVEN WATCHING ME.
I DID KNOW THAT.
LIAR.

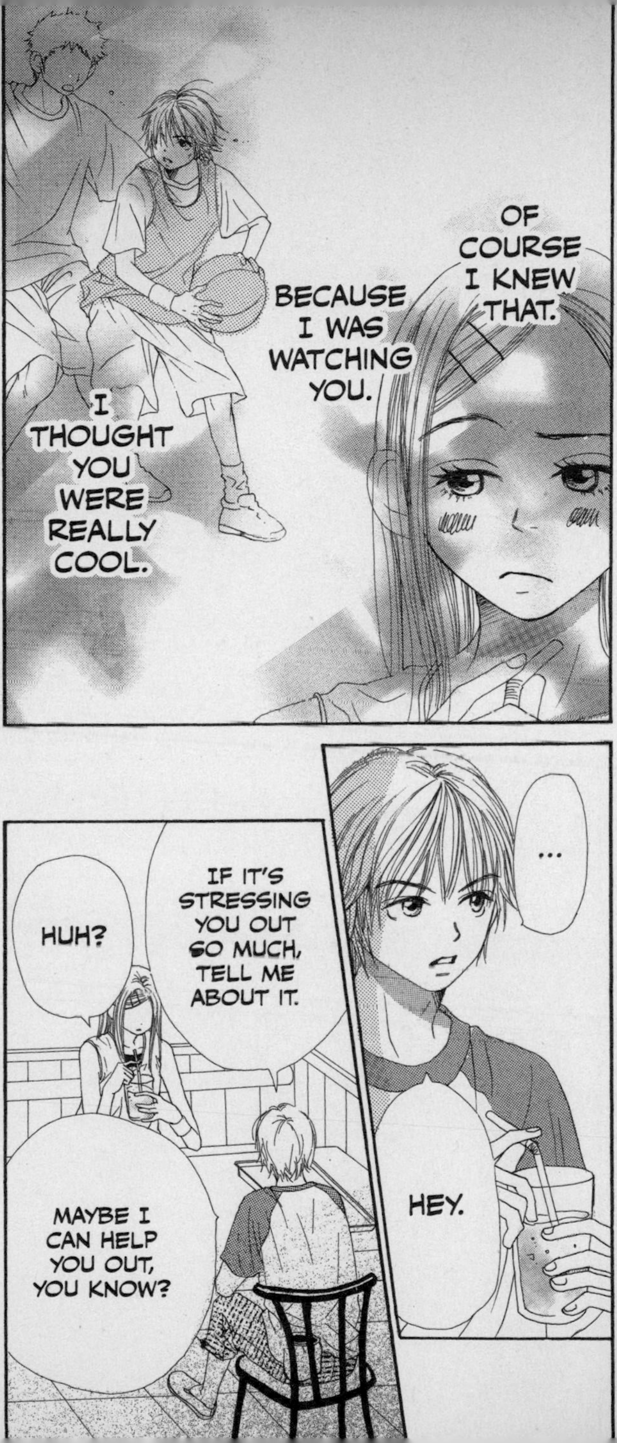
OF COURSE I KNEW THAT.
BECAUSE I WAS WATCHING YOU.
I THOUGHT YOU WERE REALLY COOL.
...
HEY.
IF IT'S STRESSING YOU OUT SO MUCH, TELL ME ABOUT IT.
HUH?
MAYBE I CAN HELP YOU OUT, YOU KNOW?

②

I'm starting to seem like someone who's got a poop fetish or something.

The number of times poop has come up in this space is... well, a lot.

The first edition of Vol. 4 came with special stickers, and when I submitted the designs I sneaked a poop in there, but it was rejected.

Well, of course. Where would you stick a poop?

ha ha ha ha
I really must seem like I have a poop fetish, doesn't it?

Poop is what makes a man.

I hereby appoint you Minister of Poop!

What am I saying?!

Let's zip those lips.

...I haven't been drinking or anything, okay?

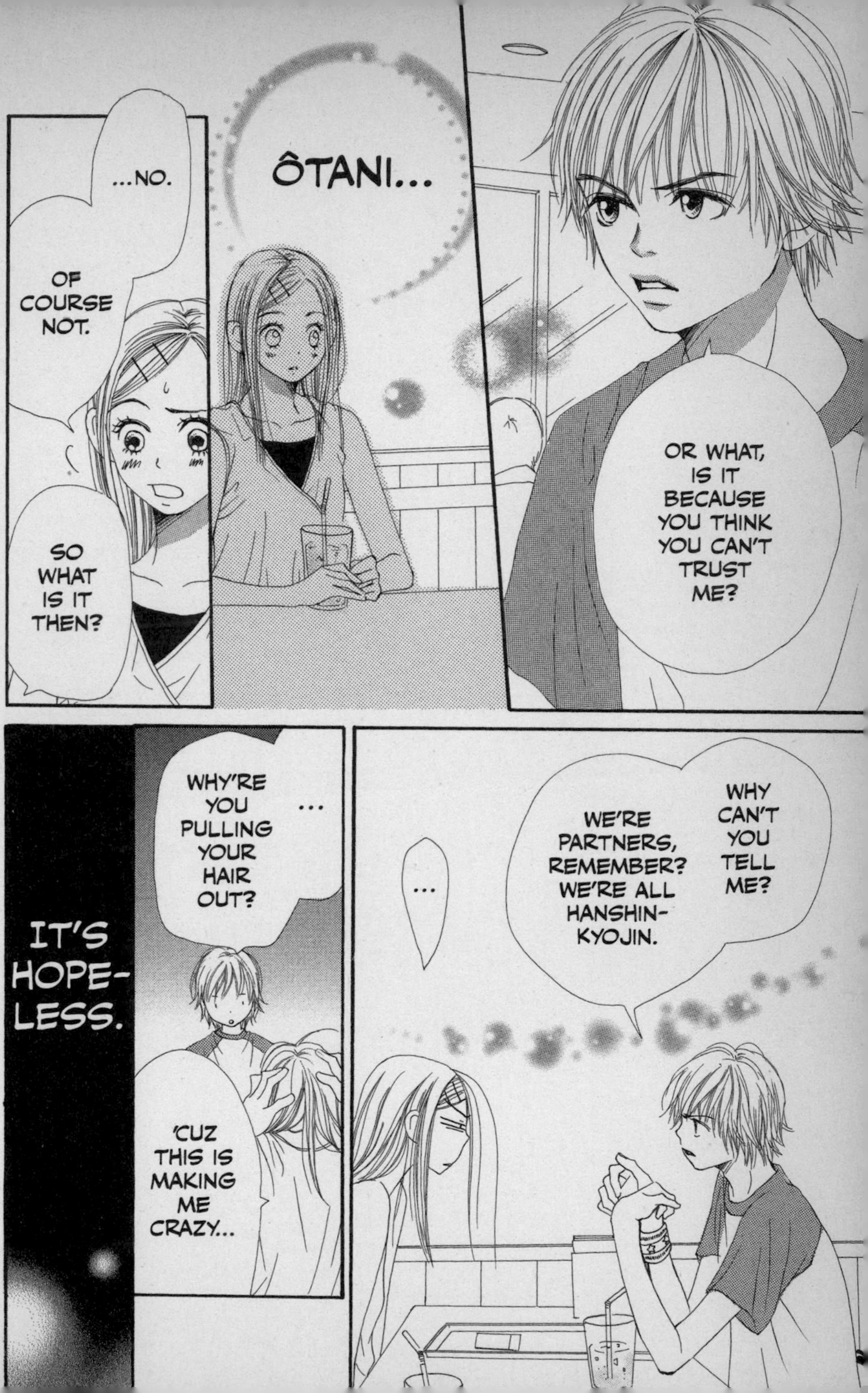
OR WHAT, IS IT BECAUSE YOU THINK YOU CAN'T TRUST ME?
ÔTANI...
...NO.
OF COURSE NOT.
SO WHAT IS IT THEN?
WHY CAN'T YOU TELL ME?
WE'RE PARTNERS, REMEMBER? WE'RE ALL HANSHIN-KYOJIN.
...
...
WHY'RE YOU PULLING YOUR HAIR OUT?
'CUZ THIS IS MAKING ME CRAZY...
IT'S HOPE-LESS.

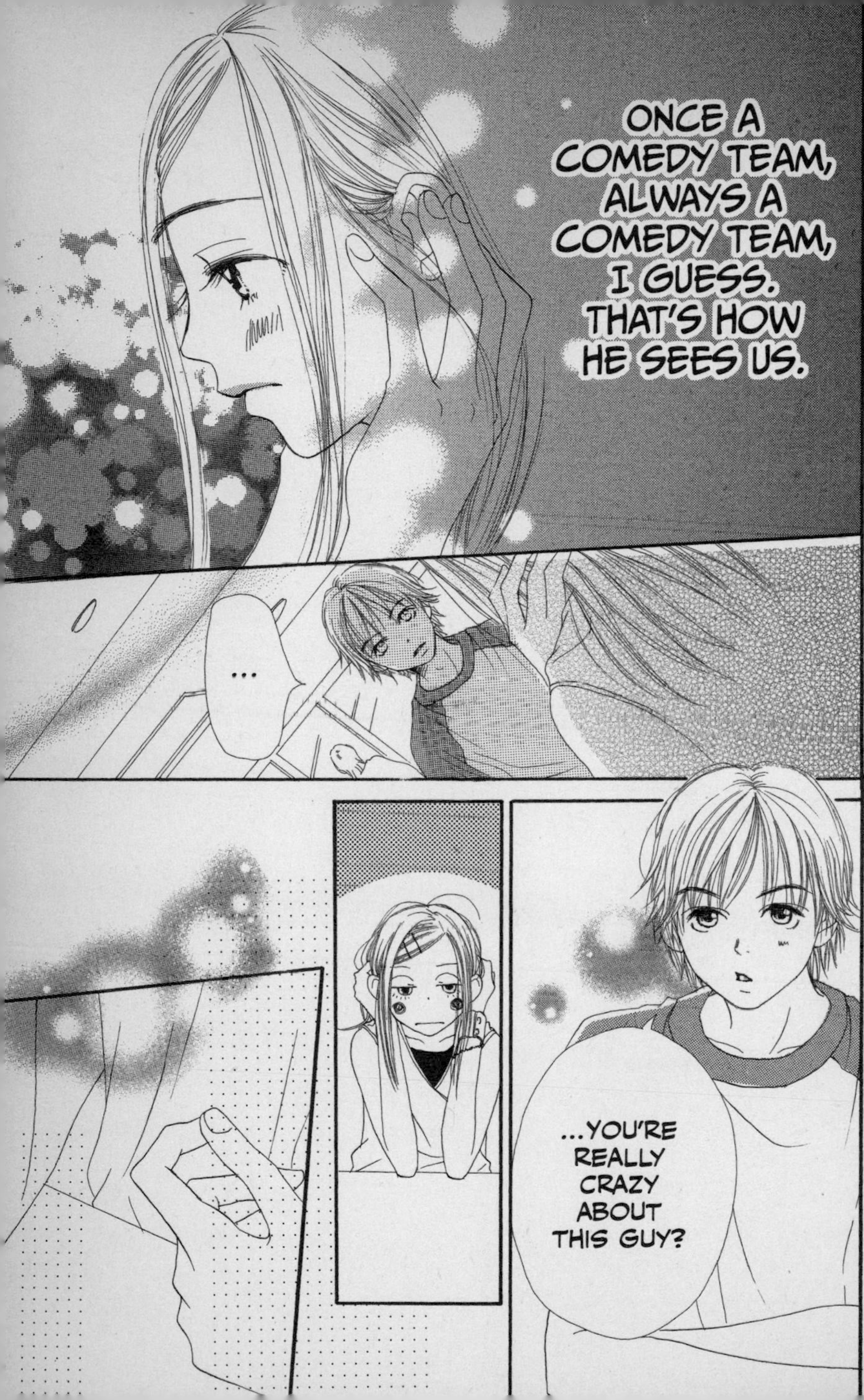
ONCE A COMEDY TEAM, ALWAYS A COMEDY TEAM, I GUESS. THAT'S HOW HE SEES US.
...
...YOU'RE REALLY CRAZY ABOUT THIS GUY?

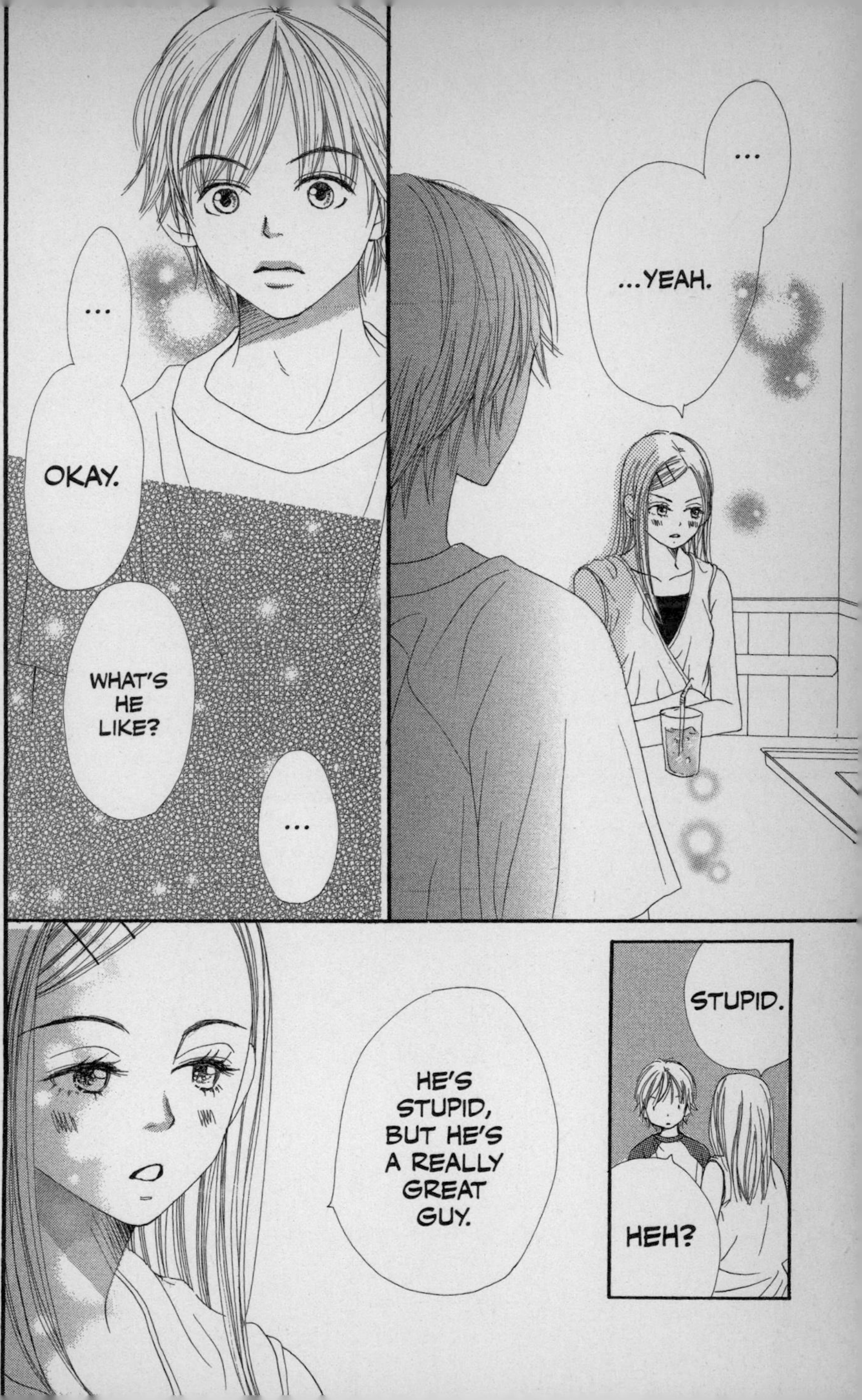
...
...YEAH.
...
OKAY.
WHAT'S HE LIKE?
...
STUPID.
HEH?
HE'S STUPID, BUT HE'S A REALLY GREAT GUY.

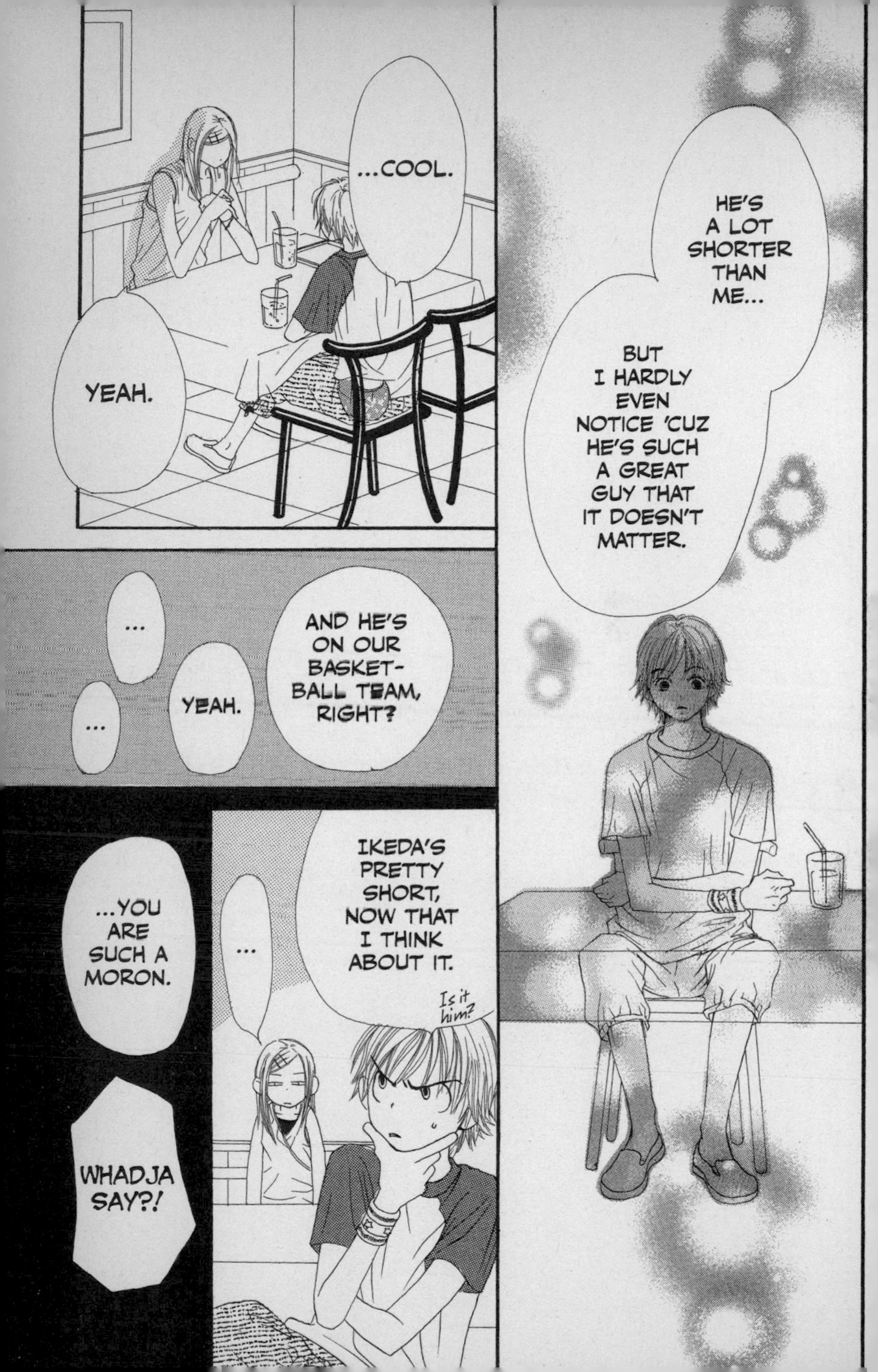
HE'S A LOT SHORTER THAN ME...
BUT I HARDLY EVEN NOTICE 'CUZ HE'S SUCH A GREAT GUY THAT IT DOESN'T MATTER.
...COOL.
YEAH.
AND HE'S ON OUR BASKETBALL TEAM, RIGHT?
YEAH.
...
...
IKEDA'S PRETTY SHORT, NOW THAT I THINK ABOUT IT.
...
Is it him?
...YOU ARE SUCH A MORON.
WHADJA SAY?!

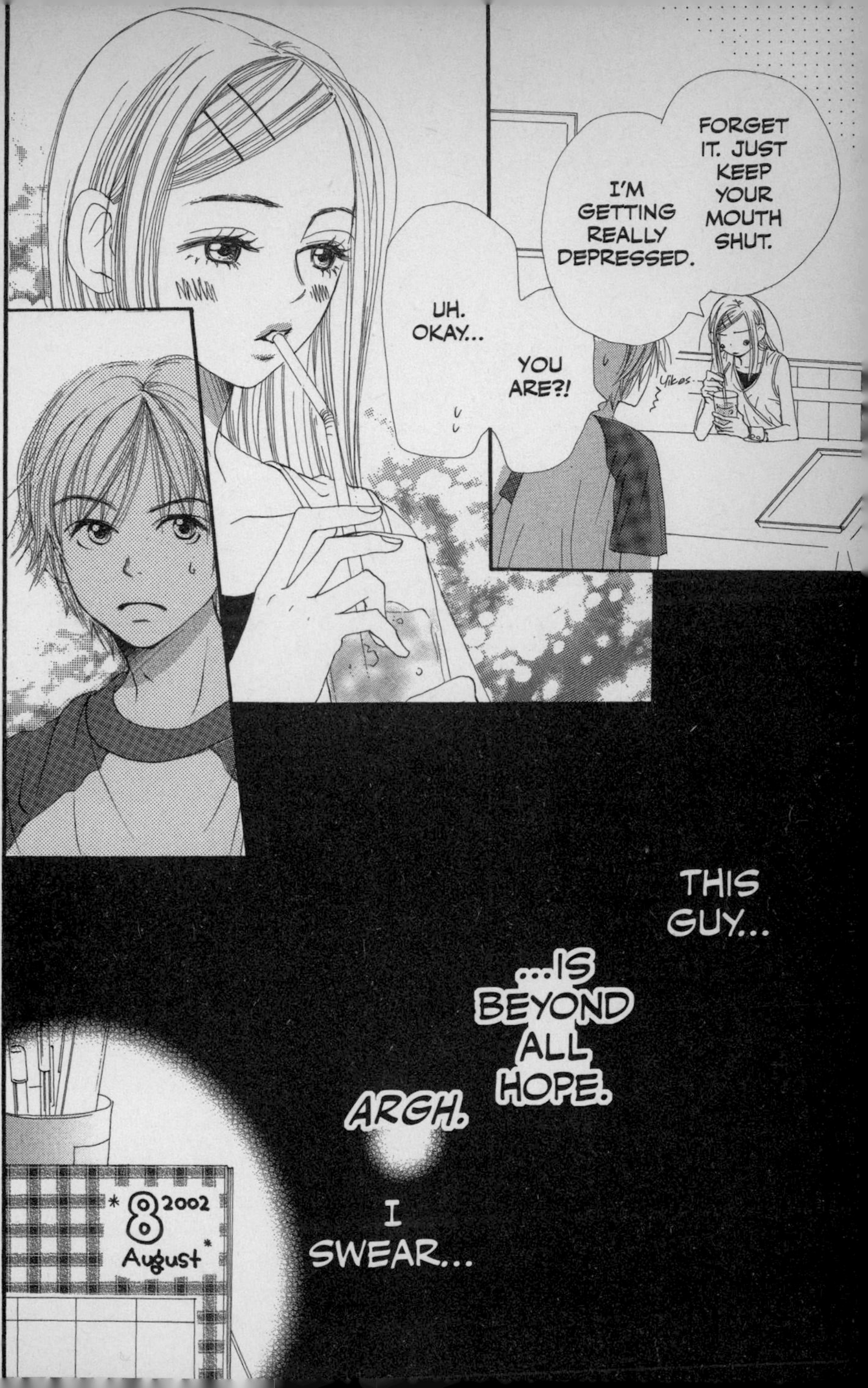
FORGET IT. JUST KEEP YOUR MOUTH SHUT.
I'M GETTING REALLY DEPRESSED.
Yikes...
YOU ARE?!
UH. OKAY...
THIS GUY...
...IS BEYOND ALL HOPE.
ARGH.
I SWEAR...
8 2002 August

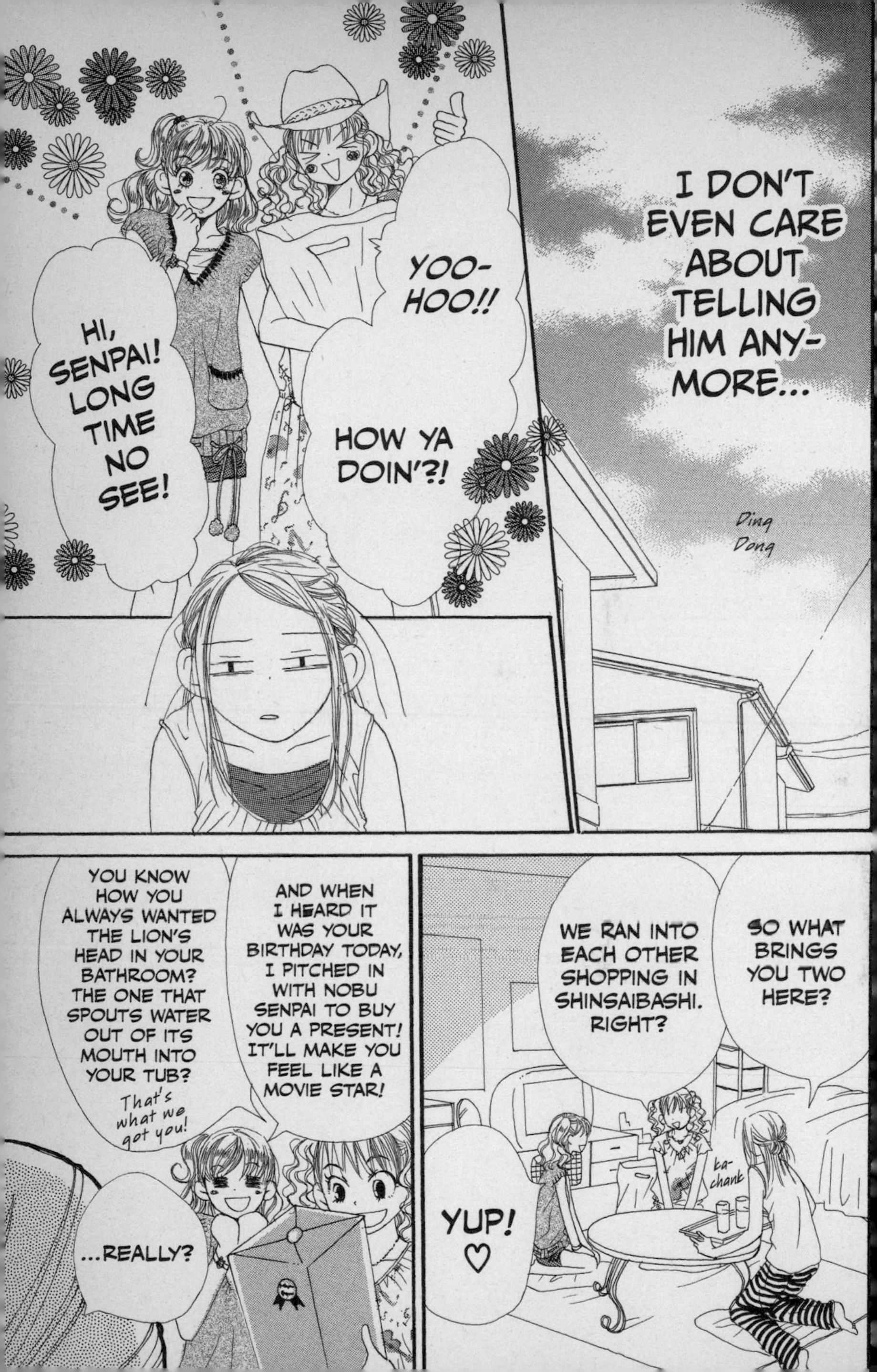
I DON'T EVEN CARE ABOUT TELLING HIM ANY-MORE...
Ding Dong
YOO-HOO!!
HOW YA DOIN'?!
HI, SENPAI! LONG TIME NO SEE!
SO WHAT BRINGS YOU TWO HERE?
WE RAN INTO EACH OTHER SHOPPING IN SHINSAIBASHI. RIGHT?
ka-chank
YUP! ♡
AND WHEN I HEARD IT WAS YOUR BIRTHDAY TODAY, I PITCHED IN WITH NOBU SENPAI TO BUY YOU A PRESENT! IT'LL MAKE YOU FEEL LIKE A MOVIE STAR!
YOU KNOW HOW YOU ALWAYS WANTED THE LION'S HEAD IN YOUR BATHROOM? THE ONE THAT SPOUTS WATER OUT OF ITS MOUTH INTO YOUR TUB?
That's what we got you!
...REALLY?

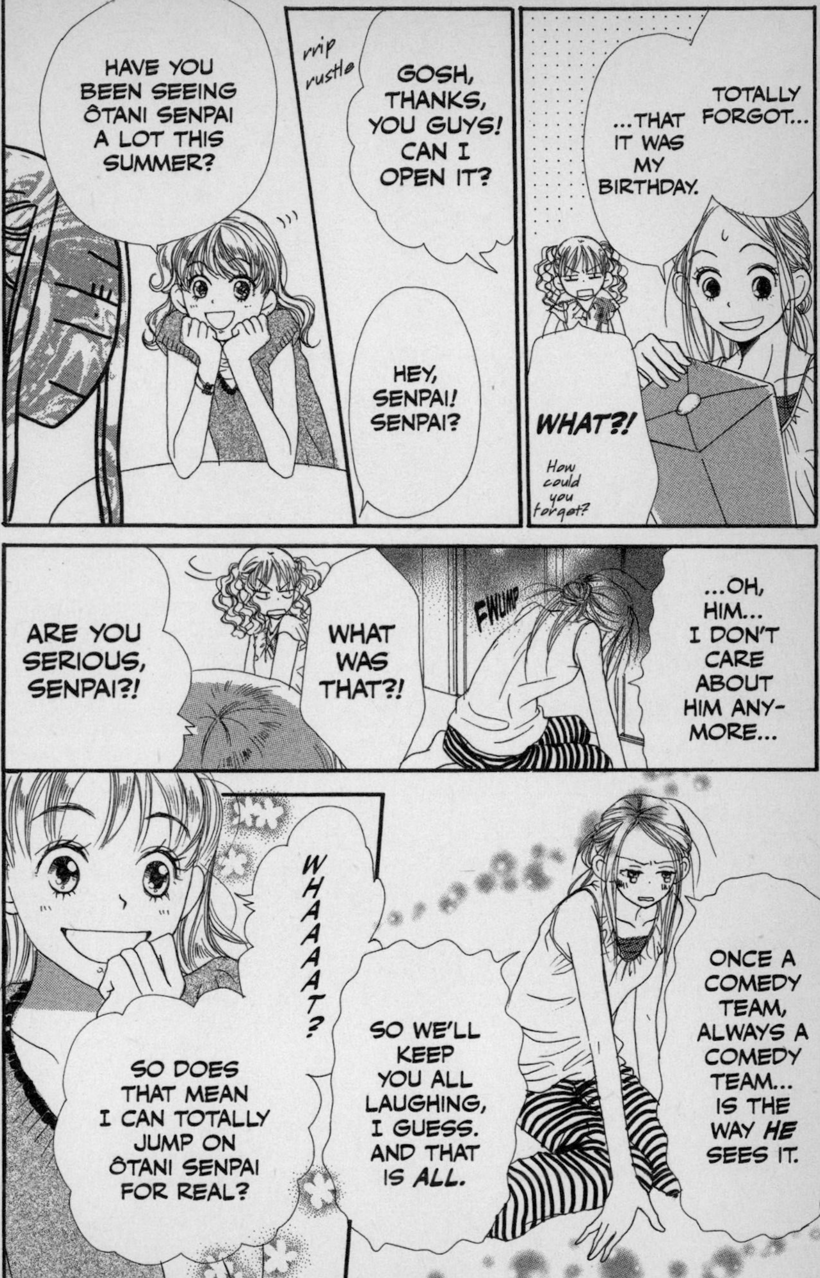
TOTALLY FORGOT...
...THAT IT WAS MY BIRTHDAY.
WHAT?!
How could you forget?
rrip rustle
GOSH, THANKS, YOU GUYS! CAN I OPEN IT?
HEY, SENPAI! SENPAI?
HAVE YOU BEEN SEEING ÔTANI SENPAI A LOT THIS SUMMER?
...OH, HIM... I DON'T CARE ABOUT HIM ANYMORE...
FWUMP
WHAT WAS THAT?!
ARE YOU SERIOUS, SENPAI?!
ONCE A COMEDY TEAM, ALWAYS A COMEDY TEAM... IS THE WAY *HE* SEES IT.
SO WE'LL KEEP YOU ALL LAUGHING, I GUESS. AND THAT IS *ALL*.
WHAAAAAT?
SO DOES THAT MEAN I CAN TOTALLY JUMP ON ÔTANI SENPAI FOR REAL?

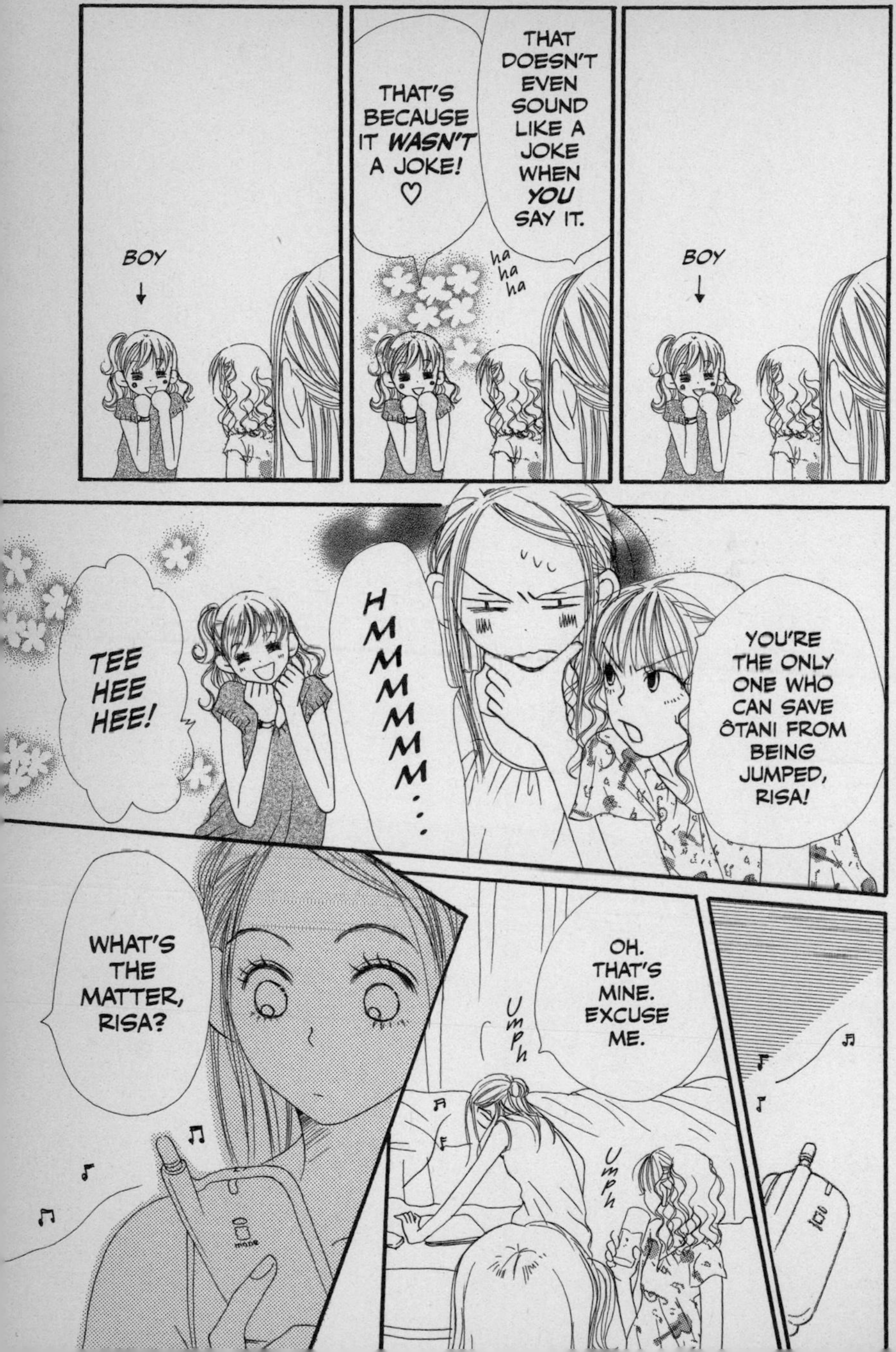
BOY
THAT DOESN'T EVEN SOUND LIKE A JOKE WHEN YOU SAY IT.
THAT'S BECAUSE IT WASN'T A JOKE! ♡
ha ha ha
BOY
YOU'RE THE ONLY ONE WHO CAN SAVE ŌTANI FROM BEING JUMPED, RISA!
HMMMMMM...
TEE HEE HEE!
OH. THAT'S MINE. EXCUSE ME.
Umph
Umph
WHAT'S THE MATTER, RISA?

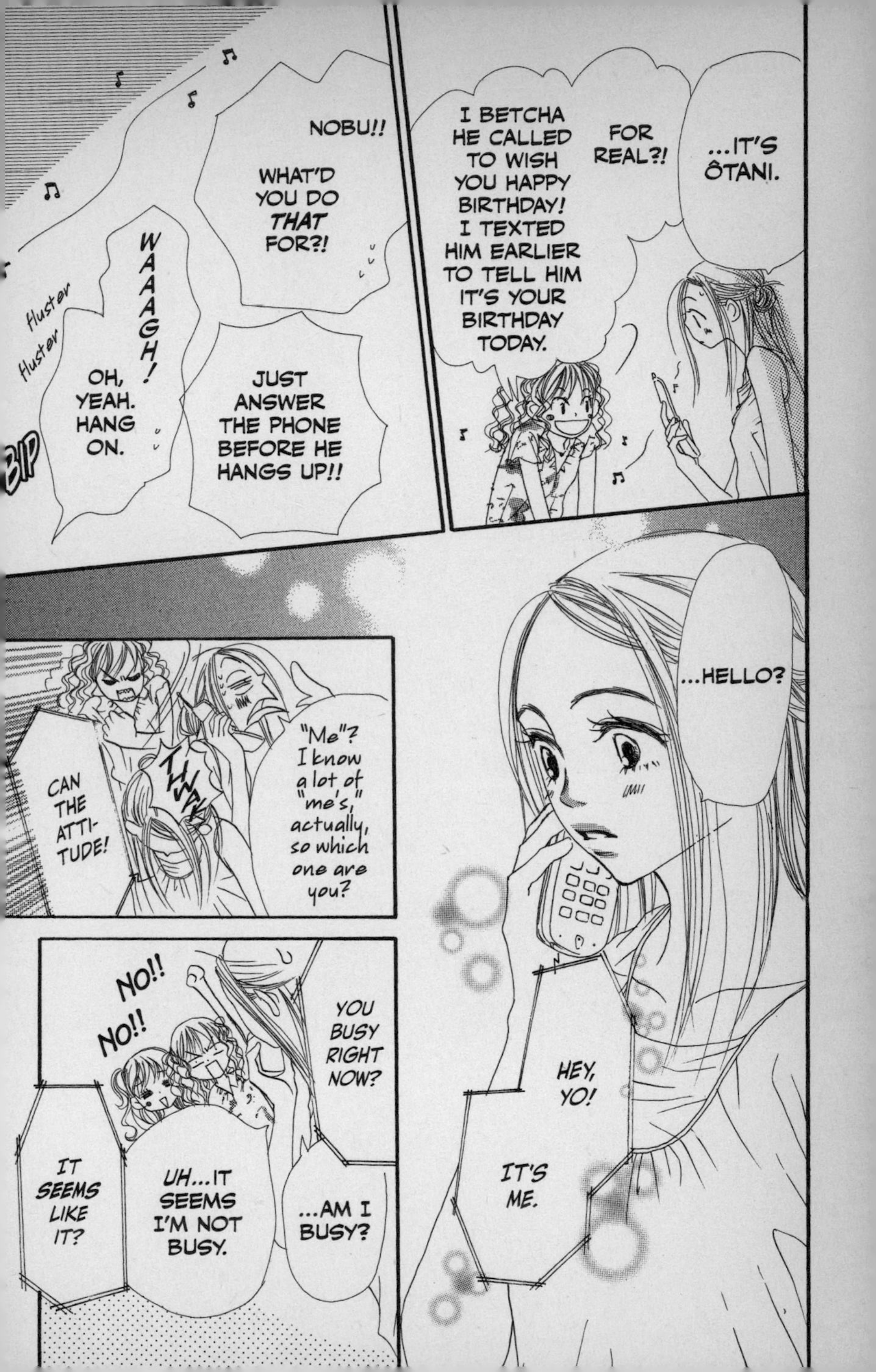
...IT'S ÔTANI.
FOR REAL?!
I BETCHA HE CALLED TO WISH YOU HAPPY BIRTHDAY! I TEXTED HIM EARLIER TO TELL HIM IT'S YOUR BIRTHDAY TODAY.
NOBU!!
WHAT'D YOU DO *THAT* FOR?!
WAAAAGH!
JUST ANSWER THE PHONE BEFORE HE HANGS UP!!
OH, YEAH. HANG ON.
Fluster Fluster
BIP
...HELLO?
HEY, YO!
IT'S ME.
"Me"? I know a lot of "me's," actually, so which one are you?
CAN THE ATTI-TUDE!
YOU BUSY RIGHT NOW?
NO!! NO!!
...AM I BUSY?
UH...IT SEEMS I'M NOT BUSY.
IT SEEMS LIKE IT?

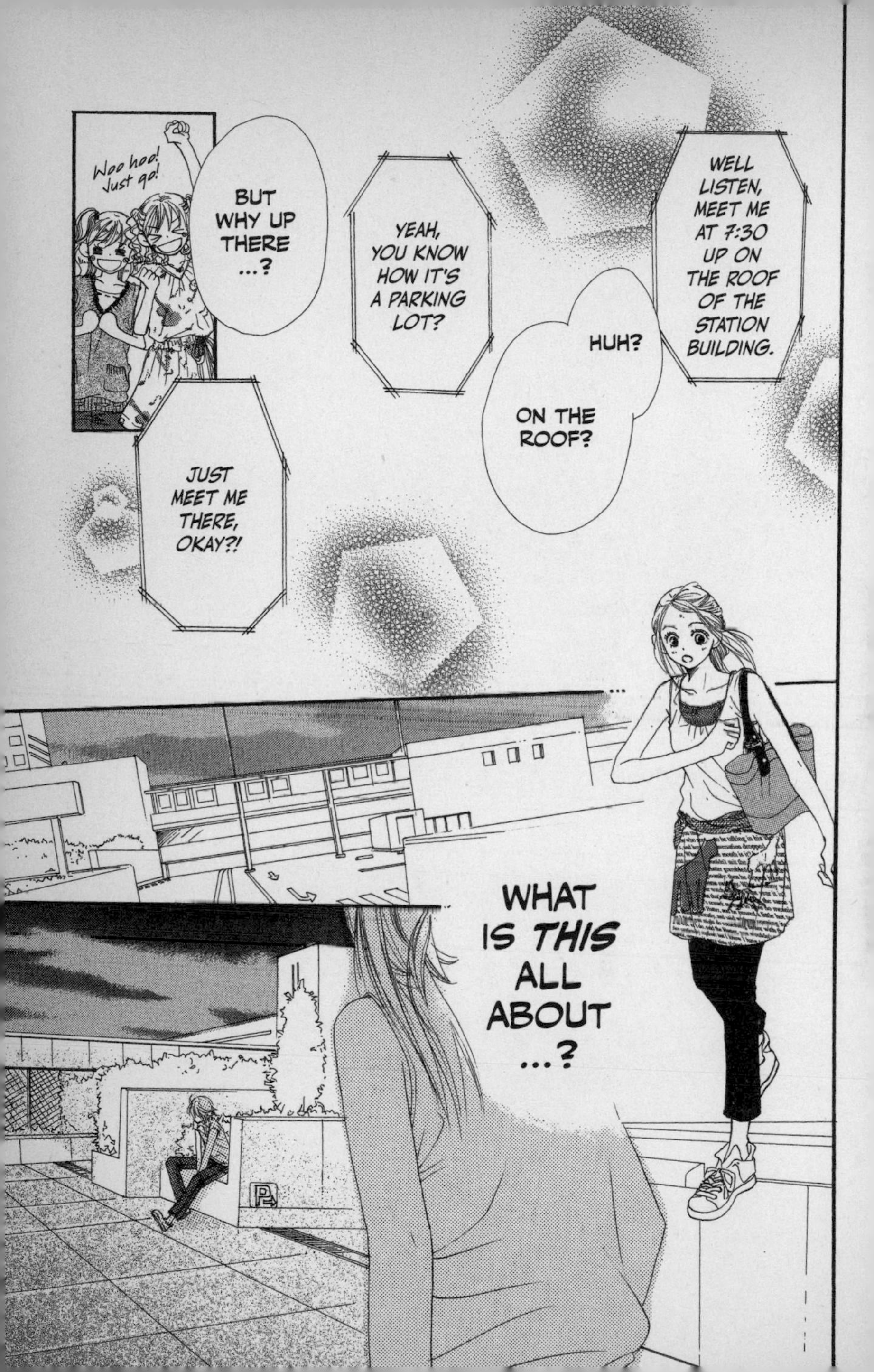
WELL LISTEN, MEET ME AT 7:30 UP ON THE ROOF OF THE STATION BUILDING.
HUH?
ON THE ROOF?
YEAH, YOU KNOW HOW IT'S A PARKING LOT?
BUT WHY UP THERE ...?
Woo hoo! Just go!
JUST MEET ME THERE, OKAY?!
...
WHAT IS *THIS* ALL ABOUT ...?

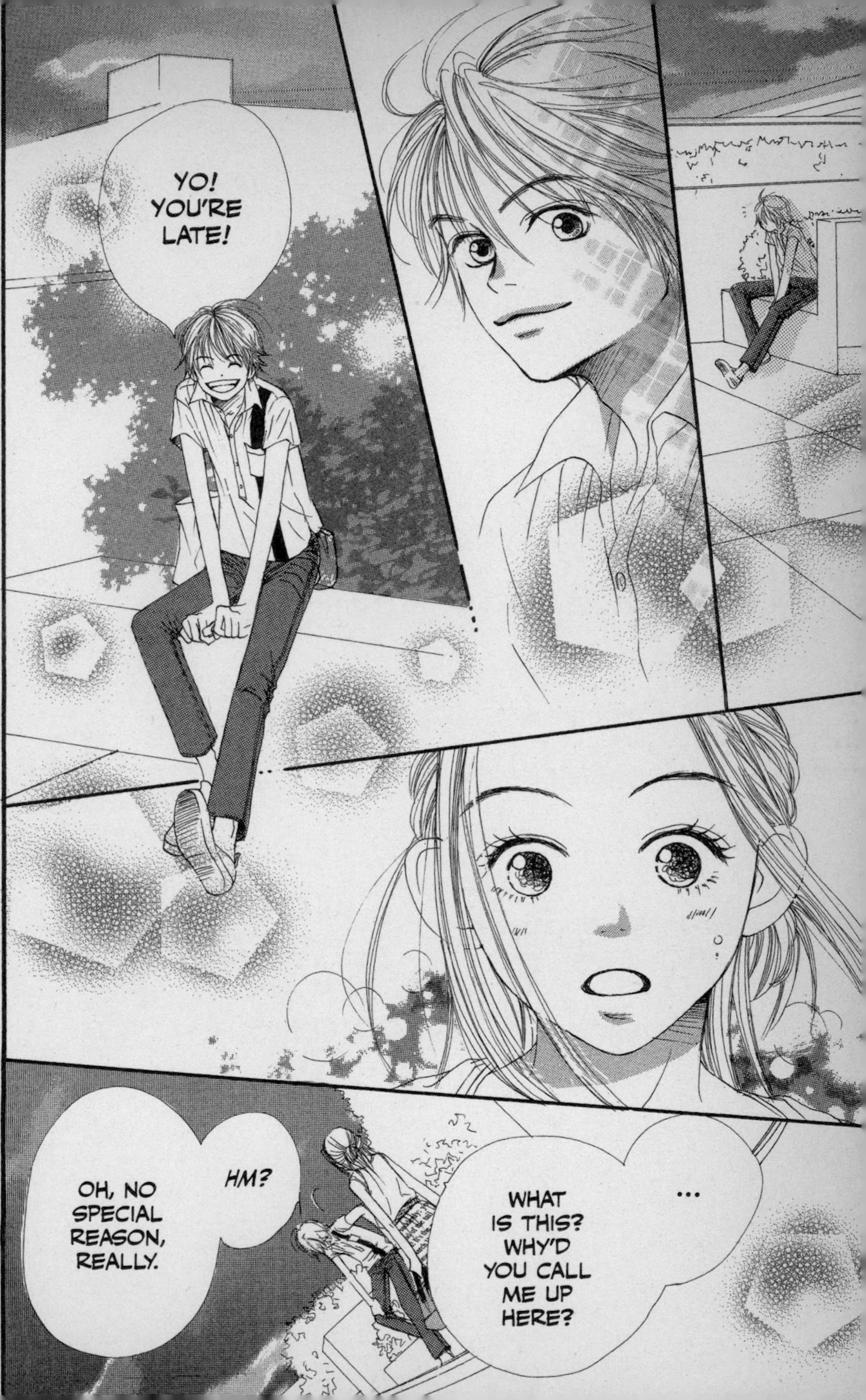
YO! YOU'RE LATE!
...
WHAT IS THIS? WHY'D YOU CALL ME UP HERE?
HM?
OH, NO SPECIAL REASON, REALLY.

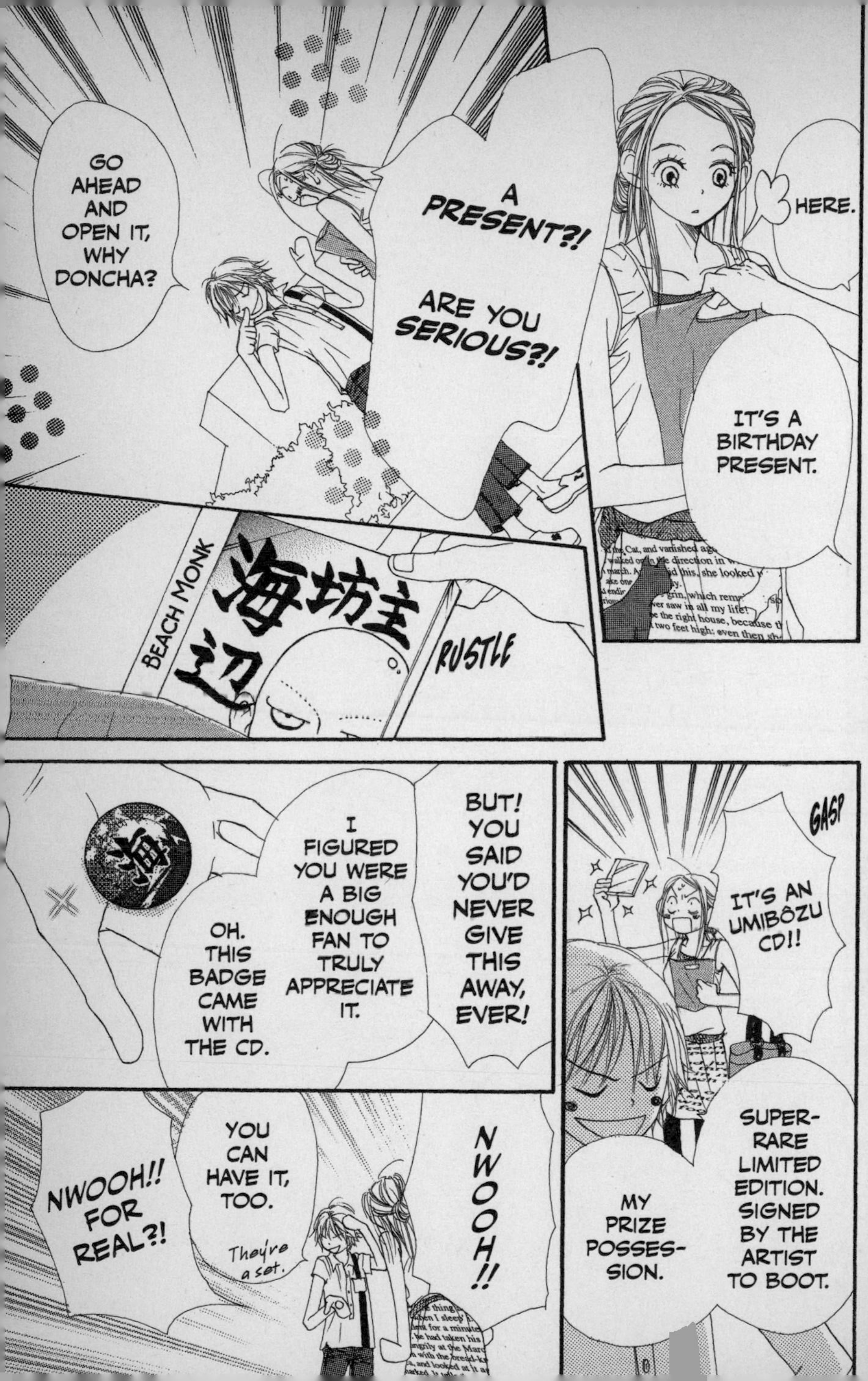
HERE.
IT'S A BIRTHDAY PRESENT.
A PRESENT?!
ARE YOU SERIOUS?!
GO AHEAD AND OPEN IT, WHY DONCHA?
海坊主辺
BEACH MONK
RUSTLE
GASP
IT'S AN UMIBÔZU CD!!
SUPER-RARE LIMITED EDITION. SIGNED BY THE ARTIST TO BOOT.
MY PRIZE POSSESSION.
BUT! YOU SAID YOU'D NEVER GIVE THIS AWAY, EVER!
I FIGURED YOU WERE A BIG ENOUGH FAN TO TRULY APPRECIATE IT.
OH. THIS BADGE CAME WITH THE CD.
海
NWOOH!!
YOU CAN HAVE IT, TOO.
They're a set.
NWOOH!! FOR REAL?!

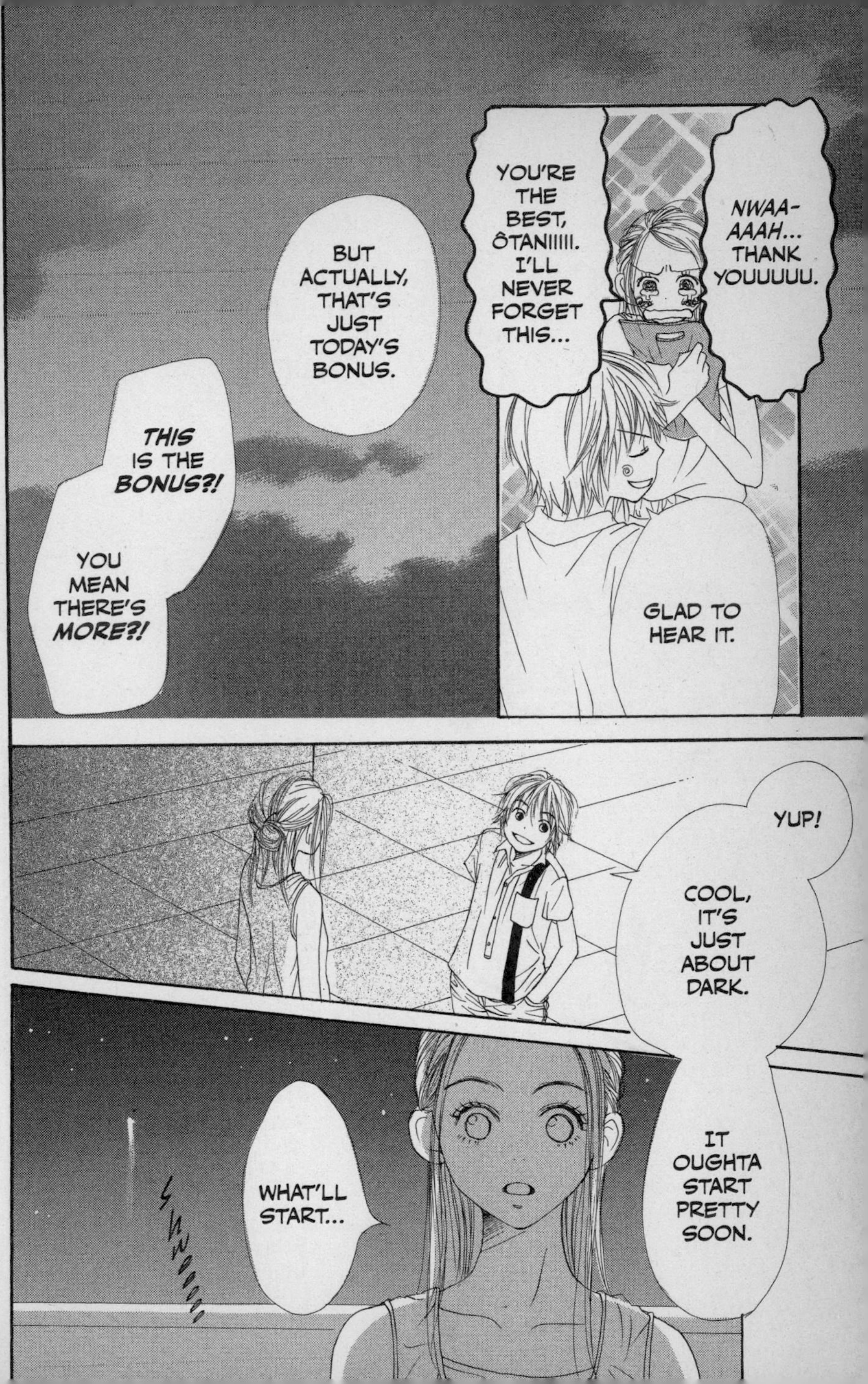
NWAA-AAAH... THANK YOUUUUUU.
YOU'RE THE BEST, ÔTANIIIII. I'LL NEVER FORGET THIS...
GLAD TO HEAR IT.
BUT ACTUALLY, THAT'S JUST TODAY'S BONUS.
THIS IS THE BONUS?!
YOU MEAN THERE'S MORE?!
YUP!
COOL, IT'S JUST ABOUT DARK.
IT OUGHTA START PRETTY SOON.
WHAT'LL START...

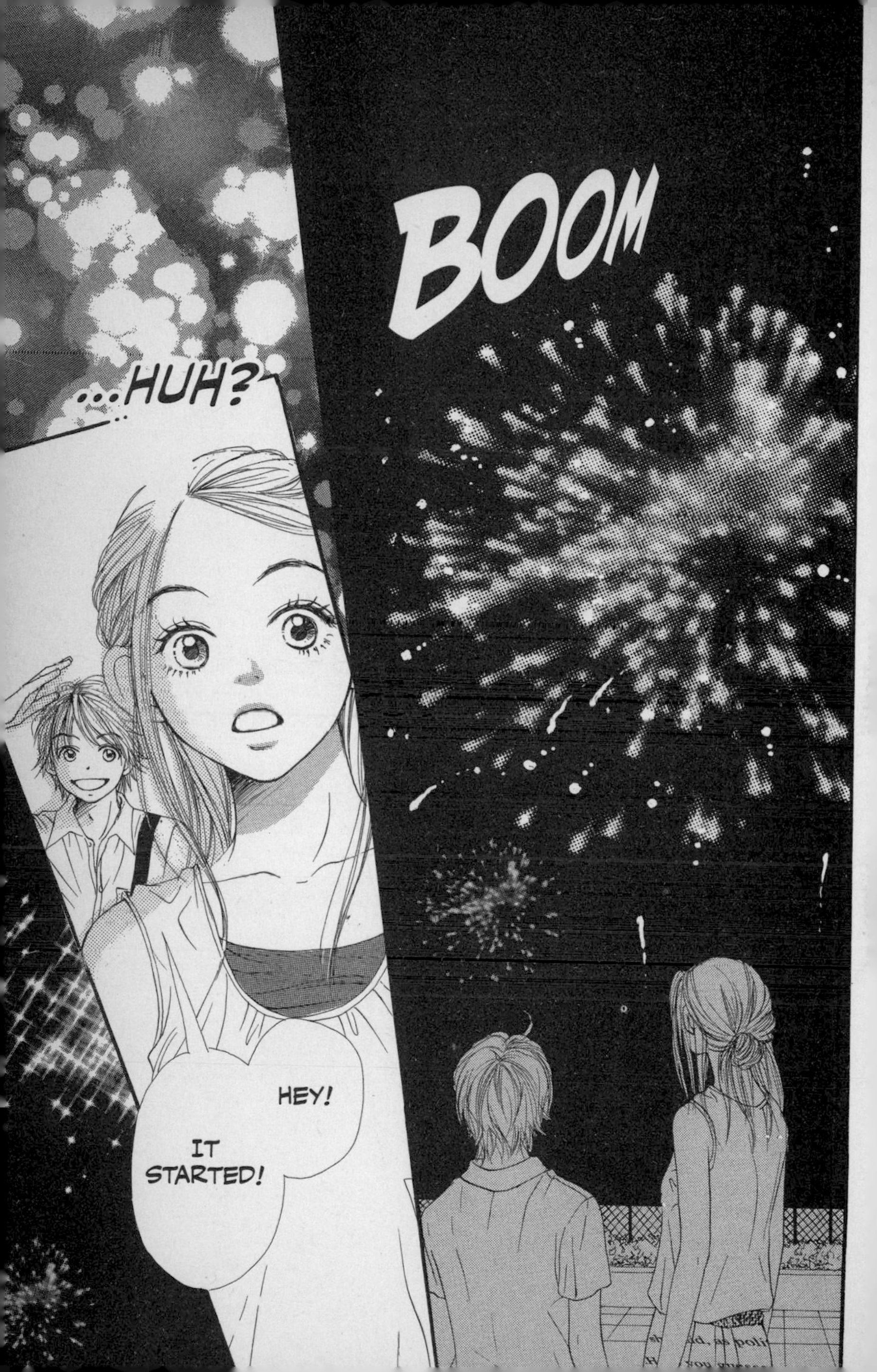
BOOM
...HUH?
HEY!
IT STARTED!

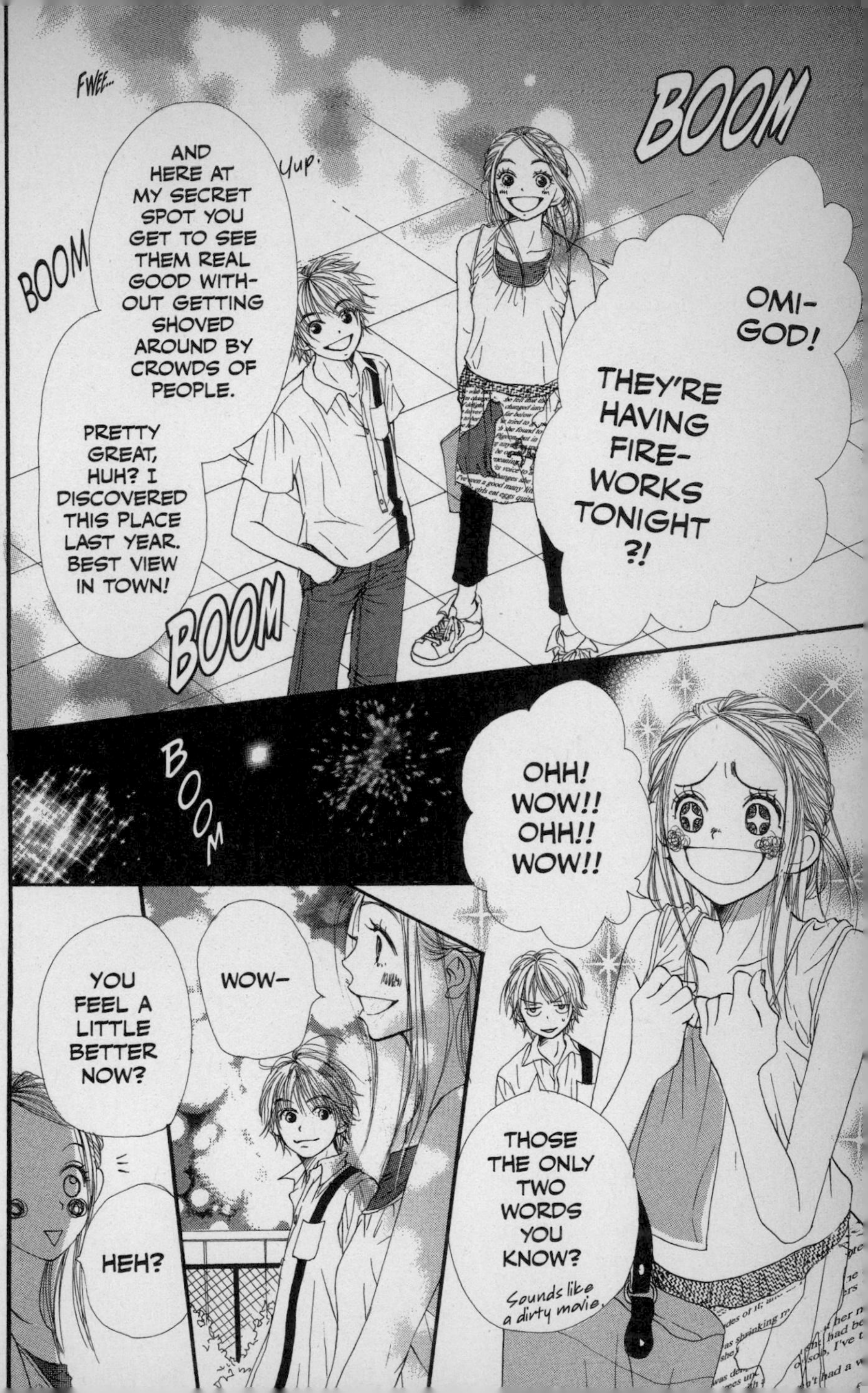
BOOM
OMI-GOD!
THEY'RE HAVING FIRE-WORKS TONIGHT?!
Yup.
FWEE...
AND HERE AT MY SECRET SPOT YOU GET TO SEE THEM REAL GOOD WITH-OUT GETTING SHOVED AROUND BY CROWDS OF PEOPLE.
BOOM
PRETTY GREAT, HUH? I DISCOVERED THIS PLACE LAST YEAR. BEST VIEW IN TOWN!
BOOM
OHH! WOW!! OHH!! WOW!!
BOOM
THOSE THE ONLY TWO WORDS YOU KNOW?
Sounds like a dirty movie.
WOW-
YOU FEEL A LITTLE BETTER NOW?
HEH?

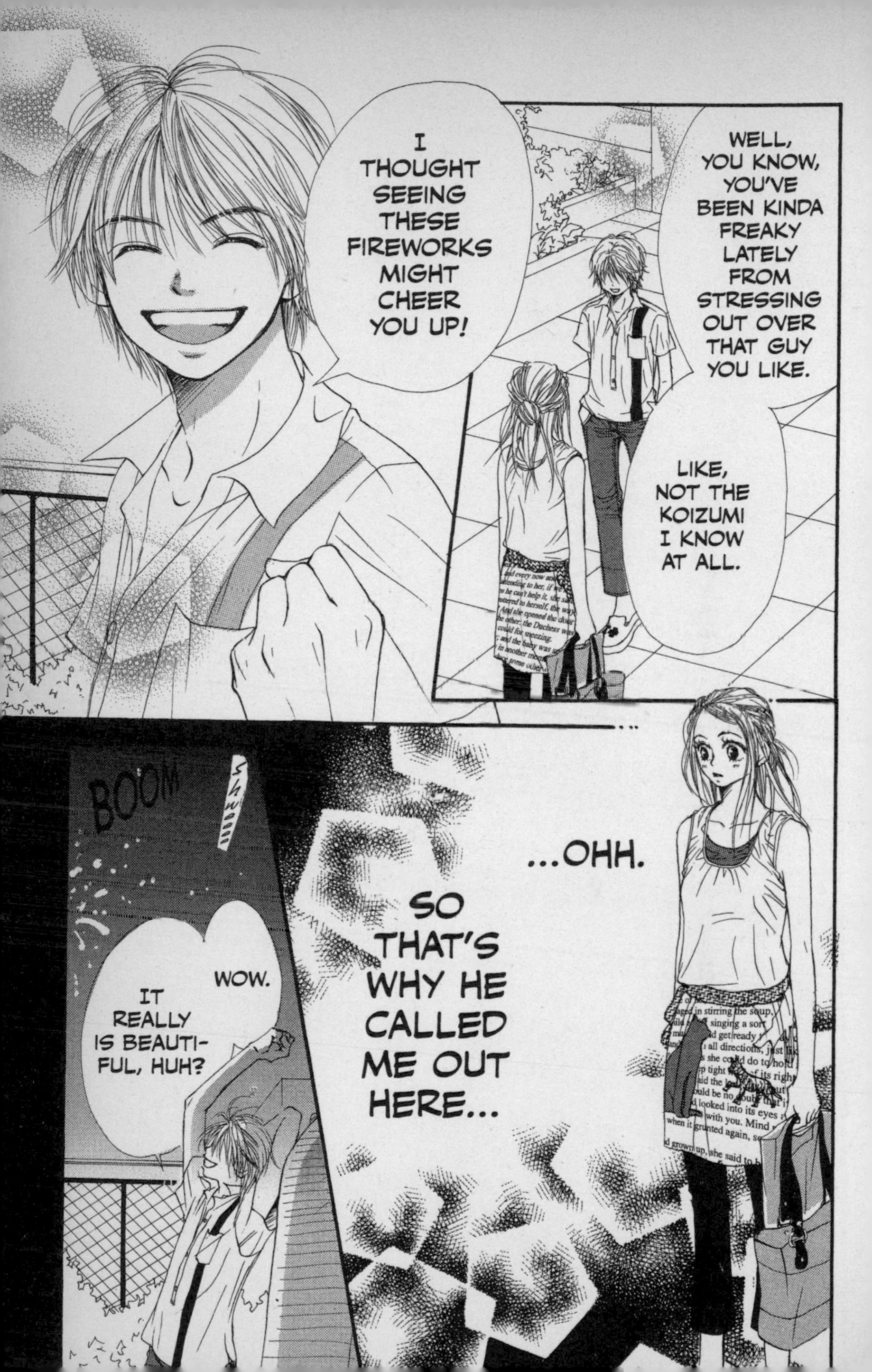
WELL, YOU KNOW, YOU'VE BEEN KINDA FREAKY LATELY FROM STRESSING OUT OVER THAT GUY YOU LIKE.
LIKE, NOT THE KOIZUMI I KNOW AT ALL.
I THOUGHT SEEING THESE FIREWORKS MIGHT CHEER YOU UP!
...OHH.
SO THAT'S WHY HE CALLED ME OUT HERE...
BOOM
WOW.
IT REALLY IS BEAUTIFUL, HUH?

...YEAH.
HE'S THE BEST.
I REALLY LOVE THIS GUY.
AND RIGHT NOW ...
...I FEEL LIKE I CAN TELL HIM THAT.
...

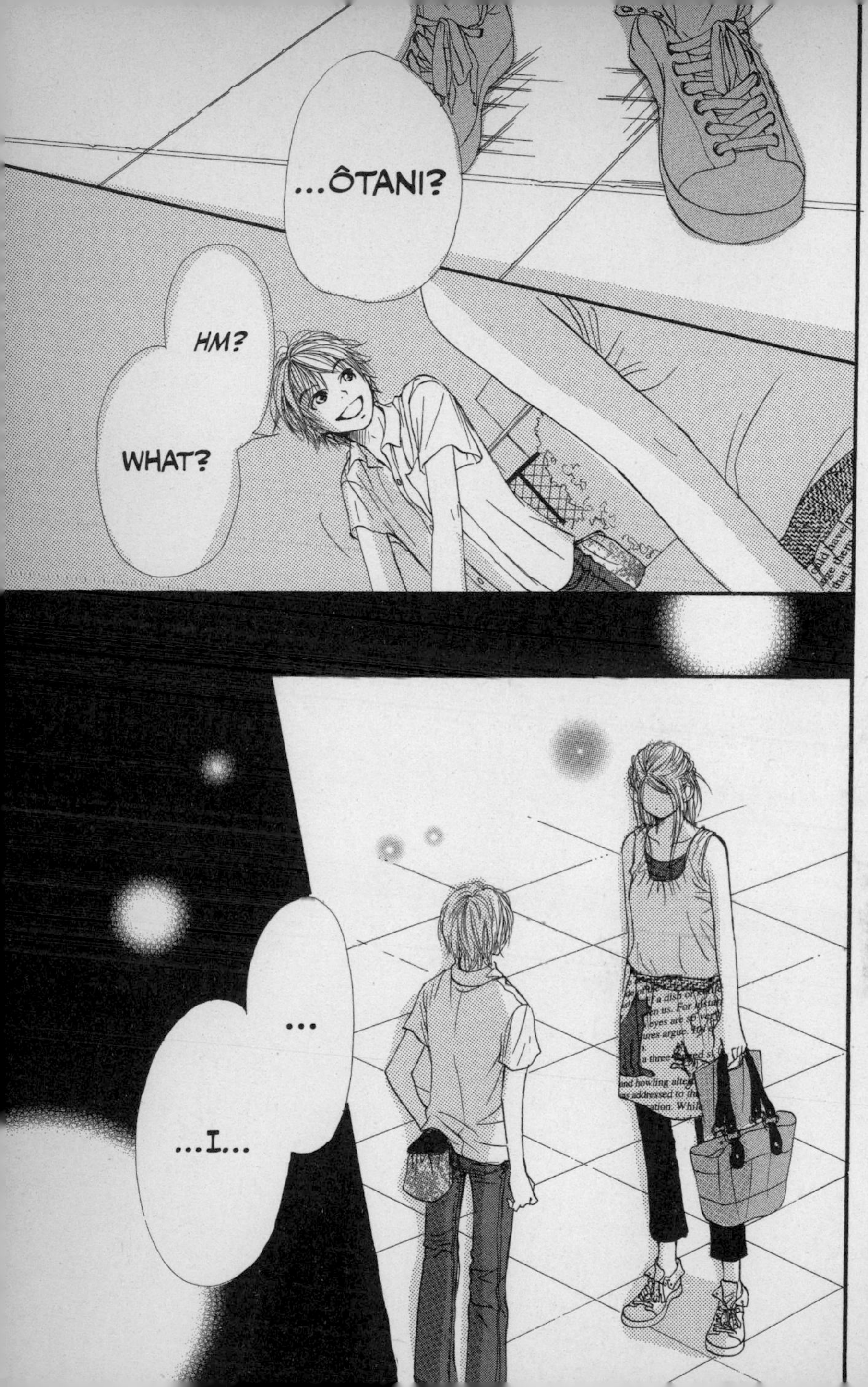
...ÔTANI?
HM? WHAT?
...
...I...

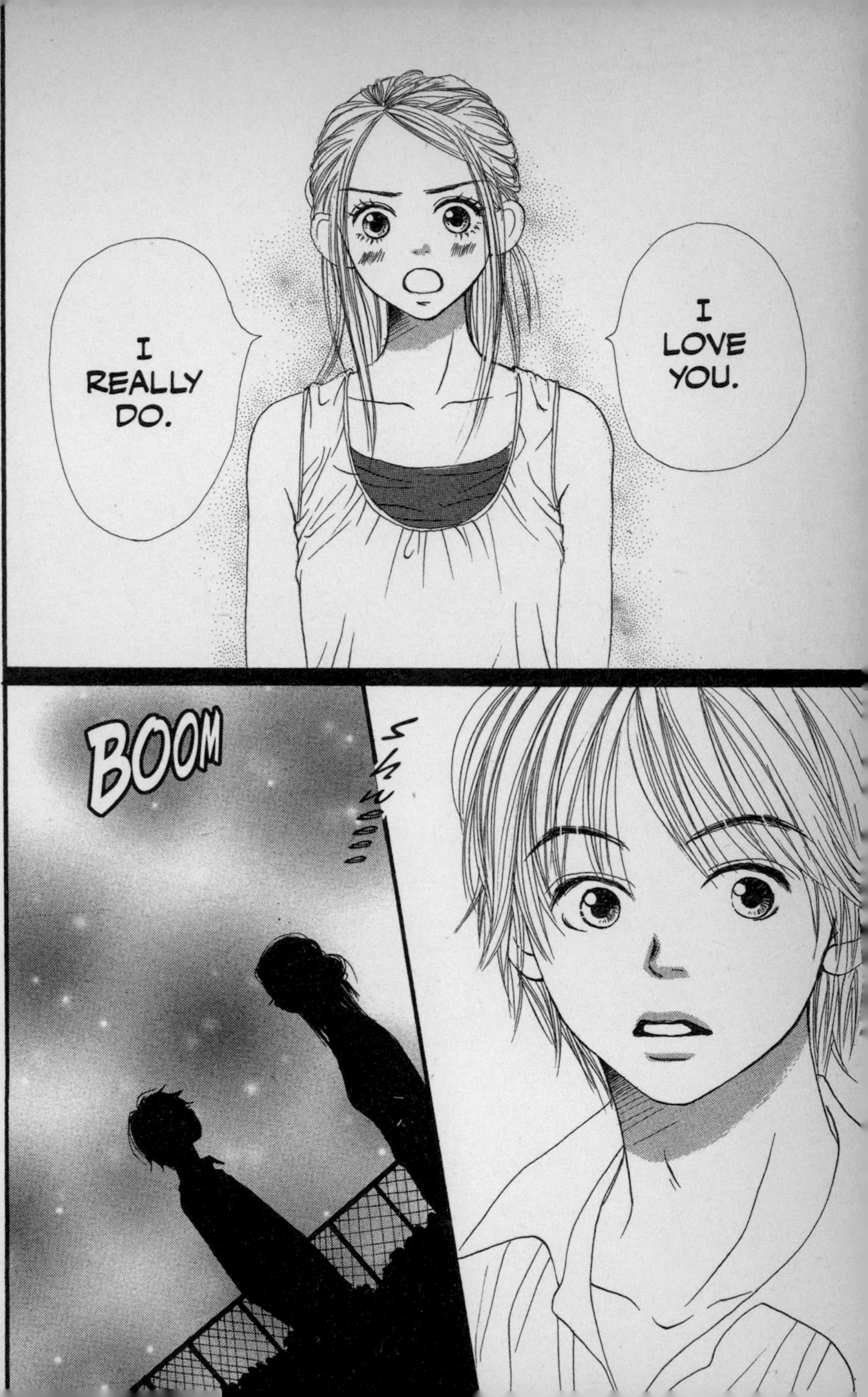
I LOVE YOU.
I REALLY DO.
BOOM

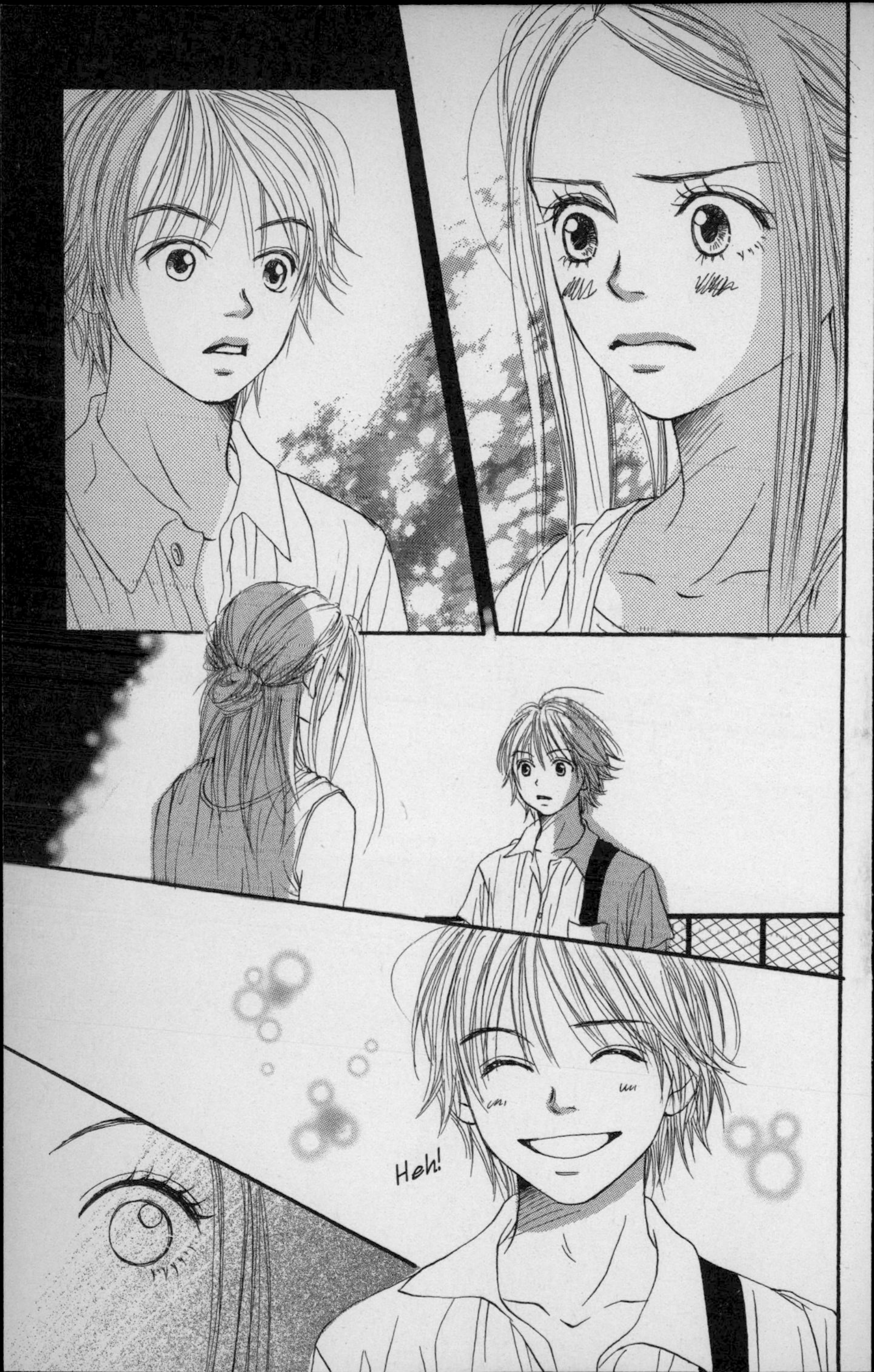
Heh!

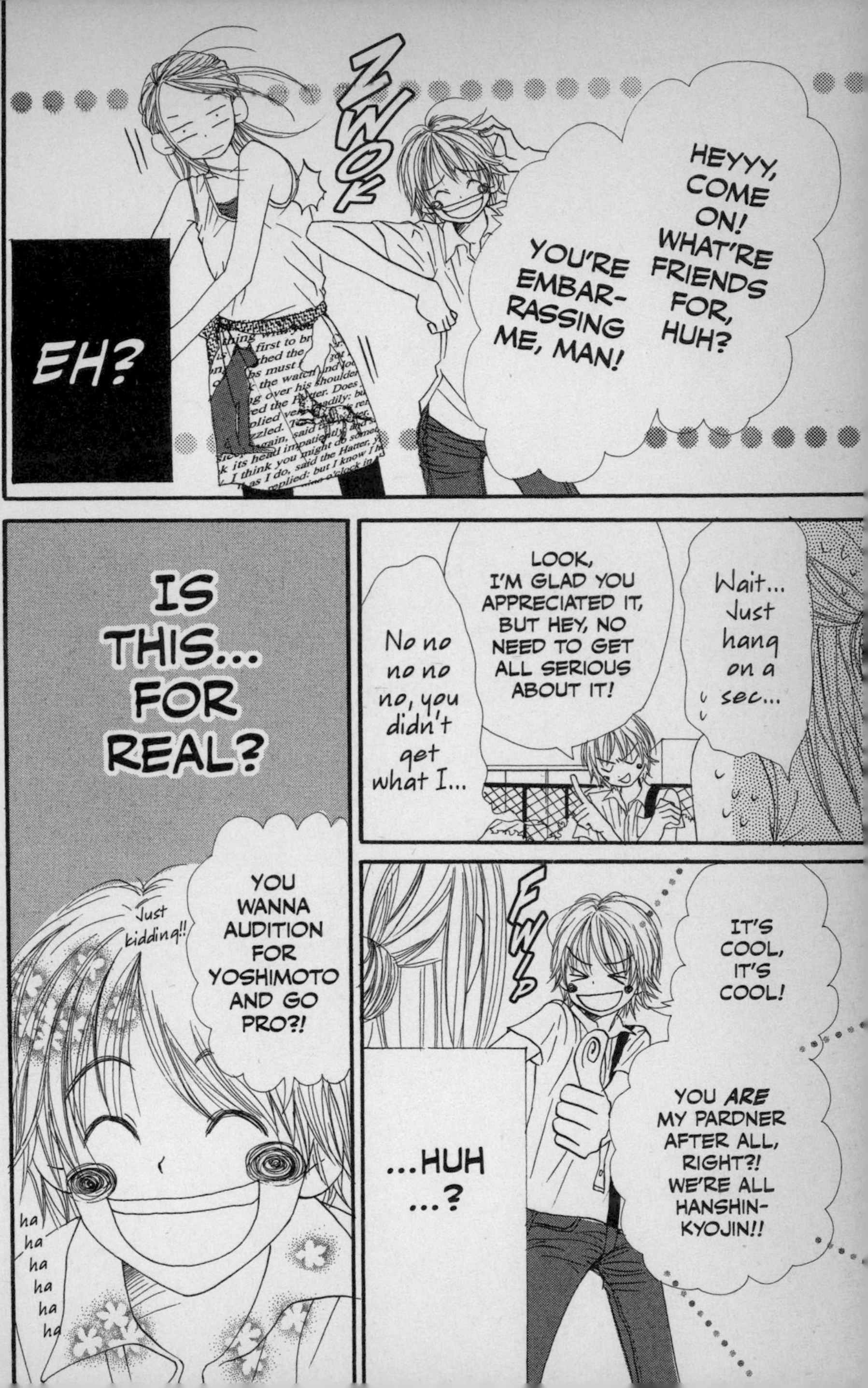
HEYYY, COME ON! WHAT'RE FRIENDS FOR, HUH?
YOU'RE EMBAR-RASSING ME, MAN!
ZWOOF
EH?
Wait... Just hang on a sec...
LOOK, I'M GLAD YOU APPRECIATED IT, BUT HEY, NO NEED TO GET ALL SERIOUS ABOUT IT!
No no no no no, you didn't get what I...
IT'S COOL, IT'S COOL!
FWIP
YOU *ARE* MY PARDNER AFTER ALL, RIGHT?! WE'RE ALL HANSHIN-KYOJIN!!
...HUH ...?
IS THIS... FOR REAL?
YOU WANNA AUDITION FOR YOSHIMOTO AND GO PRO?!
Just kidding!!
ha ha ha ha ha ha ha

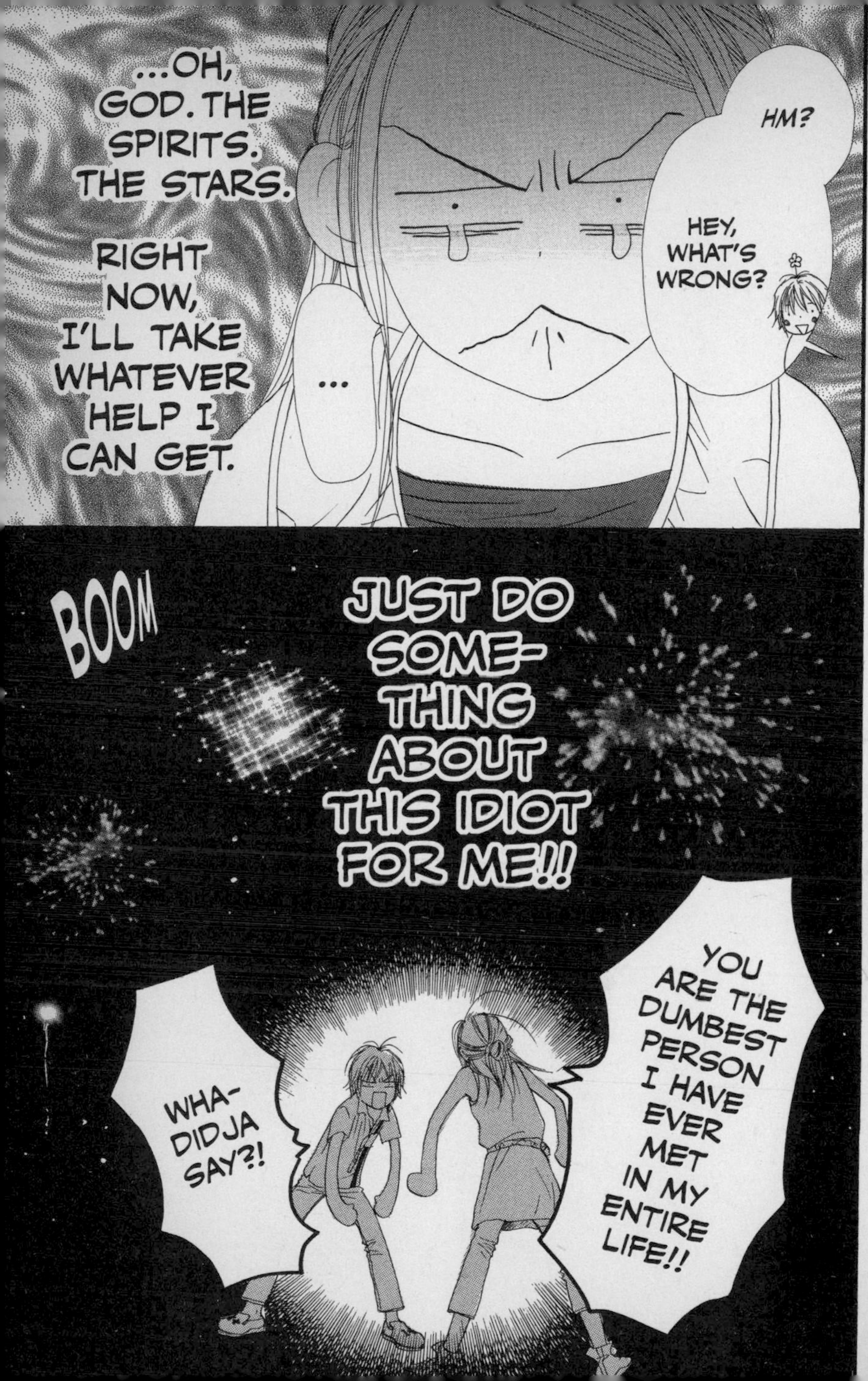
HM?
HEY, WHAT'S WRONG?
...
...OH, GOD. THE SPIRITS. THE STARS.
RIGHT NOW, I'LL TAKE WHATEVER HELP I CAN GET.
BOOM
JUST DO SOME-THING ABOUT THIS IDIOT FOR ME!!
YOU ARE THE DUMBEST PERSON I HAVE EVER MET IN MY ENTIRE LIFE!!
WHA-DIDJA SAY?!

CHAPTER 15

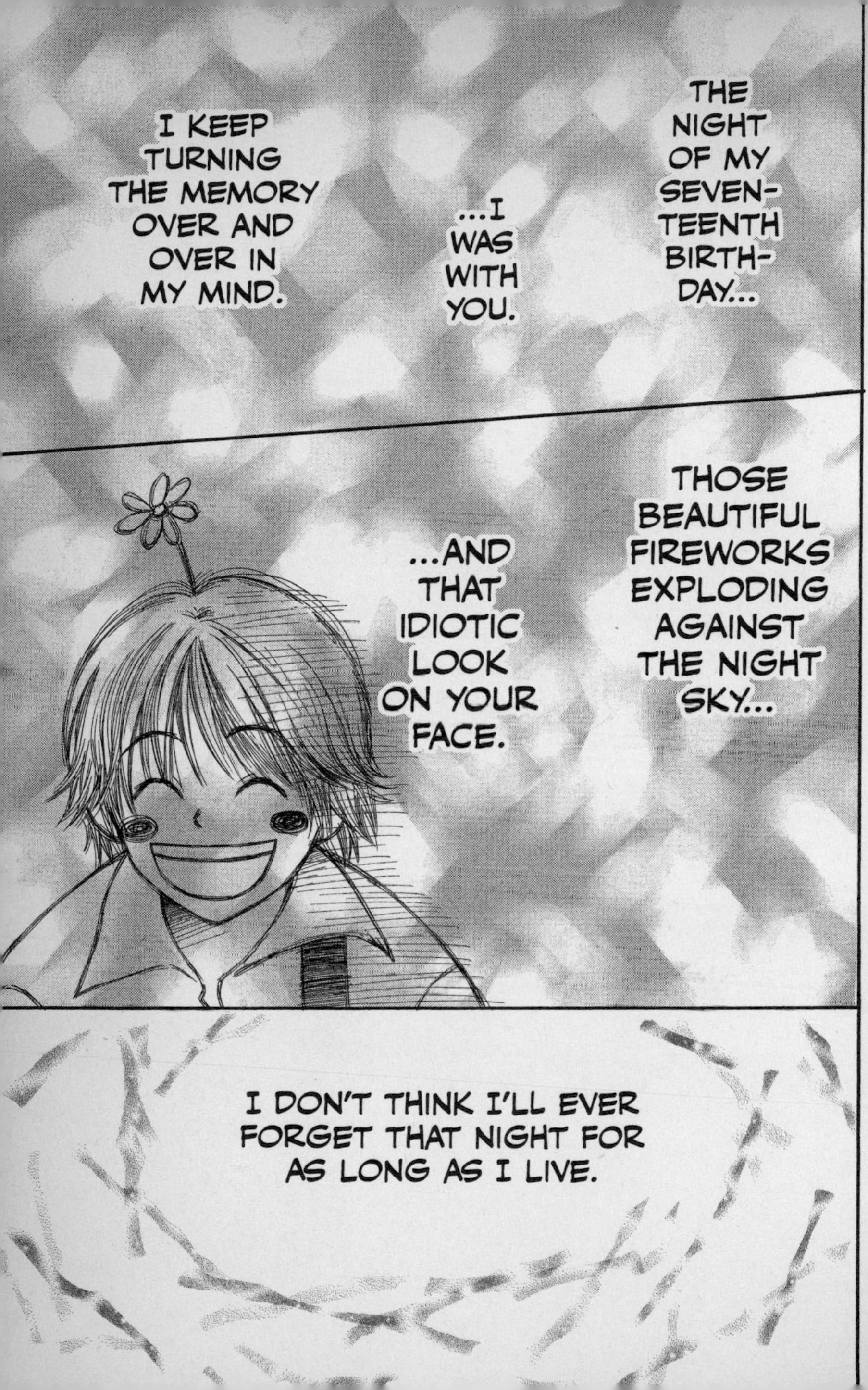
THE NIGHT OF MY SEVENTEENTH BIRTHDAY...
...I WAS WITH YOU.
I KEEP TURNING THE MEMORY OVER AND OVER IN MY MIND.
THOSE BEAUTIFUL FIREWORKS EXPLODING AGAINST THE NIGHT SKY...
...AND THAT IDIOTIC LOOK ON YOUR FACE.
I DON'T THINK I'LL EVER FORGET THAT NIGHT FOR AS LONG AS I LIVE.

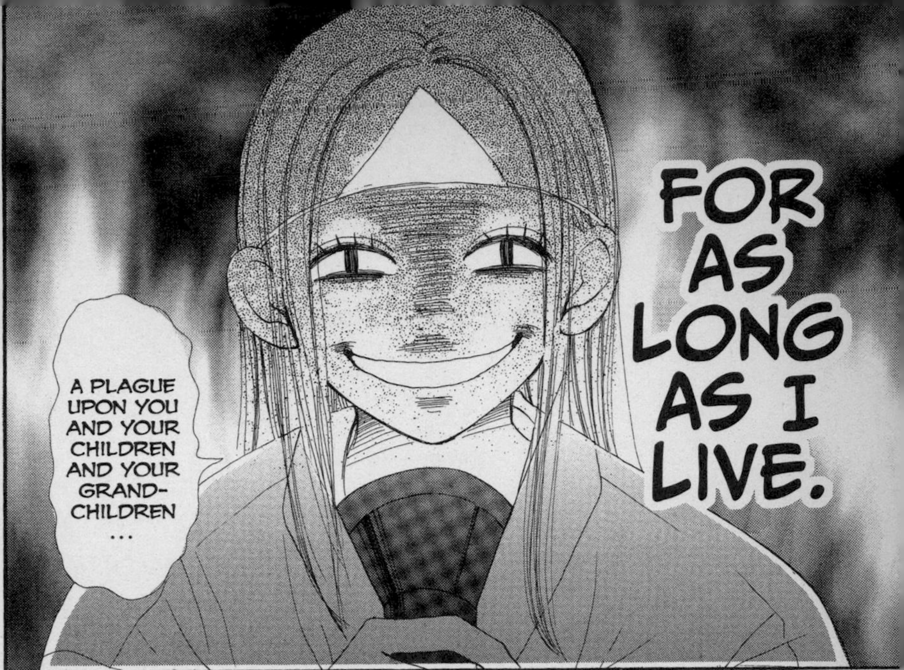
A PLAGUE UPON YOU AND YOUR CHILDREN AND YOUR GRAND-CHILDREN ...
FOR AS LONG AS I LIVE.

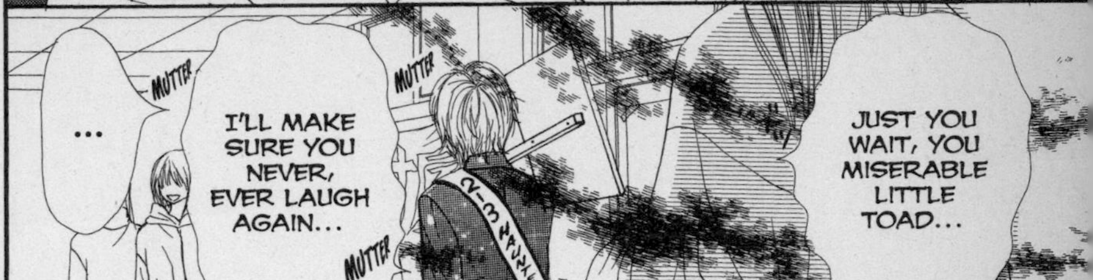
JUST YOU WAIT, YOU MISERABLE LITTLE TOAD...
MUTTER
MUTTER
I'LL MAKE SURE YOU NEVER, EVER LAUGH AGAIN...
MUTTER
...

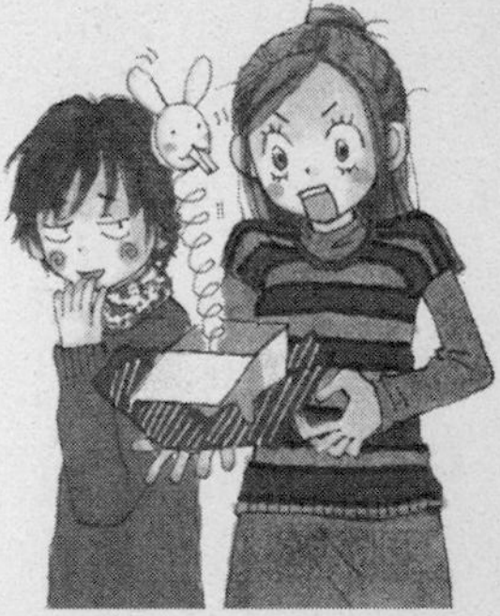

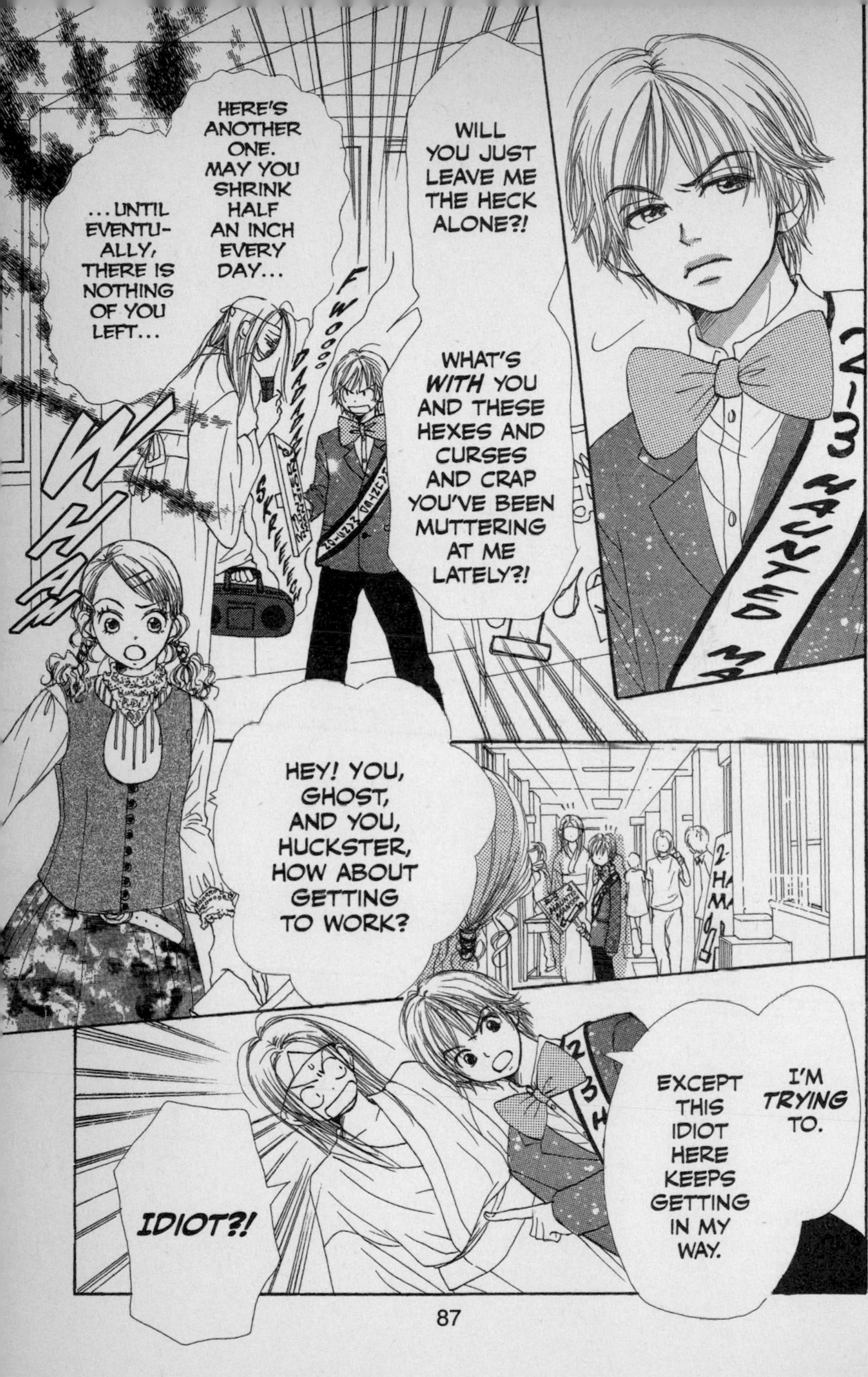
2-3 HAUNTED MA
WILL YOU JUST LEAVE ME THE HECK ALONE?!
WHAT'S *WITH* YOU AND THESE HEXES AND CURSES AND CRAP YOU'VE BEEN MUTTERING AT ME LATELY?!
HERE'S ANOTHER ONE. MAY YOU SHRINK HALF AN INCH EVERY DAY...
...UNTIL EVENTU-ALLY, THERE IS NOTHING OF YOU LEFT...
WHAM
HEY! YOU, GHOST, AND YOU, HUCKSTER, HOW ABOUT GETTING TO WORK?
I'M *TRYING* TO.
EXCEPT THIS IDIOT HERE KEEPS GETTING IN MY WAY.
IDIOT?!

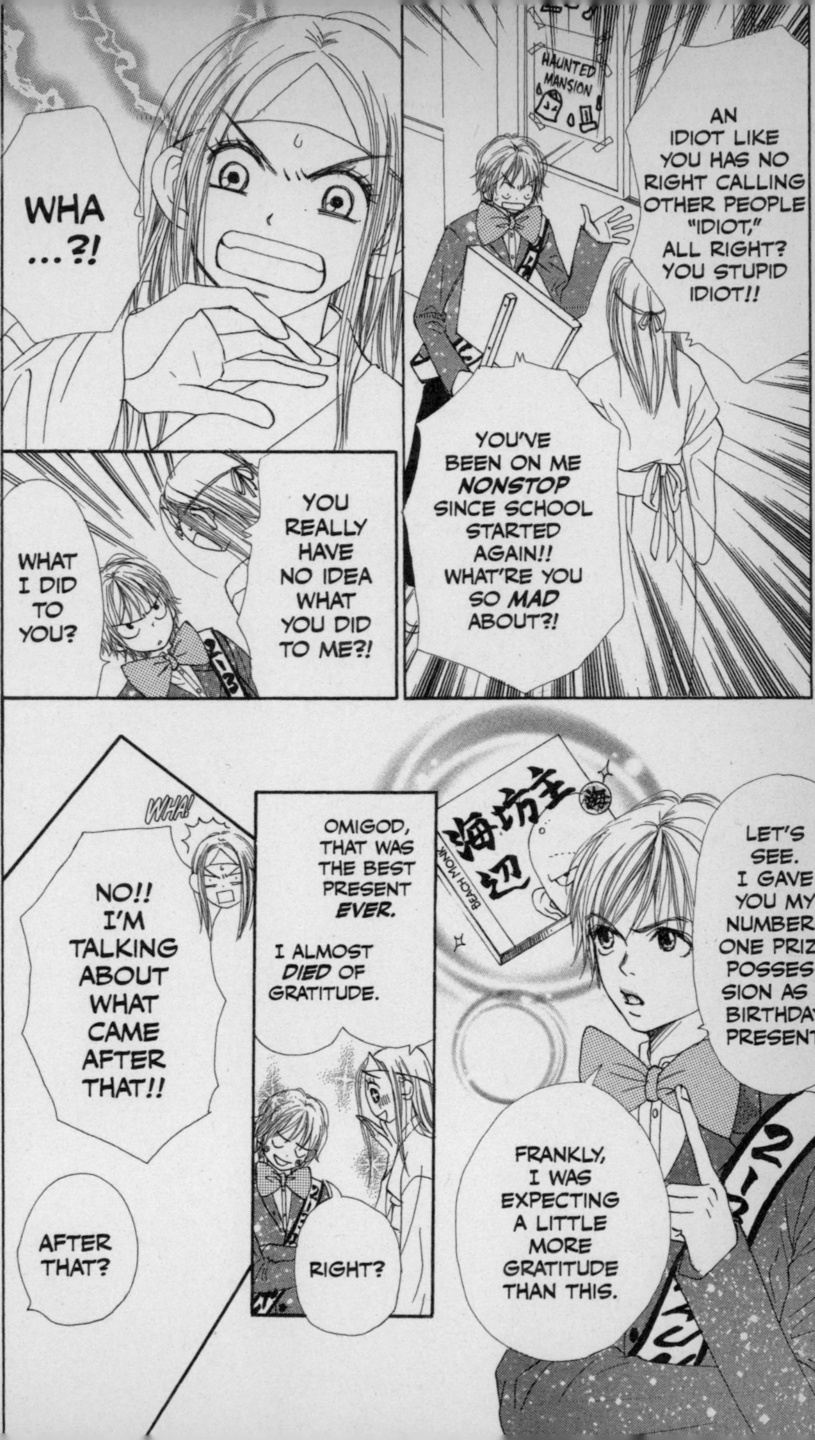
HAUNTED MANSION
AN IDIOT LIKE YOU HAS NO RIGHT CALLING OTHER PEOPLE "IDIOT," ALL RIGHT? YOU STUPID IDIOT!!
YOU'VE BEEN ON ME NONSTOP SINCE SCHOOL STARTED AGAIN!! WHAT'RE YOU SO MAD ABOUT?!
WHA ...?!
YOU REALLY HAVE NO IDEA WHAT YOU DID TO ME?!
WHAT I DID TO YOU?
LET'S SEE. I GAVE YOU MY NUMBER-ONE PRIZE POSSESSION AS A BIRTHDAY PRESENT.
BEACH MONK
FRANKLY, I WAS EXPECTING A LITTLE MORE GRATITUDE THAN THIS.
OMIGOD, THAT WAS THE BEST PRESENT EVER.
I ALMOST DIED OF GRATITUDE.
RIGHT?
WHA!
NO!! I'M TALKING ABOUT WHAT CAME AFTER THAT!!
AFTER THAT?

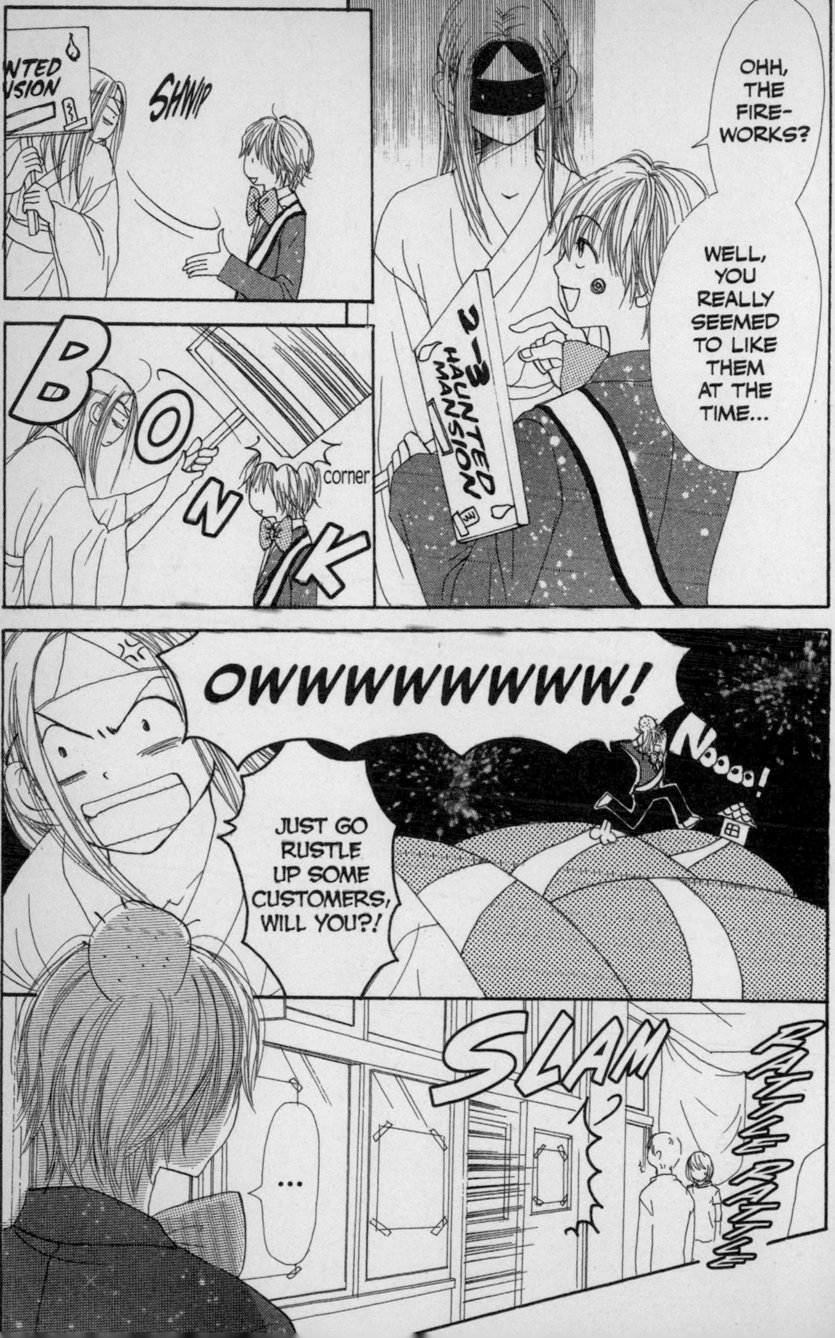
OHH, THE FIRE-WORKS?
WELL, YOU REALLY SEEMED TO LIKE THEM AT THE TIME...
2-3 HAUNTED MANSION
SHWIP
BONK
corner
OWWWWWWWW!
Noooo!
JUST GO RUSTLE UP SOME CUSTOMERS, WILL YOU?!
SLAM
...

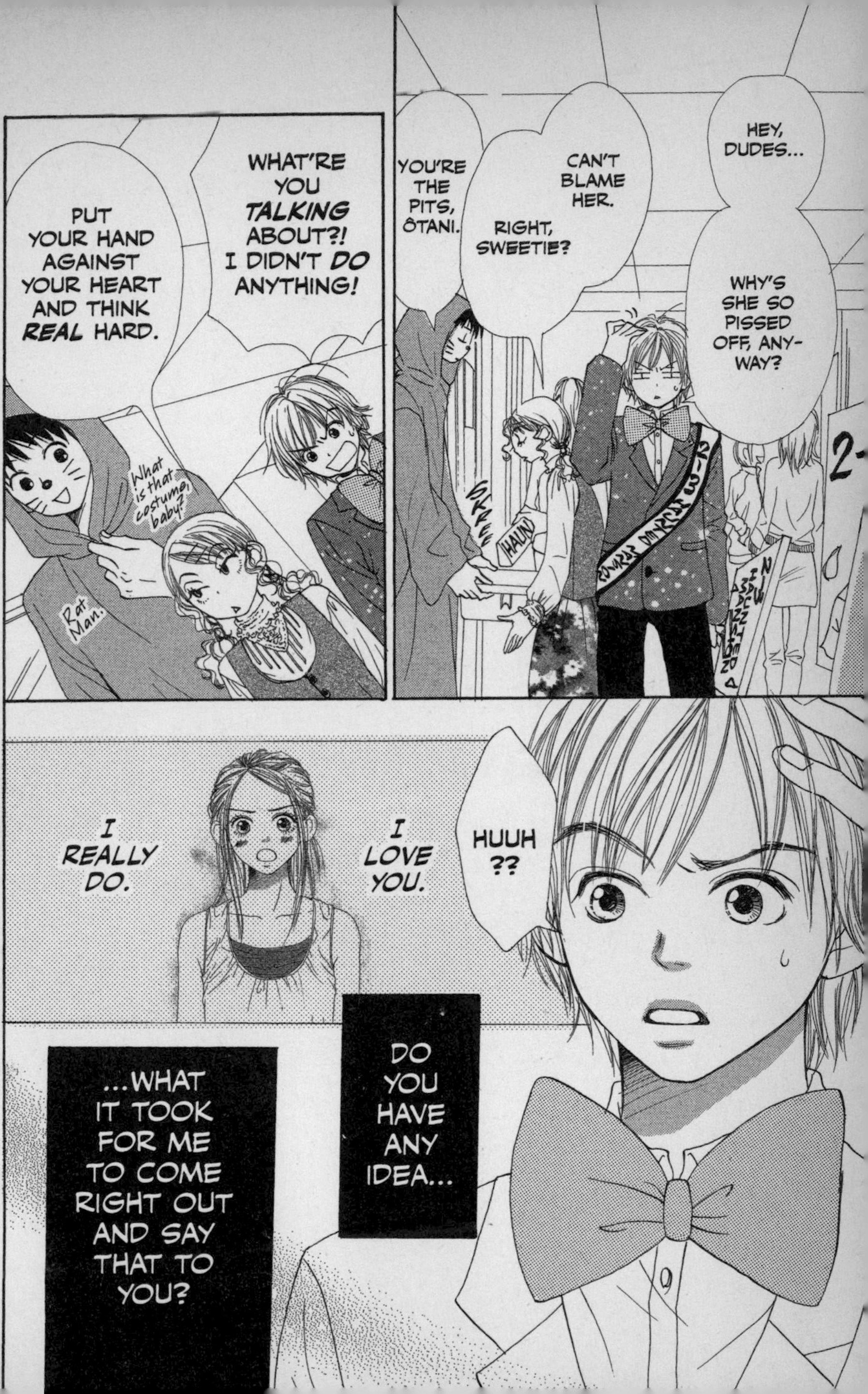
HEY, DUDES...
WHY'S SHE SO PISSED OFF, ANYWAY?
CAN'T BLAME HER.
RIGHT, SWEETIE?
YOU'RE THE PITS, ÔTANI.
WHAT'RE YOU *TALKING* ABOUT?! I DIDN'T *DO* ANYTHING!
PUT YOUR HAND AGAINST YOUR HEART AND THINK ***REAL*** HARD.
What is that costume, baby?
Rat Man.
HUUH ??
I LOVE YOU.
I REALLY DO.
DO YOU HAVE ANY IDEA...
...WHAT IT TOOK FOR ME TO COME RIGHT OUT AND SAY THAT TO YOU?

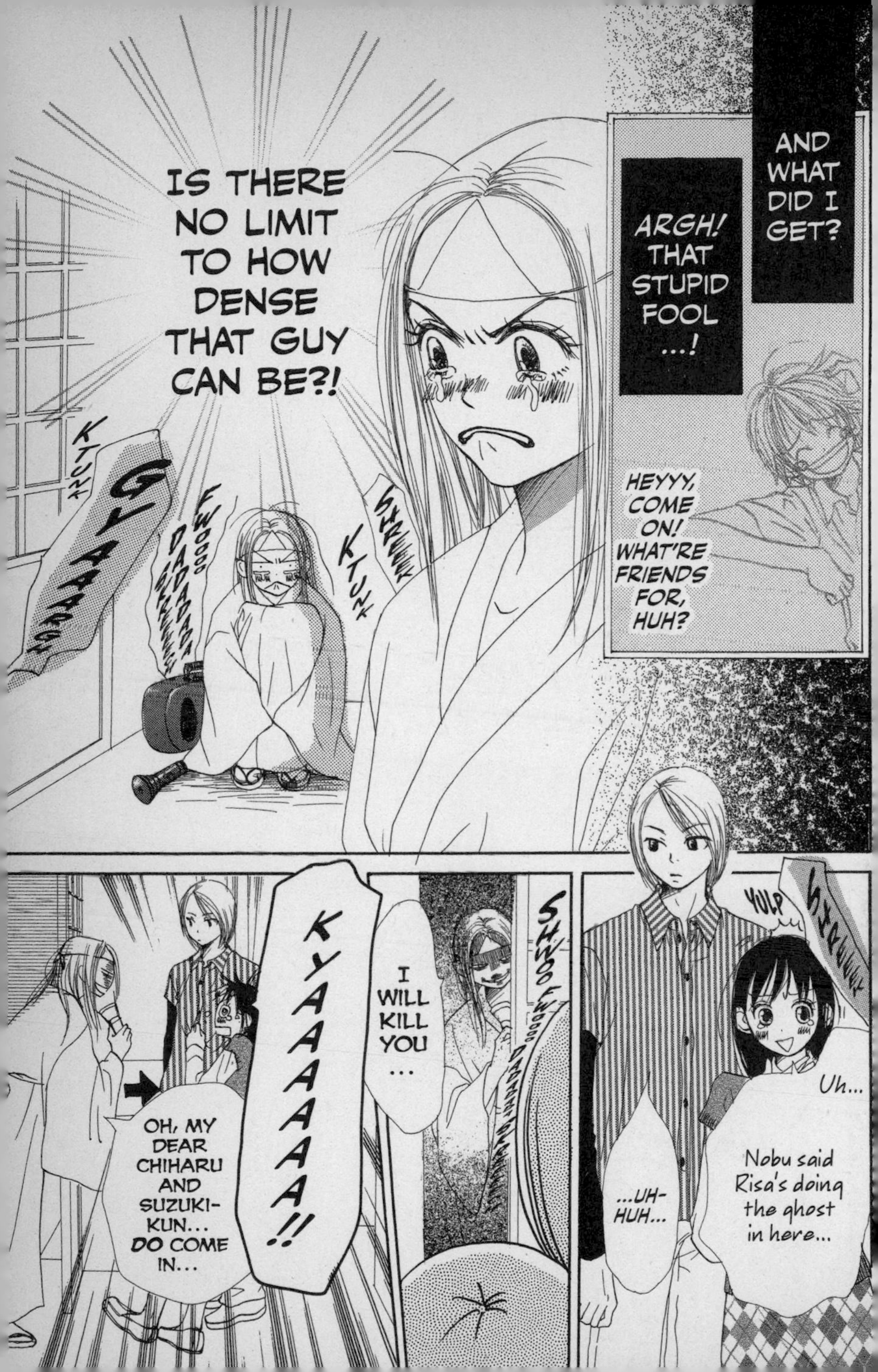
AND WHAT DID I GET?
ARGH! THAT STUPID FOOL ...!
HEYYY, COME ON! WHAT'RE FRIENDS FOR, HUH?
IS THERE NO LIMIT TO HOW DENSE THAT GUY CAN BE?!
KTUNK
KTUNK
GYAAAARGH
YULP
Uh...
Nobu said Risa's doing the ghost in here...
...UH-HUH...
I WILL KILL YOU ...
KYAAAAAAAA!!
OH, MY DEAR CHIHARU AND SUZUKI-KUN... DO COME IN...

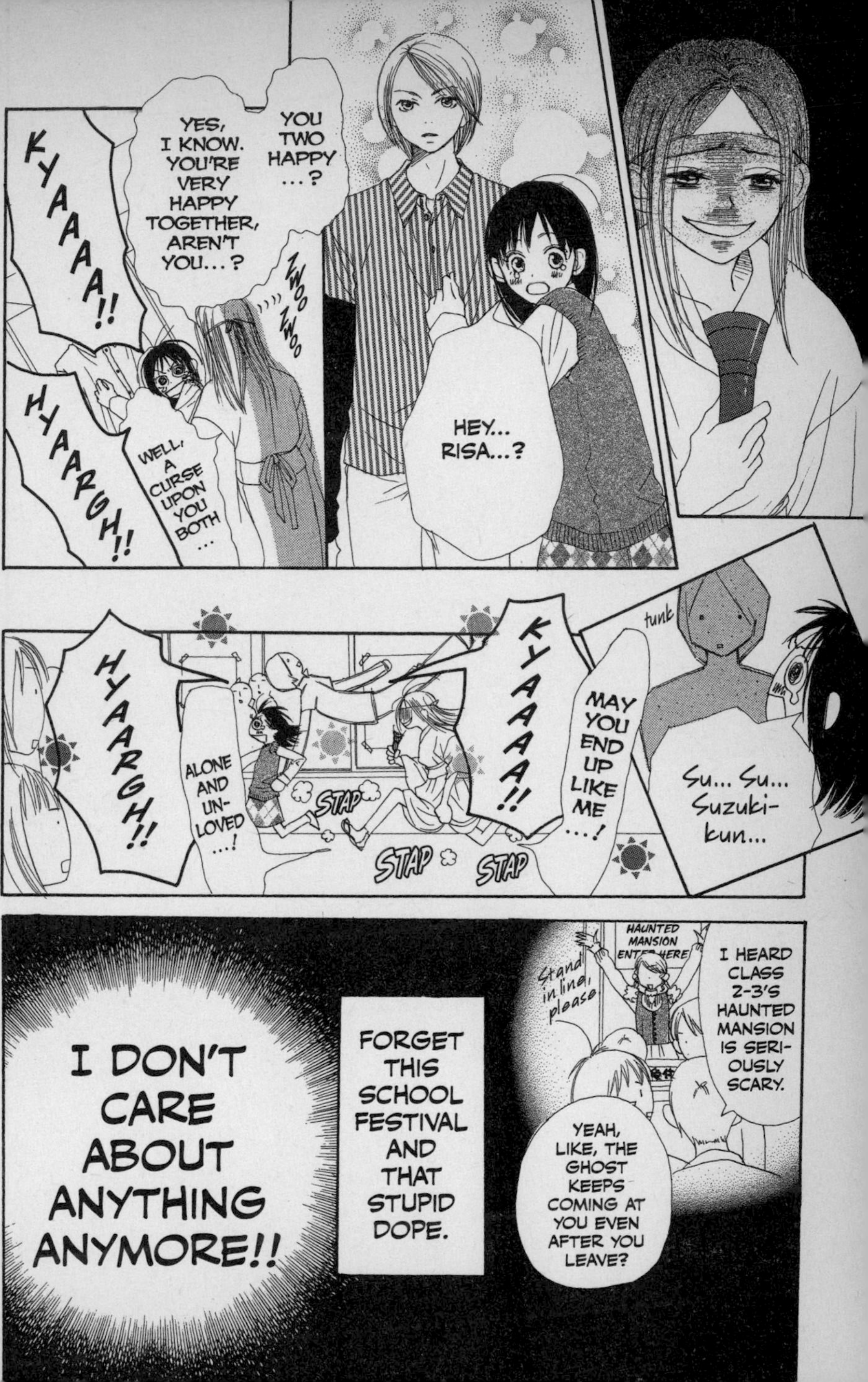
YOU TWO HAPPY . . . ?
YES, I KNOW. YOU'RE VERY HAPPY TOGETHER, AREN'T YOU . . . ?
ZWOO ZWOO
HEY... RISA...?
WELL, A CURSE UPON YOU BOTH . . .
KYAAAAA!!
HYAARGH!!
tunk
Su... Su... Suzuki-kun...
KYAAAAA!!
MAY YOU END UP LIKE ME . . . !
STAP
STAP
HYAARGH!!
ALONE AND UN-LOVED . . . !
STAP
HAUNTED MANSION ENTER HERE
I HEARD CLASS 2-3'S HAUNTED MANSION IS SERI-OUSLY SCARY.
Stand in line, please
YEAH, LIKE, THE GHOST KEEPS COMING AT YOU EVEN AFTER YOU LEAVE?
FORGET THIS SCHOOL FESTIVAL AND THAT STUPID DOPE.
I DON'T CARE ABOUT ANYTHING ANYMORE!!

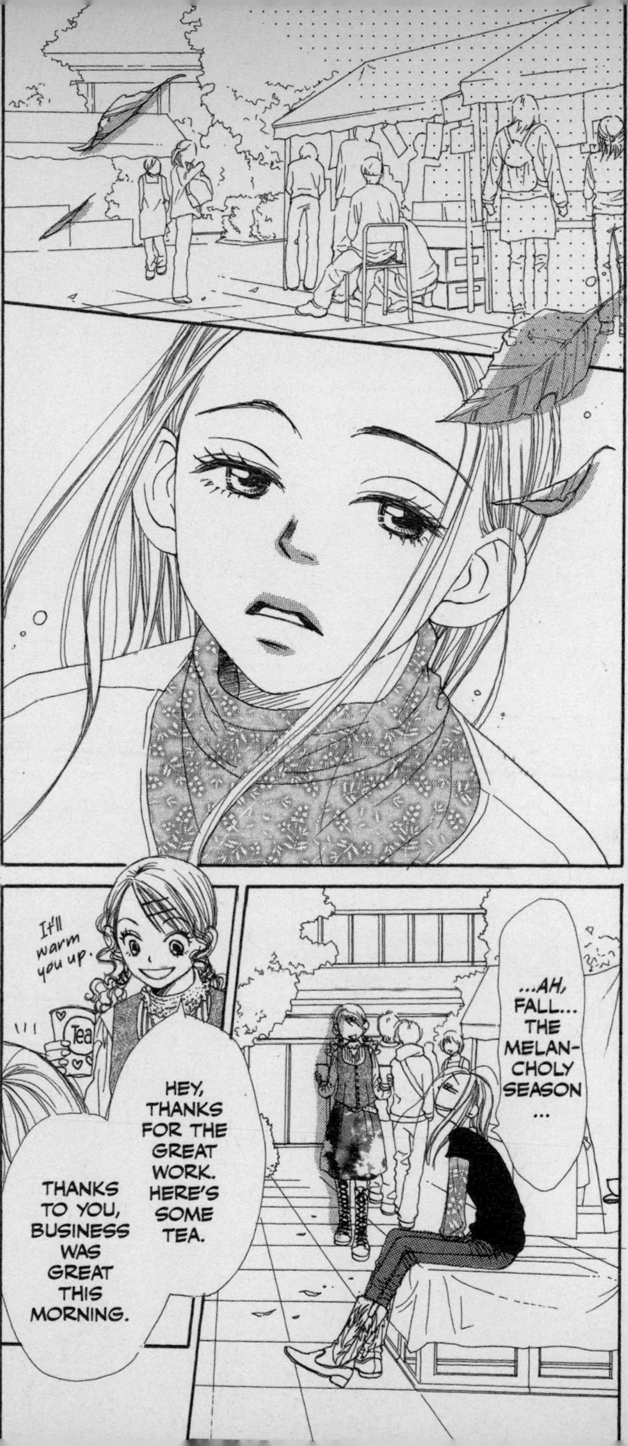
...AH, FALL... THE MELAN-CHOLY SEASON ...
HEY, THANKS FOR THE GREAT WORK. HERE'S SOME TEA.
THANKS TO YOU, BUSINESS WAS GREAT THIS MORNING.
It'll warm you up.
Tea

3

I'll write about something normal for a change.

It turns out there really is a "Tokimeki Beach" in Osaka. I found out after this was published. I knew there was a Pichipichi Beach... So anyway, I went to Tokimeki Beach this summer to watch some fireworks.

It's technically within Osaka Prefecture, but so far south it's practically in Wakayama, so I got a ride.

The fireworks were really beautiful.

Cars...are pretty wonderful.

But I don't have a driver's license.

I can't even get through crowds of people, so I just don't feel I can make my way through crowds of cars. I plan to live my life sitting in somebody else's passenger's seat.

Can anybody give me a ride?

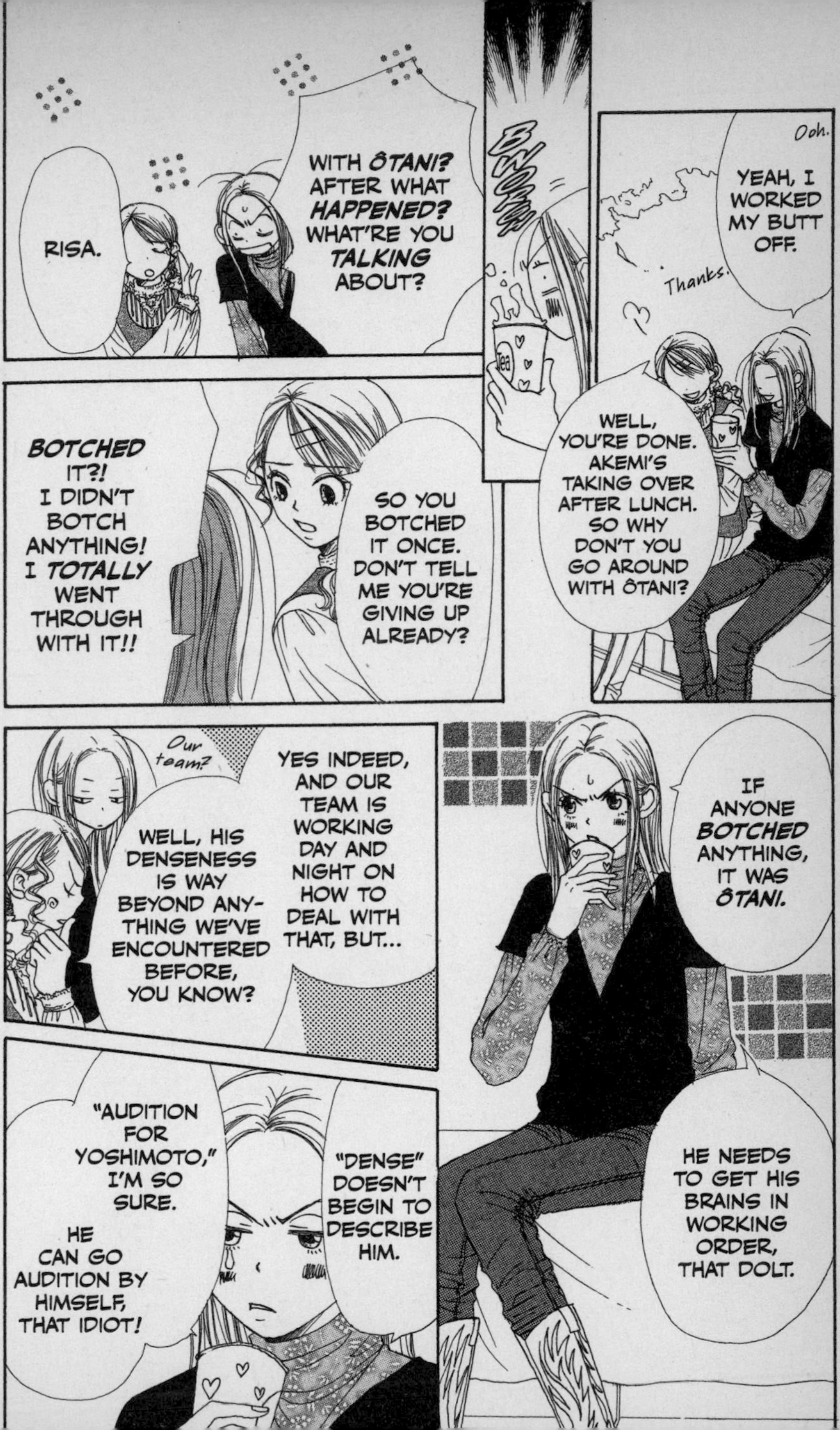
Ooh.
YEAH, I WORKED MY BUTT OFF.
Thanks.
WELL, YOU'RE DONE. AKEMI'S TAKING OVER AFTER LUNCH. SO WHY DON'T YOU GO AROUND WITH ÔTANI?
BWOOM
WITH ÔTANI? AFTER WHAT HAPPENED? WHAT'RE YOU TALKING ABOUT?
RISA.
SO YOU BOTCHED IT ONCE. DON'T TELL ME YOU'RE GIVING UP ALREADY?
BOTCHED IT?! I DIDN'T BOTCH ANYTHING! I TOTALLY WENT THROUGH WITH IT!!
IF ANYONE BOTCHED ANYTHING, IT WAS ÔTANI.
HE NEEDS TO GET HIS BRAINS IN WORKING ORDER, THAT DOLT.
YES INDEED, AND OUR TEAM IS WORKING DAY AND NIGHT ON HOW TO DEAL WITH THAT, BUT...
Our team?
WELL, HIS DENSENESS IS WAY BEYOND ANY-THING WE'VE ENCOUNTERED BEFORE, YOU KNOW?
"DENSE" DOESN'T BEGIN TO DESCRIBE HIM.
"AUDITION FOR YOSHIMOTO," I'M SO SURE.
HE CAN GO AUDITION BY HIMSELF, THAT IDIOT!

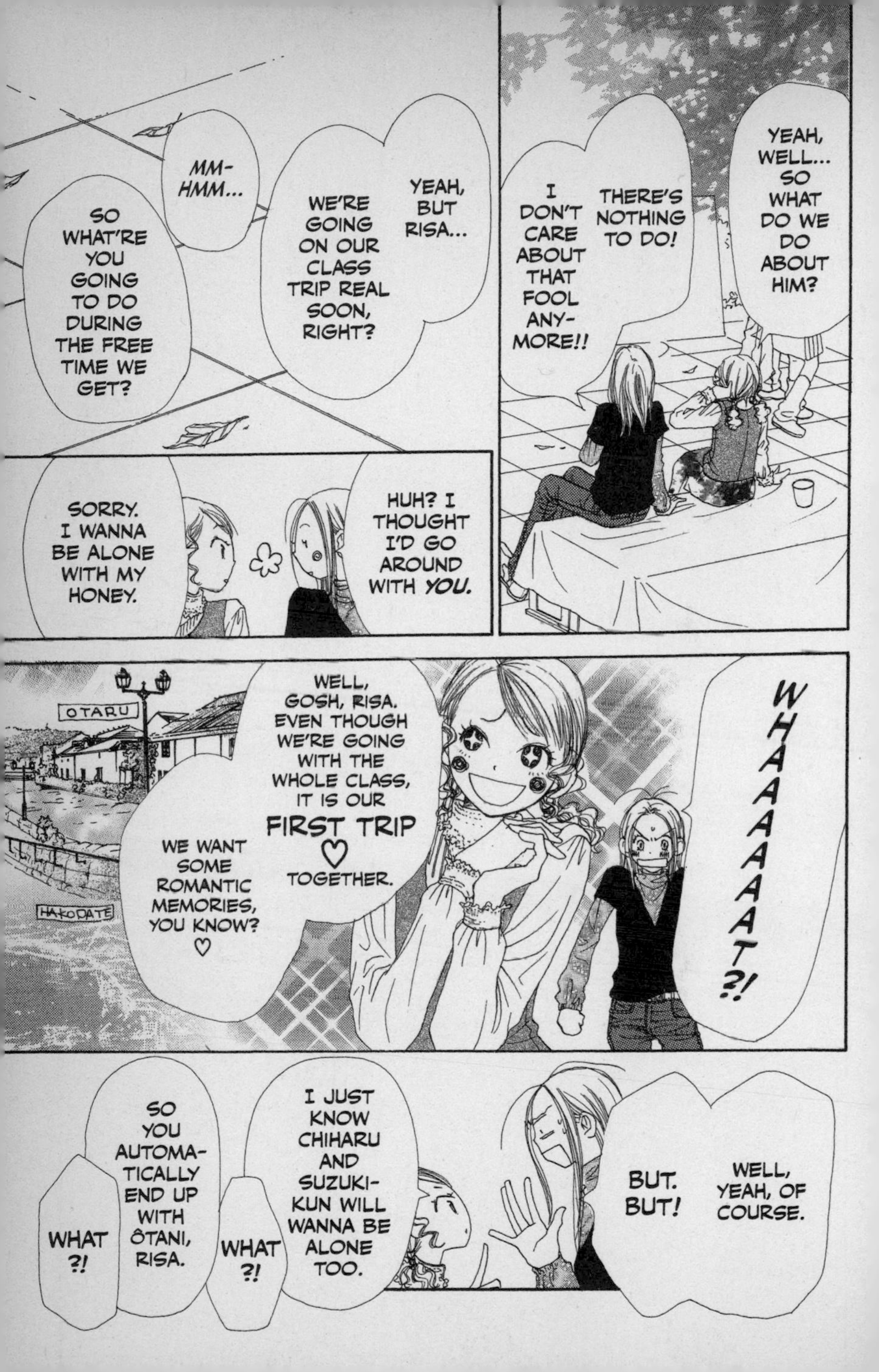
YEAH, WELL... SO WHAT DO WE DO ABOUT HIM?
THERE'S NOTHING TO DO!
I DON'T CARE ABOUT THAT FOOL ANYMORE!!
YEAH, BUT RISA...
WE'RE GOING ON OUR CLASS TRIP REAL SOON, RIGHT?
MM-HMM...
SO WHAT'RE YOU GOING TO DO DURING THE FREE TIME WE GET?
HUH? I THOUGHT I'D GO AROUND WITH YOU.
SORRY. I WANNA BE ALONE WITH MY HONEY.
WHAAAAAAAT?!
WELL, GOSH, RISA. EVEN THOUGH WE'RE GOING WITH THE WHOLE CLASS, IT IS OUR FIRST TRIP ♡ TOGETHER.
WE WANT SOME ROMANTIC MEMORIES, YOU KNOW? ♡
OTARU
HAKODATE
WELL, YEAH, OF COURSE.
BUT. BUT!
I JUST KNOW CHIHARU AND SUZUKI-KUN WILL WANNA BE ALONE TOO.
WHAT?!
SO YOU AUTOMATICALLY END UP WITH ŌTANI, RISA.
WHAT?!

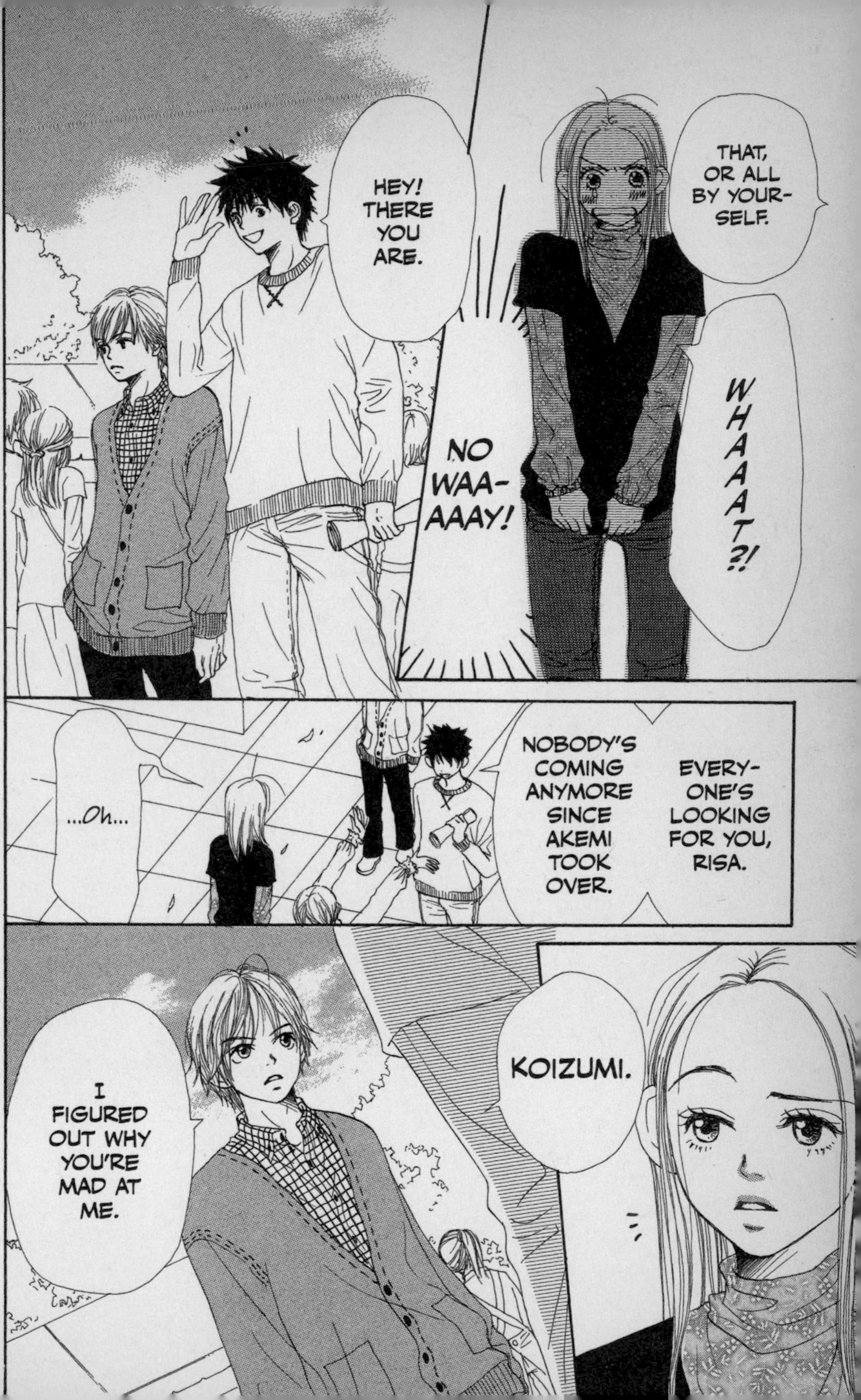
THAT, OR ALL BY YOUR-SELF.
WHAAAAT?!
NO WAA-AAAY!
HEY! THERE YOU ARE.
EVERY-ONE'S LOOKING FOR YOU, RISA.
NOBODY'S COMING ANYMORE SINCE AKEMI TOOK OVER.
...Oh...
KOIZUMI.
I FIGURED OUT WHY YOU'RE MAD AT ME.

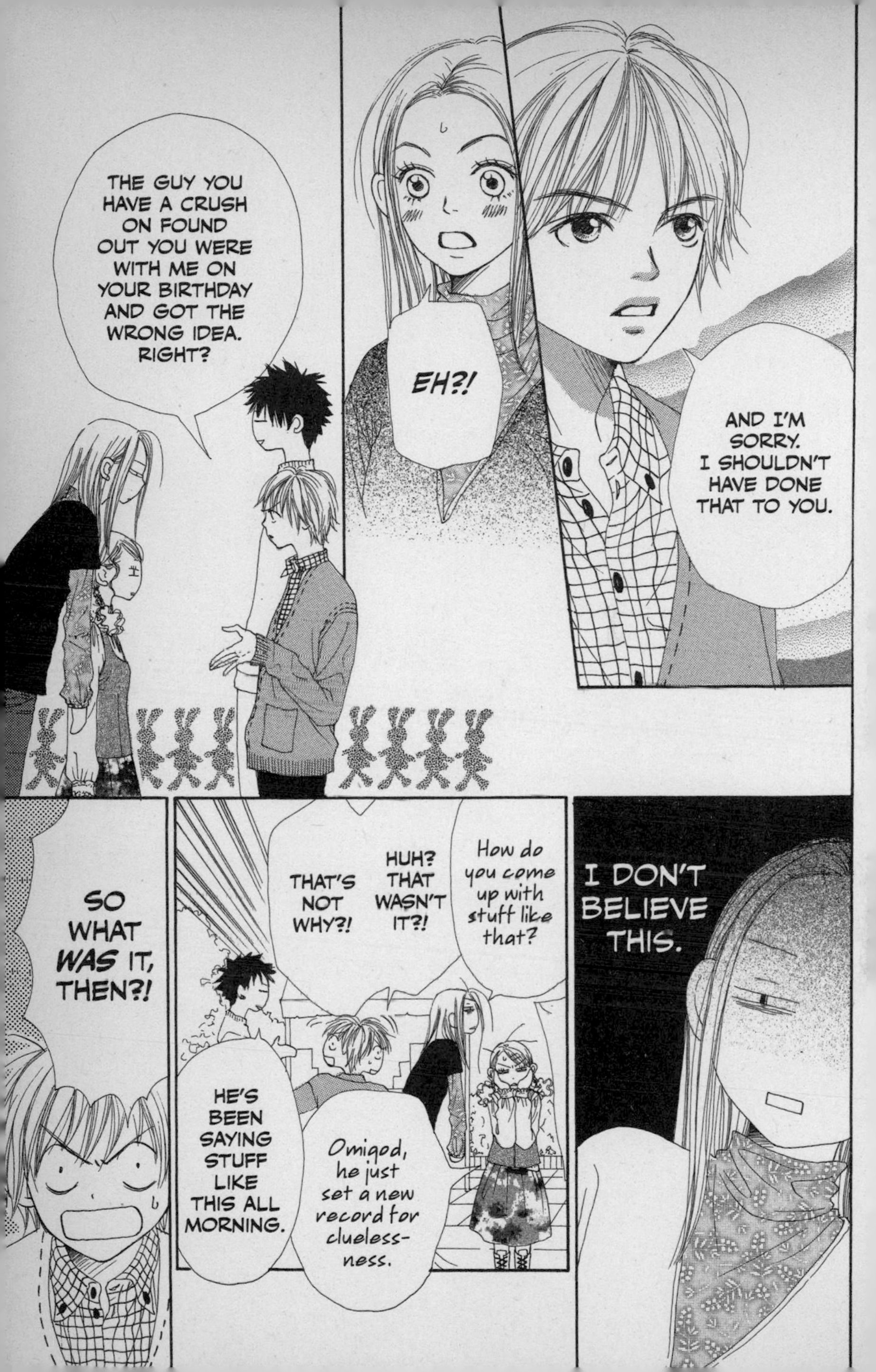
AND I'M SORRY. I SHOULDN'T HAVE DONE THAT TO YOU.
EH?!
THE GUY YOU HAVE A CRUSH ON FOUND OUT YOU WERE WITH ME ON YOUR BIRTHDAY AND GOT THE WRONG IDEA. RIGHT?
I DON'T BELIEVE THIS.
How do you come up with stuff like that?
HUH? THAT WASN'T IT?!
THAT'S NOT WHY?!
Omigod, he just set a new record for clueless-ness.
HE'S BEEN SAYING STUFF LIKE THIS ALL MORNING.
SO WHAT *WAS* IT, THEN?!

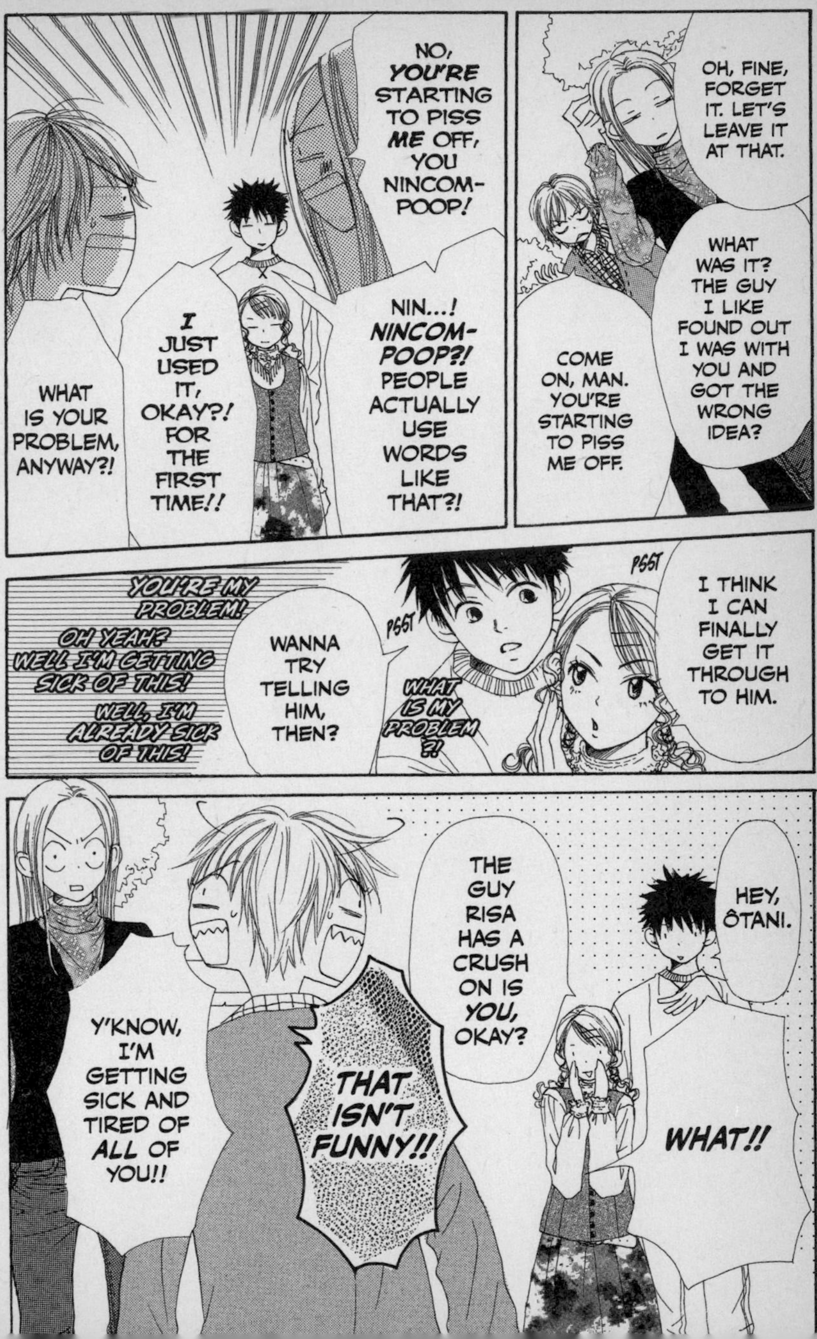
OH, FINE, FORGET IT. LET'S LEAVE IT AT THAT.
WHAT WAS IT? THE GUY I LIKE FOUND OUT I WAS WITH YOU AND GOT THE WRONG IDEA?
COME ON, MAN. YOU'RE STARTING TO PISS ME OFF.
NO, *YOU'RE* STARTING TO PISS *ME* OFF, YOU NINCOMPOOP!
NIN...! *NINCOMPOOP?!* PEOPLE ACTUALLY USE WORDS LIKE THAT?!
I JUST USED IT, OKAY?! FOR THE FIRST TIME!!
WHAT IS YOUR PROBLEM, ANYWAY?!
PSST
I THINK I CAN FINALLY GET IT THROUGH TO HIM.
PSST
WHAT IS MY PROBLEM?!
WANNA TRY TELLING HIM, THEN?
YOU'RE MY PROBLEM!
OH YEAH? WELL I'M GETTING SICK OF THIS!
WELL, I'M ALREADY SICK OF THIS!
HEY, ŌTANI.
THE GUY RISA HAS A CRUSH ON IS *YOU*, OKAY?
WHAT!!
THAT ISN'T FUNNY!!
Y'KNOW, I'M GETTING SICK AND TIRED OF *ALL* OF YOU!!

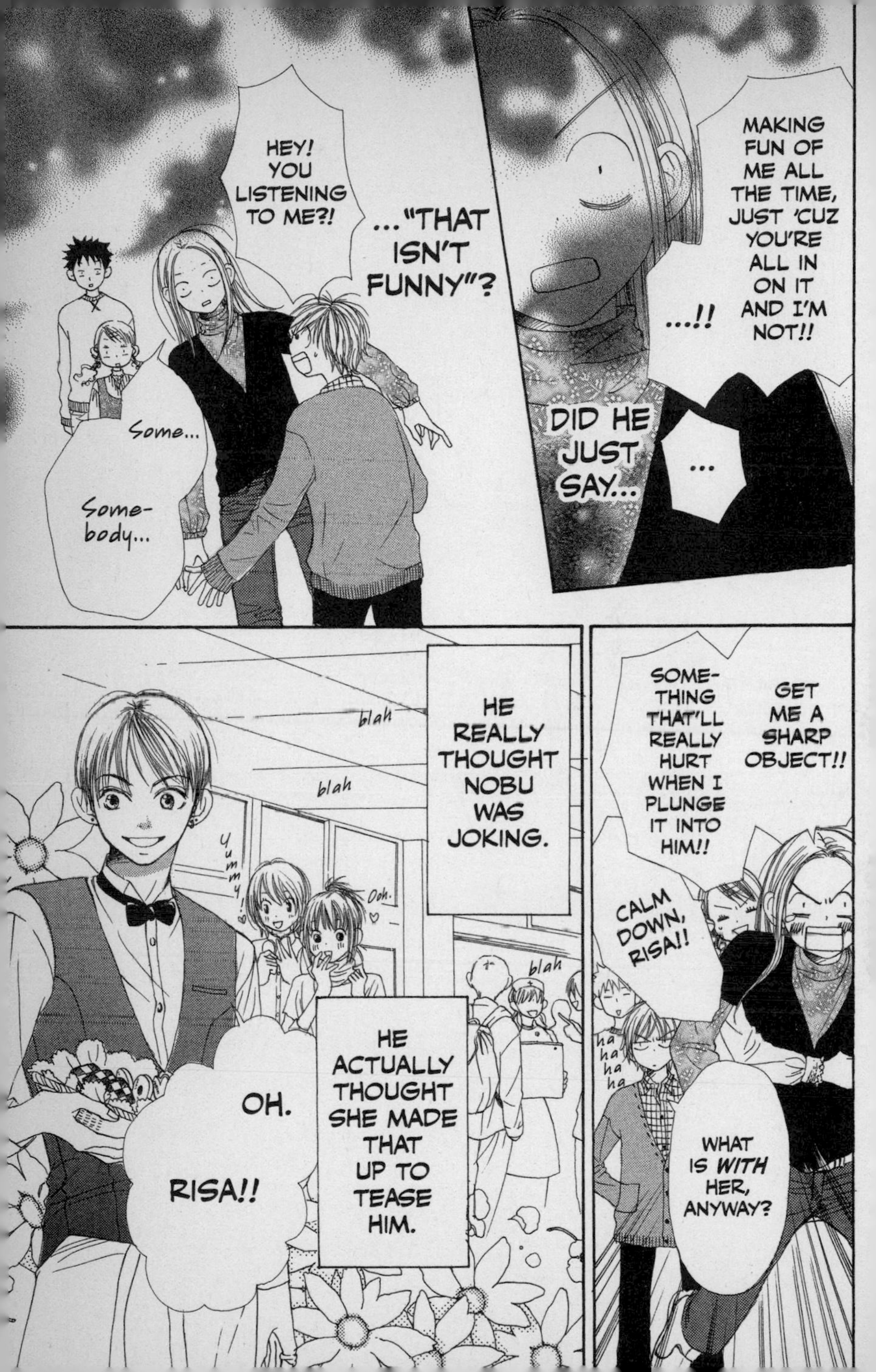
MAKING FUN OF ME ALL THE TIME, JUST 'CUZ YOU'RE ALL IN ON IT AND I'M NOT!!
...!!
DID HE JUST SAY...
...
..."THAT ISN'T FUNNY"?
HEY! YOU LISTENING TO ME?!
Some...
Some-body...
GET ME A SHARP OBJECT!!
SOME-THING THAT'LL REALLY HURT WHEN I PLUNGE IT INTO HIM!!
CALM DOWN, RISA!!
ha ha ha ha
WHAT IS *WITH* HER, ANYWAY?
HE REALLY THOUGHT NOBU WAS JOKING.
blah
blah
Yummy!
Ooh.
blah
HE ACTUALLY THOUGHT SHE MADE THAT UP TO TEASE HIM.
OH.
RISA!!

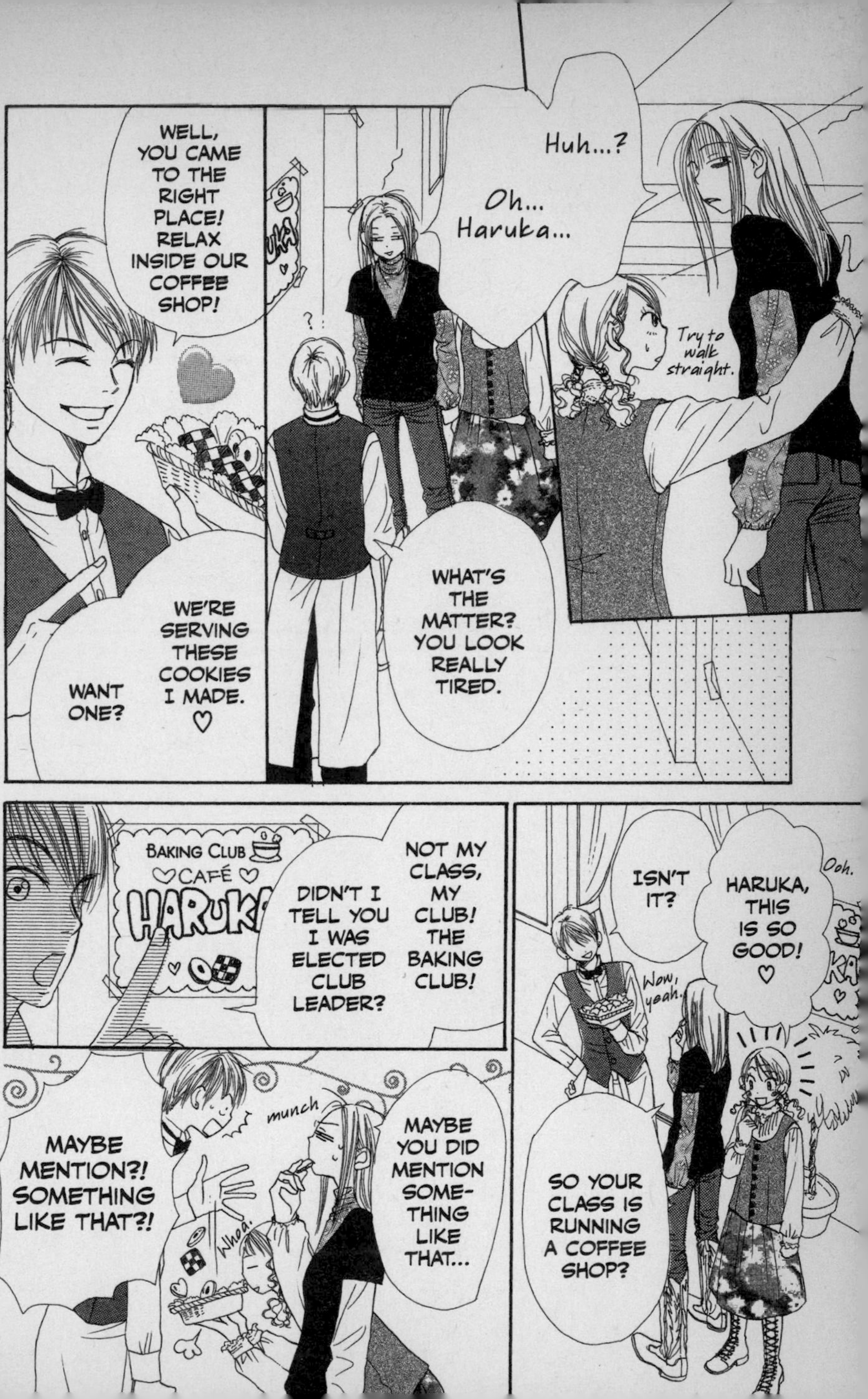
Huh...?
Oh... Haruka...
Try to walk straight.
WHAT'S THE MATTER? YOU LOOK REALLY TIRED.
WELL, YOU CAME TO THE RIGHT PLACE! RELAX INSIDE OUR COFFEE SHOP!
WE'RE SERVING THESE COOKIES I MADE. ♡
WANT ONE?
Ooh.
HARUKA, THIS IS SO GOOD! ♡
Wow, yeah.
ISN'T IT?
SO YOUR CLASS IS RUNNING A COFFEE SHOP?
NOT MY CLASS, MY CLUB! THE BAKING CLUB!
DIDN'T I TELL YOU I WAS ELECTED CLUB LEADER?
BAKING CLUB
♡CAFÉ♡
HARUKA
MAYBE YOU DID MENTION SOMETHING LIKE THAT...
munch
MAYBE MENTION?! SOMETHING LIKE THAT?!
Whoa.

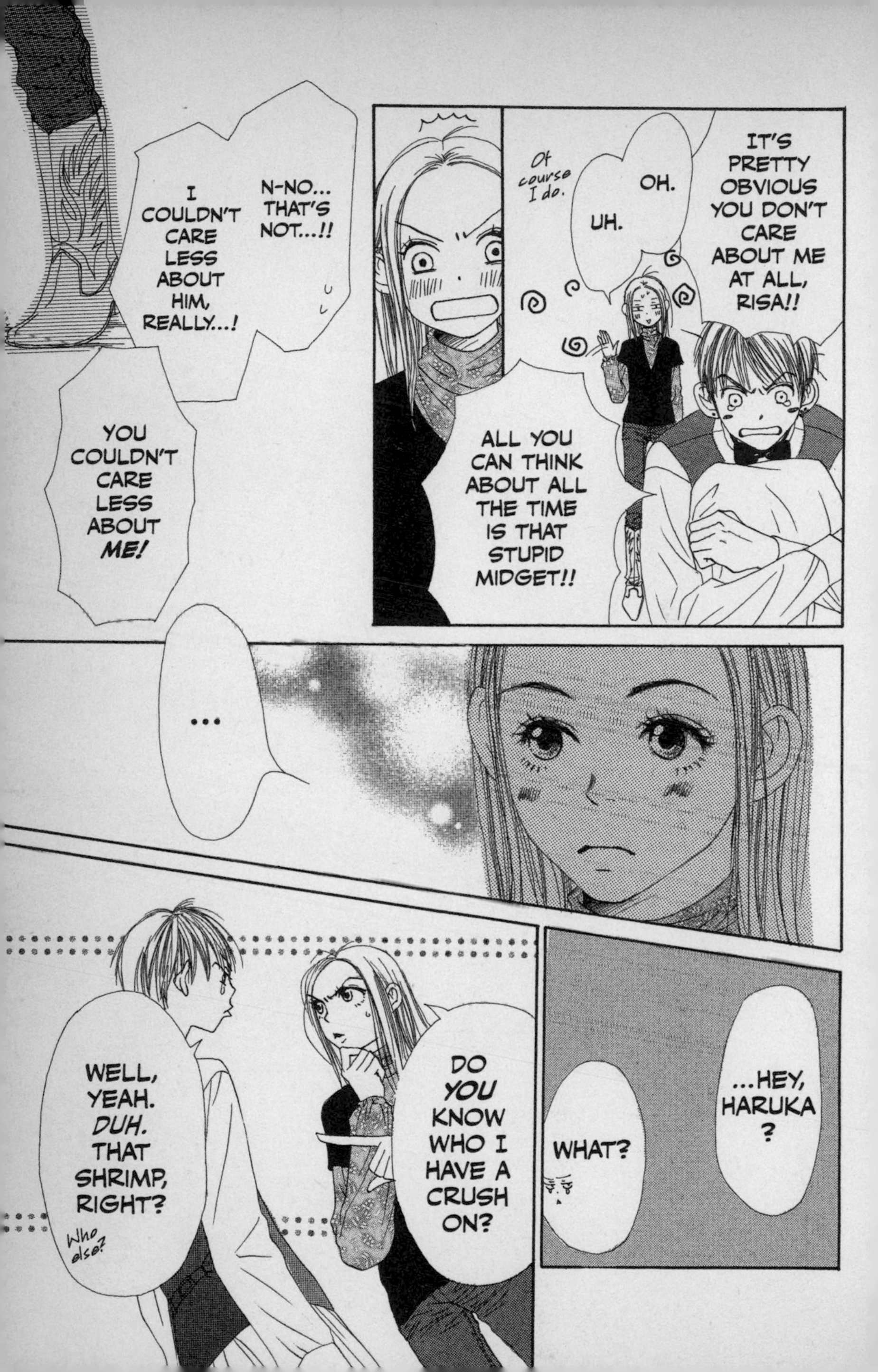
IT'S PRETTY OBVIOUS YOU DON'T CARE ABOUT ME AT ALL, RISA!!
UH.
OH.
Of course I do.
ALL YOU CAN THINK ABOUT ALL THE TIME IS THAT STUPID MIDGET!!
N-NO... THAT'S NOT...!!
I COULDN'T CARE LESS ABOUT HIM, REALLY...!
YOU COULDN'T CARE LESS ABOUT *ME!*
...
...HEY, HARUKA?
WHAT?
DO *YOU* KNOW WHO I HAVE A CRUSH ON?
WELL, YEAH. *DUH.* THAT SHRIMP, RIGHT?
Who else?

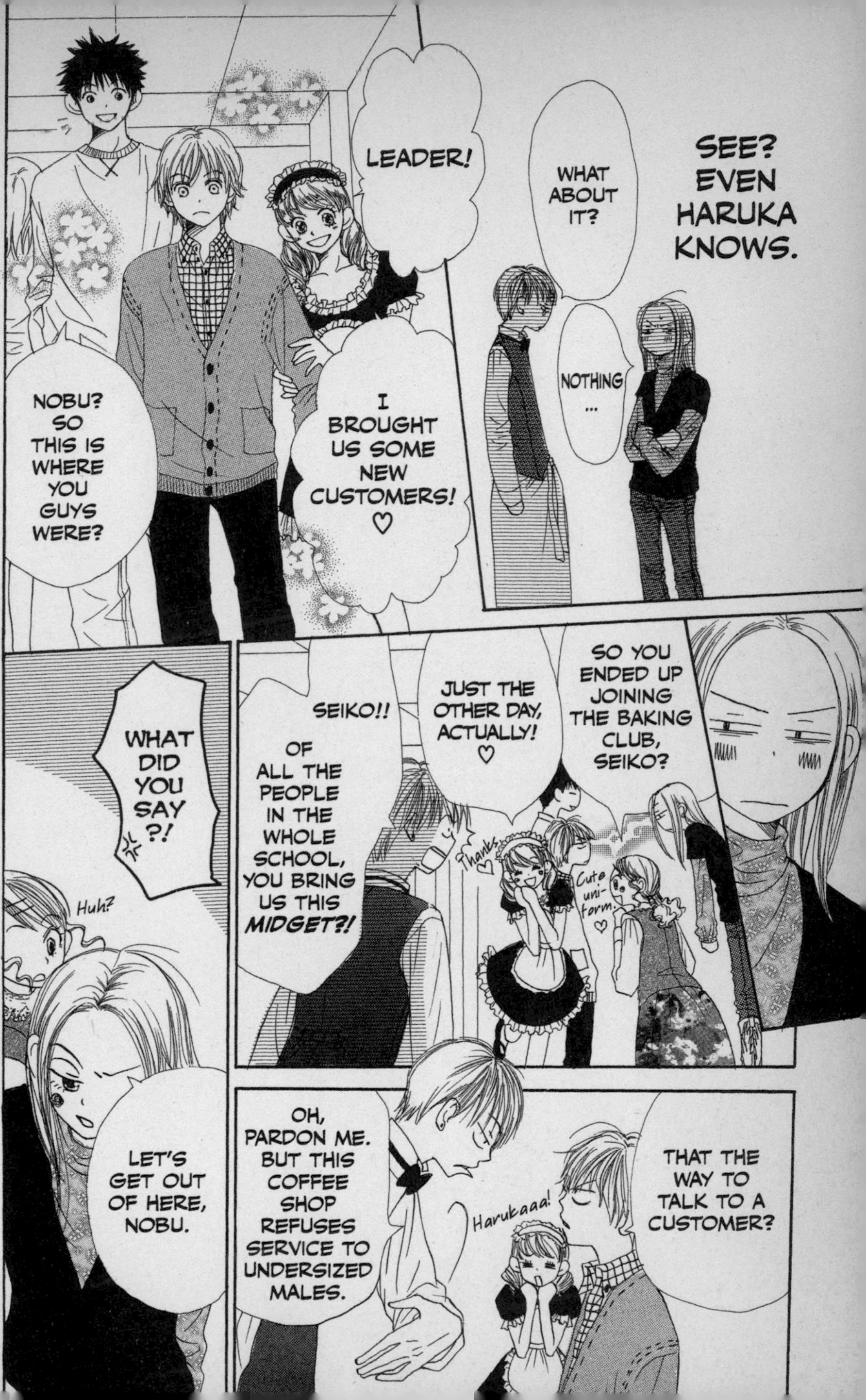
SEE? EVEN HARUKA KNOWS.
WHAT ABOUT IT?
NOTHING ...
LEADER!
I BROUGHT US SOME NEW CUSTOMERS! ♡
NOBU? SO THIS IS WHERE YOU GUYS WERE?
SO YOU ENDED UP JOINING THE BAKING CLUB, SEIKO?
JUST THE OTHER DAY, ACTUALLY! ♡
Thanks ♡
Cute uniform. ♡
SEIKO!!
OF ALL THE PEOPLE IN THE WHOLE SCHOOL, YOU BRING US THIS *MIDGET?!*
THAT THE WAY TO TALK TO A CUSTOMER?
Harukaaa!
OH, PARDON ME. BUT THIS COFFEE SHOP REFUSES SERVICE TO UNDERSIZED MALES.
WHAT DID YOU SAY ?!
Huh?
LET'S GET OUT OF HERE, NOBU.

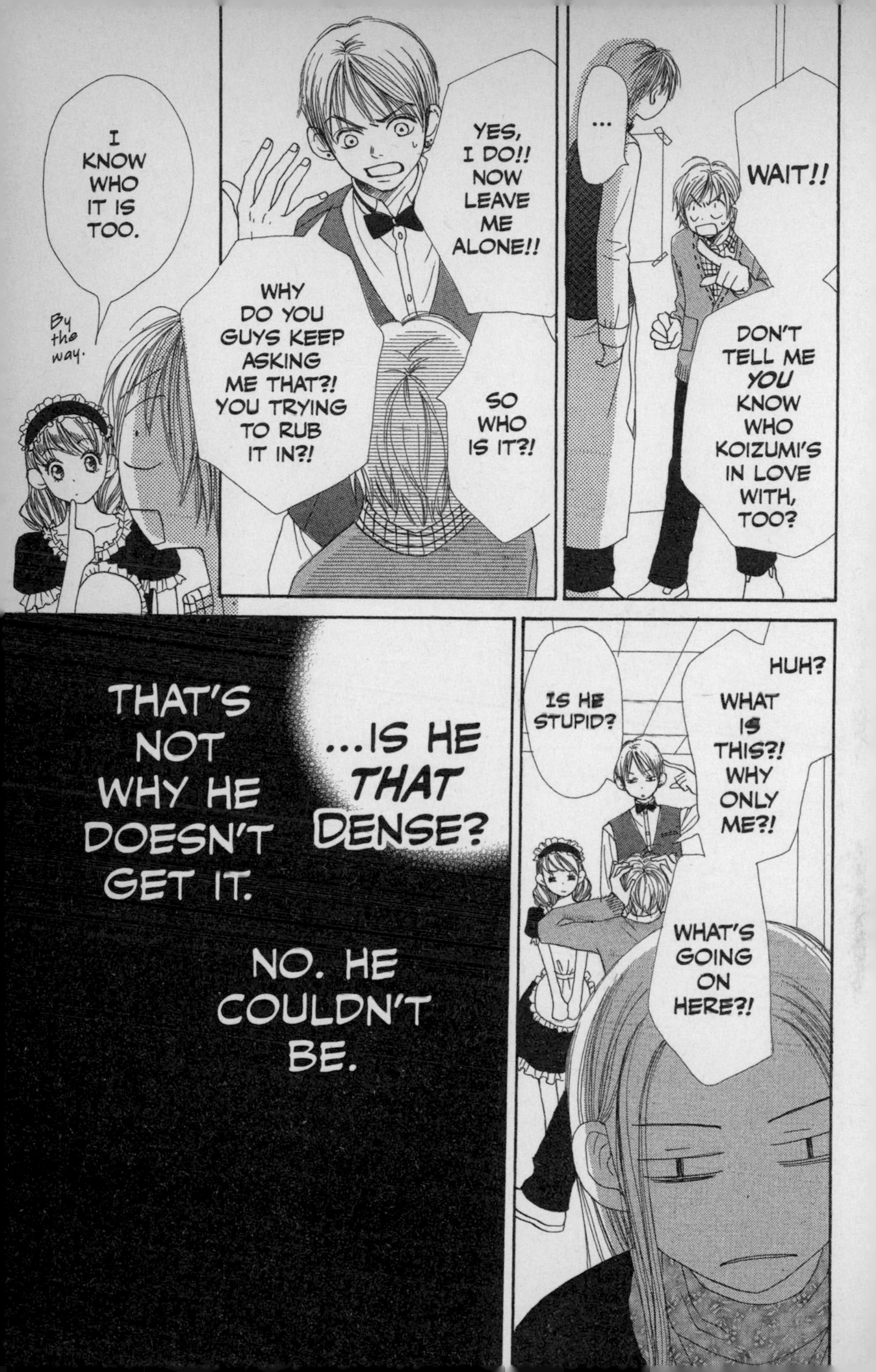
WAIT!!
...
DON'T TELL ME *YOU* KNOW WHO KOIZUMI'S IN LOVE WITH, TOO?
YES, I DO!! NOW LEAVE ME ALONE!!
SO WHO IS IT?!
WHY DO YOU GUYS KEEP ASKING ME THAT?! YOU TRYING TO RUB IT IN?!
I KNOW WHO IT IS TOO.
By the way.
HUH?
WHAT IS THIS?! WHY ONLY ME?!
IS HE STUPID?
WHAT'S GOING ON HERE?!
...IS HE *THAT* DENSE?
THAT'S NOT WHY HE DOESN'T GET IT.
NO. HE COULDN'T BE.

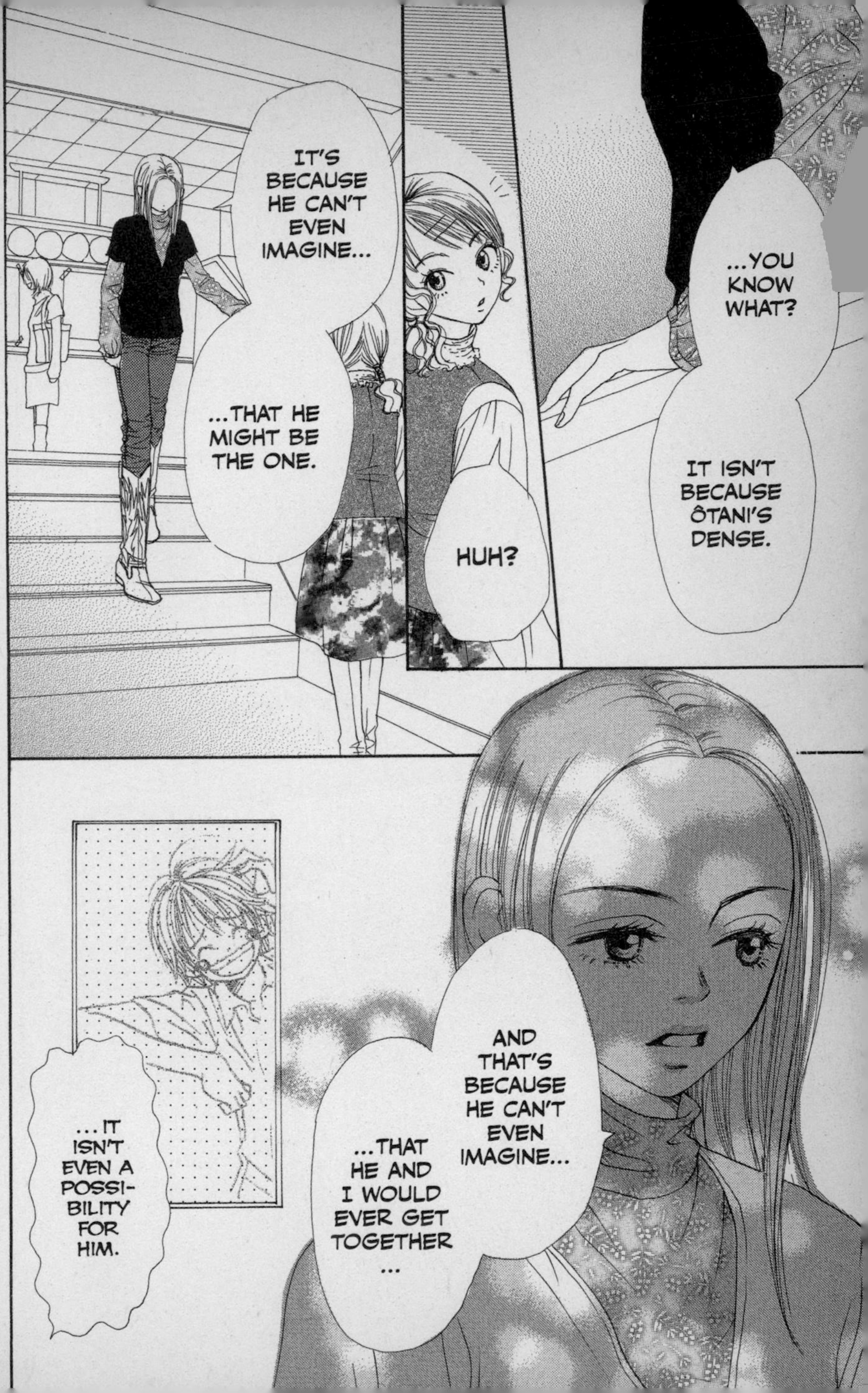
...YOU KNOW WHAT?
IT ISN'T BECAUSE ÔTANI'S DENSE.
HUH?
IT'S BECAUSE HE CAN'T EVEN IMAGINE...
...THAT HE MIGHT BE THE ONE.
AND THAT'S BECAUSE HE CAN'T EVEN IMAGINE...
...THAT HE AND I WOULD EVER GET TOGETHER...
...IT ISN'T EVEN A POSSI-BILITY FOR HIM.

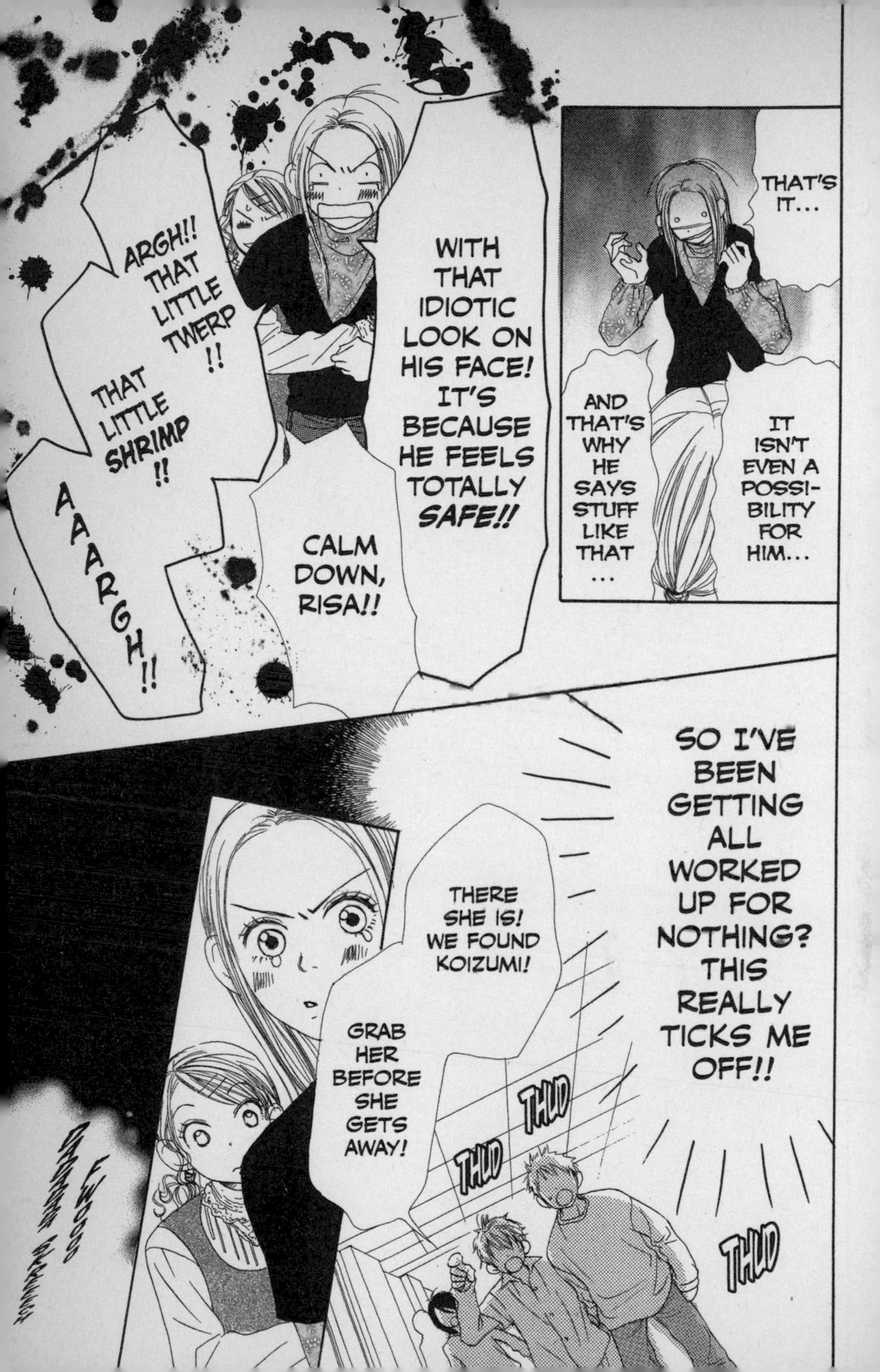
THAT'S IT...
IT ISN'T EVEN A POSSI-BILITY FOR HIM...
AND THAT'S WHY HE SAYS STUFF LIKE THAT ...
WITH THAT IDIOTIC LOOK ON HIS FACE! IT'S BECAUSE HE FEELS TOTALLY SAFE!!
ARGH!! THAT LITTLE TWERP !!
THAT LITTLE SHRIMP !!
AAAARGH!!
CALM DOWN, RISA!!
SO I'VE BEEN GETTING ALL WORKED UP FOR NOTHING? THIS REALLY TICKS ME OFF!!
THERE SHE IS! WE FOUND KOIZUMI!
GRAB HER BEFORE SHE GETS AWAY!
THUD
THUD
THUD

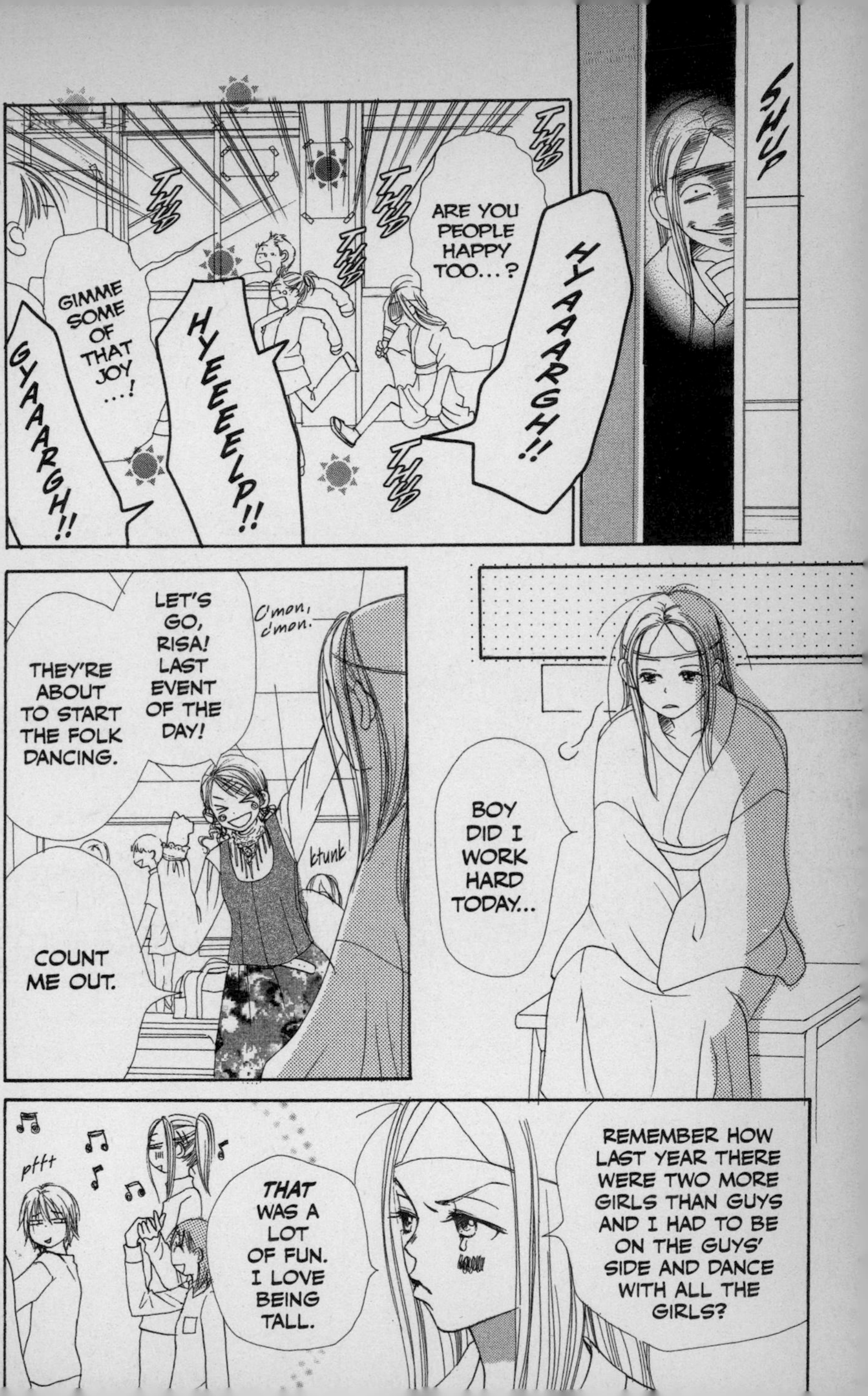
SHUP
HYAAARGH!!
ARE YOU PEOPLE HAPPY TOO...?
HYEEEELP!!
GIMME SOME OF THAT JOY...!
GYAAARGH!!
BOY DID I WORK HARD TODAY...
LET'S GO, RISA! LAST EVENT OF THE DAY!
C'mon, c'mon.
THEY'RE ABOUT TO START THE FOLK DANCING.
ktunk
COUNT ME OUT.
REMEMBER HOW LAST YEAR THERE WERE TWO MORE GIRLS THAN GUYS AND I HAD TO BE ON THE GUYS' SIDE AND DANCE WITH ALL THE GIRLS?
THAT WAS A LOT OF FUN. I LOVE BEING TALL.
pfft

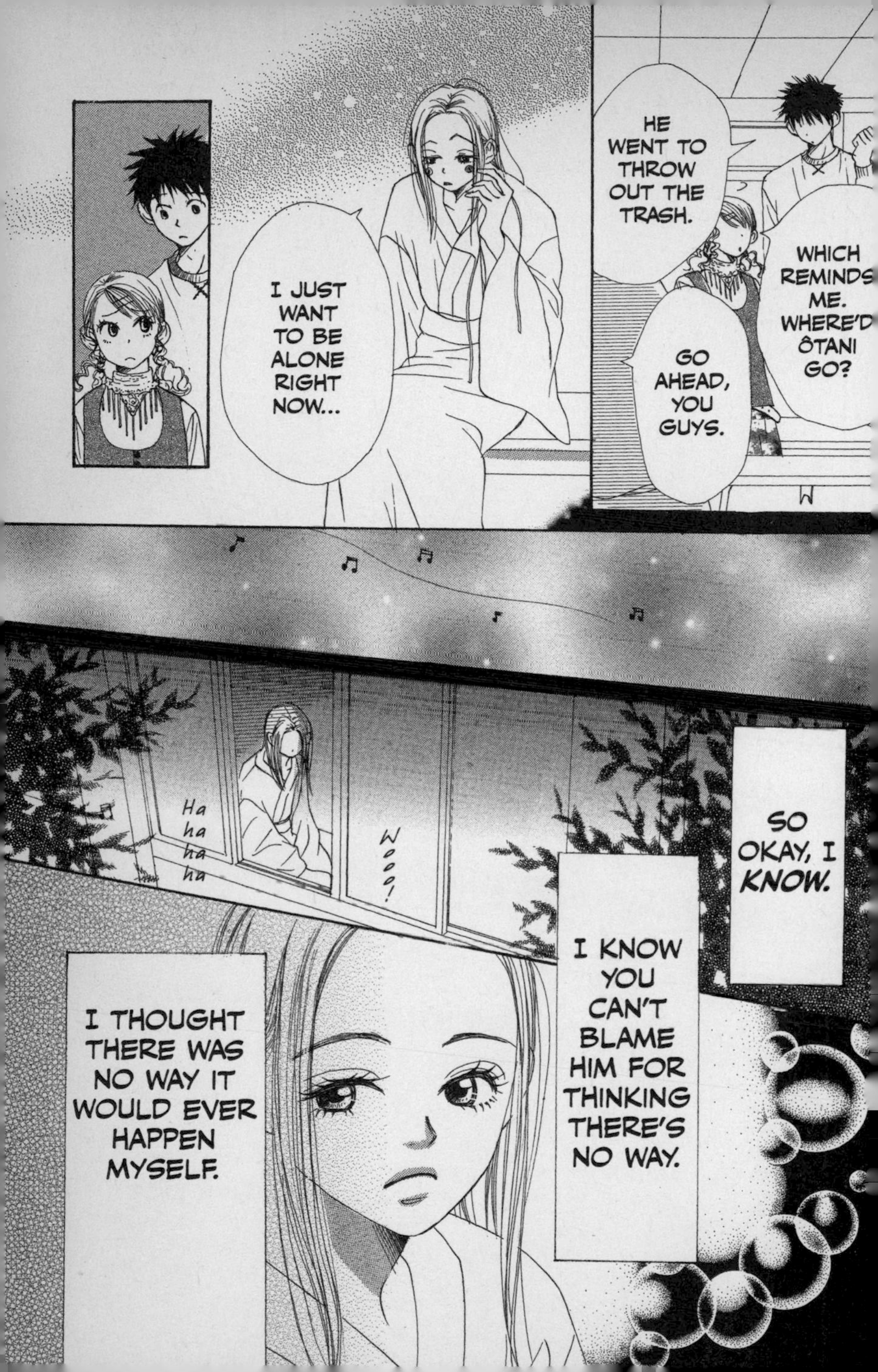
WHICH REMINDS ME. WHERE'D ŌTANI GO?
HE WENT TO THROW OUT THE TRASH.
GO AHEAD, YOU GUYS.
I JUST WANT TO BE ALONE RIGHT NOW...
Wooo!
Ha ha ha ha
SO OKAY, I *KNOW.*
I KNOW YOU CAN'T BLAME HIM FOR THINKING THERE'S NO WAY.
I THOUGHT THERE WAS NO WAY IT WOULD EVER HAPPEN MYSELF.

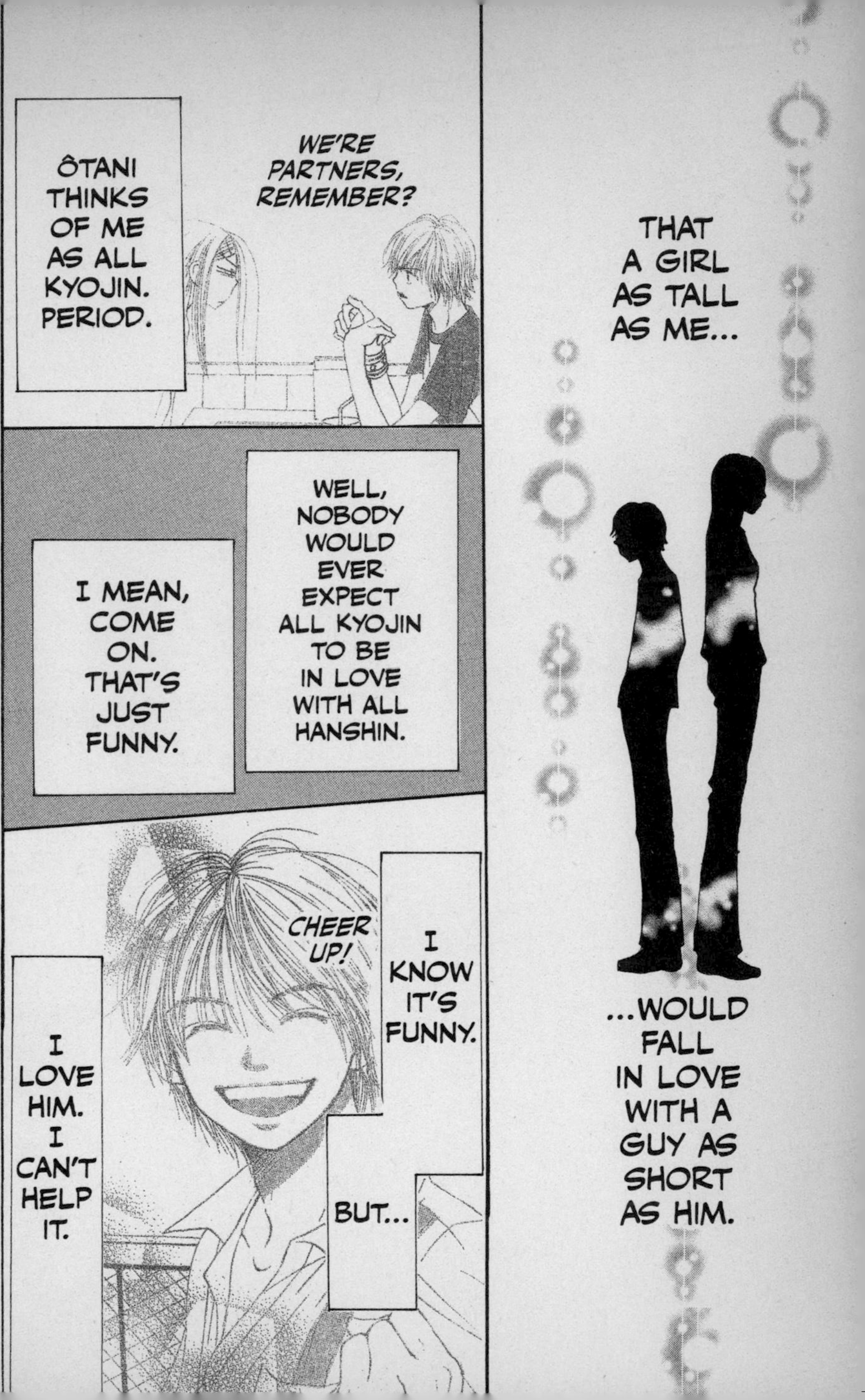
THAT A GIRL AS TALL AS ME...
...WOULD FALL IN LOVE WITH A GUY AS SHORT AS HIM.
WE'RE PARTNERS, REMEMBER?
ÔTANI THINKS OF ME AS ALL KYOJIN. PERIOD.
WELL, NOBODY WOULD EVER EXPECT ALL KYOJIN TO BE IN LOVE WITH ALL HANSHIN.
I MEAN, COME ON. THAT'S JUST FUNNY.
I KNOW IT'S FUNNY.
CHEER UP!
BUT...
I LOVE HIM. I CAN'T HELP IT.

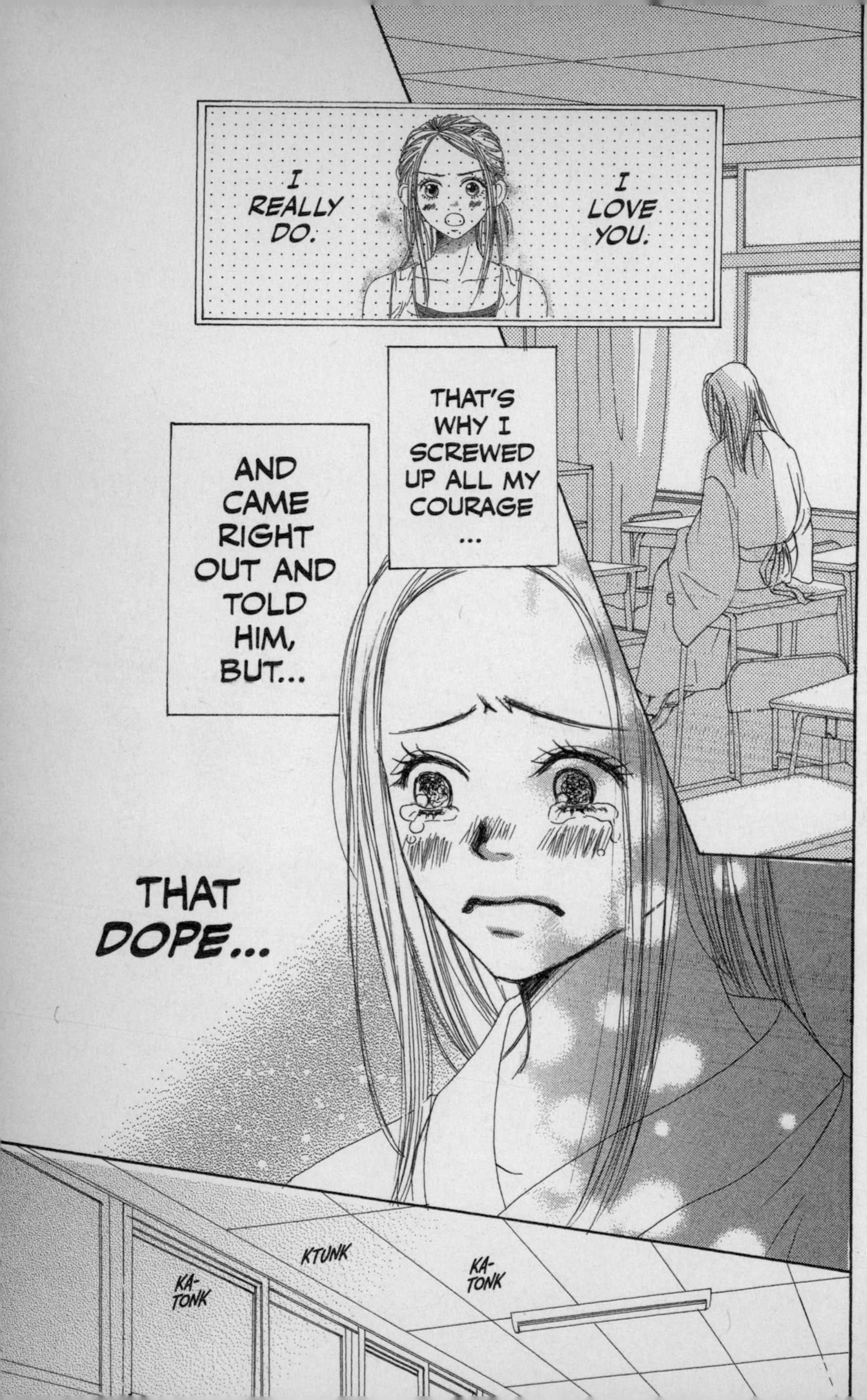
I LOVE YOU.
I REALLY DO.
THAT'S WHY I SCREWED UP ALL MY COURAGE ...
AND CAME RIGHT OUT AND TOLD HIM, BUT...
THAT DOPE...
KA-TONK
KTUNK
KA-TONK

KTUNK

GYAA-
AAARGH
!!

...Oh.
It's
you...

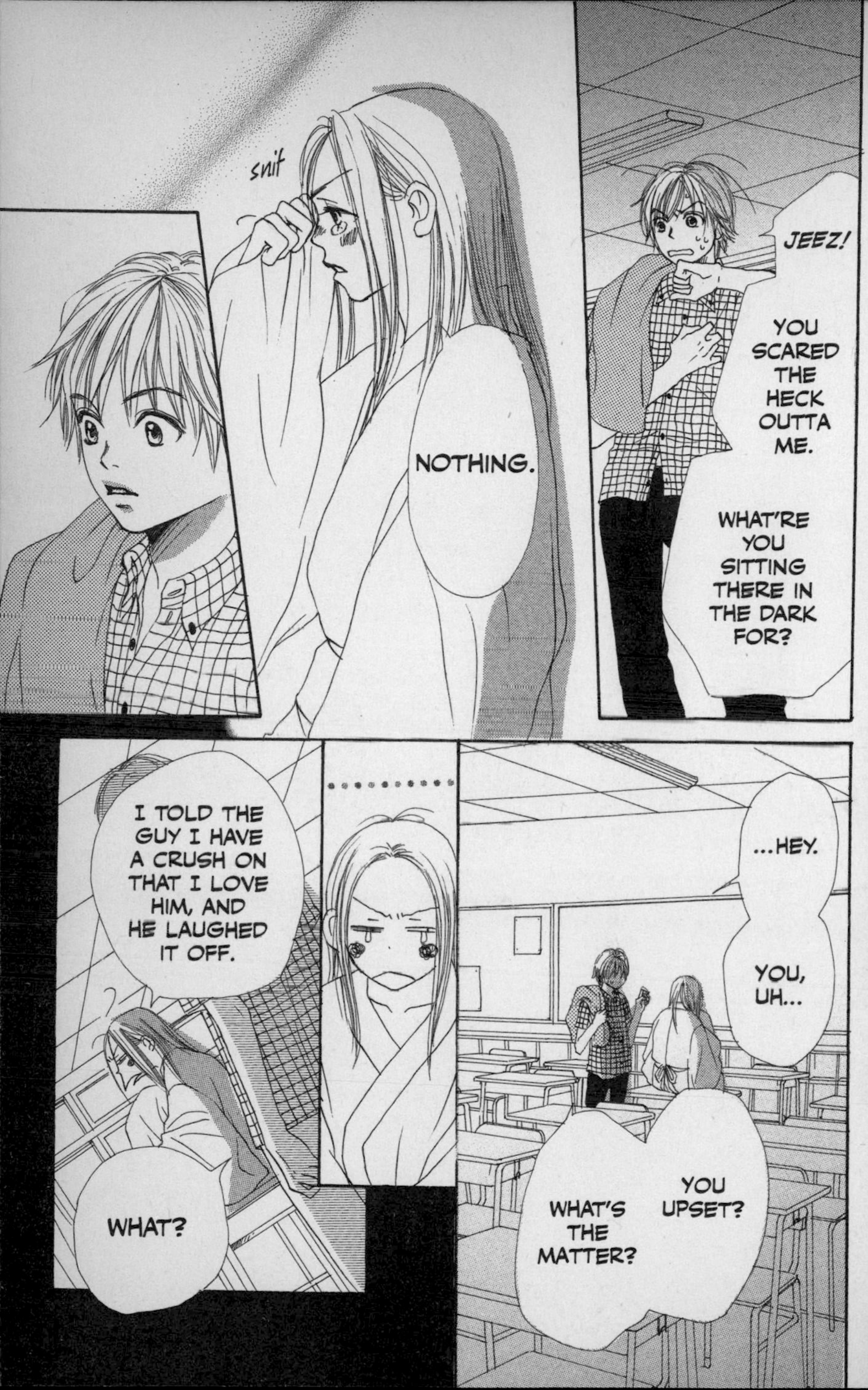
JEEZ!
YOU SCARED THE HECK OUTTA ME.
WHAT'RE YOU SITTING THERE IN THE DARK FOR?
snif
NOTHING.
...HEY.
YOU, UH...
YOU UPSET?
WHAT'S THE MATTER?
I TOLD THE GUY I HAVE A CRUSH ON THAT I LOVE HIM, AND HE LAUGHED IT OFF.
WHAT?

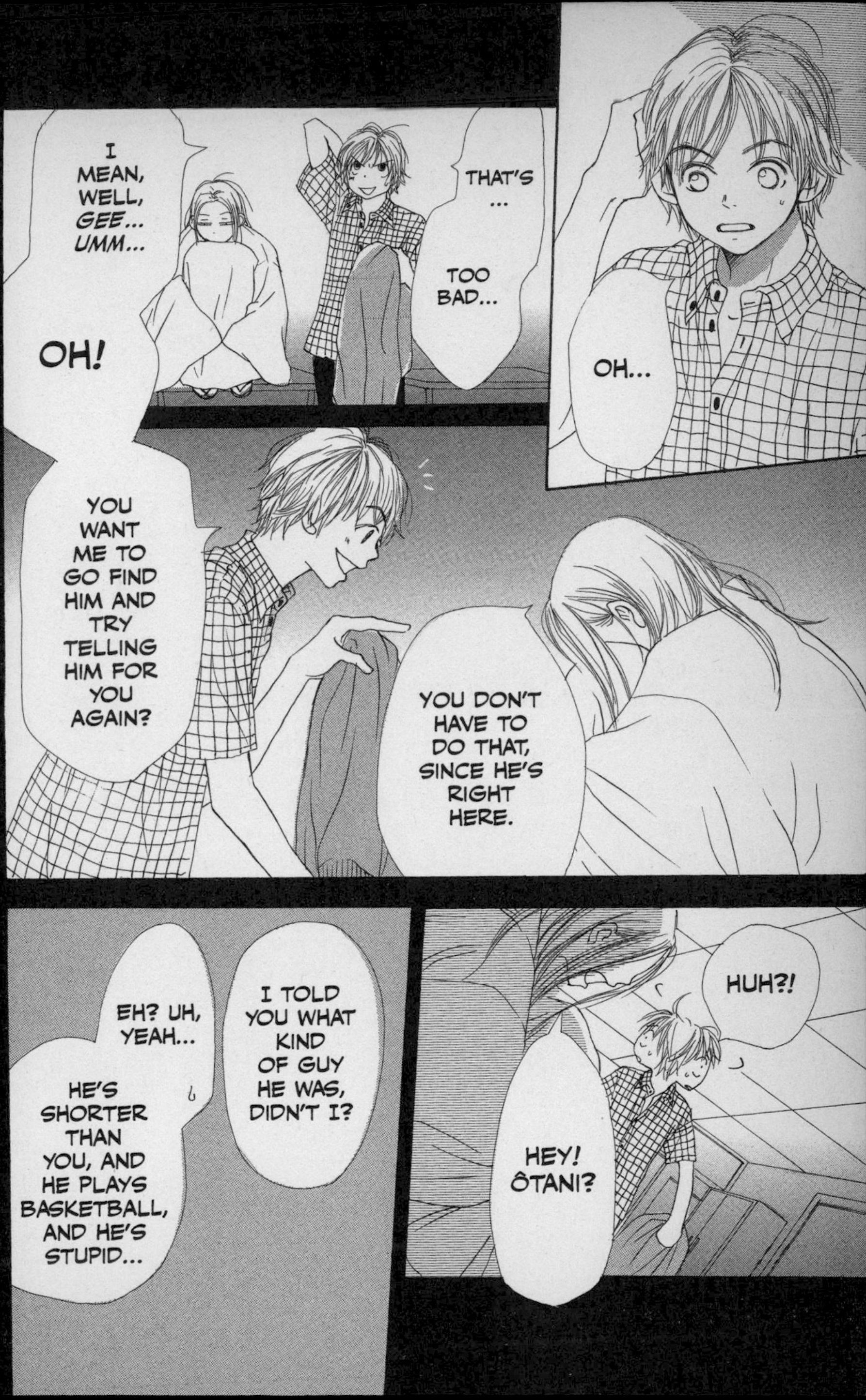
OH...
THAT'S ...
TOO BAD...
I MEAN, WELL, GEE... UMM...
OH!
YOU WANT ME TO GO FIND HIM AND TRY TELLING HIM FOR YOU AGAIN?
YOU DON'T HAVE TO DO THAT, SINCE HE'S RIGHT HERE.
HUH?!
HEY! ÔTANI?
I TOLD YOU WHAT KIND OF GUY HE WAS, DIDN'T I?
EH? UH, YEAH...
HE'S SHORTER THAN YOU, AND HE PLAYS BASKETBALL, AND HE'S STUPID...

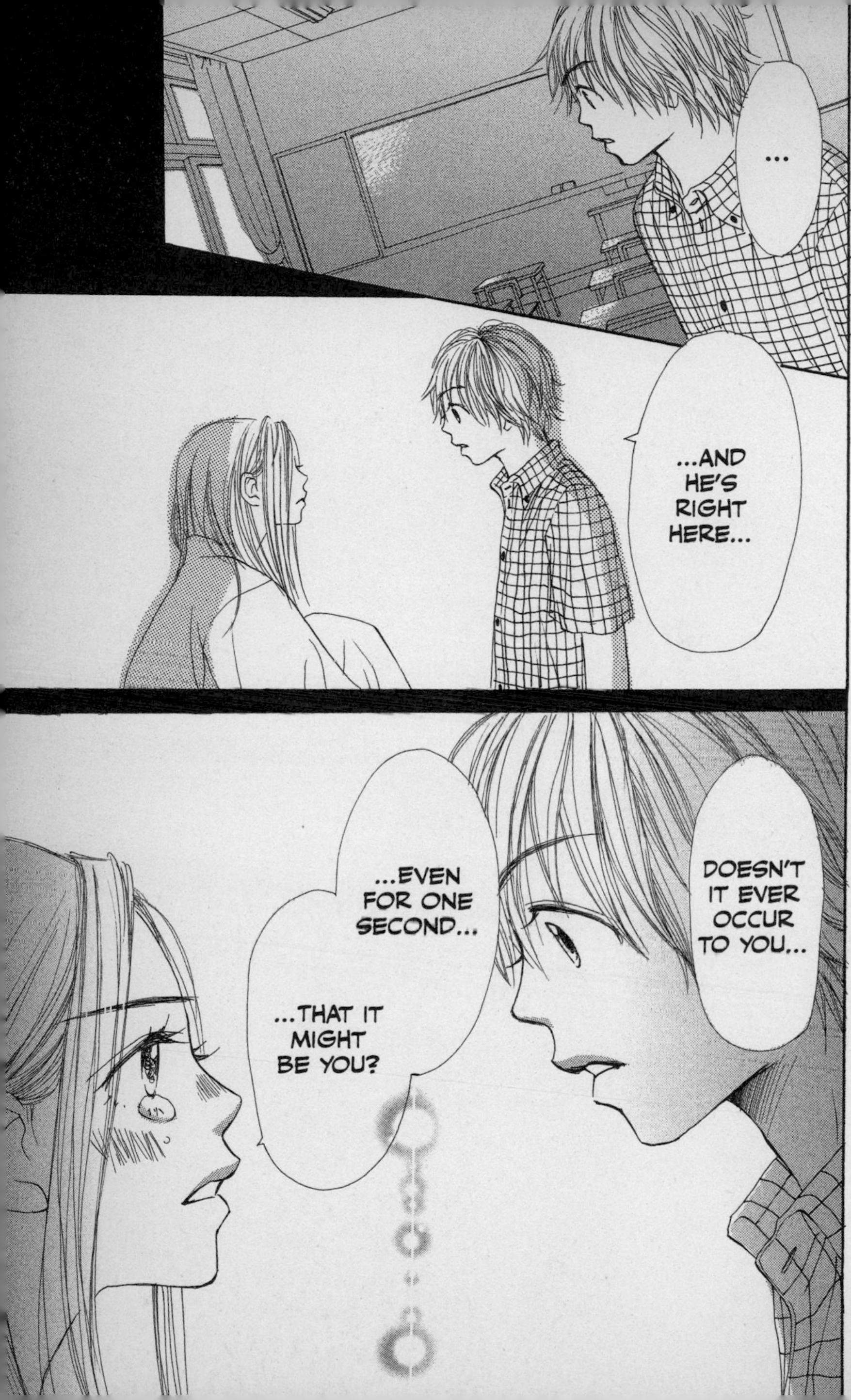
...
...AND HE'S RIGHT HERE...
DOESN'T IT EVER OCCUR TO YOU...
...EVEN FOR ONE SECOND...
...THAT IT MIGHT BE YOU?

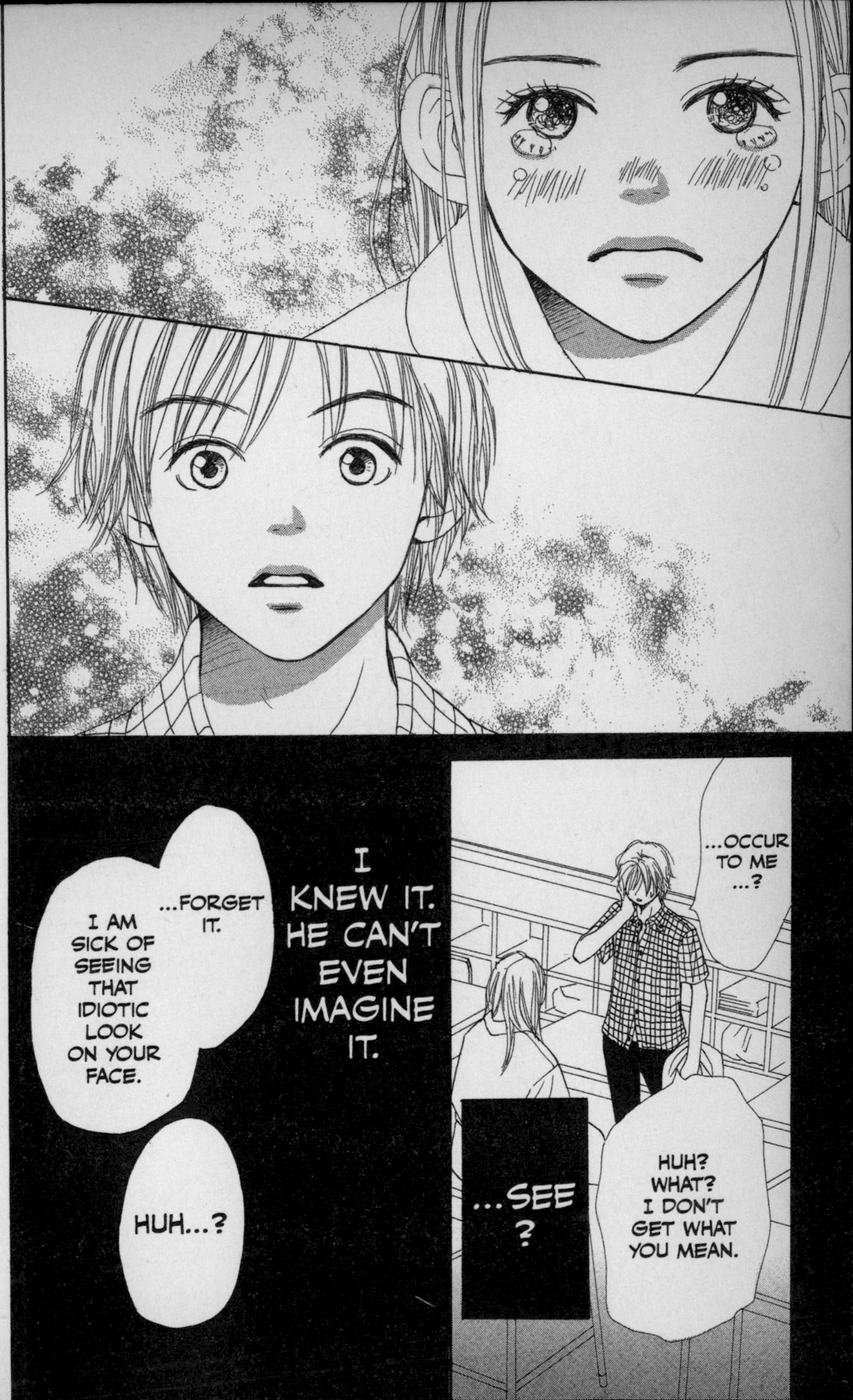
...OCCUR TO ME ...?
HUH? WHAT? I DON'T GET WHAT YOU MEAN.
...SEE ?
I KNEW IT. HE CAN'T EVEN IMAGINE IT.
...FORGET IT.
I AM SICK OF SEEING THAT IDIOTIC LOOK ON YOUR FACE.
HUH...?

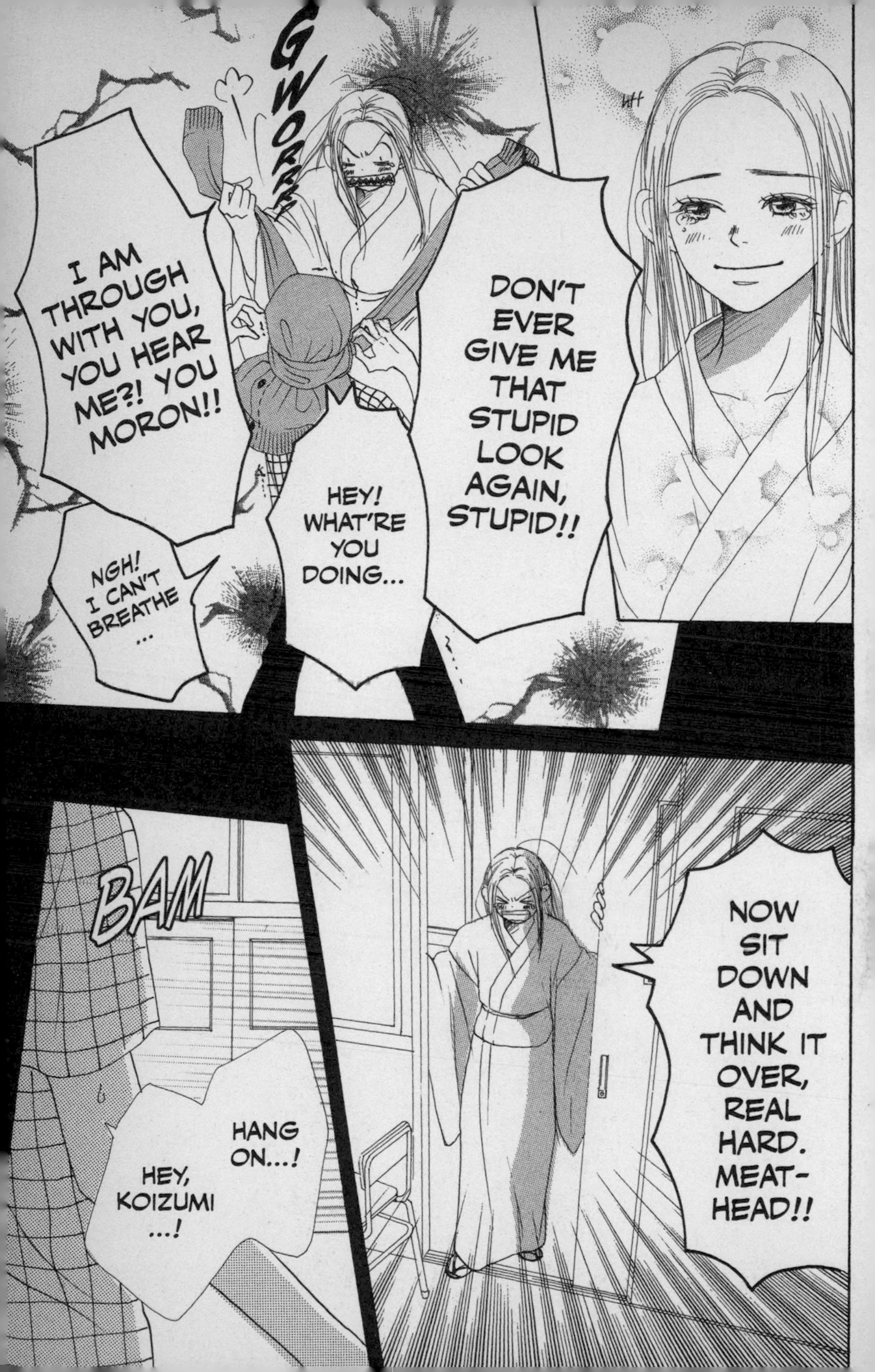
GWORRR
DON'T EVER GIVE ME THAT STUPID LOOK AGAIN, STUPID!!
I AM THROUGH WITH YOU, YOU HEAR ME?! YOU MORON!!
HEY! WHAT'RE YOU DOING...
NGH! I CAN'T BREATHE ...
NOW SIT DOWN AND THINK IT OVER, REAL HARD. MEAT-HEAD!!
BAM
HANG ON...!
HEY, KOIZUMI ...!

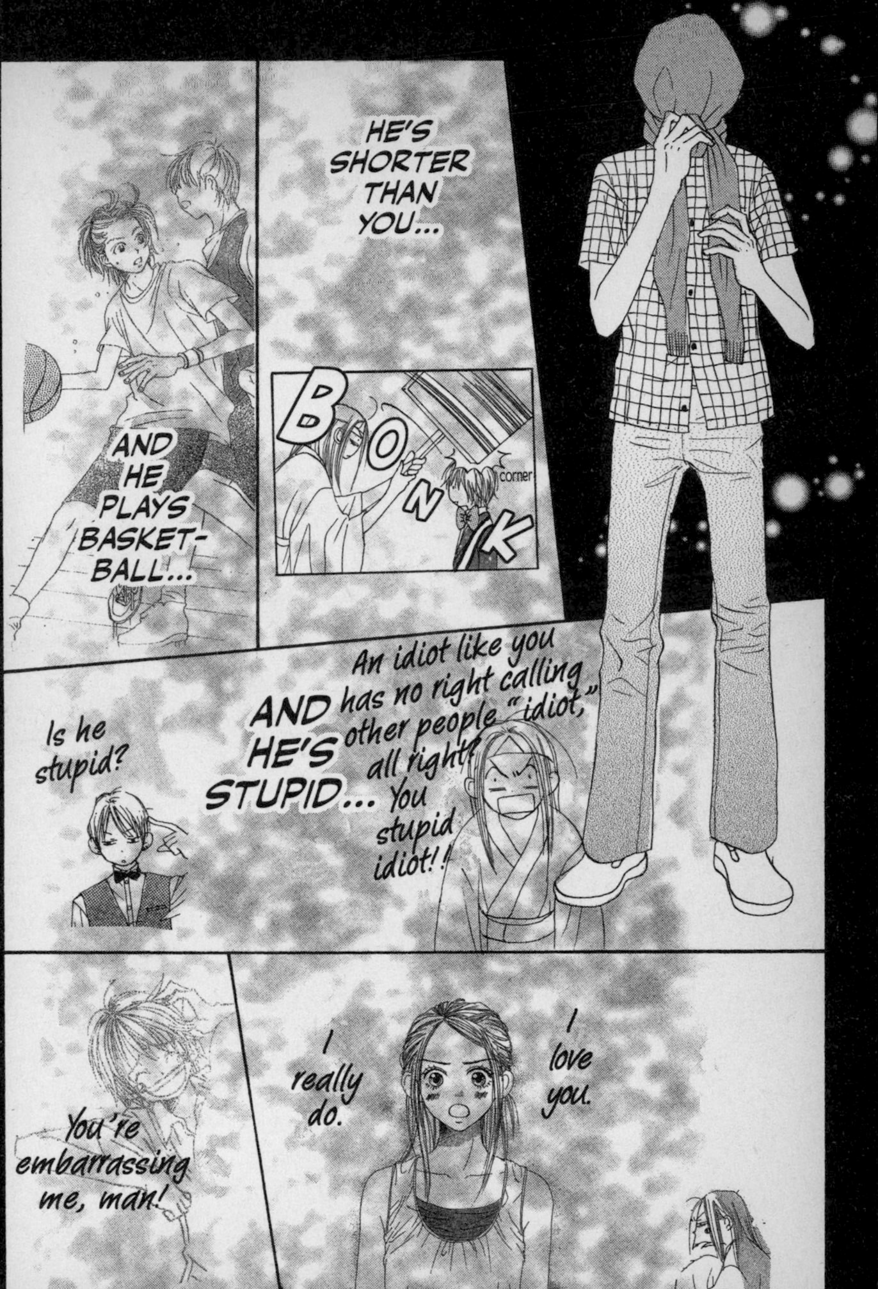
HE'S SHORTER THAN YOU...
BONK
corner
AND HE PLAYS BASKET-BALL...
An idiot like you has no right calling other people "idiot," all right?
You stupid idiot!!
AND HE'S STUPID...
Is he stupid?
I love you.
I really do.
You're embarrassing me, man!

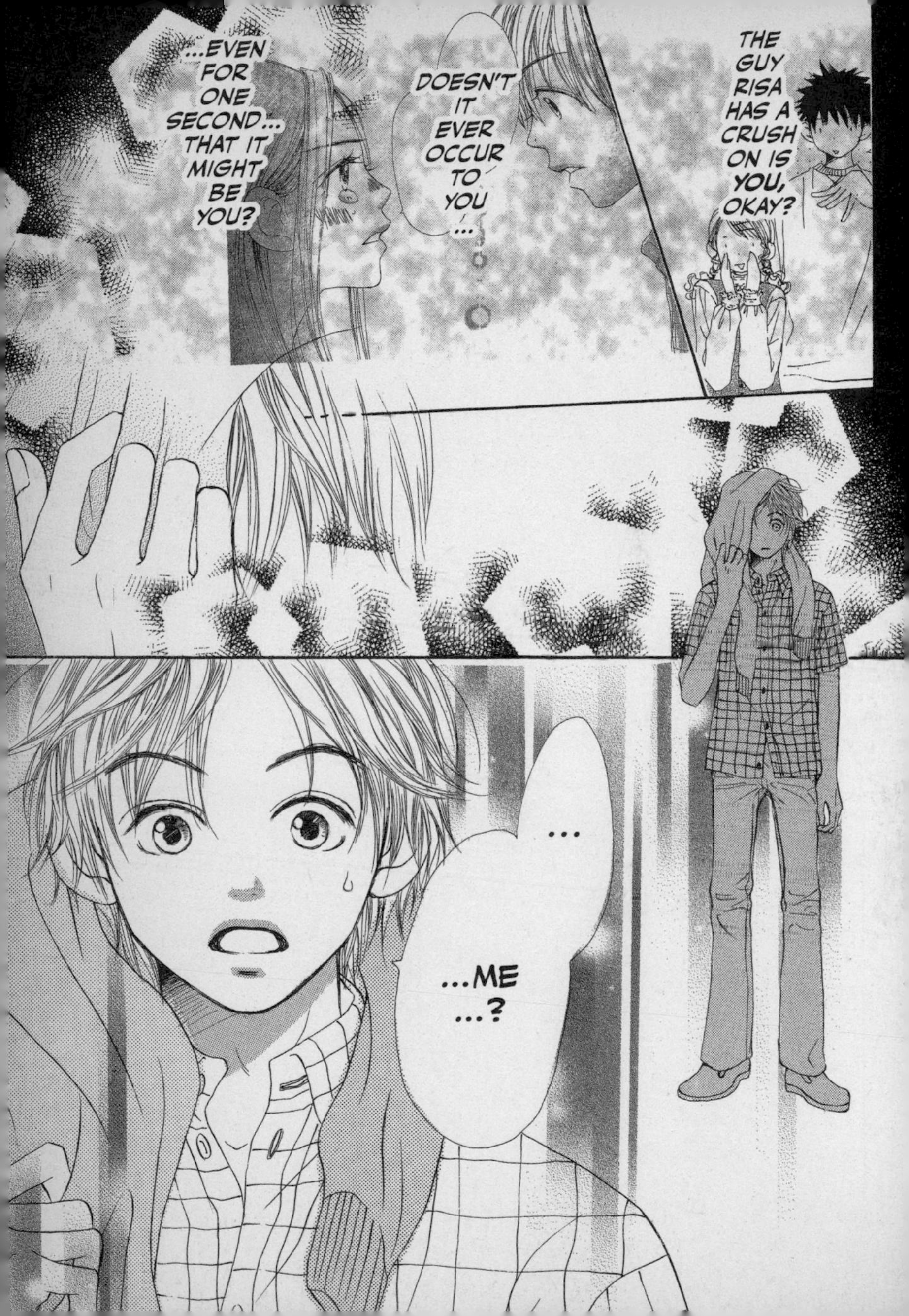
THE GUY RISA HAS A CRUSH ON IS YOU, OKAY?
DOESN'T IT EVER OCCUR TO YOU...
...EVEN FOR ONE SECOND... THAT IT MIGHT BE YOU?
...
...ME ...?

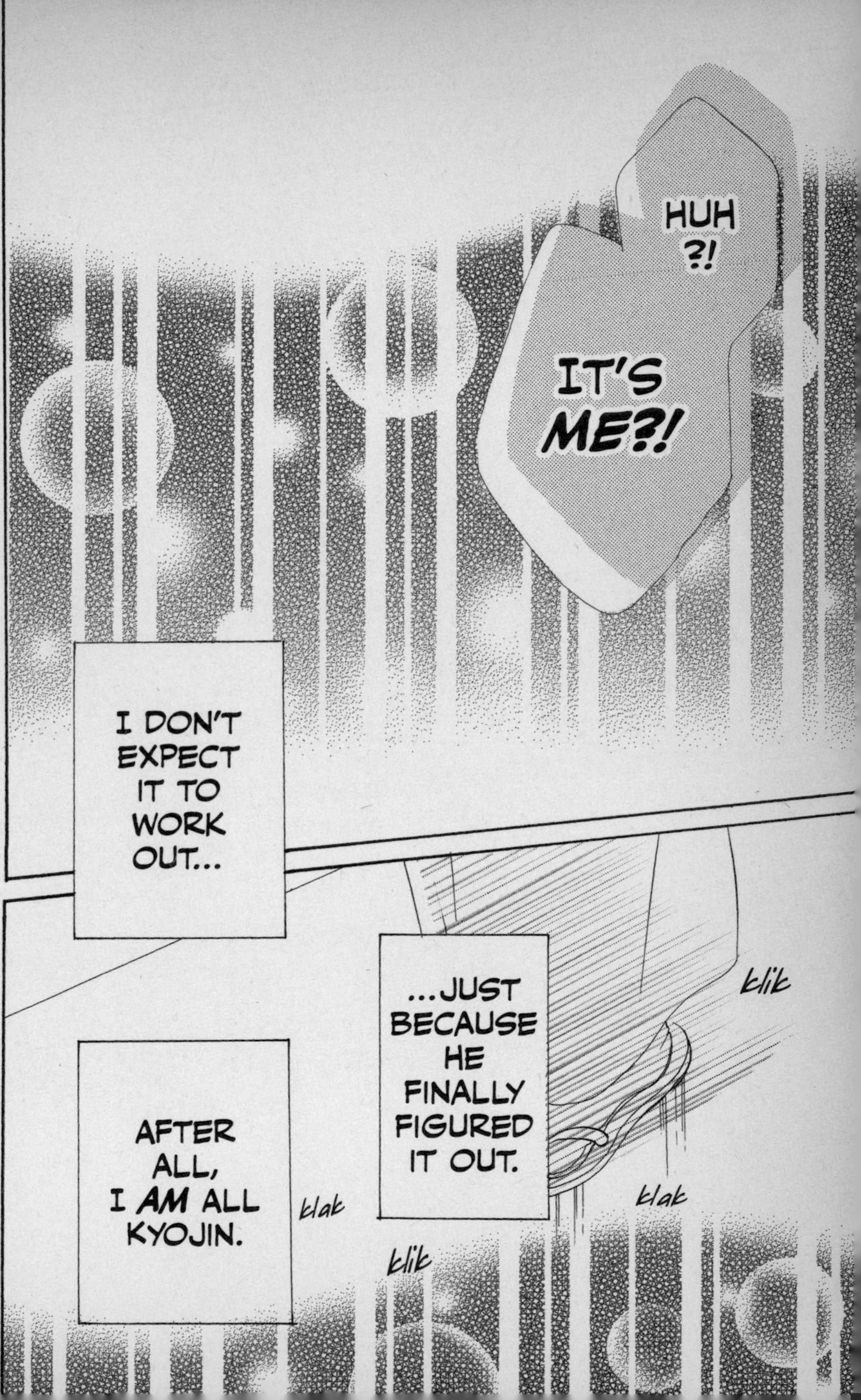
HUH ?!
IT'S ME?!
I DON'T EXPECT IT TO WORK OUT...
...JUST BECAUSE HE FINALLY FIGURED IT OUT.
klik
klak
klak
klik
AFTER ALL, I AM ALL KYOJIN.

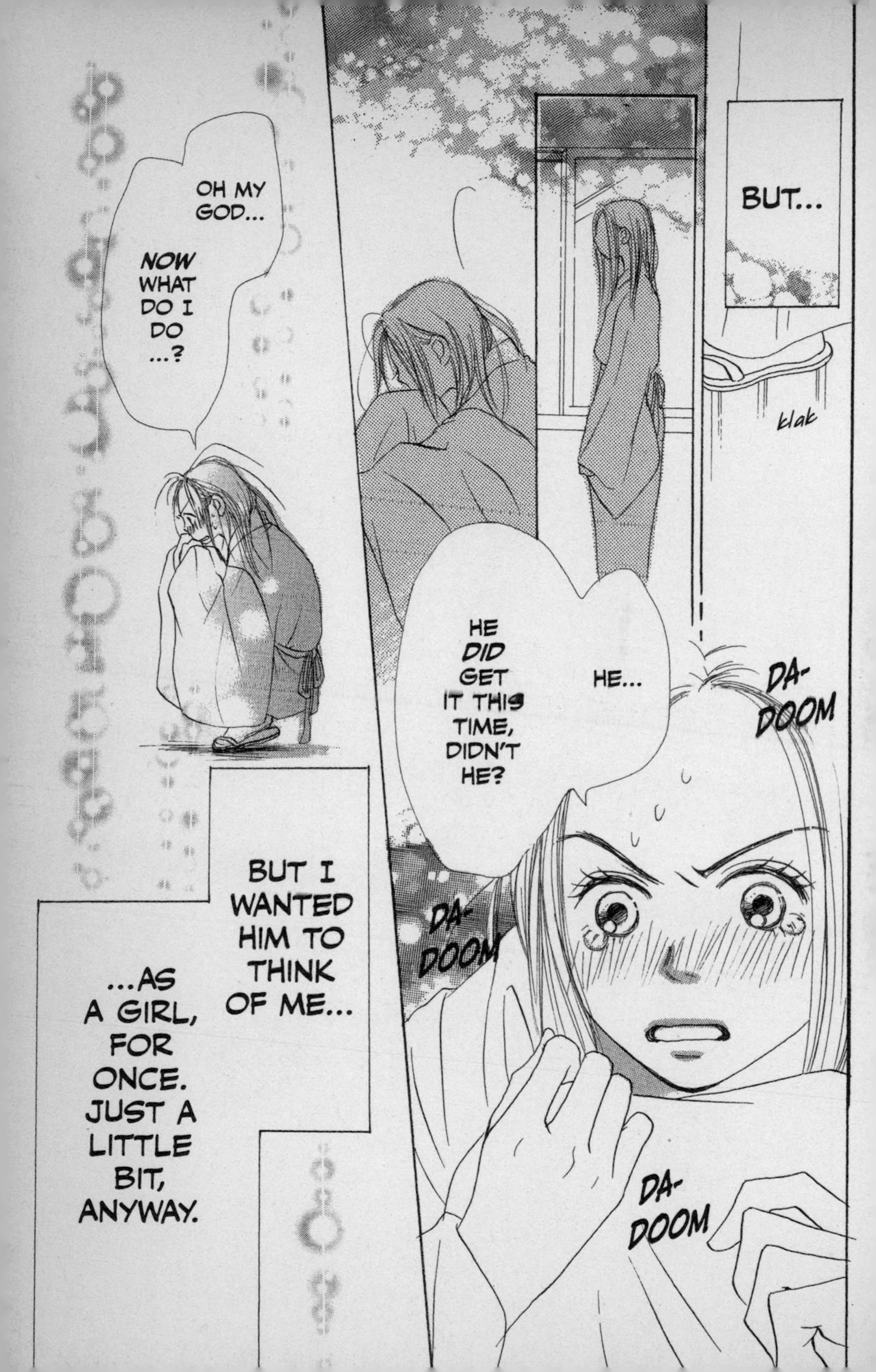
BUT...
klak
HE...
HE DID GET IT THIS TIME, DIDN'T HE?
DA-DOOM
DA-DOOM
DA-DOOM
OH MY GOD... NOW WHAT DO I DO ...?
BUT I WANTED HIM TO THINK OF ME...
...AS A GIRL, FOR ONCE. JUST A LITTLE BIT, ANYWAY.

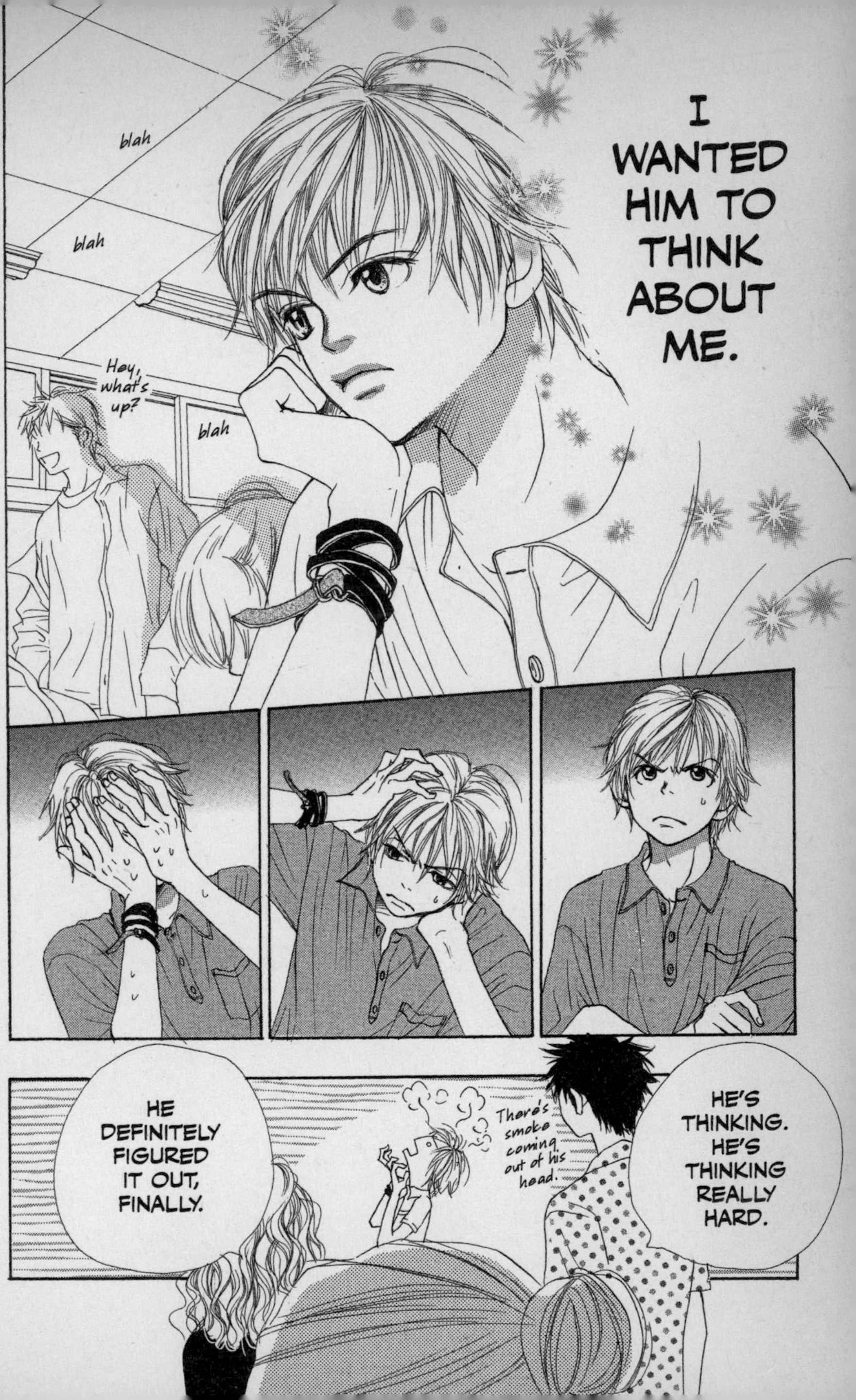
I WANTED HIM TO THINK ABOUT ME.
blah
blah
Hey, what's up?
blah
HE'S THINKING. HE'S THINKING REALLY HARD.
There's smoke coming out of his head.
HE DEFINITELY FIGURED IT OUT, FINALLY.

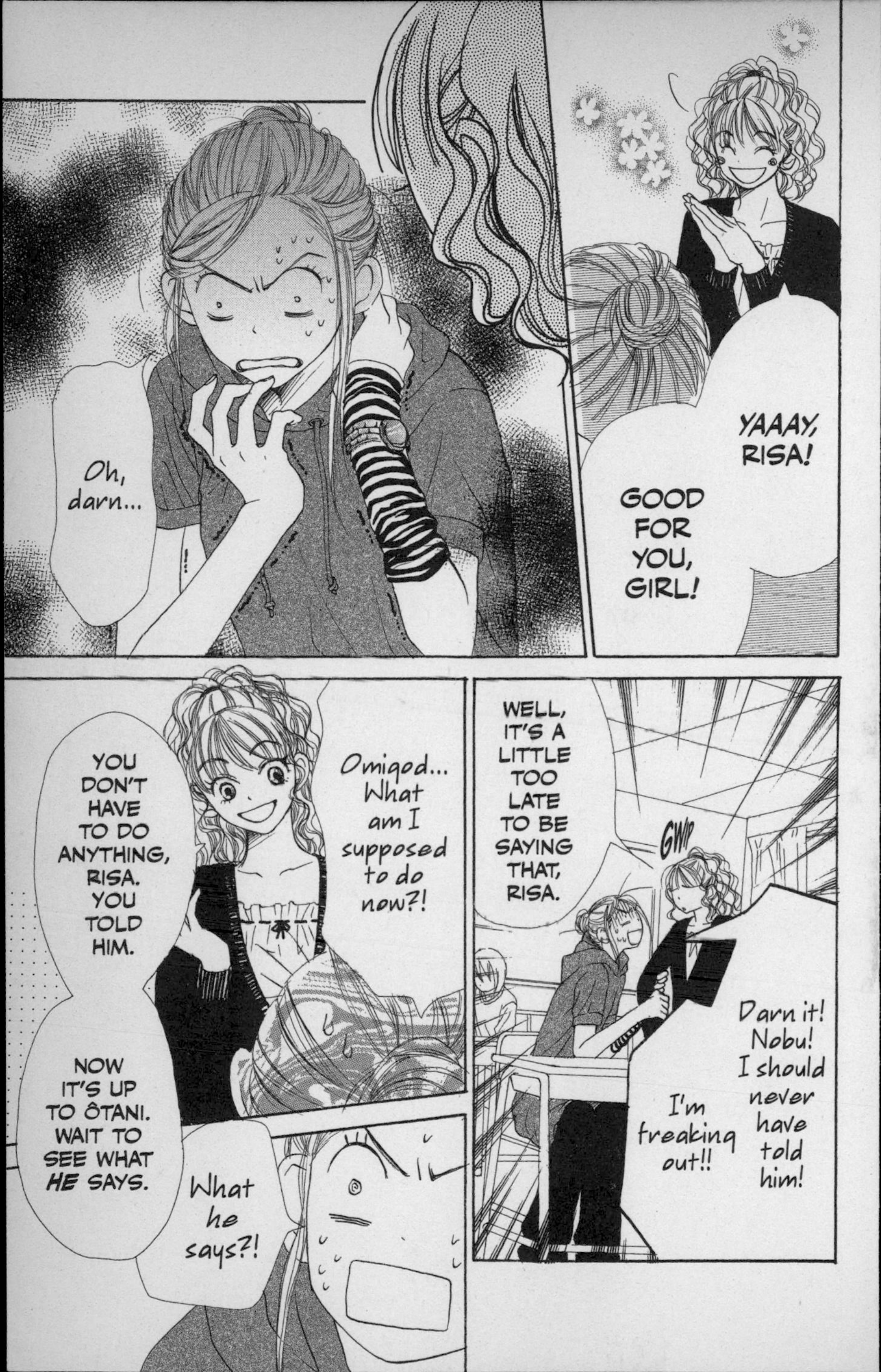
YAAAY, RISA!
GOOD FOR YOU, GIRL!
Oh, darn...
WELL, IT'S A LITTLE TOO LATE TO BE SAYING THAT, RISA.
GWIP
Darn it! Nobu! I should never have told him!
I'm freaking out!!
Omigod... What am I supposed to do now?!
YOU DON'T HAVE TO DO ANYTHING, RISA. YOU TOLD HIM.
NOW IT'S UP TO ÔTANI. WAIT TO SEE WHAT HE SAYS.
What he says?!

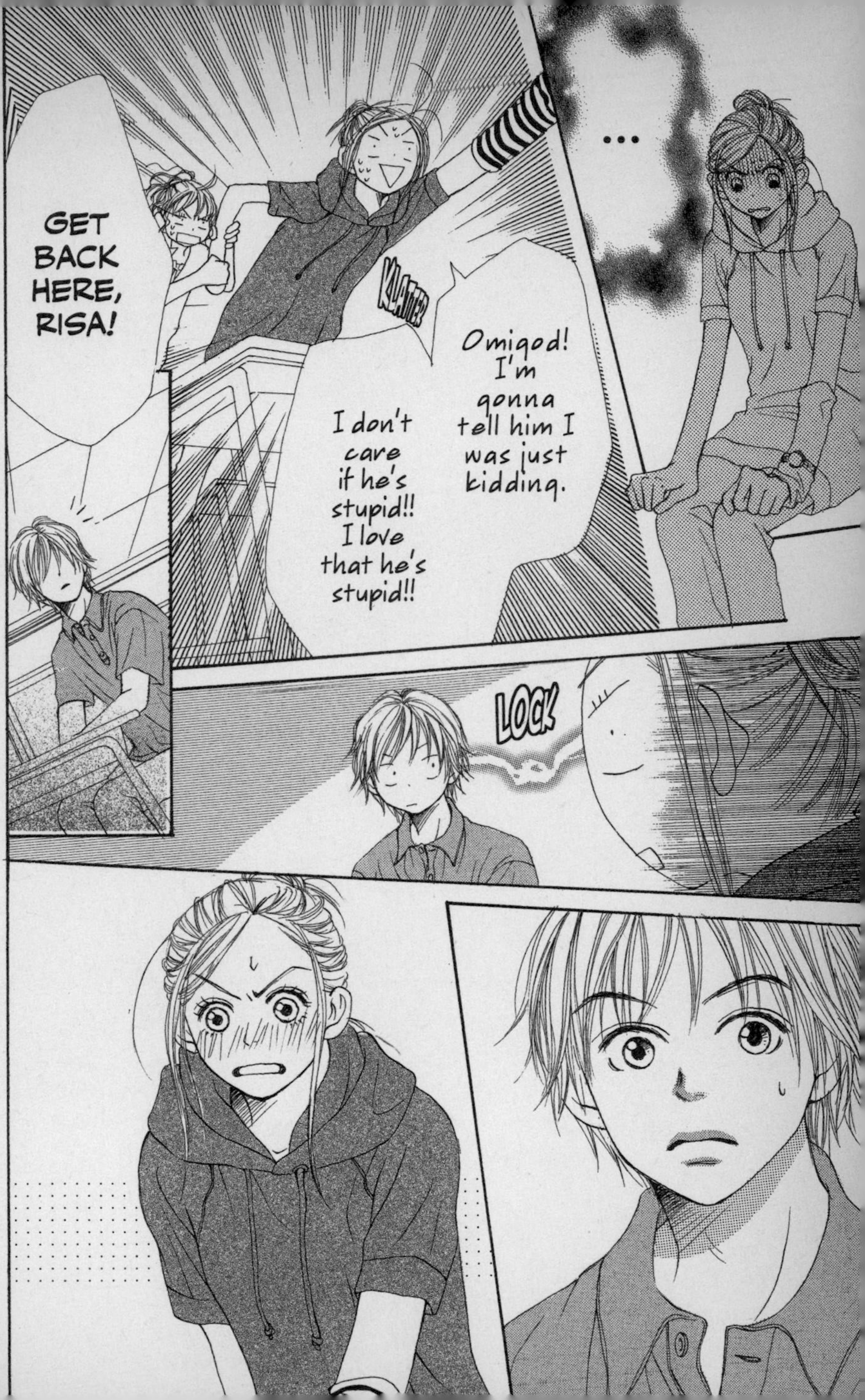
...
Omigod! I'm gonna tell him I was just kidding.
I don't care if he's stupid!! I love that he's stupid!!
KLATTER
GET BACK HERE, RISA!
LOCK

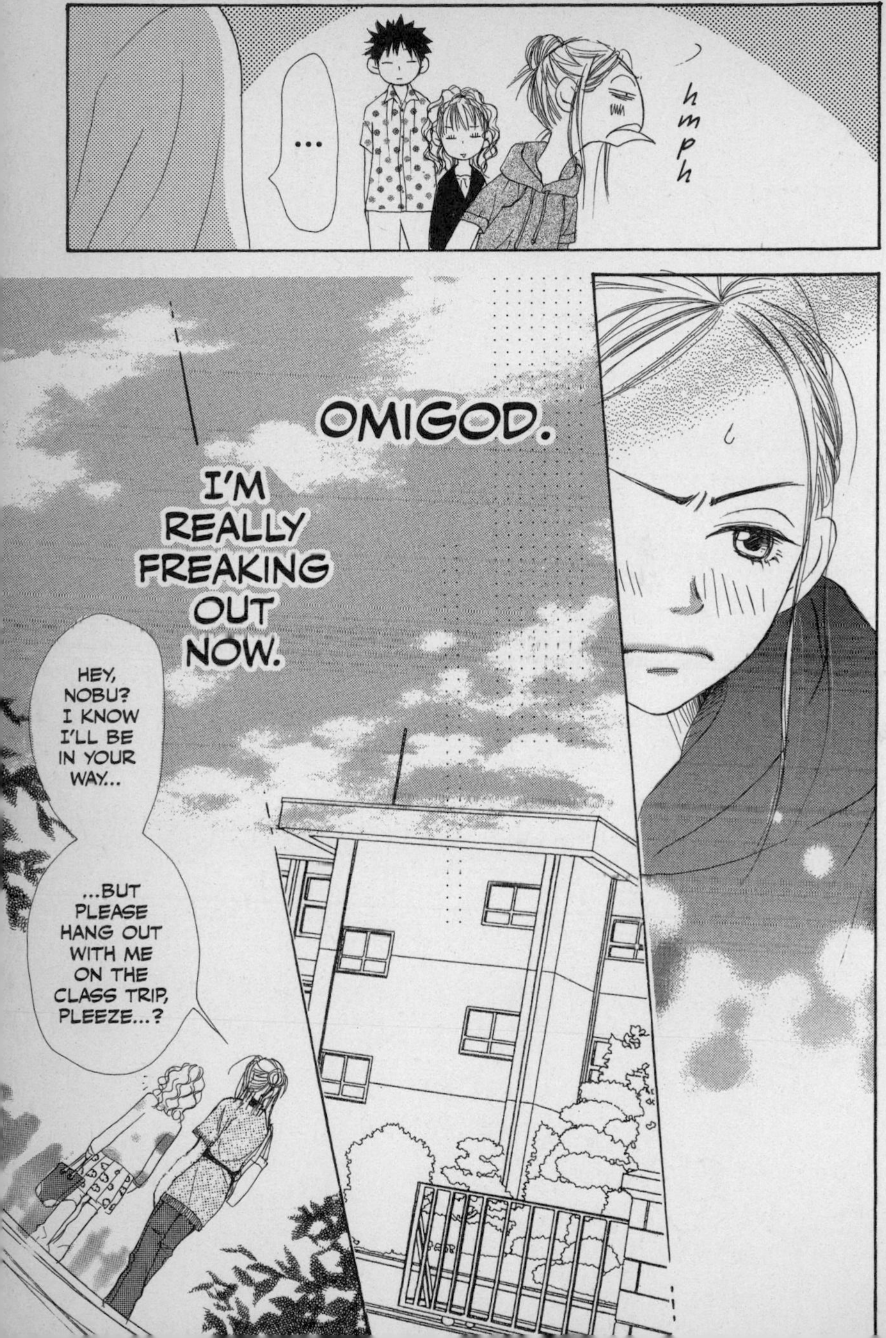
hmph
...
OMIGOD.
I'M REALLY FREAKING OUT NOW.
HEY, NOBU? I KNOW I'LL BE IN YOUR WAY...
...BUT PLEASE HANG OUT WITH ME ON THE CLASS TRIP, PLEEZE...?

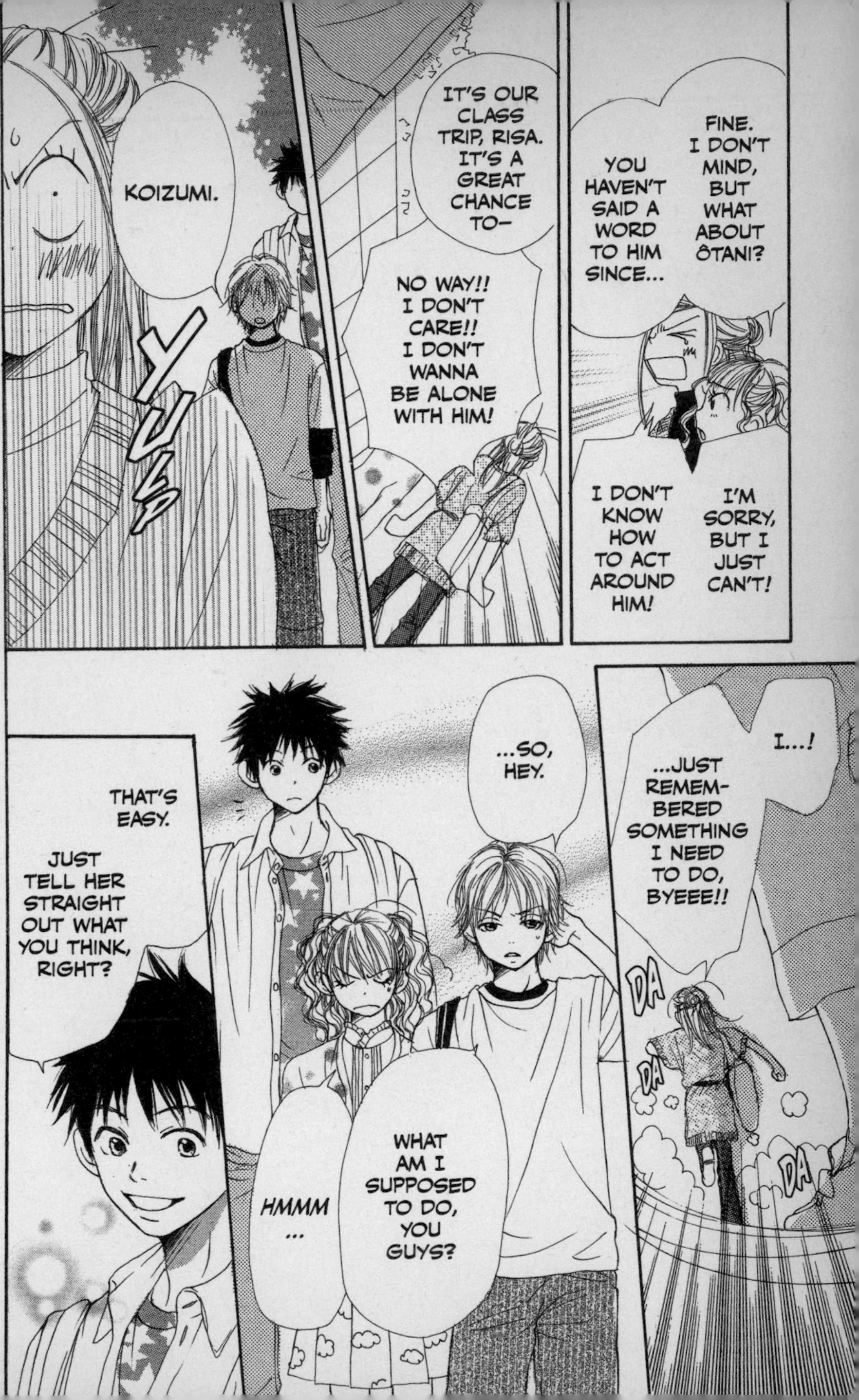
FINE. I DON'T MIND, BUT WHAT ABOUT ÔTANI?
YOU HAVEN'T SAID A WORD TO HIM SINCE...
I'M SORRY, BUT I JUST CAN'T!
I DON'T KNOW HOW TO ACT AROUND HIM!
IT'S OUR CLASS TRIP, RISA. IT'S A GREAT CHANCE TO–
NO WAY!! I DON'T CARE!! I DON'T WANNA BE ALONE WITH HIM!
KOIZUMI.
I...!
...JUST REMEM-BERED SOMETHING I NEED TO DO, BYEEE!!
DA
DA
DA
...SO, HEY.
WHAT AM I SUPPOSED TO DO, YOU GUYS?
HMMM...
THAT'S EASY.
JUST TELL HER STRAIGHT OUT WHAT YOU THINK, RIGHT?

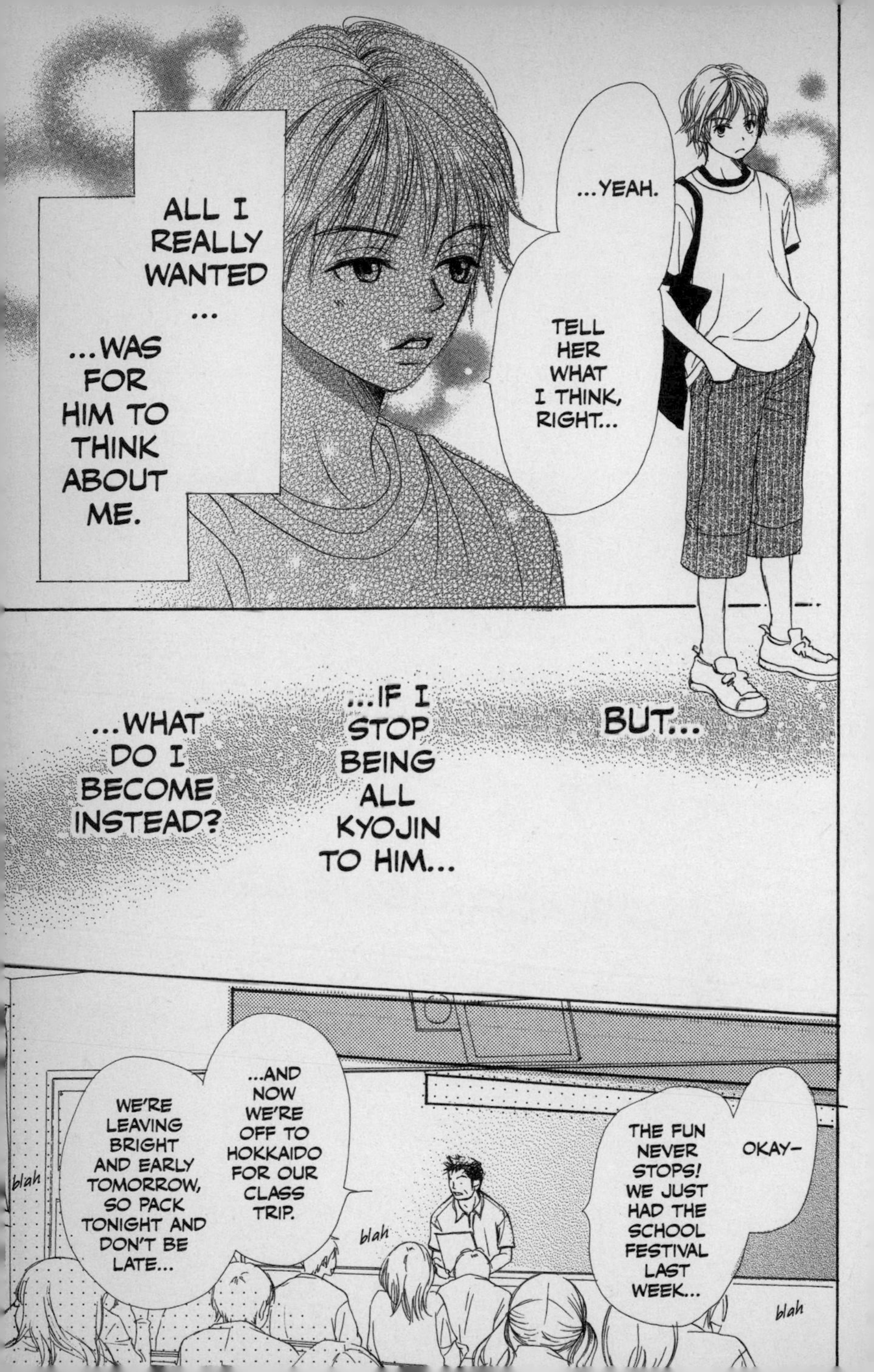
...YEAH.
TELL HER WHAT I THINK, RIGHT...
ALL I REALLY WANTED ...
...WAS FOR HIM TO THINK ABOUT ME.
BUT...
...IF I STOP BEING ALL KYOJIN TO HIM...
...WHAT DO I BECOME INSTEAD?
OKAY—
THE FUN NEVER STOPS! WE JUST HAD THE SCHOOL FESTIVAL LAST WEEK...
blah
...AND NOW WE'RE OFF TO HOKKAIDO FOR OUR CLASS TRIP.
blah
WE'RE LEAVING BRIGHT AND EARLY TOMORROW, SO PACK TONIGHT AND DON'T BE LATE...
blah

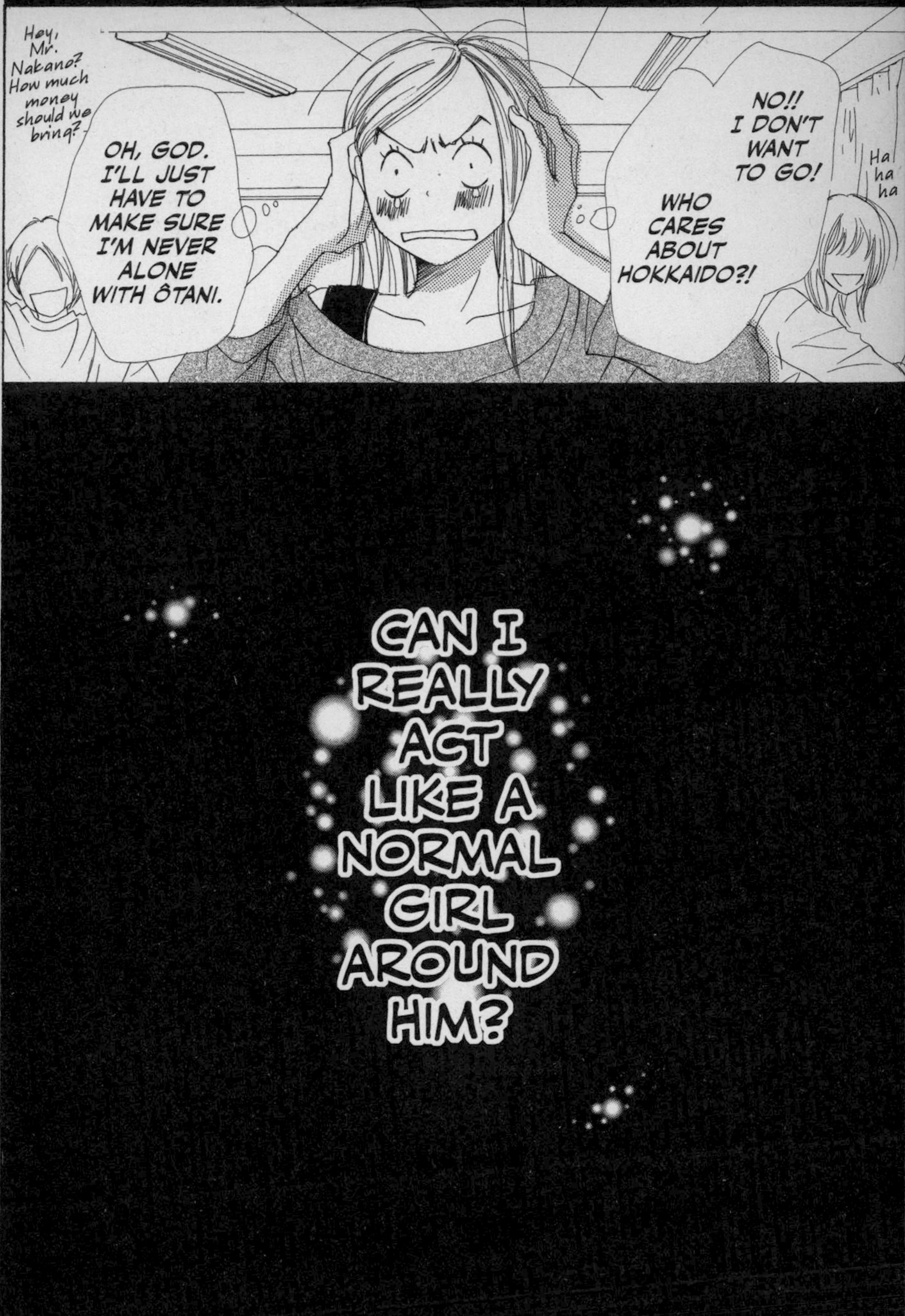
Ha ha ha
NO!! I DON'T WANT TO GO!
WHO CARES ABOUT HOKKAIDO?!
OH, GOD. I'LL JUST HAVE TO MAKE SURE I'M NEVER ALONE WITH ÔTANI.
Hey, Mr. Nakano? How much money should we bring?
CAN I REALLY ACT LIKE A NORMAL GIRL AROUND HIM?

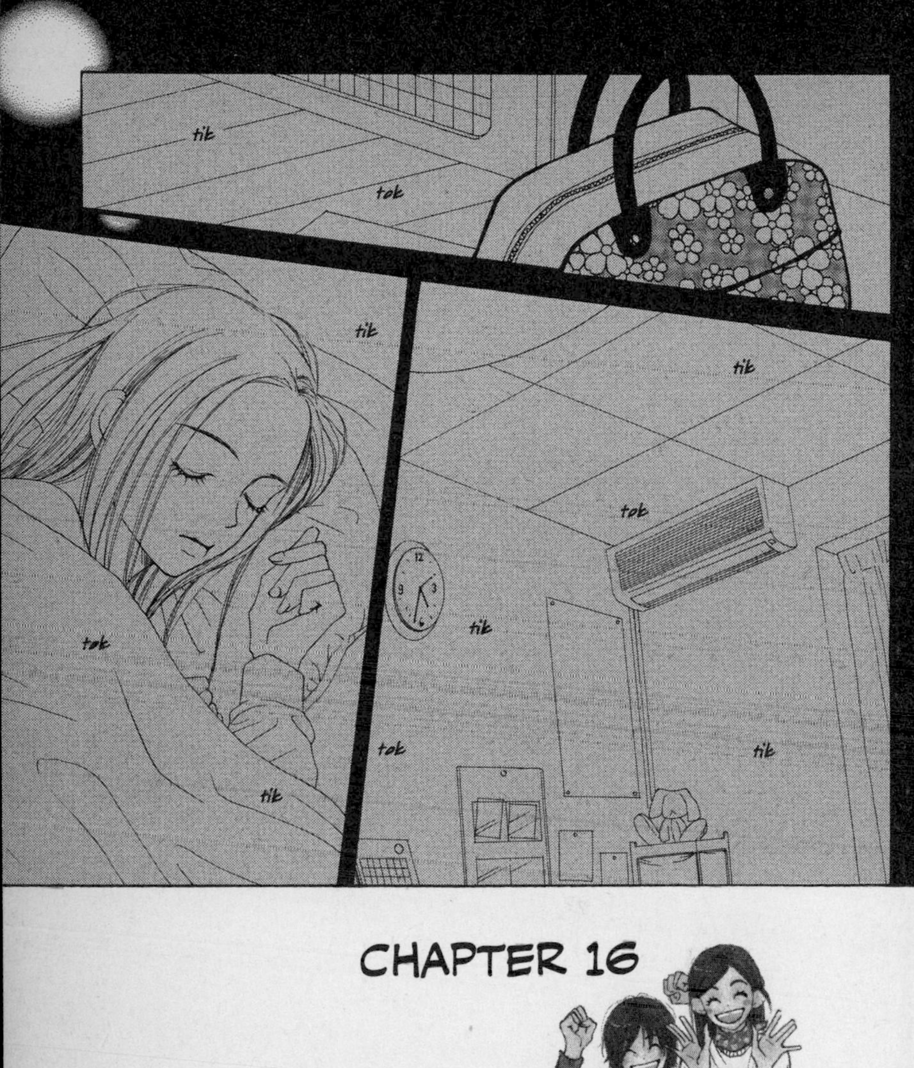
tik
tok
tik
tok
tik
tok
tik
tik
tok
tik

CHAPTER 16

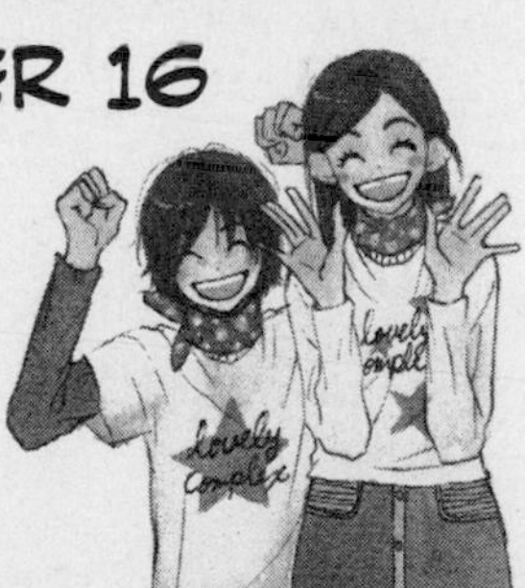
lovely complex

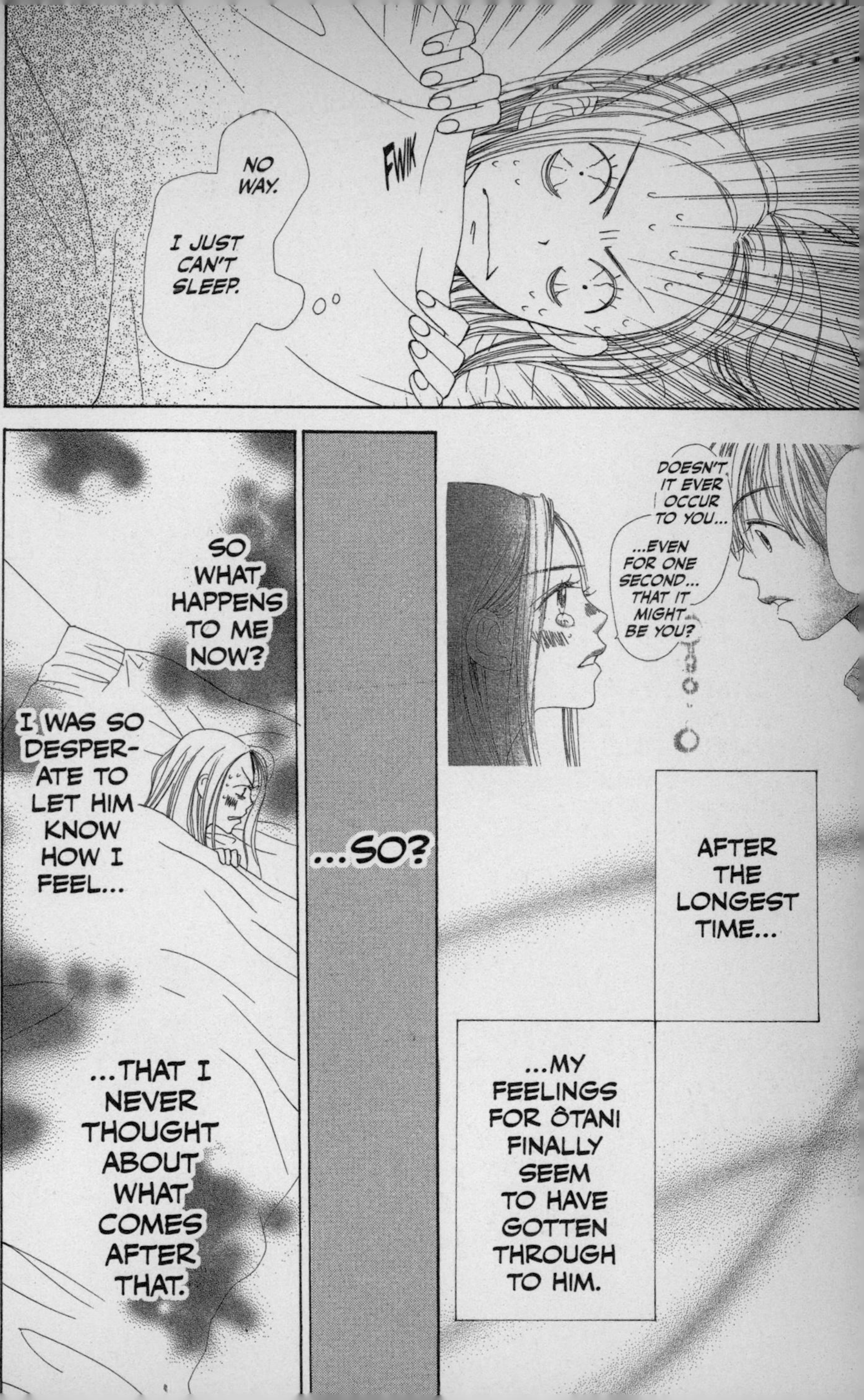
NO WAY.
I JUST CAN'T SLEEP.
FWIK
DOESN'T IT EVER OCCUR TO YOU...
...EVEN FOR ONE SECOND... THAT IT MIGHT BE YOU?
AFTER THE LONGEST TIME...
...MY FEELINGS FOR ÔTANI FINALLY SEEM TO HAVE GOTTEN THROUGH TO HIM.
...SO?
SO WHAT HAPPENS TO ME NOW?
I WAS SO DESPERATE TO LET HIM KNOW HOW I FEEL...
...THAT I NEVER THOUGHT ABOUT WHAT COMES AFTER THAT.

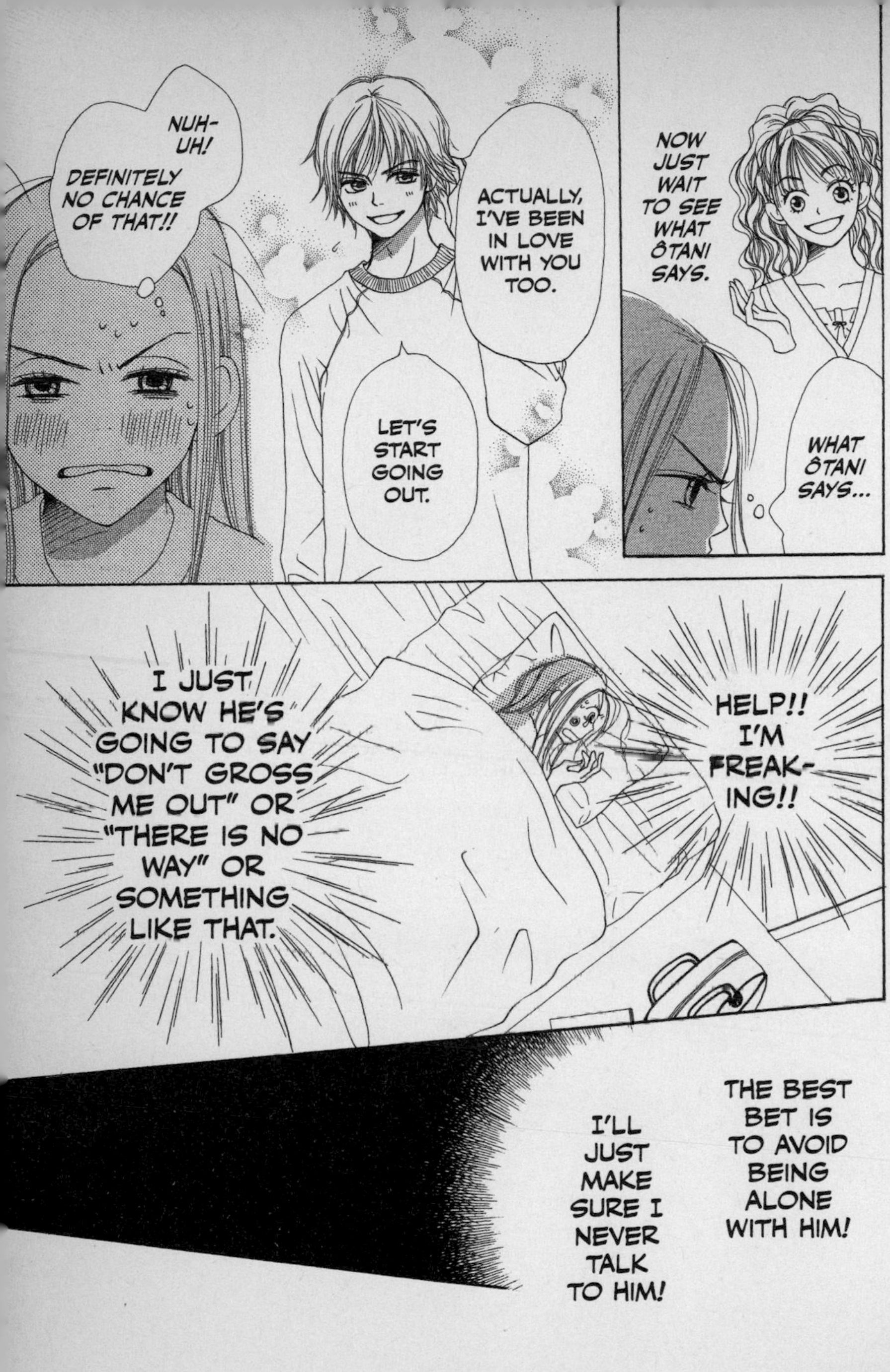
NOW JUST WAIT TO SEE WHAT ŌTANI SAYS.
WHAT ŌTANI SAYS...
ACTUALLY, I'VE BEEN IN LOVE WITH YOU TOO.
LET'S START GOING OUT.
NUH-UH! DEFINITELY NO CHANCE OF THAT!!
HELP!! I'M FREAK-ING!!
I JUST KNOW HE'S GOING TO SAY "DON'T GROSS ME OUT" OR "THERE IS NO WAY" OR SOMETHING LIKE THAT.
THE BEST BET IS TO AVOID BEING ALONE WITH HIM!
I'LL JUST MAKE SURE I NEVER TALK TO HIM!

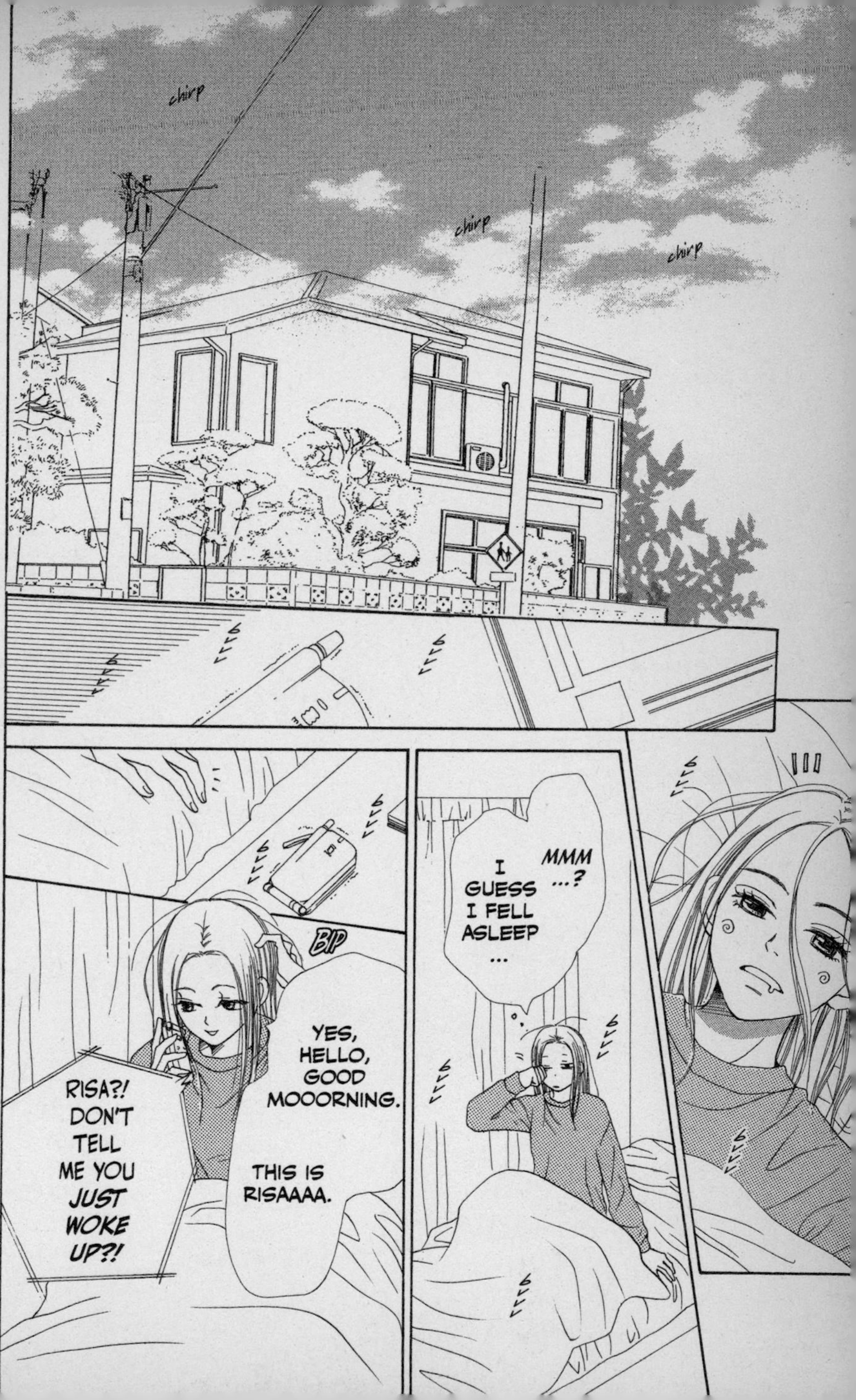
chirp
chirp
chirp
MMM ...?
I GUESS I FELL ASLEEP ...
BIP
YES, HELLO, GOOD MOOORNING.
THIS IS RISAAAA.
RISA?! DON'T TELL ME YOU JUST WOKE UP?!

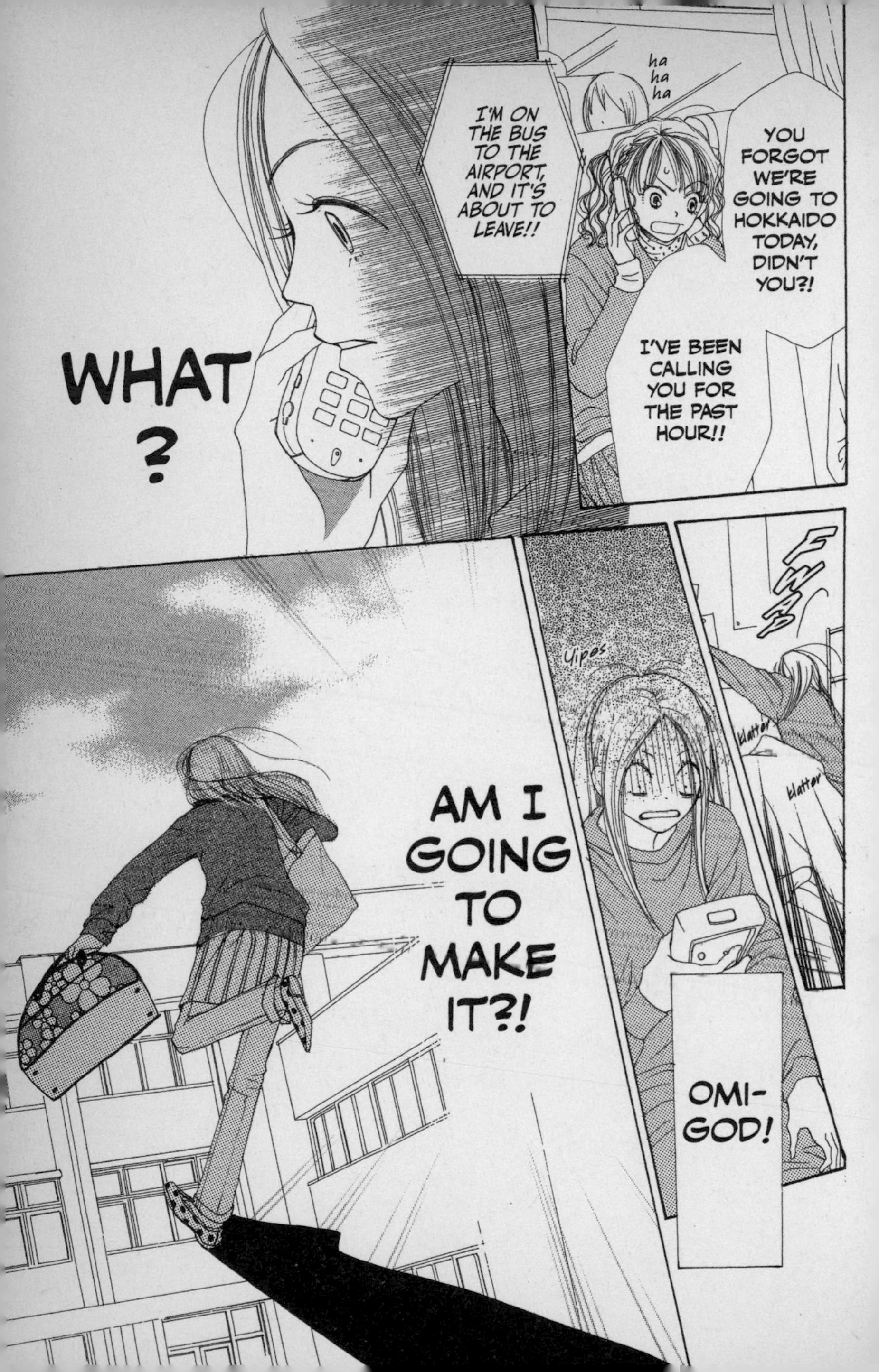
ha ha ha
I'M ON THE BUS TO THE AIRPORT, AND IT'S ABOUT TO LEAVE!!
YOU FORGOT WE'RE GOING TO HOKKAIDO TODAY, DIDN'T YOU?!
I'VE BEEN CALLING YOU FOR THE PAST HOUR!!
WHAT?
FWAP
klatter
klatter
Yipes
OMI-GOD!
AM I GOING TO MAKE IT?!

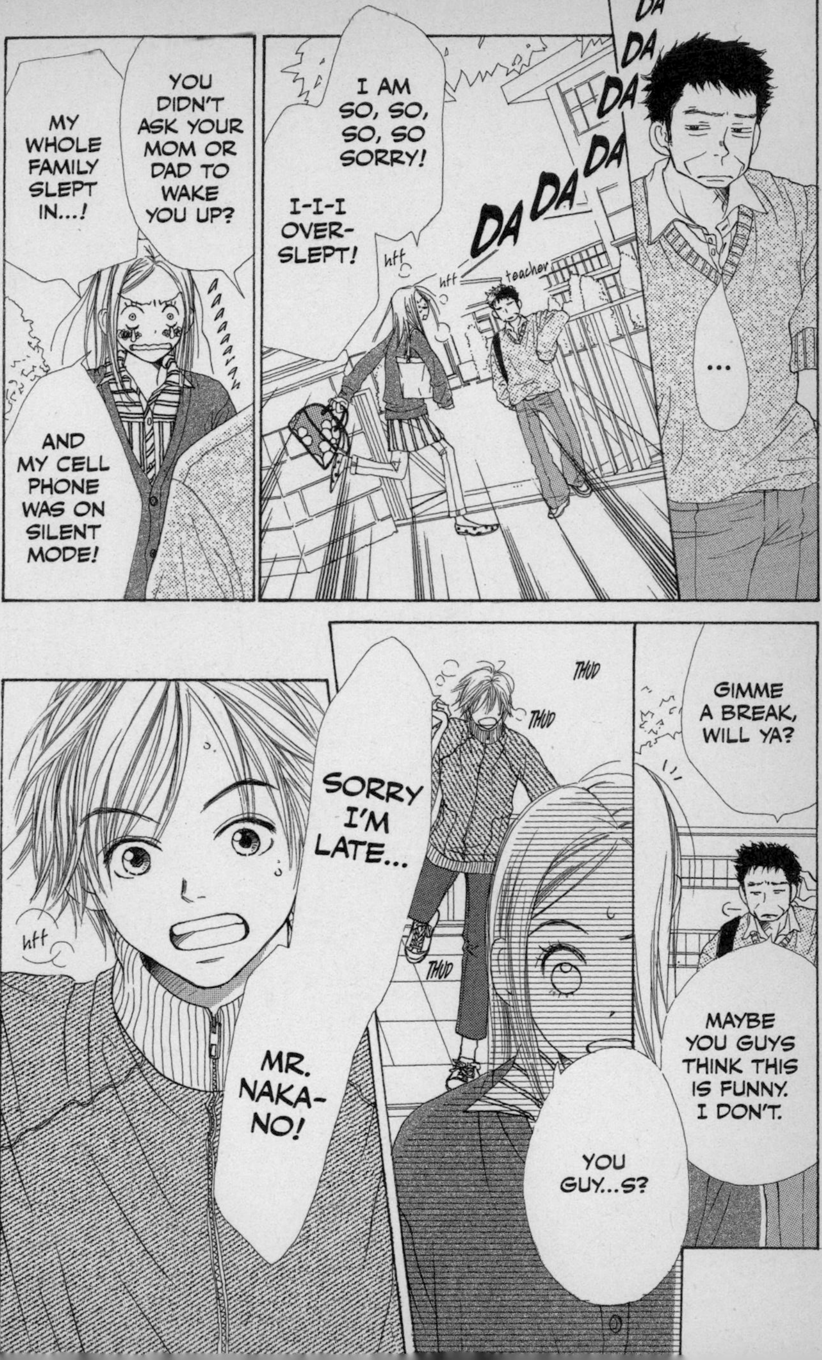
DA DA DA DA DA DA
teacher
...
hff
hff
I AM SO, SO, SO, SO SORRY!
I-I-I OVER-SLEPT!
YOU DIDN'T ASK YOUR MOM OR DAD TO WAKE YOU UP?
MY WHOLE FAMILY SLEPT IN...!
AND MY CELL PHONE WAS ON SILENT MODE!
GIMME A BREAK, WILL YA?
MAYBE YOU GUYS THINK THIS IS FUNNY. I DON'T.
YOU GUY...S?
THUD
THUD
THUD
SORRY I'M LATE...
MR. NAKA-NO!
hff

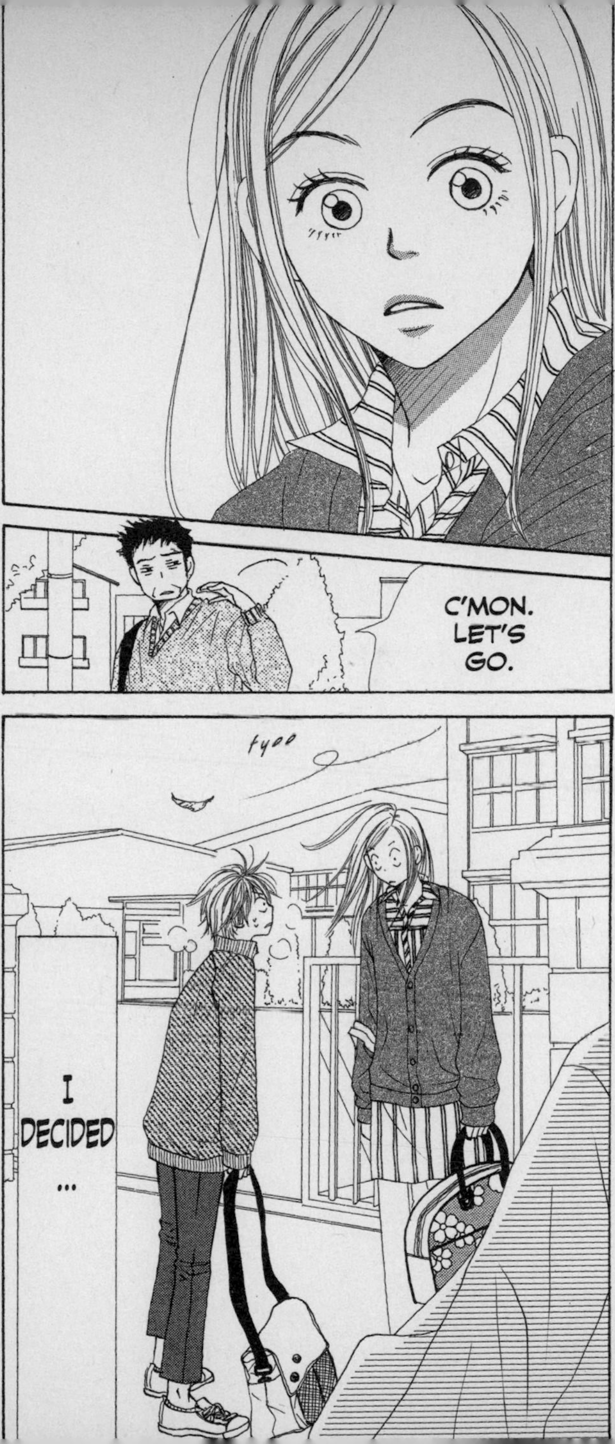
C'MON. LET'S GO.
fyoo
I DECIDED ...

4

This is the last of these for this volume.

I didn't realize people were even reading these things until those poop cartoon requests at the autograph session. Thank you so much!

Starting with the next volume, I intend to hold forth intelligently on brainy topics that will get people asking me for my views on the Japanese economy.

That is a lie.

Well, then.
I hope I get to meet you again in Vol. 5!

アヤ
Aya
January, 2003

Special Thanks

Nana Ikebe
Yuko Idomoto
Hikari Katayama
Nakahara Family
Betsuma Family
and
you

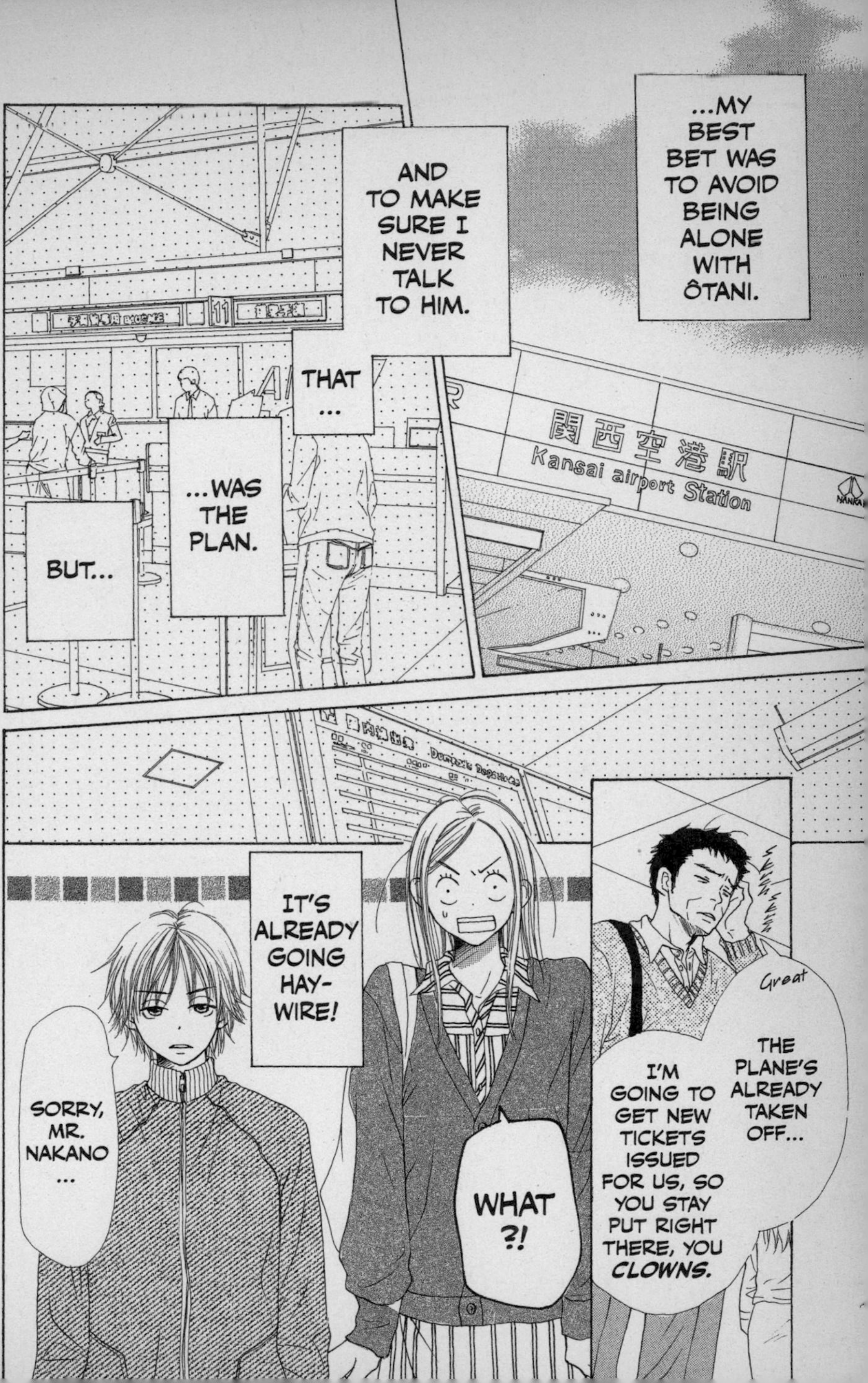
...MY BEST BET WAS TO AVOID BEING ALONE WITH ÔTANI.
AND TO MAKE SURE I NEVER TALK TO HIM.
関西空港駅
Kansai airport Station
THAT...
...WAS THE PLAN.
BUT...
Great
THE PLANE'S ALREADY TAKEN OFF...
I'M GOING TO GET NEW TICKETS ISSUED FOR US, SO YOU STAY PUT RIGHT THERE, YOU *CLOWNS.*
WHAT?!
IT'S ALREADY GOING HAY-WIRE!
SORRY, MR. NAKANO...

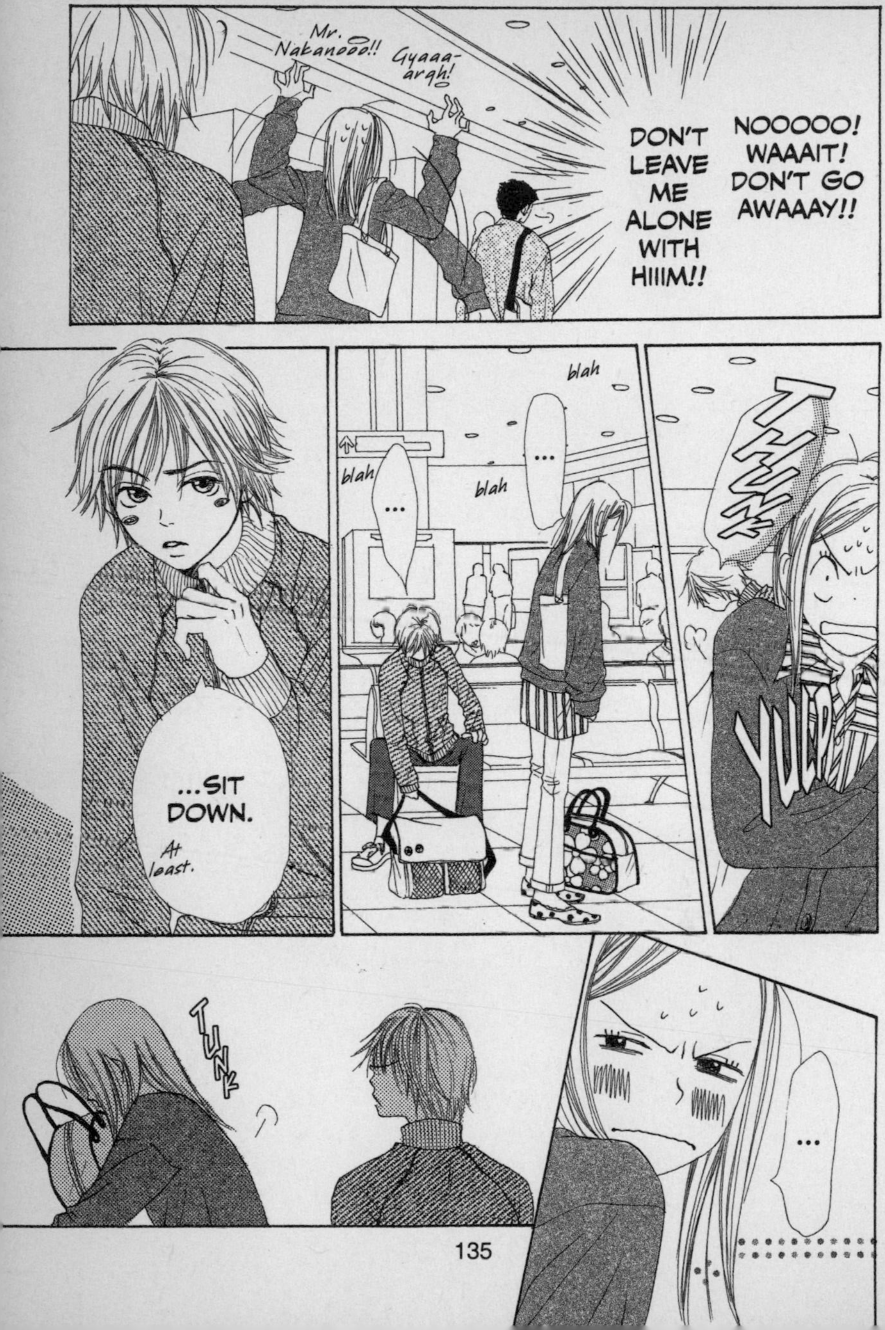
NOOOOO! WAAAIT! DON'T GO AWAAAY!!
DON'T LEAVE ME ALONE WITH HIIIM!!
Gyaaa-argh!
Mr. Nakanooo!!
THUNK
YULP
blah
...
blah
...
blah
...SIT DOWN.
At least.
...
TUNK

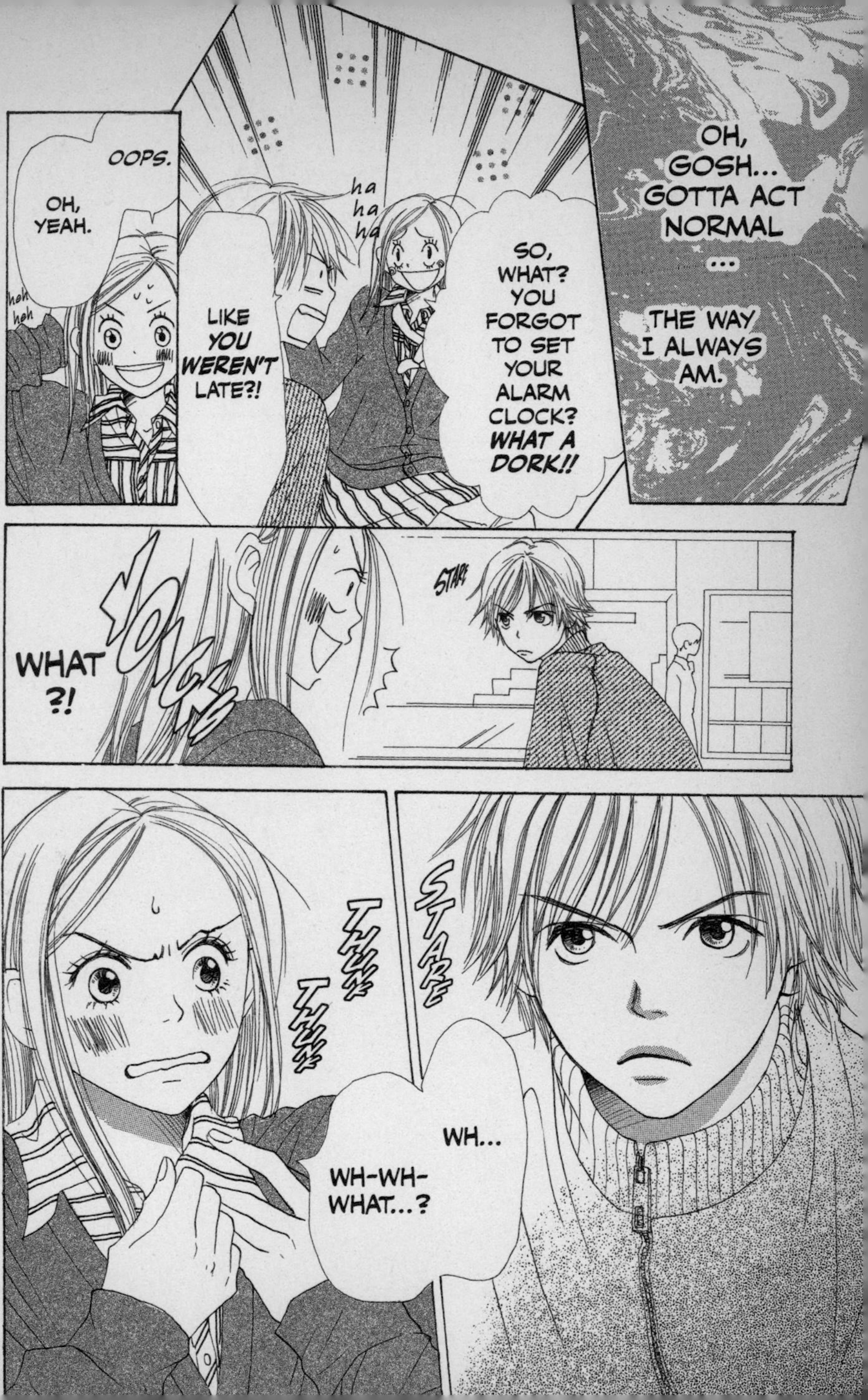
OH, GOSH... GOTTA ACT NORMAL ...
THE WAY I ALWAYS AM.
ha ha ha
SO, WHAT? YOU FORGOT TO SET YOUR ALARM CLOCK? WHAT A DORK!!
LIKE YOU WEREN'T LATE?!
OOPS.
OH, YEAH.
heh heh
STARE
WHAT ?!
STARE
THUMP
THUMP
WH...
WH-WH-WHAT...?

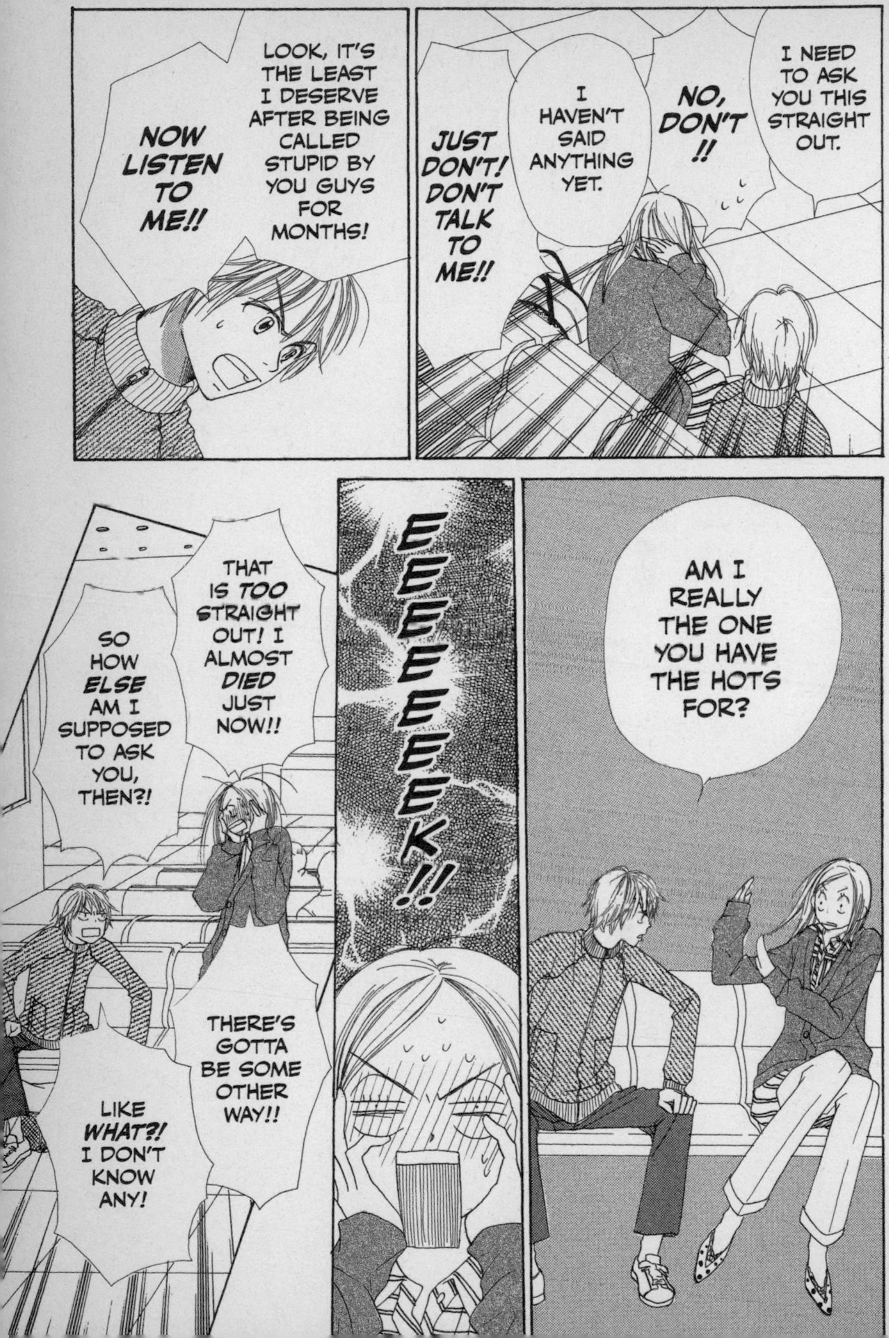
I NEED TO ASK YOU THIS STRAIGHT OUT.
NO, DON'T!!
I HAVEN'T SAID ANYTHING YET.
JUST DON'T! DON'T TALK TO ME!!
LOOK, IT'S THE LEAST I DESERVE AFTER BEING CALLED STUPID BY YOU GUYS FOR MONTHS!
NOW LISTEN TO ME!!
AM I REALLY THE ONE YOU HAVE THE HOTS FOR?
EEEEEEEEK!!
THAT IS TOO STRAIGHT OUT! I ALMOST DIED JUST NOW!!
SO HOW ELSE AM I SUPPOSED TO ASK YOU, THEN?!
THERE'S GOTTA BE SOME OTHER WAY!!
LIKE WHAT?! I DON'T KNOW ANY!

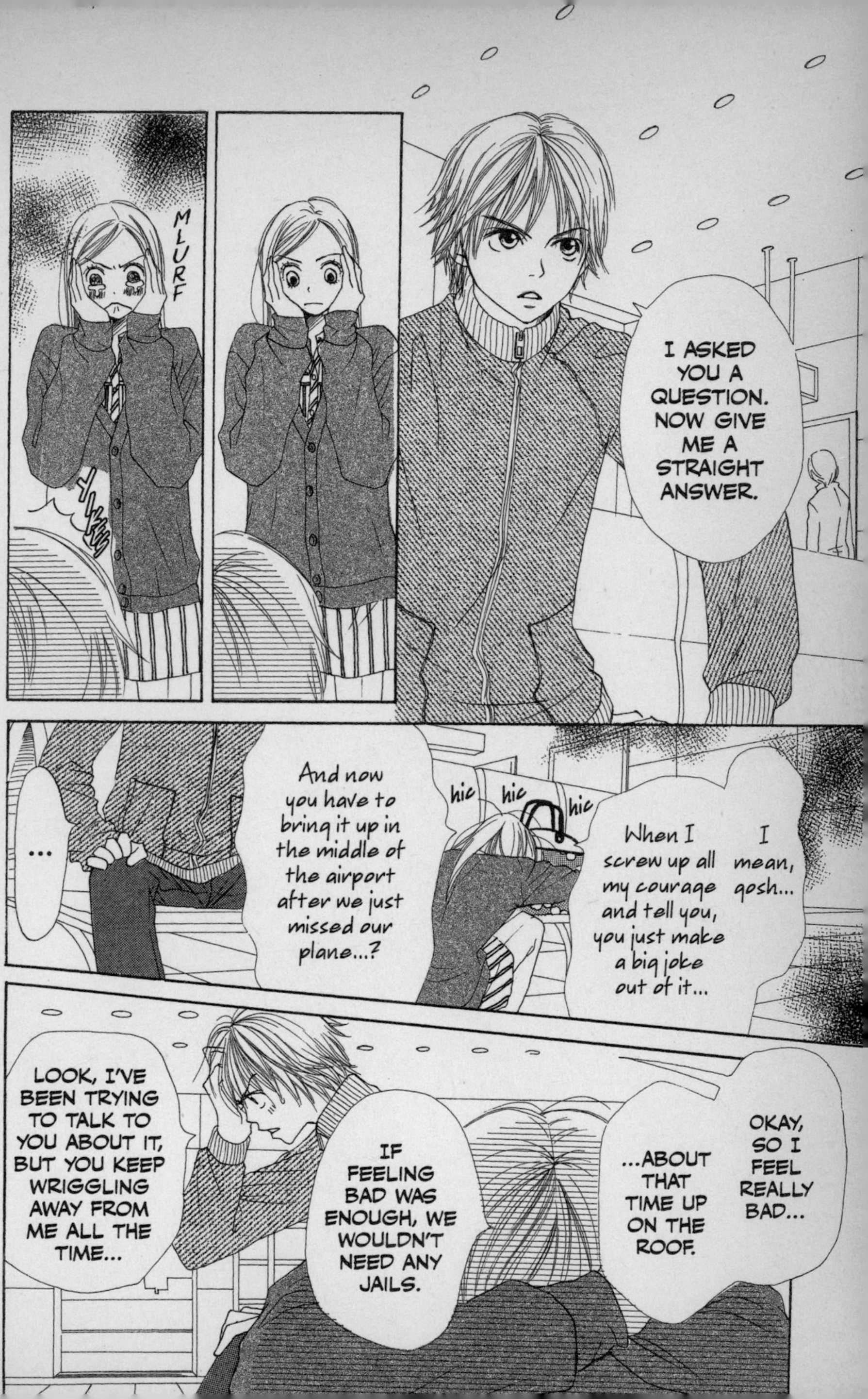
I ASKED YOU A QUESTION. NOW GIVE ME A STRAIGHT ANSWER.
MLURF
I mean, gosh...
When I screw up all my courage and tell you, you just make a big joke out of it...
hic
hic
hic
And now you have to bring it up in the middle of the airport after we just missed our plane...?
...
OKAY, SO I FEEL REALLY BAD...
...ABOUT THAT TIME UP ON THE ROOF.
IF FEELING BAD WAS ENOUGH, WE WOULDN'T NEED ANY JAILS.
LOOK, I'VE BEEN TRYING TO TALK TO YOU ABOUT IT, BUT YOU KEEP WRIGGLING AWAY FROM ME ALL THE TIME...

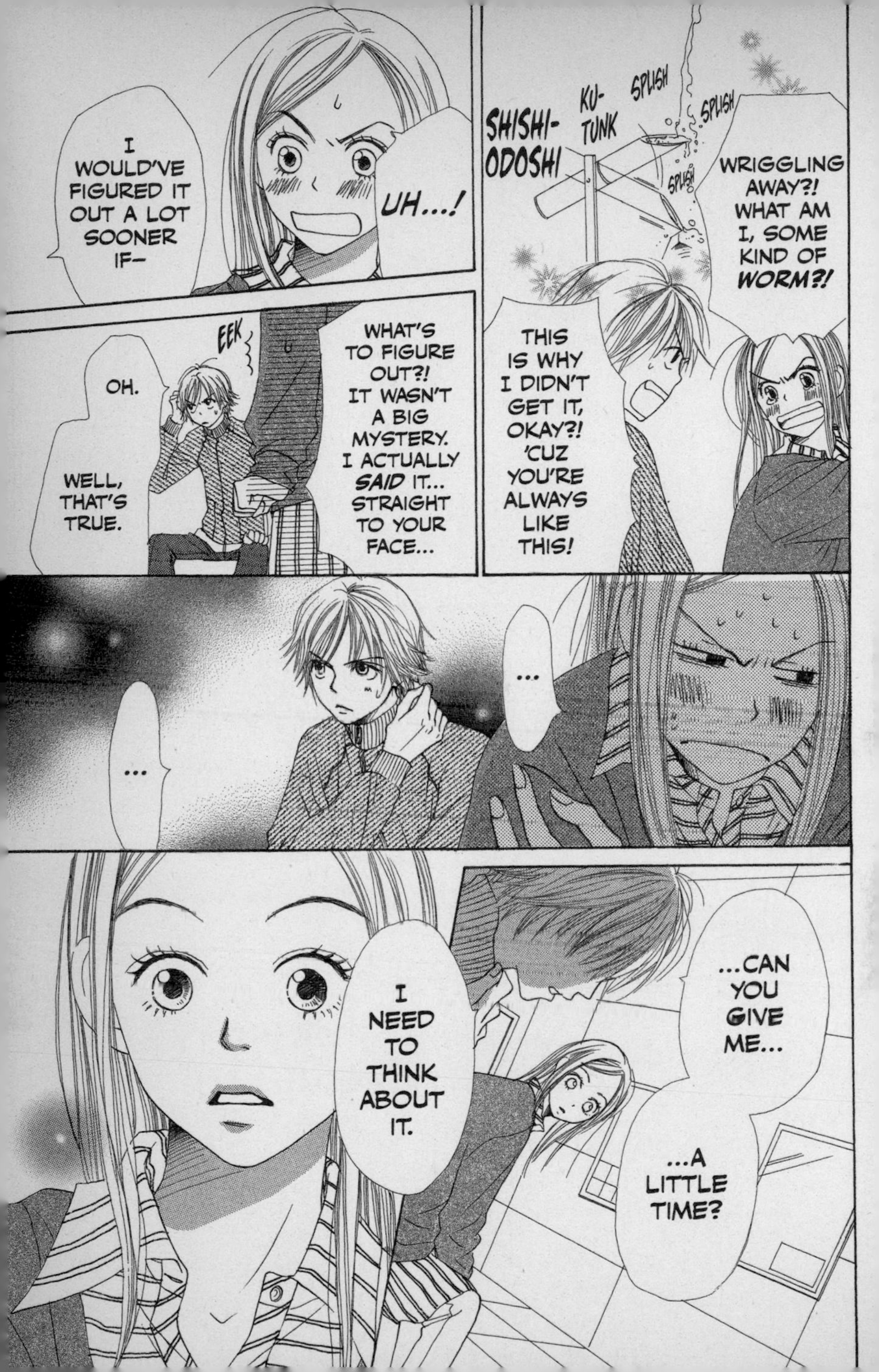
SHISHI-ODOSHI
KU-TUNK
SPLISH
SPLISH
SPLISH
WRIGGLING AWAY?! WHAT AM I, SOME KIND OF *WORM?!*
THIS IS WHY I DIDN'T GET IT, OKAY?! 'CUZ YOU'RE ALWAYS LIKE THIS!
UH...!
I WOULD'VE FIGURED IT OUT A LOT SOONER IF—
WHAT'S TO FIGURE OUT?! IT WASN'T A BIG MYSTERY. I ACTUALLY *SAID* IT... STRAIGHT TO YOUR FACE...
EEK
OH.
WELL, THAT'S TRUE.
...
...
...CAN YOU GIVE ME...
...A LITTLE TIME?
I NEED TO THINK ABOUT IT.

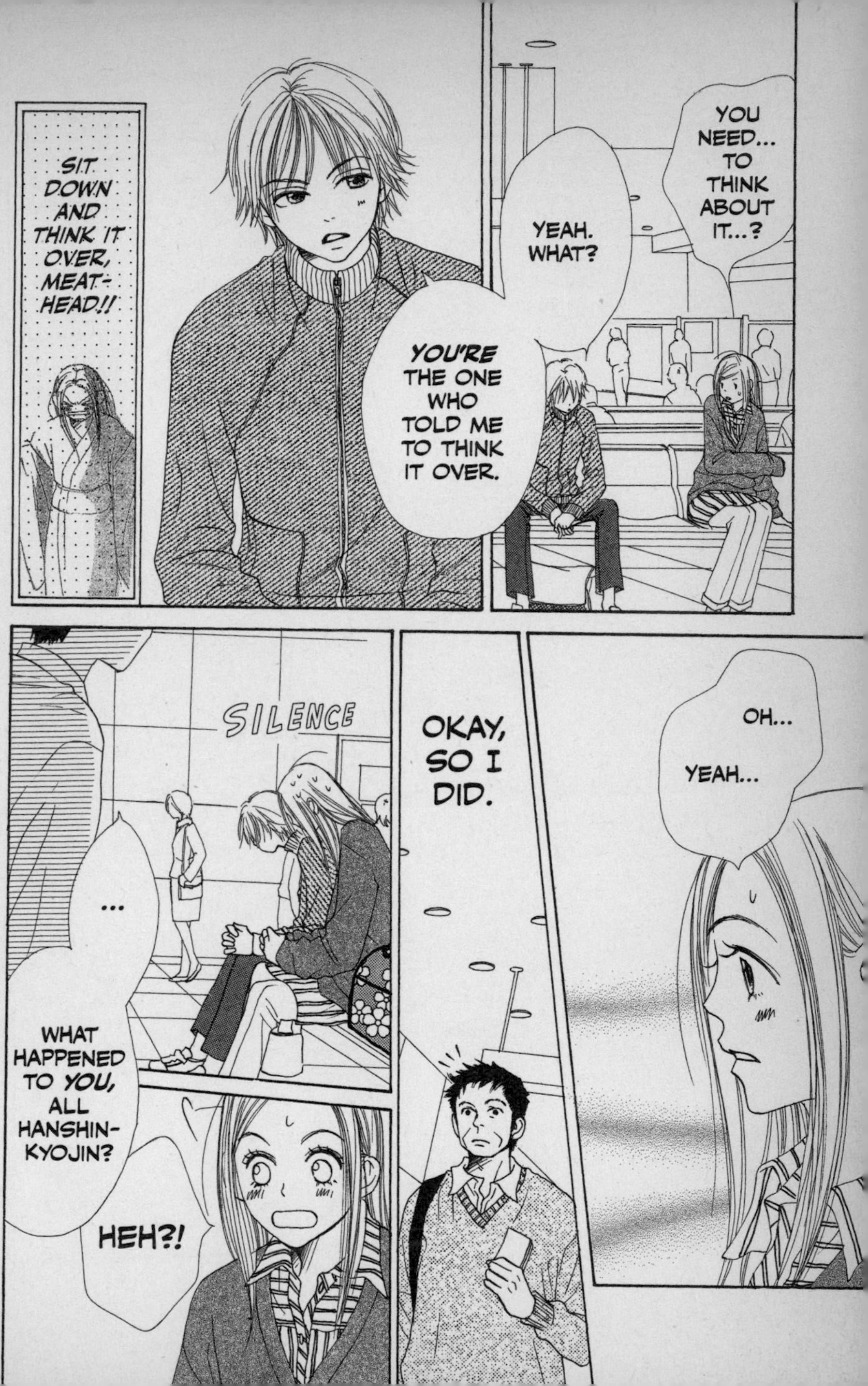
YOU NEED... TO THINK ABOUT IT...?
YEAH. WHAT?
YOU'RE THE ONE WHO TOLD ME TO THINK IT OVER.
SIT DOWN AND THINK IT OVER, MEAT-HEAD!!
OH... YEAH...
OKAY, SO I DID.
SILENCE
...
WHAT HAPPENED TO YOU, ALL HANSHIN-KYOJIN?
HEH?!

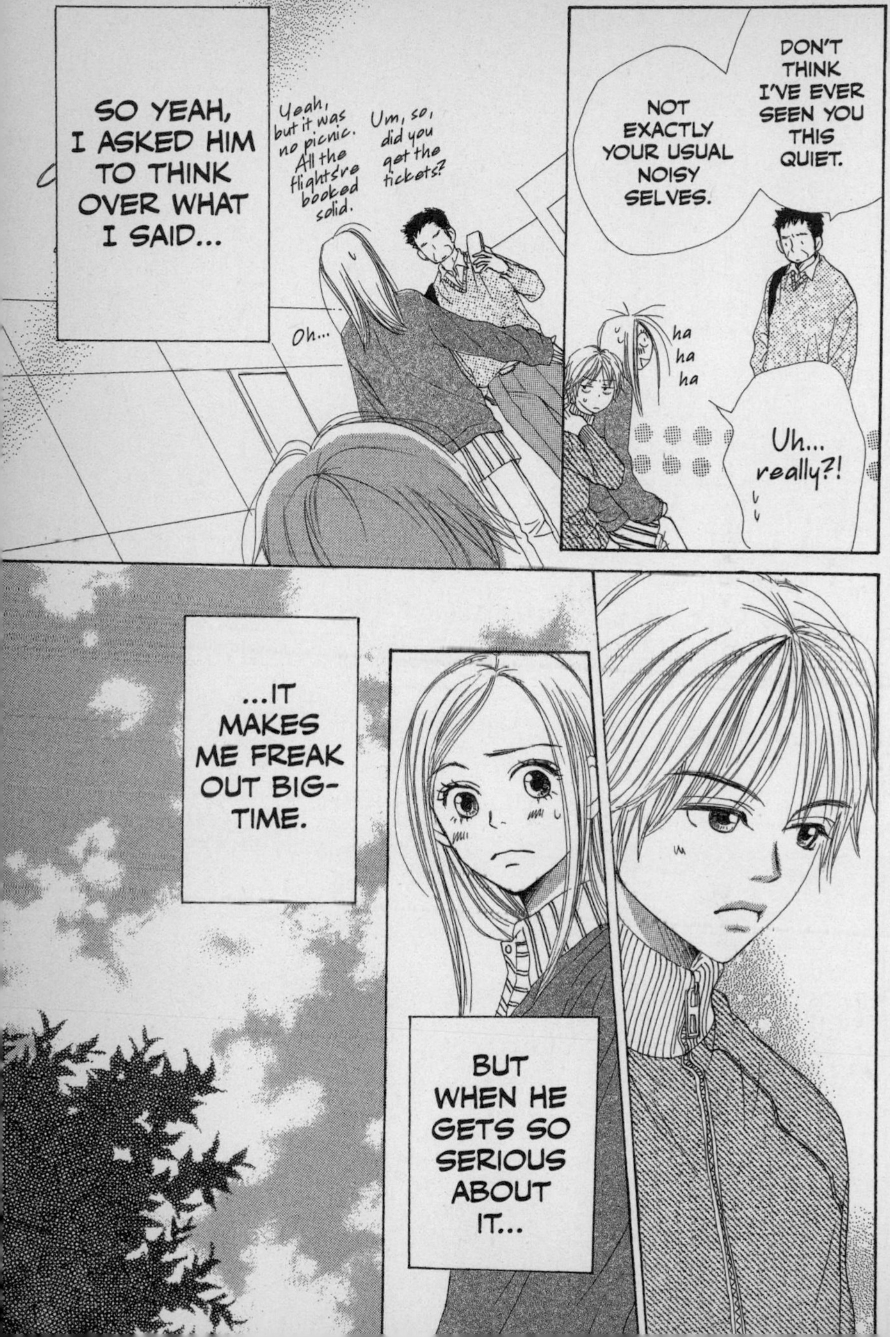
DON'T THINK I'VE EVER SEEN YOU THIS QUIET.
NOT EXACTLY YOUR USUAL NOISY SELVES.
ha ha ha
Uh... really?!
Um, so, did you get the tickets?
Yeah, but it was no picnic. All the flights're booked solid.
SO YEAH, I ASKED HIM TO THINK OVER WHAT I SAID...
Oh...
BUT WHEN HE GETS SO SERIOUS ABOUT IT...
...IT MAKES ME FREAK OUT BIG-TIME.

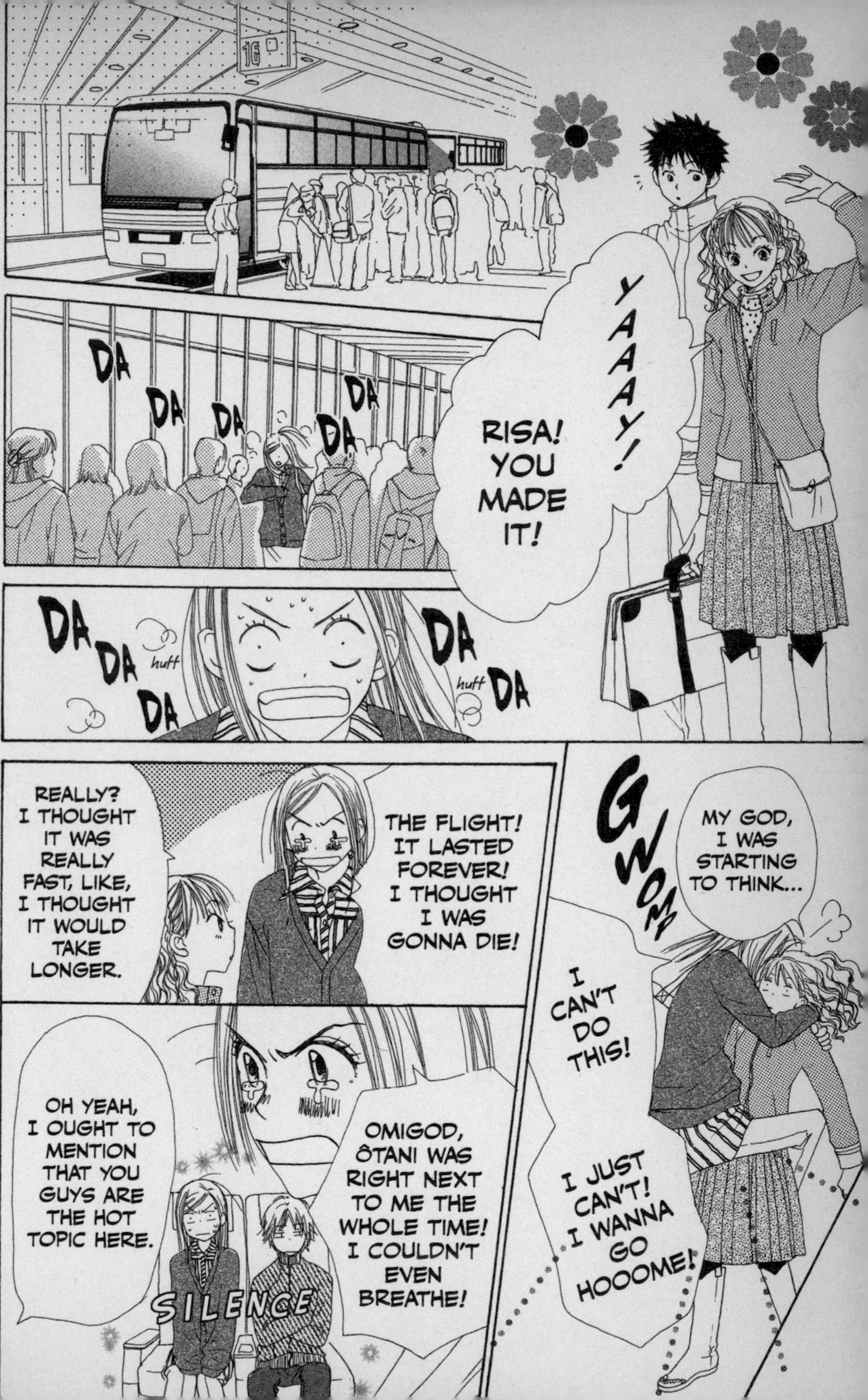
YAAAAY!
RISA! YOU MADE IT!
DA DA DA DA DA DA
DA DA DA huff
huff DA DA
GWOM
MY GOD, I WAS STARTING TO THINK...
I CAN'T DO THIS!
I JUST CAN'T! I WANNA GO HOOOME!
THE FLIGHT! IT LASTED FOREVER! I THOUGHT I WAS GONNA DIE!
REALLY? I THOUGHT IT WAS REALLY FAST, LIKE, I THOUGHT IT WOULD TAKE LONGER.
OMIGOD, ŌTANI WAS RIGHT NEXT TO ME THE WHOLE TIME! I COULDN'T EVEN BREATHE!
OH YEAH, I OUGHT TO MENTION THAT YOU GUYS ARE THE HOT TOPIC HERE.
SILENCE

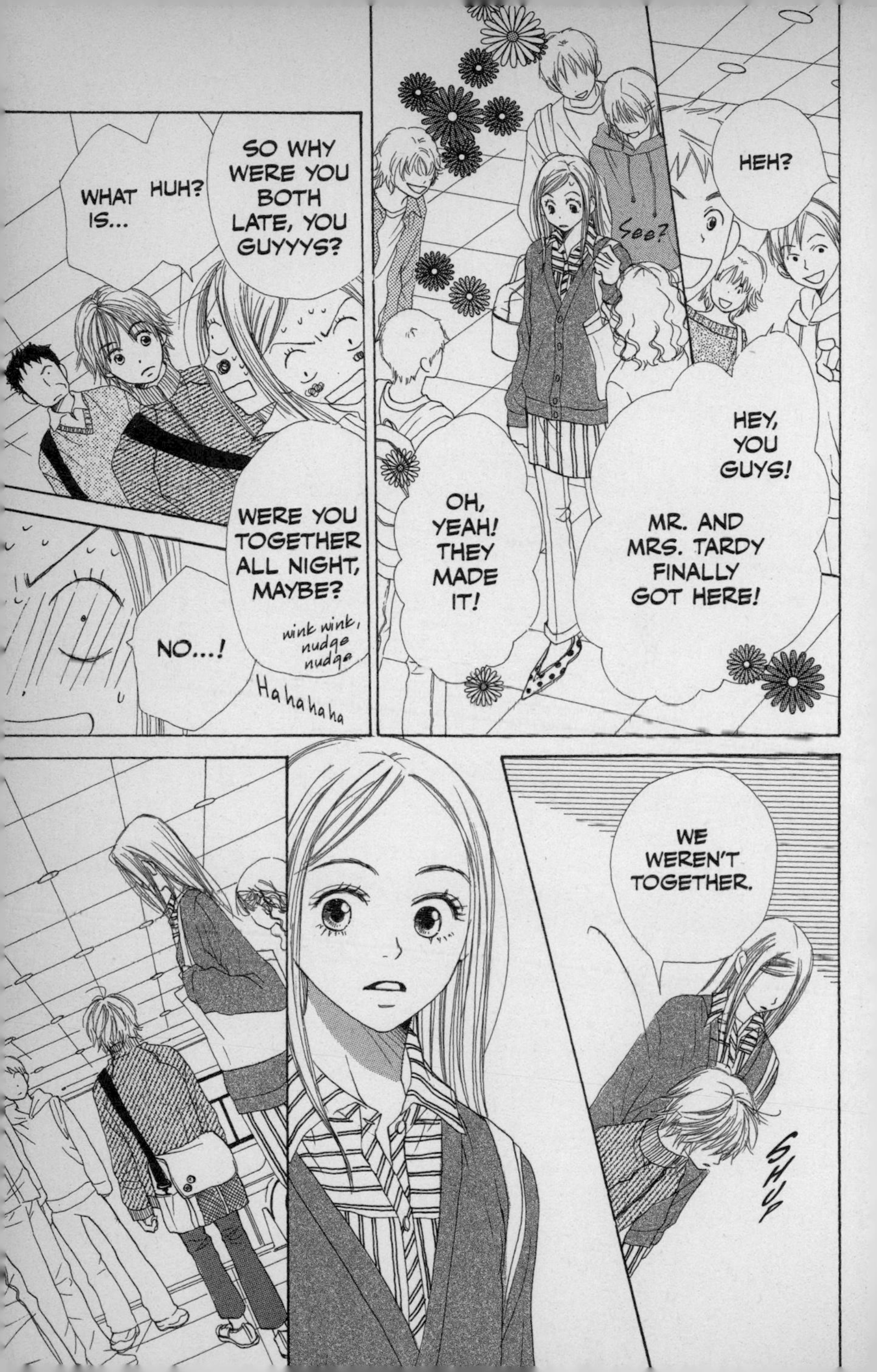
HEH?
HEY, YOU GUYS! MR. AND MRS. TARDY FINALLY GOT HERE!
OH, YEAH! THEY MADE IT!
See?
SO WHY WERE YOU BOTH LATE, YOU GUYYYS?
HUH?
WHAT IS...
WERE YOU TOGETHER ALL NIGHT, MAYBE?
wink wink, nudge nudge
NO...!
Hahahaha
WE WEREN'T TOGETHER.
SHUY

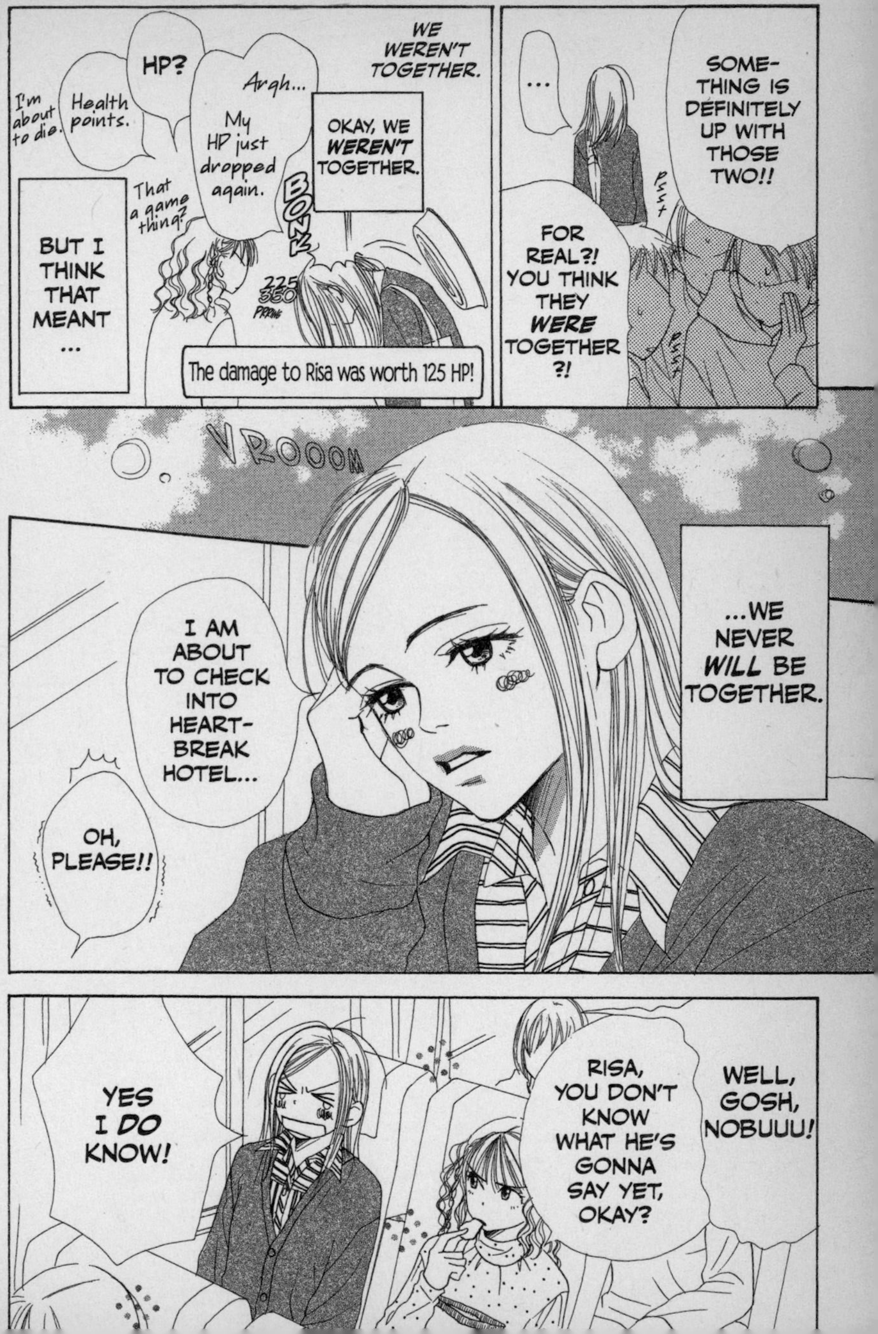
SOMETHING IS DEFINITELY UP WITH THOSE TWO!!
PSST
...
FOR REAL?! YOU THINK THEY WERE TOGETHER?!
PSST
WE WEREN'T TOGETHER.
OKAY, WE WEREN'T TOGETHER.
Argh... My HP just dropped again.
BONK
HP?
Health points.
I'm about to die.
That a game thing?
225 350
BUT I THINK THAT MEANT ...
The damage to Risa was worth 125 HP!
VROOOM
...WE NEVER WILL BE TOGETHER.
I AM ABOUT TO CHECK INTO HEARTBREAK HOTEL...
OH, PLEASE!!
WELL, GOSH, NOBUUU!
RISA, YOU DON'T KNOW WHAT HE'S GONNA SAY YET, OKAY?
YES I DO KNOW!

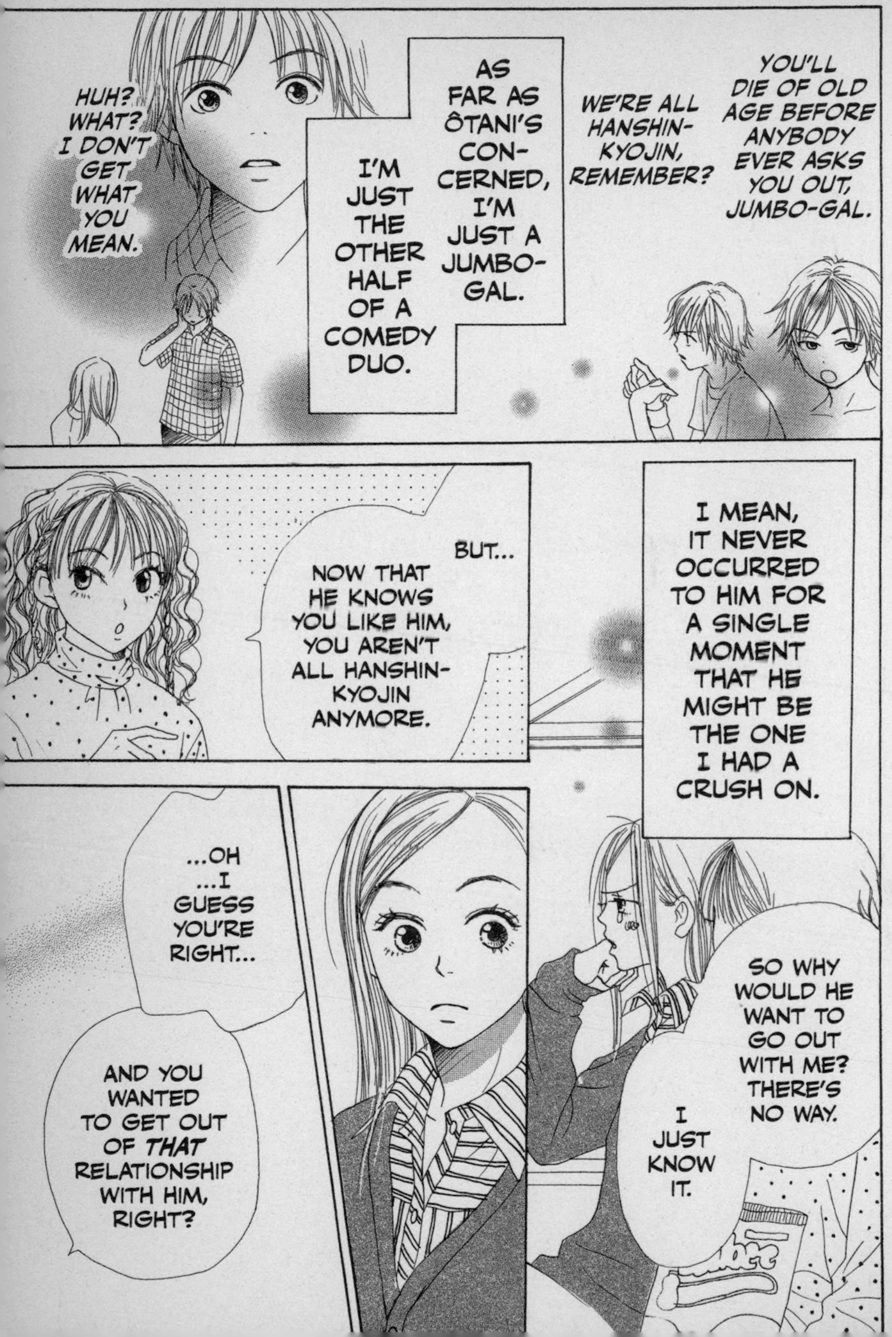
YOU'LL DIE OF OLD AGE BEFORE ANYBODY EVER ASKS YOU OUT, JUMBO-GAL.
WE'RE ALL HANSHIN-KYOJIN, REMEMBER?
AS FAR AS ÔTANI'S CONCERNED, I'M JUST A JUMBO-GAL.
I'M JUST THE OTHER HALF OF A COMEDY DUO.
HUH? WHAT? I DON'T GET WHAT YOU MEAN.
I MEAN, IT NEVER OCCURRED TO HIM FOR A SINGLE MOMENT THAT HE MIGHT BE THE ONE I HAD A CRUSH ON.
BUT...
NOW THAT HE KNOWS YOU LIKE HIM, YOU AREN'T ALL HANSHIN-KYOJIN ANYMORE.
SO WHY WOULD HE WANT TO GO OUT WITH ME? THERE'S NO WAY.
I JUST KNOW IT.
...OH ...I GUESS YOU'RE RIGHT...
AND YOU WANTED TO GET OUT OF *THAT* RELATIONSHIP WITH HIM, RIGHT?

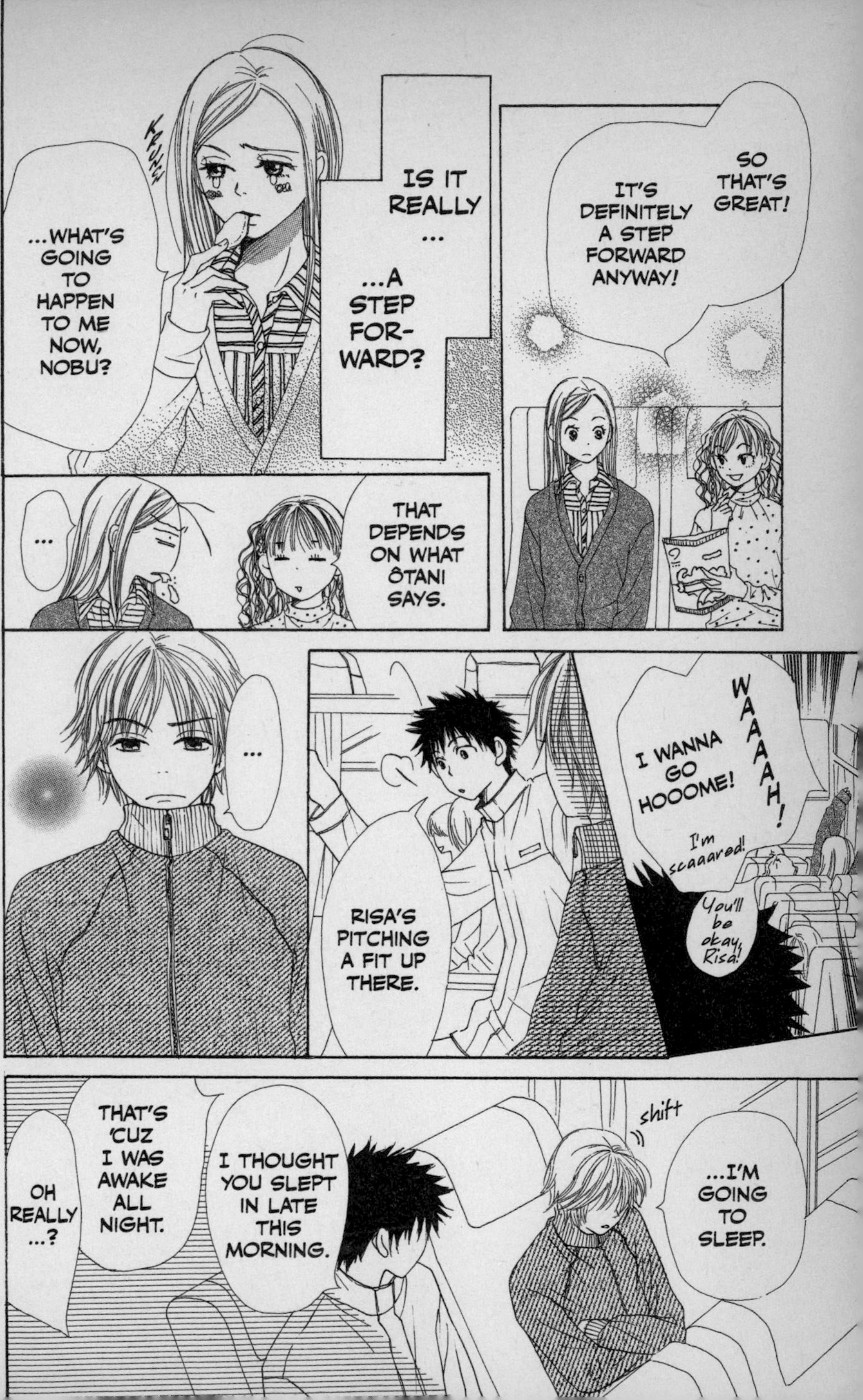
SO THAT'S GREAT!
IT'S DEFINITELY A STEP FORWARD ANYWAY!
IS IT REALLY ...
...A STEP FOR-WARD?
KRUNCH
...WHAT'S GOING TO HAPPEN TO ME NOW, NOBU?
THAT DEPENDS ON WHAT ŌTANI SAYS.
...
WAAAAH!
I WANNA GO HOOOME!
I'm scaaared!
You'll be okay, Risa!
RISA'S PITCHING A FIT UP THERE.
...
...I'M GOING TO SLEEP.
shift
I THOUGHT YOU SLEPT IN LATE THIS MORNING.
THAT'S 'CUZ I WAS AWAKE ALL NIGHT.
OH REALLY ...?

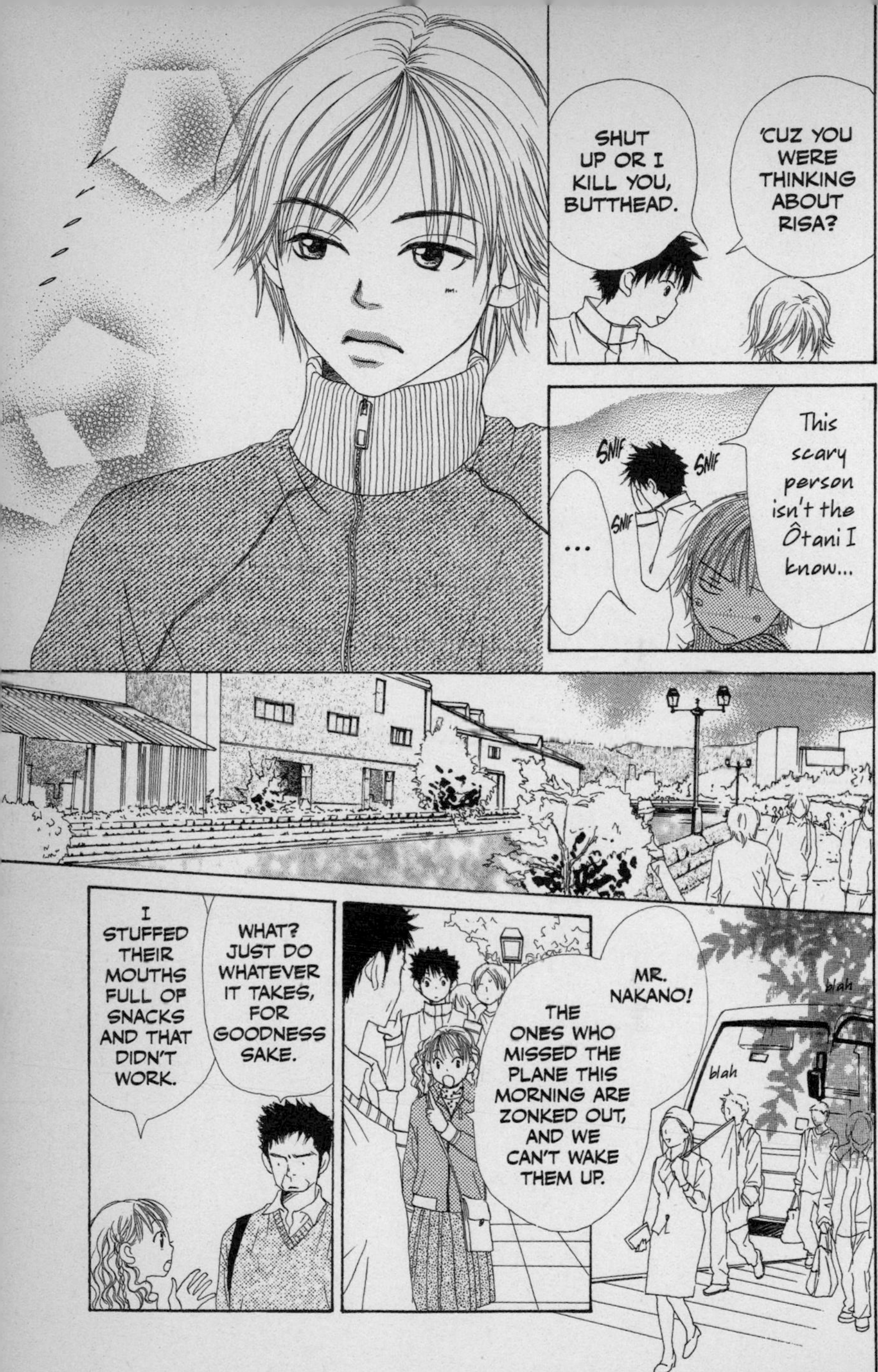

'CUZ YOU WERE THINKING ABOUT RISA?
SHUT UP OR I KILL YOU, BUTTHEAD.
This scary person isn't the Ôtani I know...
SNIF
SNIF
SNIF
...
MR. NAKANO!
THE ONES WHO MISSED THE PLANE THIS MORNING ARE ZONKED OUT, AND WE CAN'T WAKE THEM UP.
blah
blah
WHAT? JUST DO WHATEVER IT TAKES, FOR GOODNESS SAKE.
I STUFFED THEIR MOUTHS FULL OF SNACKS AND THAT DIDN'T WORK.

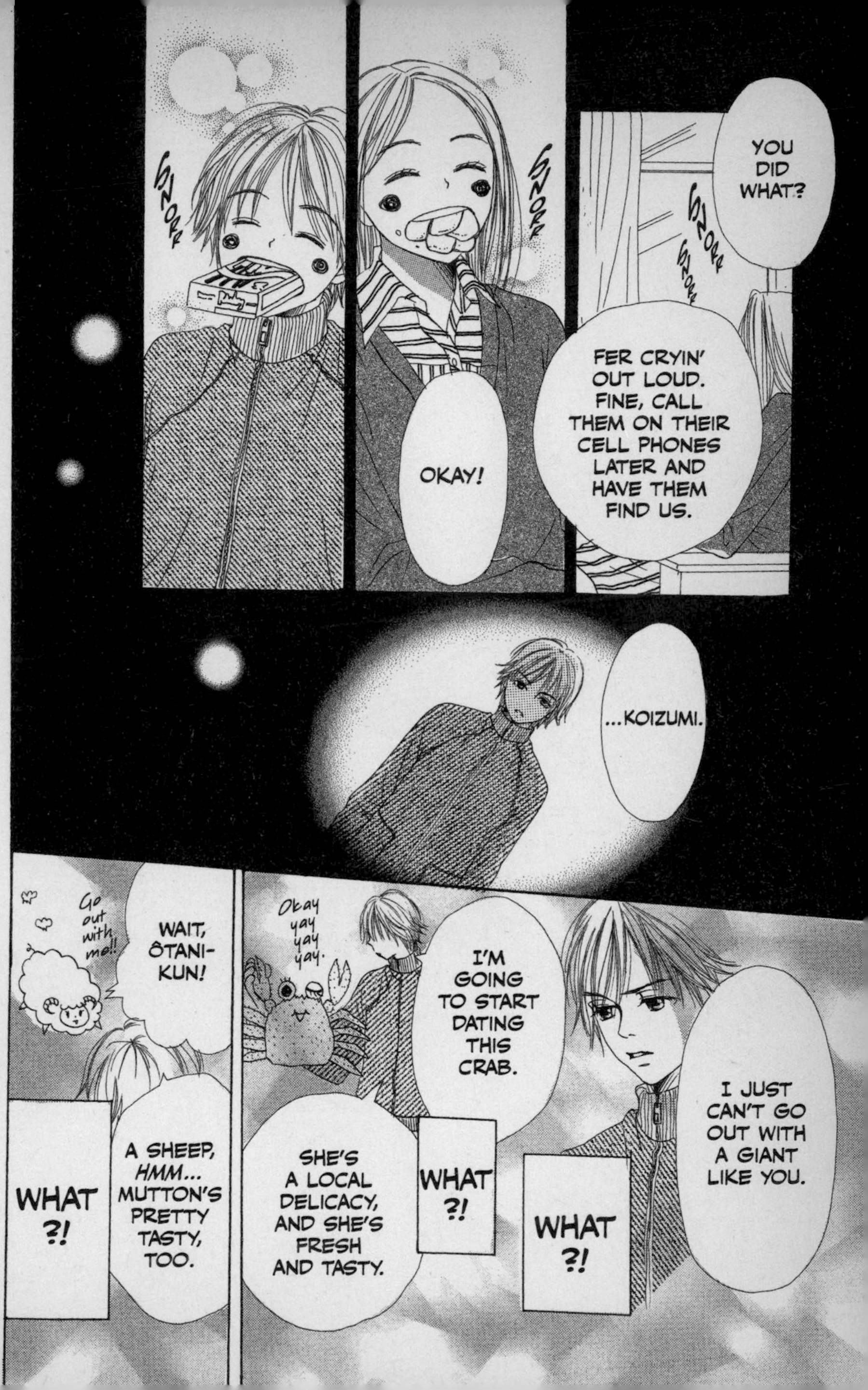
YOU DID WHAT?
SNORK
SNORK
FER CRYIN' OUT LOUD. FINE, CALL THEM ON THEIR CELL PHONES LATER AND HAVE THEM FIND US.
SNORK
OKAY!
SNORK
...KOIZUMI.
I JUST CAN'T GO OUT WITH A GIANT LIKE YOU.
WHAT ?!
I'M GOING TO START DATING THIS CRAB.
Okay yay yay yay.
SHE'S A LOCAL DELICACY, AND SHE'S FRESH AND TASTY.
WHAT ?!
WAIT, ŌTANI-KUN!
Go out with me!!
A SHEEP, *HMM*... MUTTON'S PRETTY TASTY, TOO.
WHAT ?!

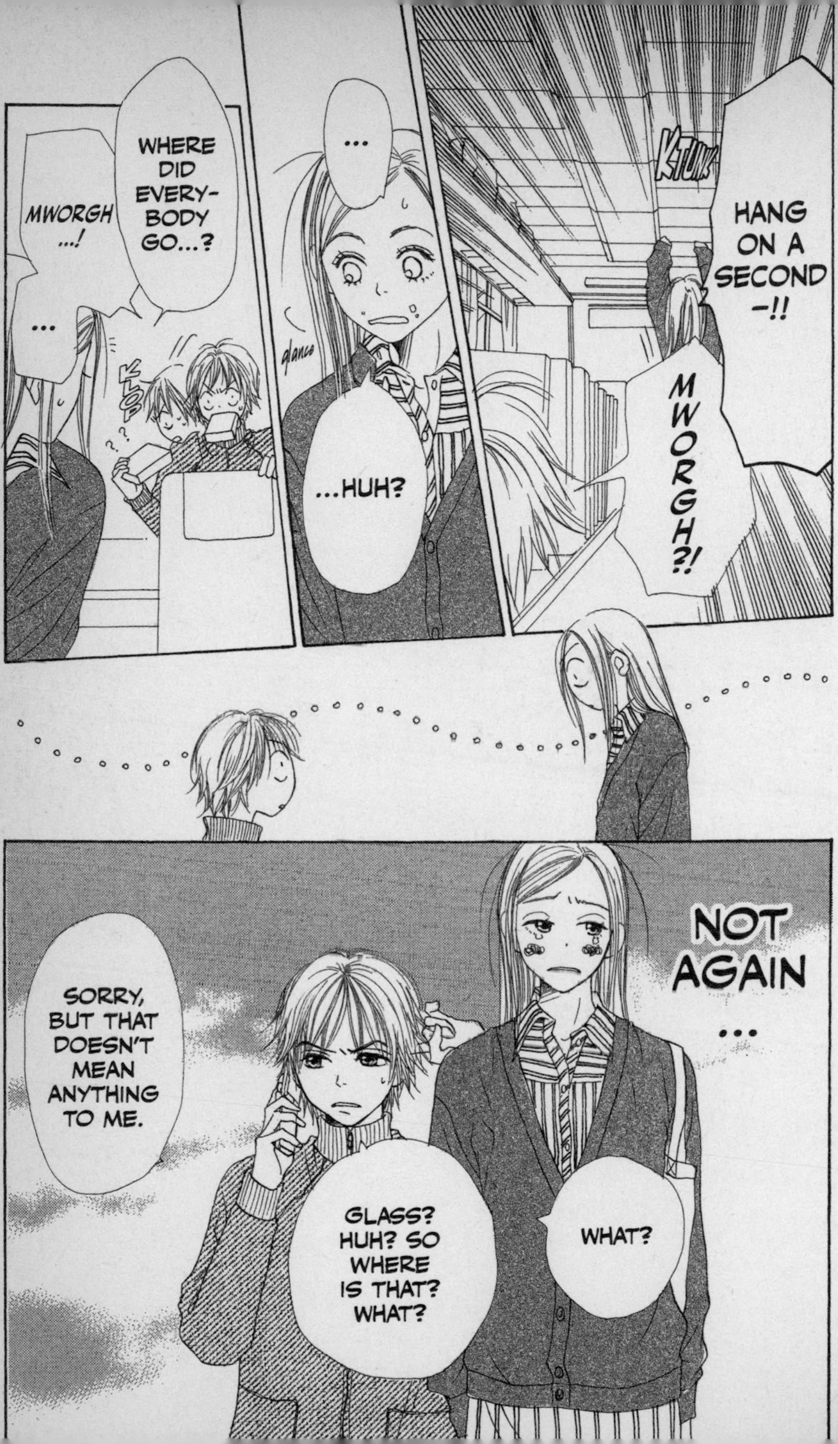
KTUK
HANG ON A SECOND—!!
MWORGH?!
...
glance
...HUH?
WHERE DID EVERY-BODY GO...?
MWORGH...!
...
KLOP
??
NOT AGAIN...
WHAT?
GLASS? HUH? SO WHERE IS THAT? WHAT?
SORRY, BUT THAT DOESN'T MEAN ANYTHING TO ME.

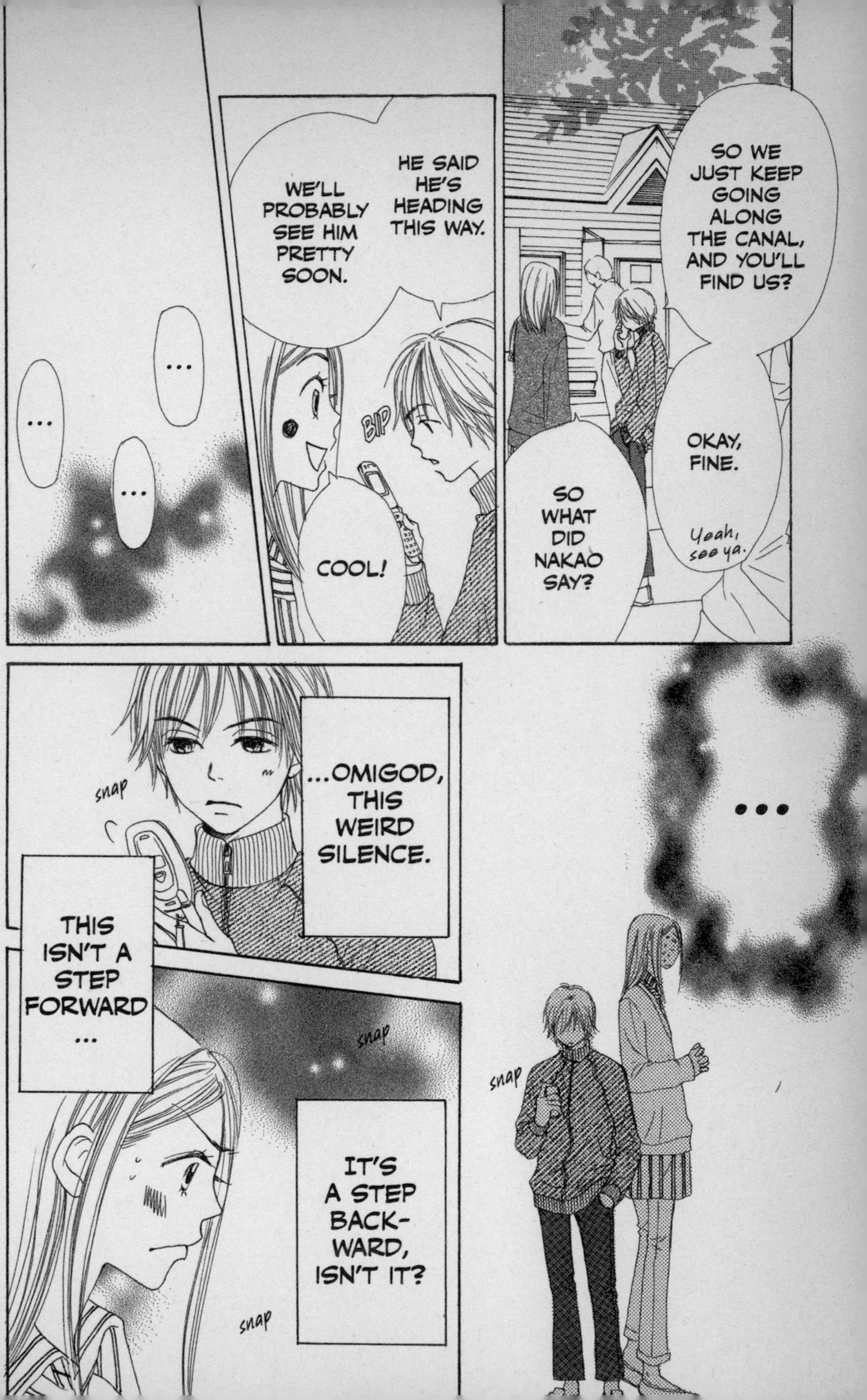
SO WE JUST KEEP GOING ALONG THE CANAL, AND YOU'LL FIND US?
OKAY, FINE.
Yeah, see ya.
SO WHAT DID NAKAO SAY?
HE SAID HE'S HEADING THIS WAY.
WE'LL PROBABLY SEE HIM PRETTY SOON.
BIP
COOL!
...
...
...
...
snap
snap
...OMIGOD, THIS WEIRD SILENCE.
THIS ISN'T A STEP FORWARD ...
snap
IT'S A STEP BACKWARD, ISN'T IT?
snap

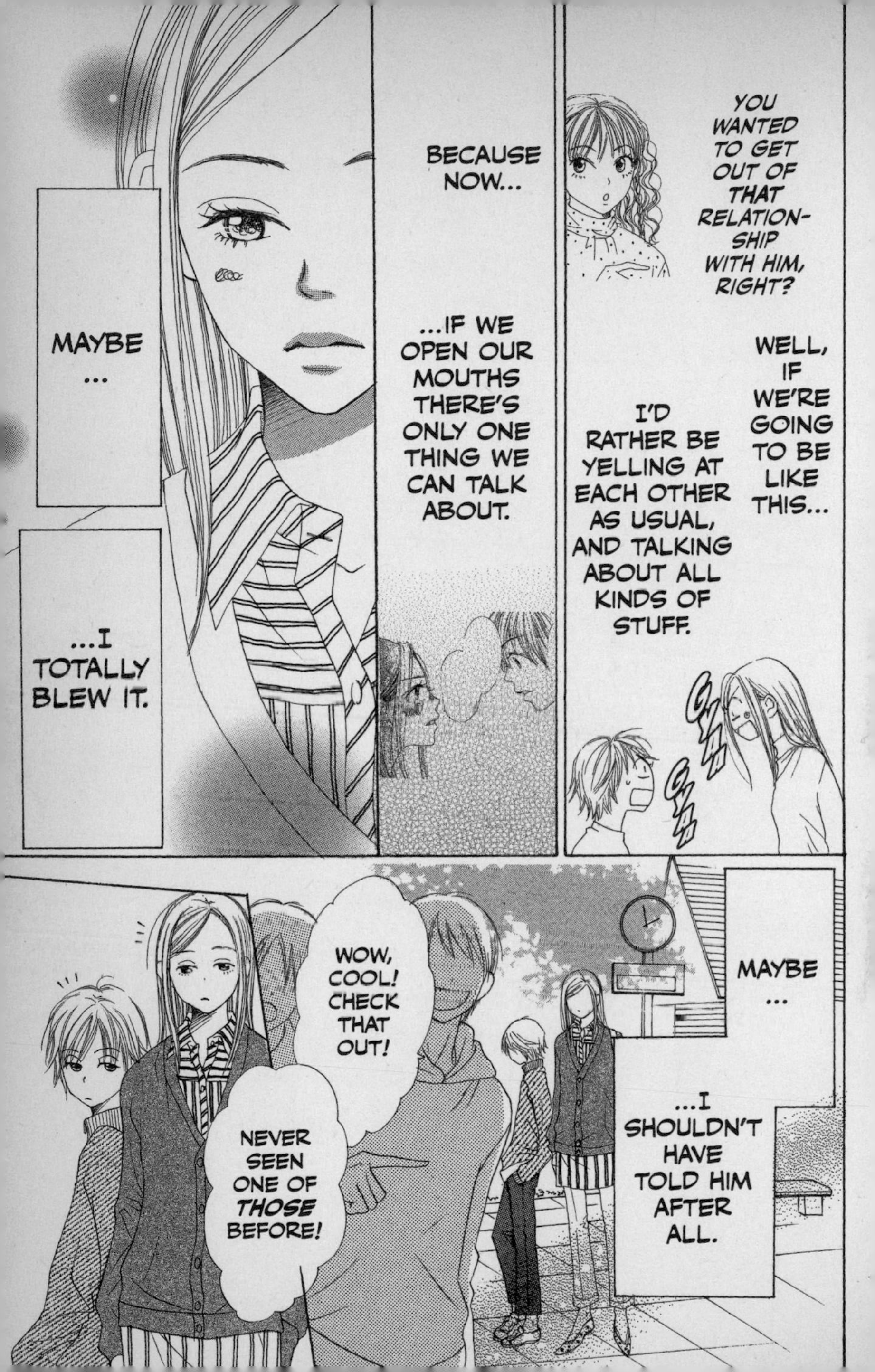
YOU WANTED TO GET OUT OF THAT RELATIONSHIP WITH HIM, RIGHT?
WELL, IF WE'RE GOING TO BE LIKE THIS...
I'D RATHER BE YELLING AT EACH OTHER AS USUAL, AND TALKING ABOUT ALL KINDS OF STUFF.
BECAUSE NOW...
...IF WE OPEN OUR MOUTHS THERE'S ONLY ONE THING WE CAN TALK ABOUT.
MAYBE ...
...I TOTALLY BLEW IT.
MAYBE ...
...I SHOULDN'T HAVE TOLD HIM AFTER ALL.
WOW, COOL! CHECK THAT OUT!
NEVER SEEN ONE OF *THOSE* BEFORE!

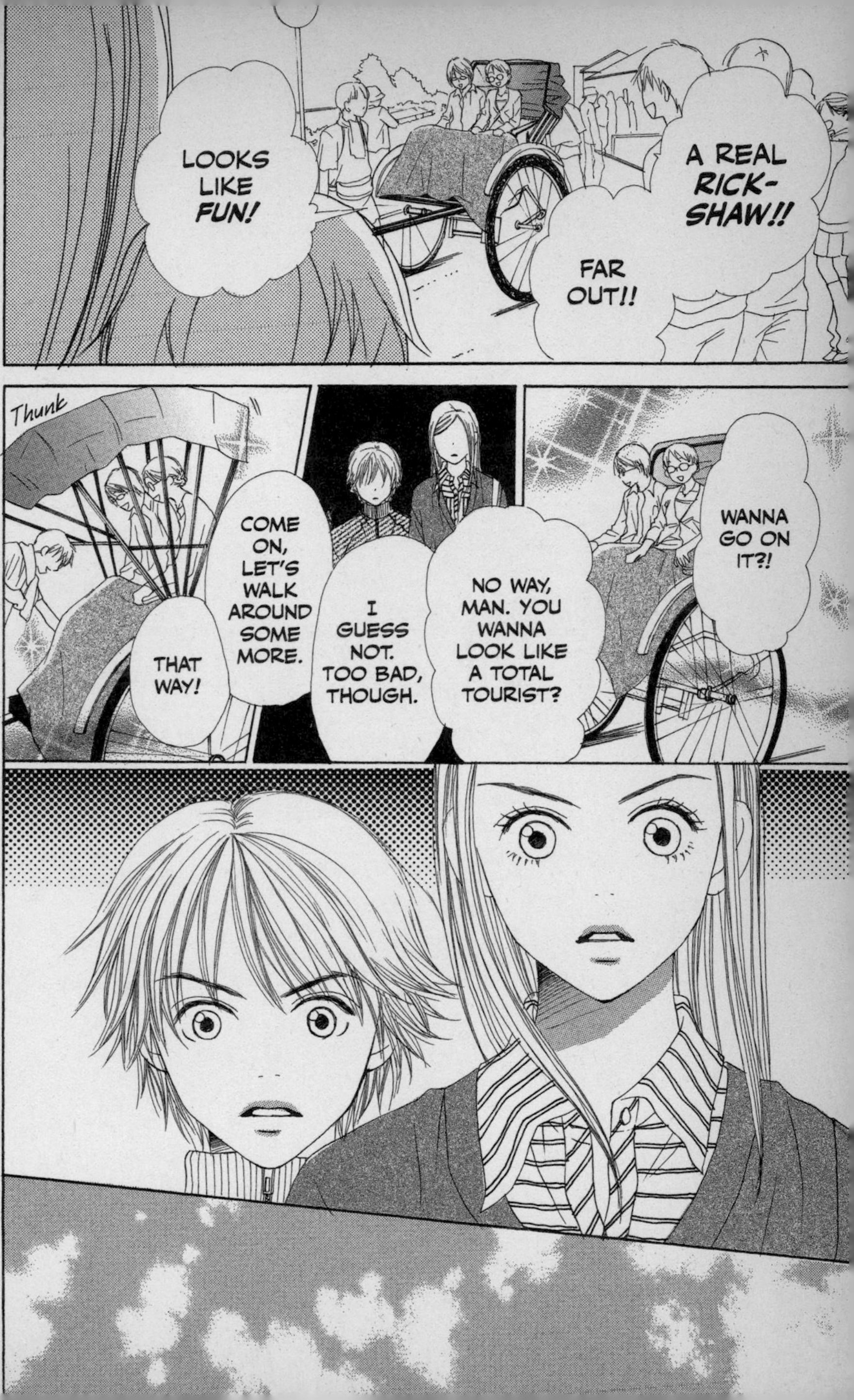
A REAL RICK-SHAW!!
FAR OUT!!
LOOKS LIKE FUN!
WANNA GO ON IT?!
NO WAY, MAN. YOU WANNA LOOK LIKE A TOTAL TOURIST?
I GUESS NOT. TOO BAD, THOUGH.
Thunk
COME ON, LET'S WALK AROUND SOME MORE.
THAT WAY!

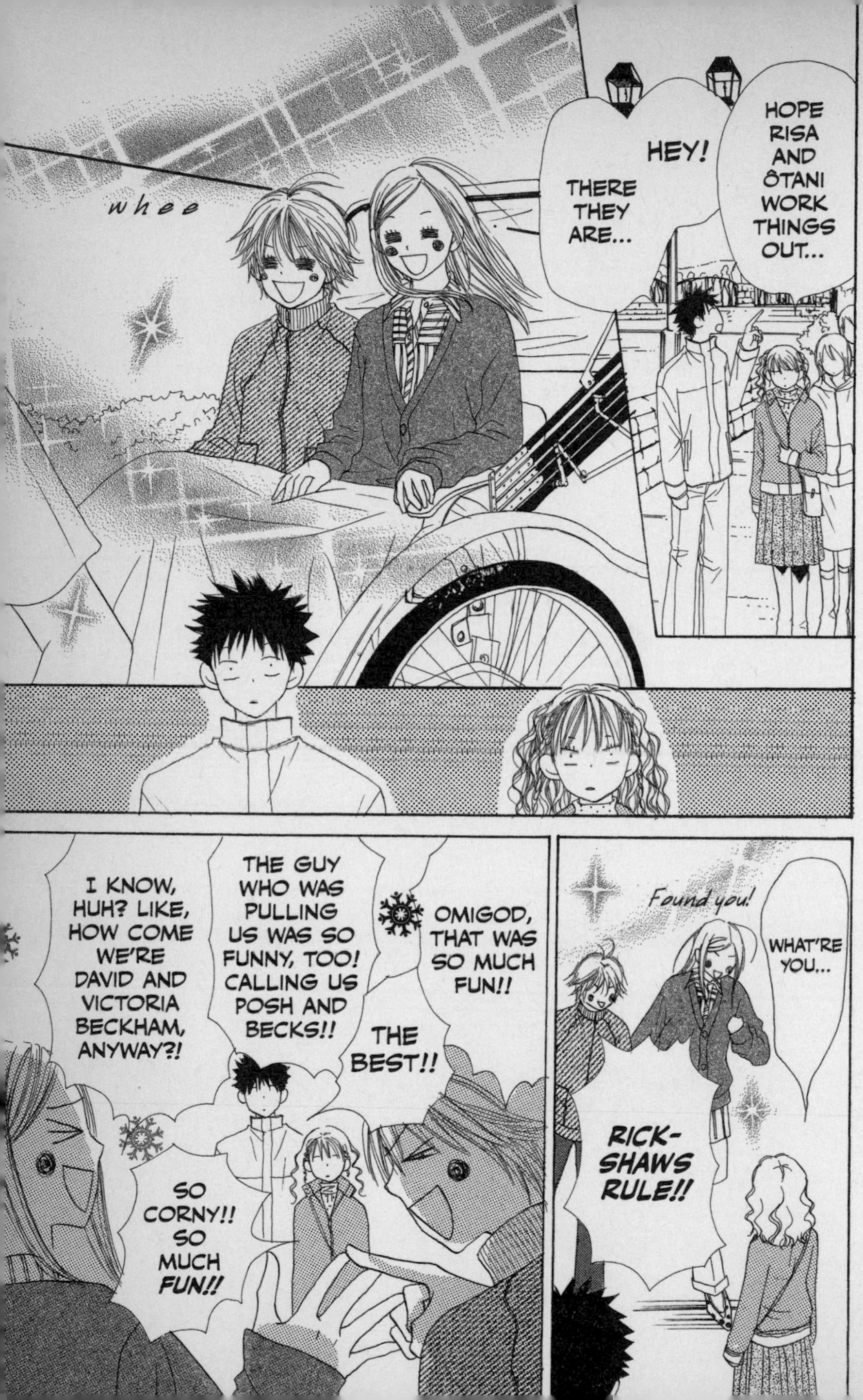
HOPE RISA AND ŌTANI WORK THINGS OUT...
HEY!
THERE THEY ARE...
whee
WHAT'RE YOU...
Found you!
RICK-SHAWS RULE!!
OMIGOD, THAT WAS SO MUCH FUN!!
THE BEST!!
THE GUY WHO WAS PULLING US WAS SO FUNNY, TOO! CALLING US POSH AND BECKS!!
I KNOW, HUH? LIKE, HOW COME WE'RE DAVID AND VICTORIA BECKHAM, ANYWAY?!
SO CORNY!! SO MUCH FUN!!

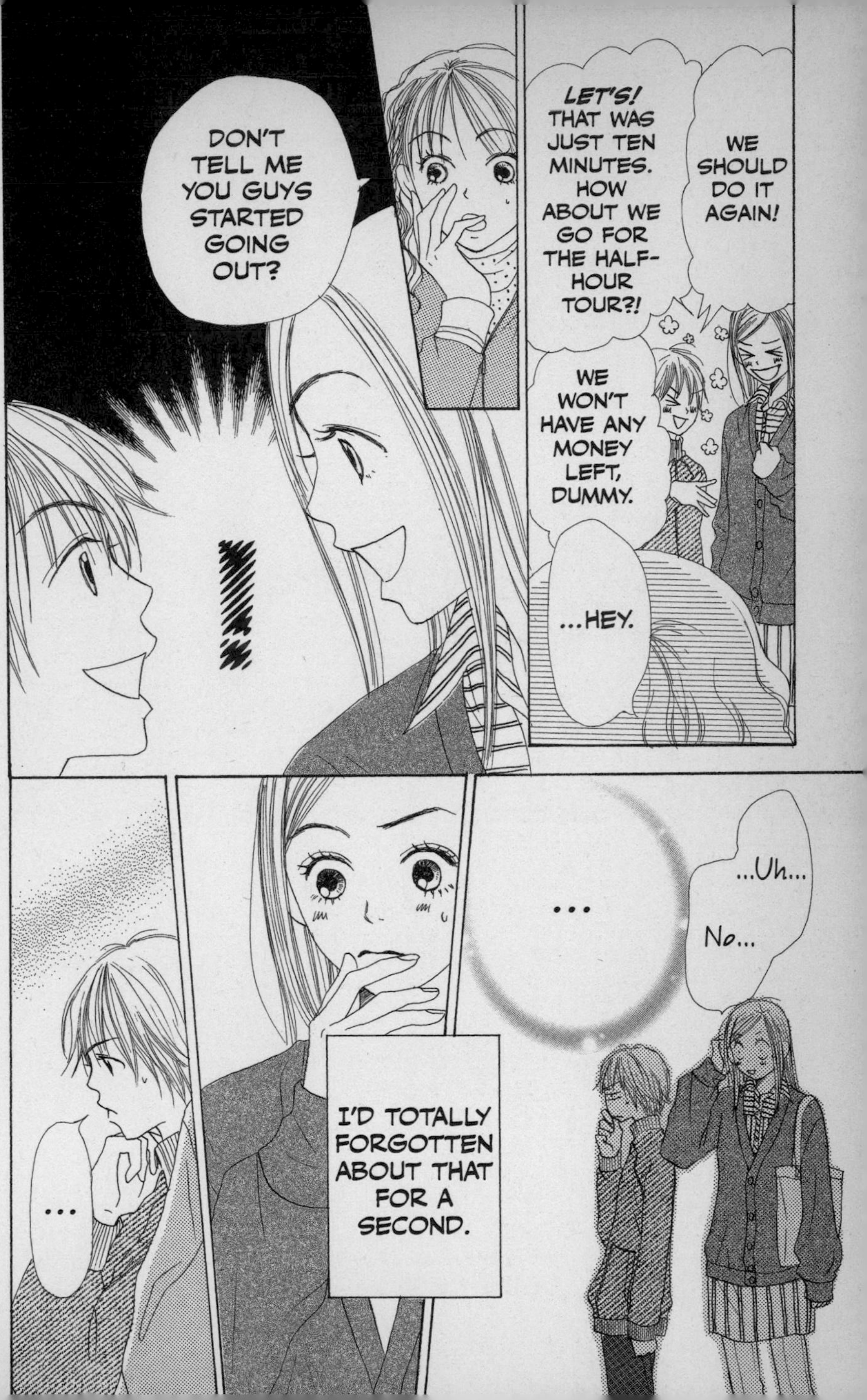
WE SHOULD DO IT AGAIN!
LET'S! THAT WAS JUST TEN MINUTES. HOW ABOUT WE GO FOR THE HALF-HOUR TOUR?!
WE WON'T HAVE ANY MONEY LEFT, DUMMY.
...HEY.
DON'T TELL ME YOU GUYS STARTED GOING OUT?
!
...Uh...
No...
...
I'D TOTALLY FORGOTTEN ABOUT THAT FOR A SECOND.
...

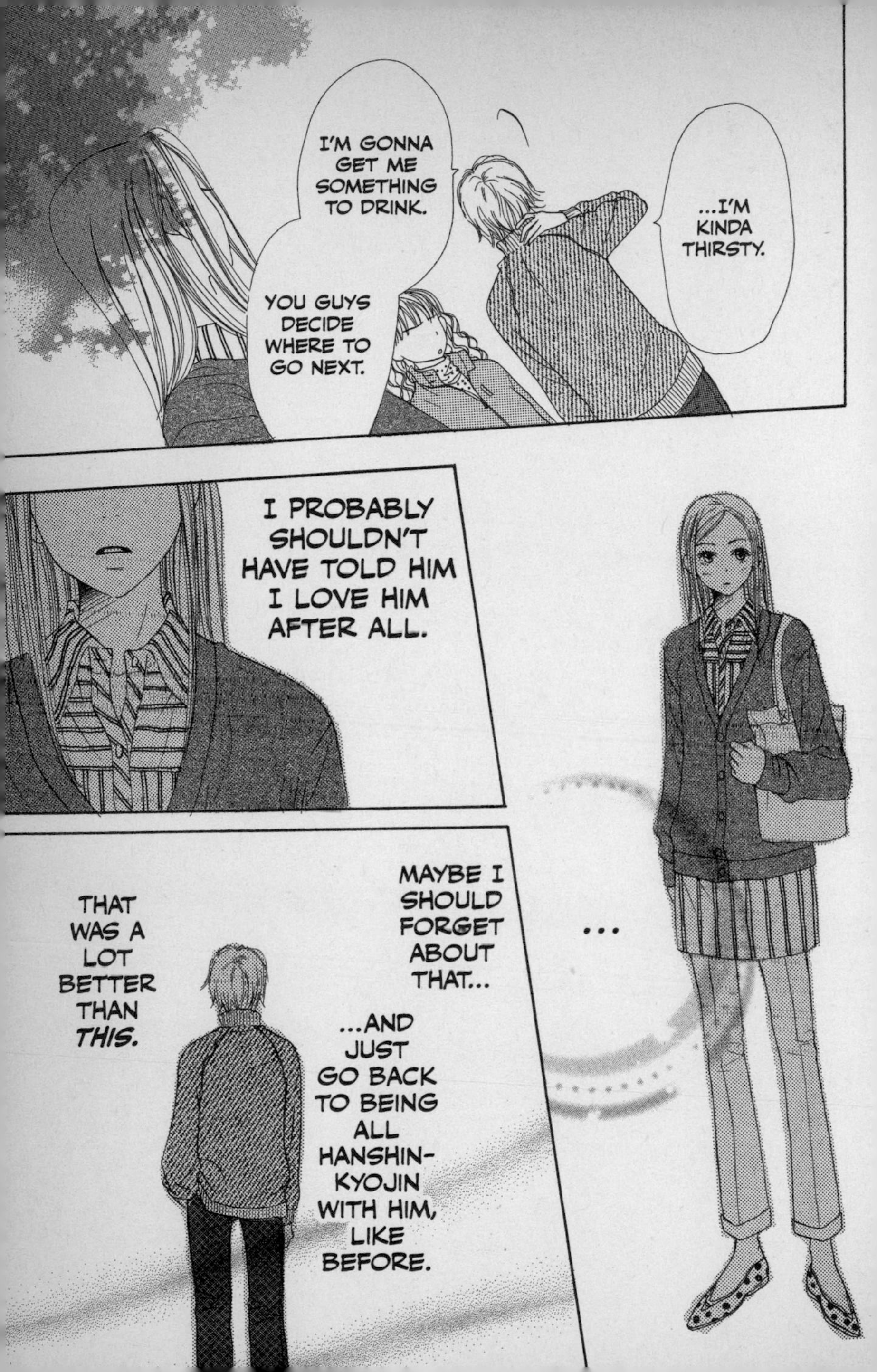
...I'M KINDA THIRSTY.
I'M GONNA GET ME SOMETHING TO DRINK.
YOU GUYS DECIDE WHERE TO GO NEXT.
...
I PROBABLY SHOULDN'T HAVE TOLD HIM I LOVE HIM AFTER ALL.
MAYBE I SHOULD FORGET ABOUT THAT...
...AND JUST GO BACK TO BEING ALL HANSHIN-KYOJIN WITH HIM, LIKE BEFORE.
THAT WAS A LOT BETTER THAN *THIS.*

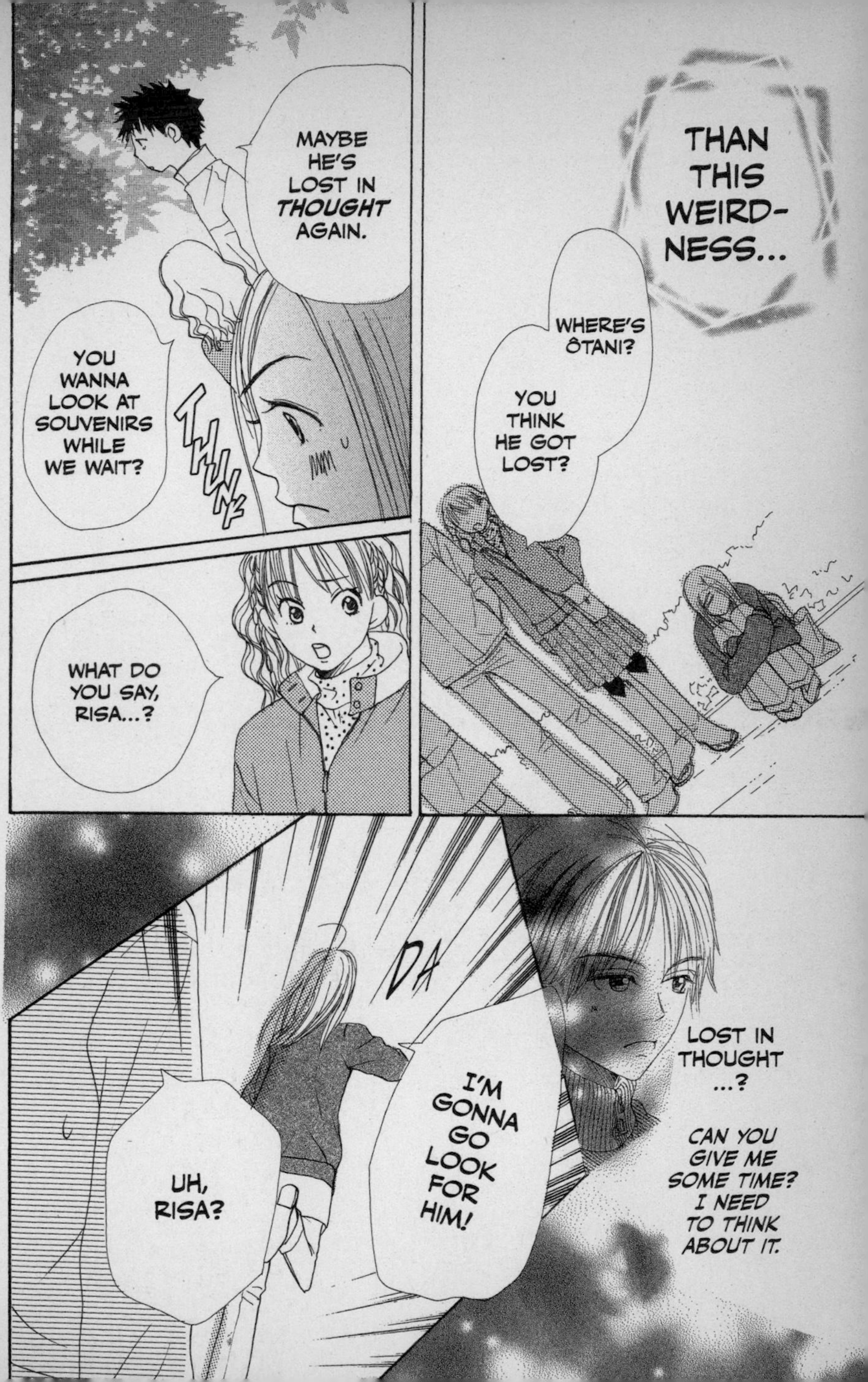

THAN THIS WEIRD-NESS...
WHERE'S ÔTANI?
YOU THINK HE GOT LOST?
MAYBE HE'S LOST IN *THOUGHT* AGAIN.
THUNK
YOU WANNA LOOK AT SOUVENIRS WHILE WE WAIT?
WHAT DO YOU SAY, RISA...?
LOST IN THOUGHT ...?
CAN YOU GIVE ME SOME TIME? I NEED TO THINK ABOUT IT.
I'M GONNA GO LOOK FOR HIM!
DA
UH, RISA?

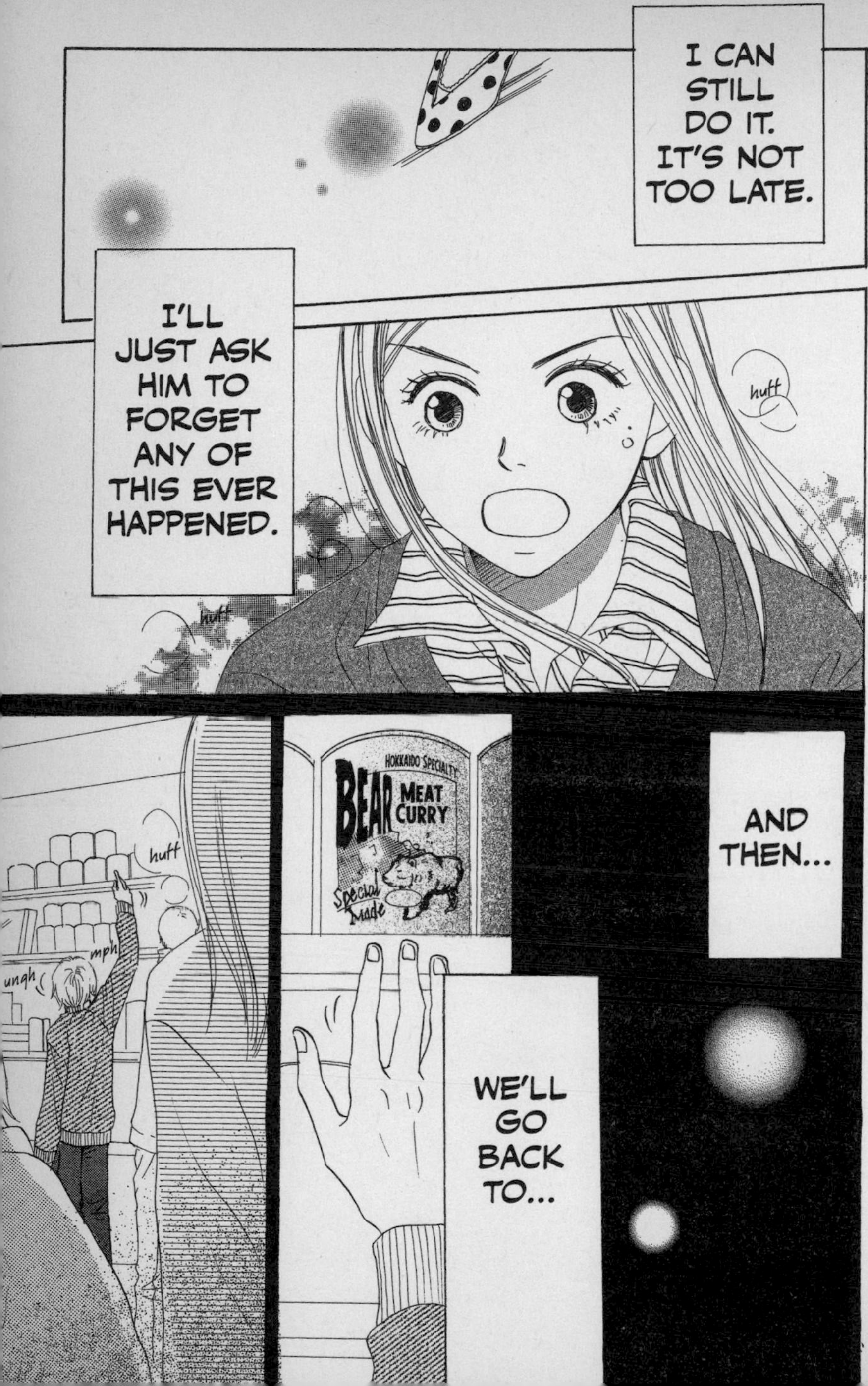
I CAN STILL DO IT. IT'S NOT TOO LATE.
I'LL JUST ASK HIM TO FORGET ANY OF THIS EVER HAPPENED.
huff
huff
AND THEN...
WE'LL GO BACK TO...
HOKKAIDO SPECIALTY
BEAR MEAT CURRY
Special Made
huff
mph
unngh

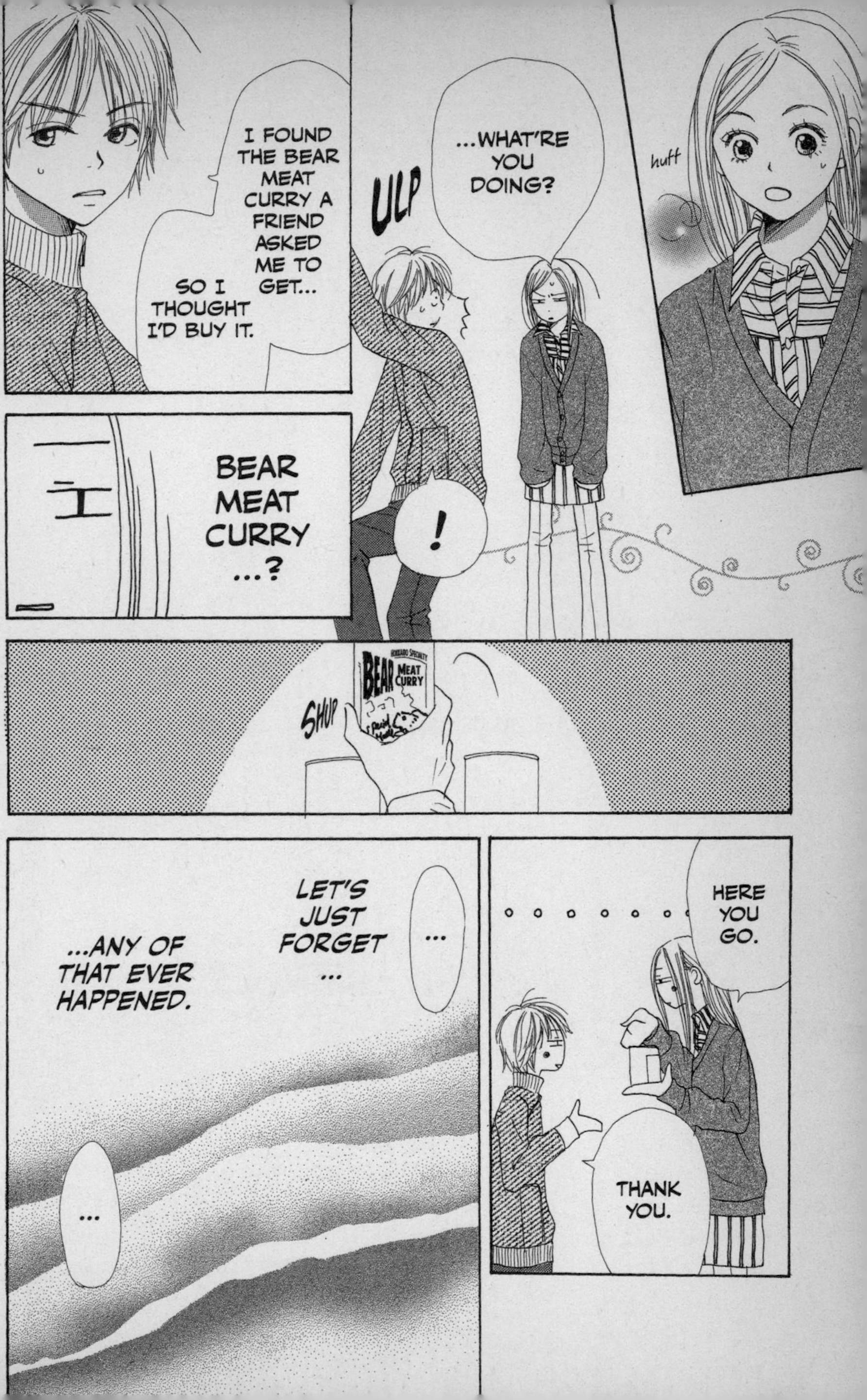
huff
ULP
...WHAT'RE YOU DOING?
!
I FOUND THE BEAR MEAT CURRY A FRIEND ASKED ME TO GET...
SO I THOUGHT I'D BUY IT.
BEAR MEAT CURRY ...?
BEAR MEAT CURRY
SHUP
....
HERE YOU GO.
THANK YOU.
...
LET'S JUST FORGET ...
...ANY OF THAT EVER HAPPENED.
...

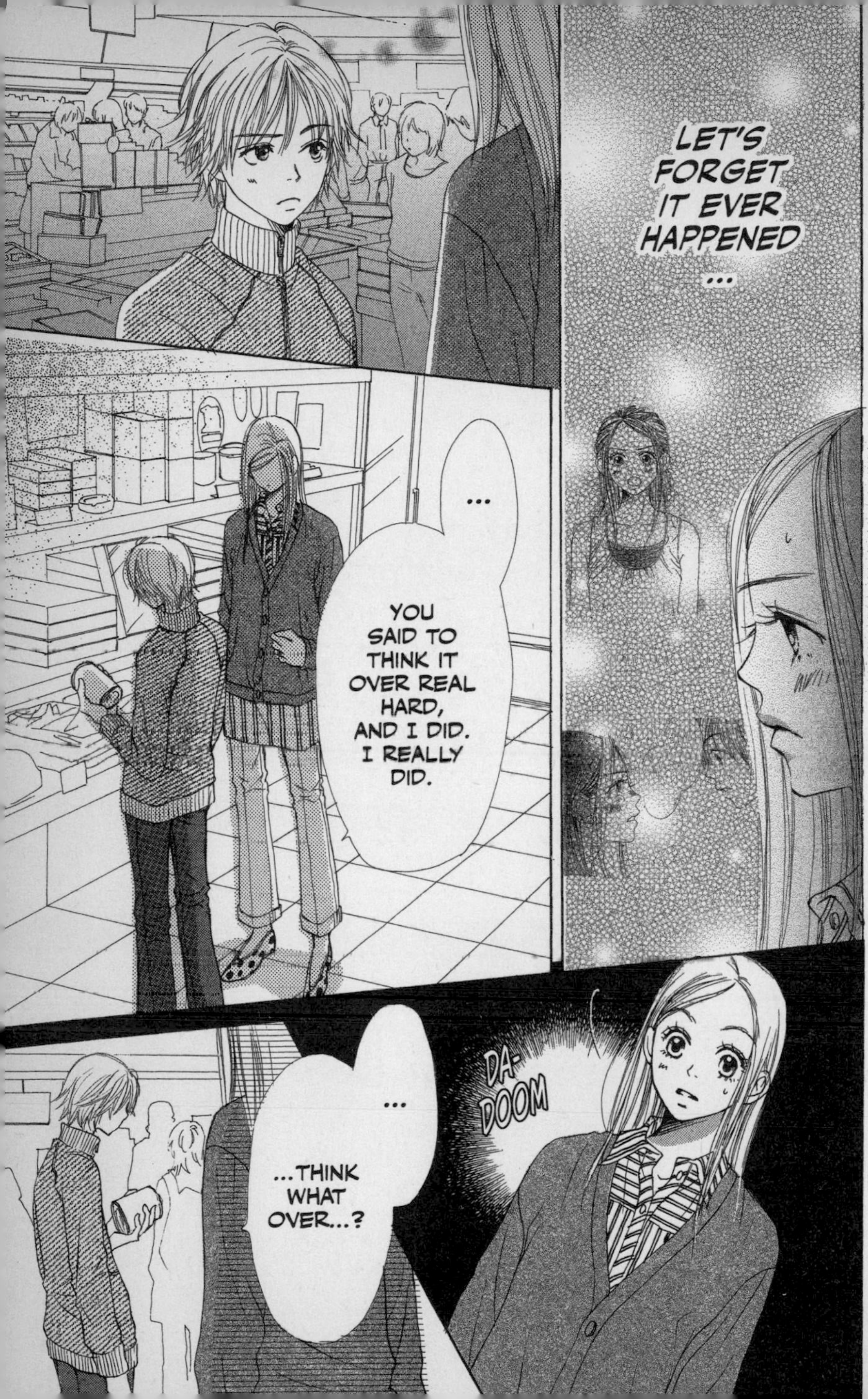
LET'S FORGET IT EVER HAPPENED ...
... YOU SAID TO THINK IT OVER REAL HARD, AND I DID. I REALLY DID.
DA-DOOM
... ...THINK WHAT OVER...?

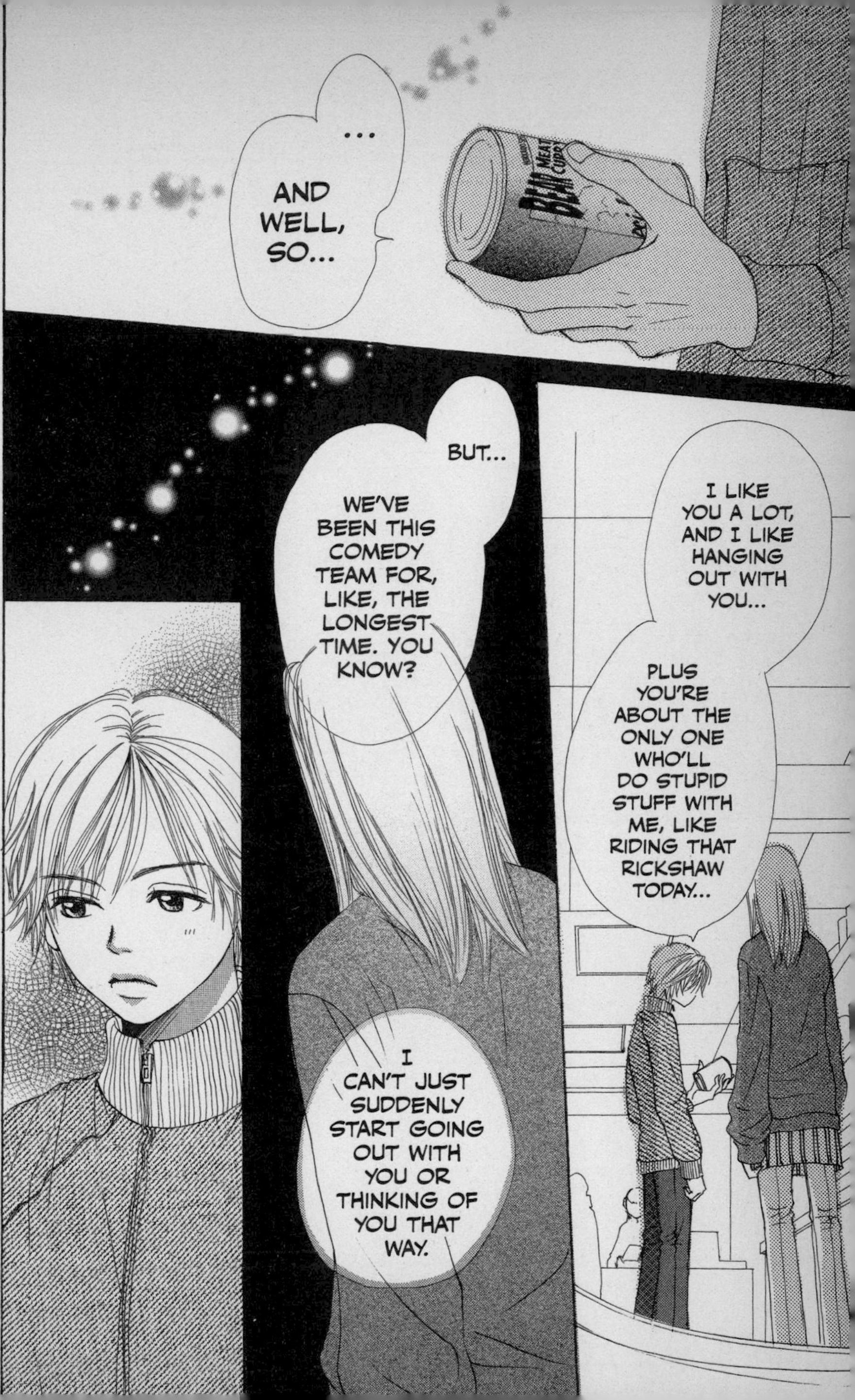
...
AND WELL, SO...
I LIKE YOU A LOT, AND I LIKE HANGING OUT WITH YOU...
PLUS YOU'RE ABOUT THE ONLY ONE WHO'LL DO STUPID STUFF WITH ME, LIKE RIDING THAT RICKSHAW TODAY...
BUT...
WE'VE BEEN THIS COMEDY TEAM FOR, LIKE, THE LONGEST TIME. YOU KNOW?
I CAN'T JUST SUDDENLY START GOING OUT WITH YOU OR THINKING OF YOU THAT WAY.

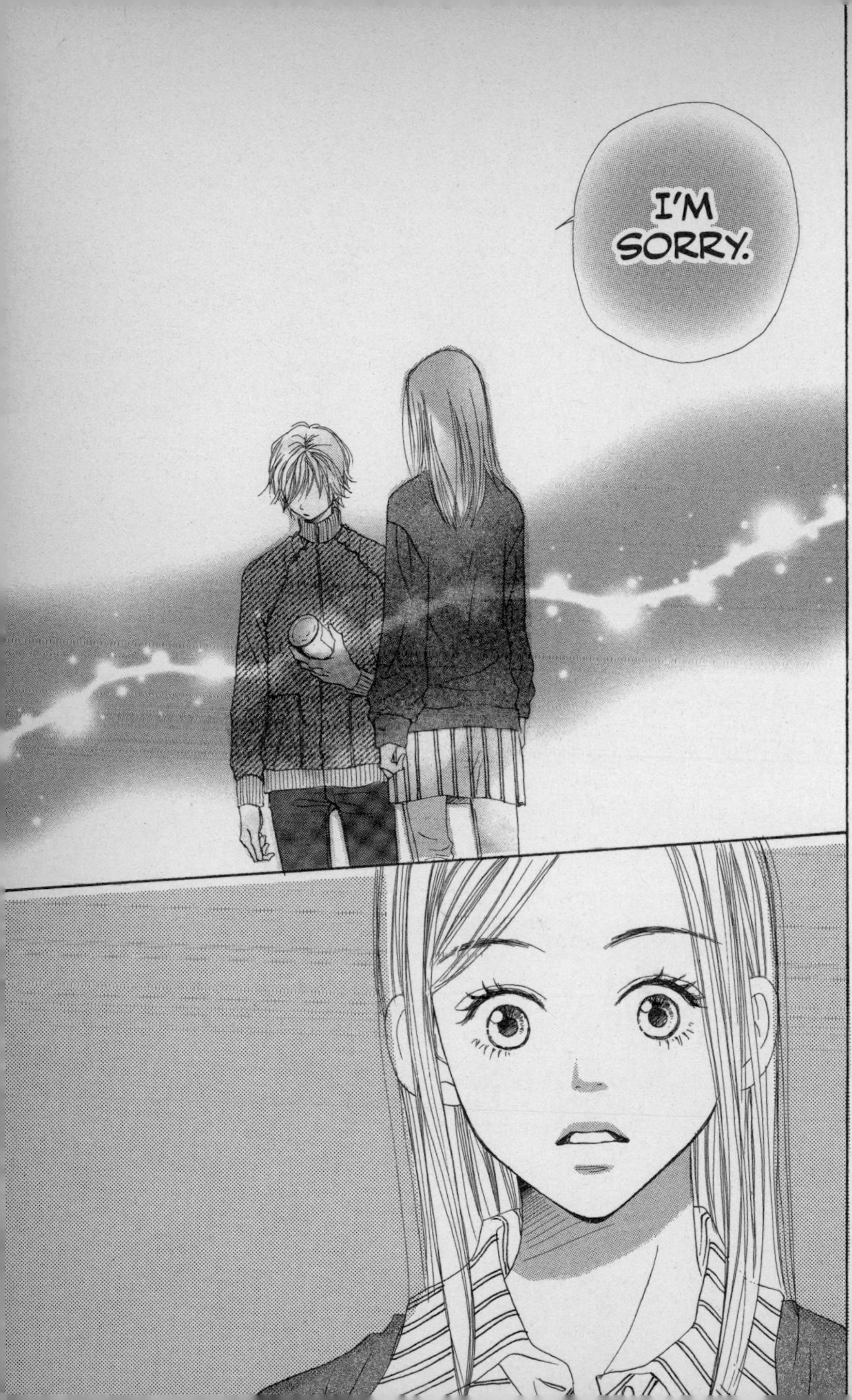
I'M SORRY.

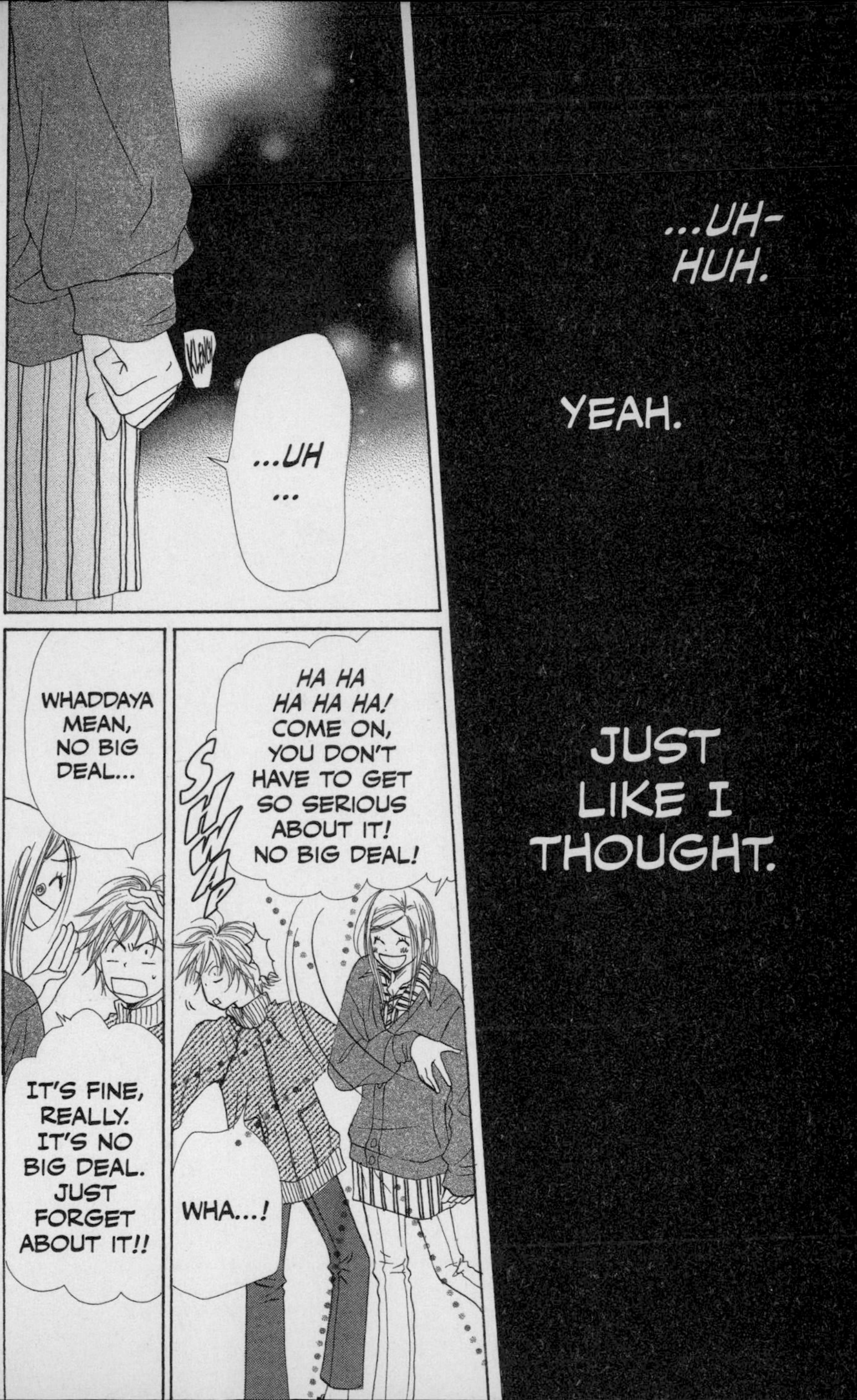
...UH-HUH.
YEAH.
JUST LIKE I THOUGHT.
KLENCH
...UH ...
HA HA HA HA HA! COME ON, YOU DON'T HAVE TO GET SO SERIOUS ABOUT IT! NO BIG DEAL!
SHWAP
WHA...!
WHADDAYA MEAN, NO BIG DEAL...
IT'S FINE, REALLY. IT'S NO BIG DEAL. JUST FORGET ABOUT IT!!

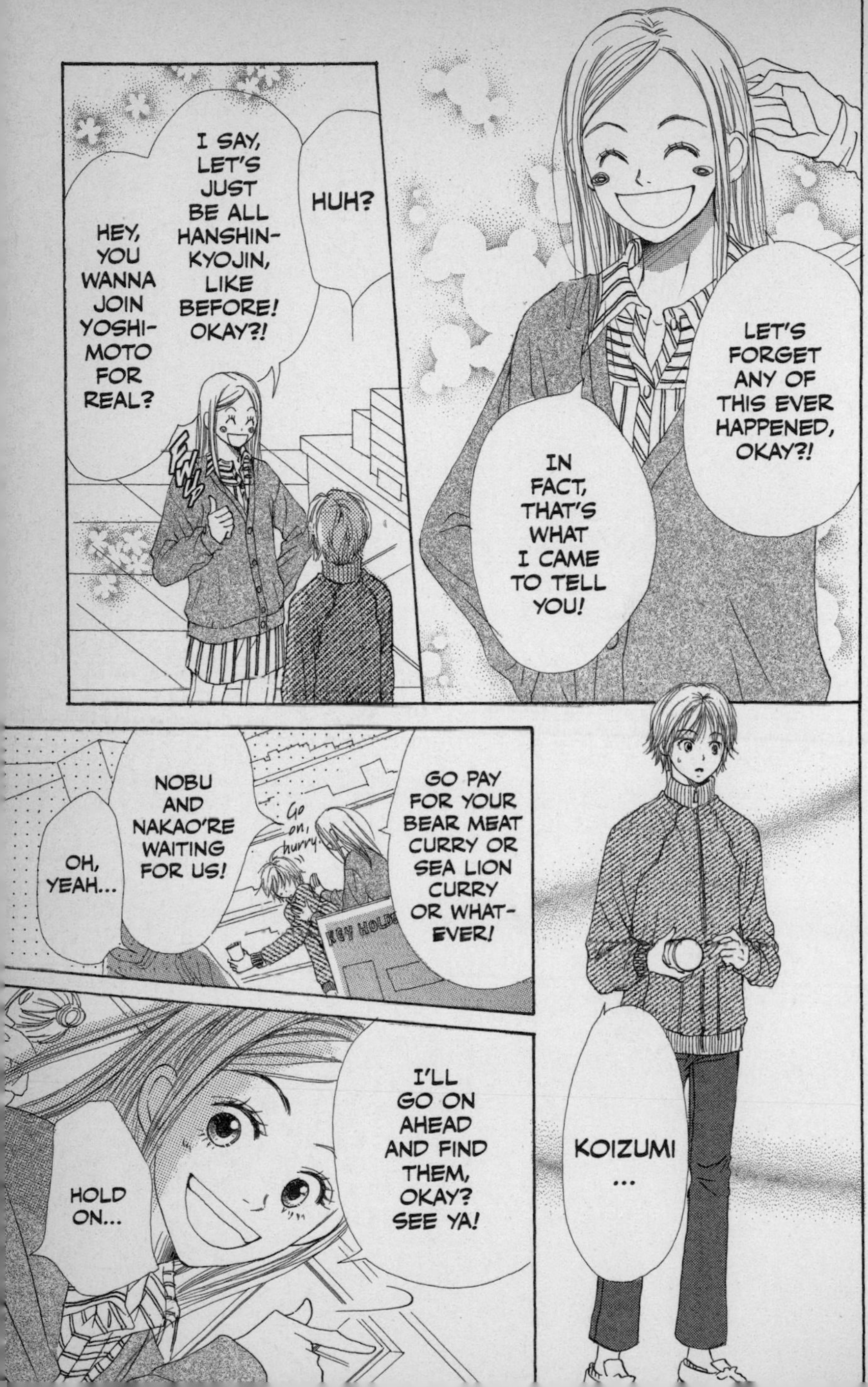
LET'S FORGET ANY OF THIS EVER HAPPENED, OKAY?!
IN FACT, THAT'S WHAT I CAME TO TELL YOU!
HUH?
I SAY, LET'S JUST BE ALL HANSHIN-KYOJIN, LIKE BEFORE! OKAY?!
HEY, YOU WANNA JOIN YOSHIMOTO FOR REAL?
KOIZUMI ...
GO PAY FOR YOUR BEAR MEAT CURRY OR SEA LION CURRY OR WHAT-EVER!
Go on, hurry
NOBU AND NAKAO'RE WAITING FOR US!
OH, YEAH...
I'LL GO ON AHEAD AND FIND THEM, OKAY? SEE YA!
HOLD ON...

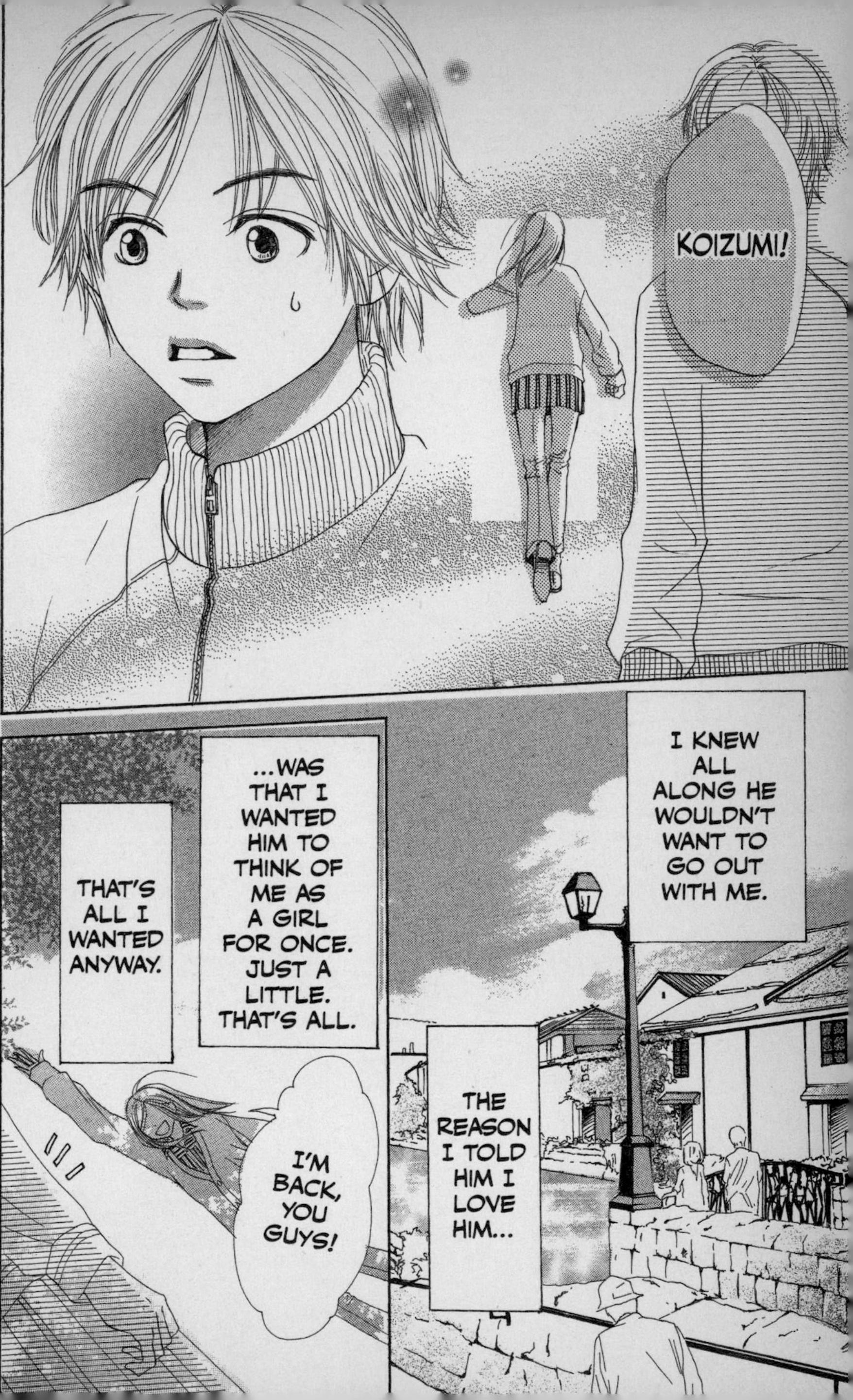
KOIZUMI!
I KNEW ALL ALONG HE WOULDN'T WANT TO GO OUT WITH ME.
THE REASON I TOLD HIM I LOVE HIM...
...WAS THAT I WANTED HIM TO THINK OF ME AS A GIRL FOR ONCE. JUST A LITTLE. THAT'S ALL.
THAT'S ALL I WANTED ANYWAY.
I'M BACK, YOU GUYS!

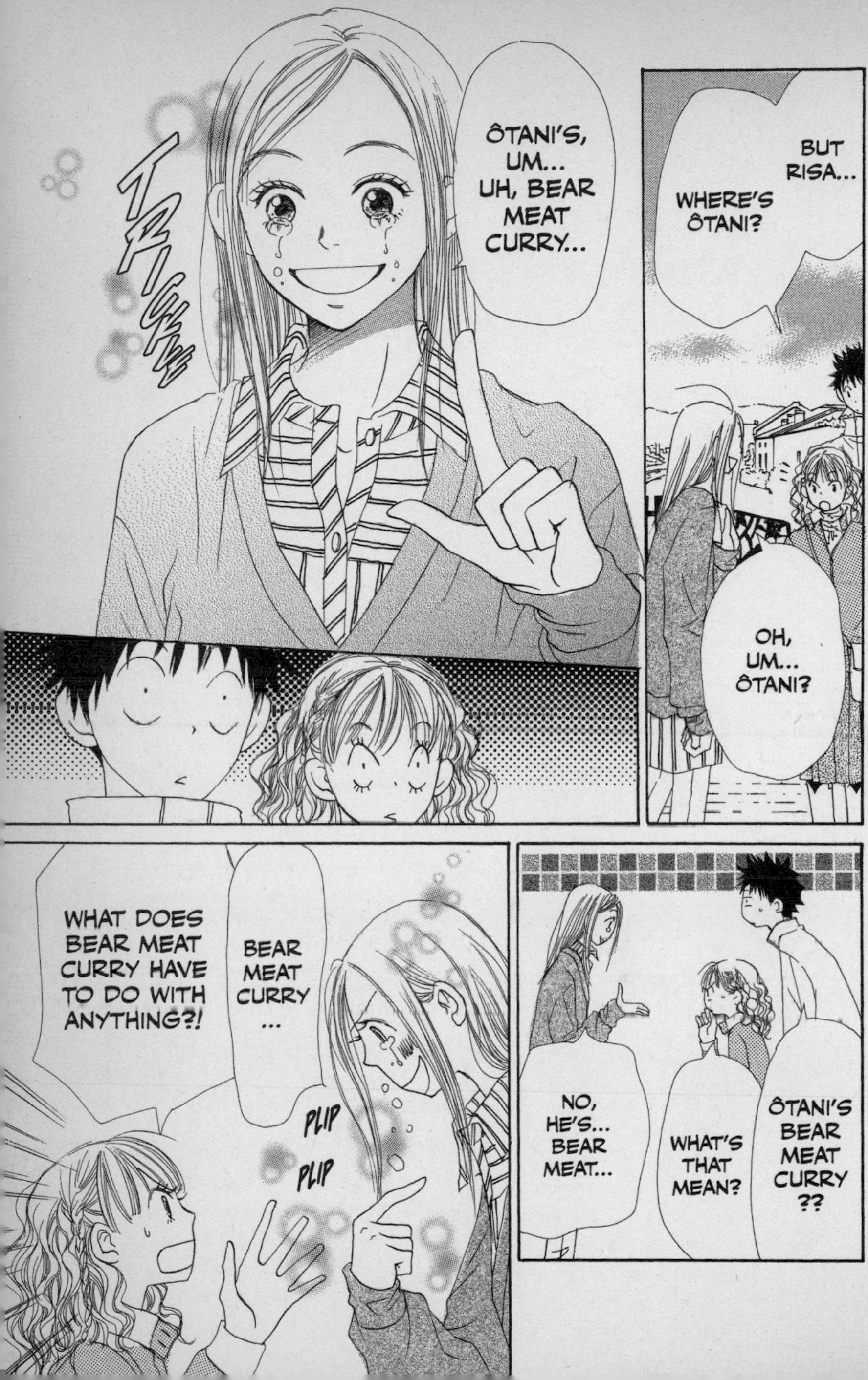
BUT RISA... WHERE'S ÔTANI?
OH, UM... ÔTANI?
ÔTANI'S, UM... UH, BEAR MEAT CURRY...
TRICKLE
ÔTANI'S BEAR MEAT CURRY ??
WHAT'S THAT MEAN?
NO, HE'S... BEAR MEAT...
BEAR MEAT CURRY ...
PLIP
PLIP
WHAT DOES BEAR MEAT CURRY HAVE TO DO WITH ANYTHING?!

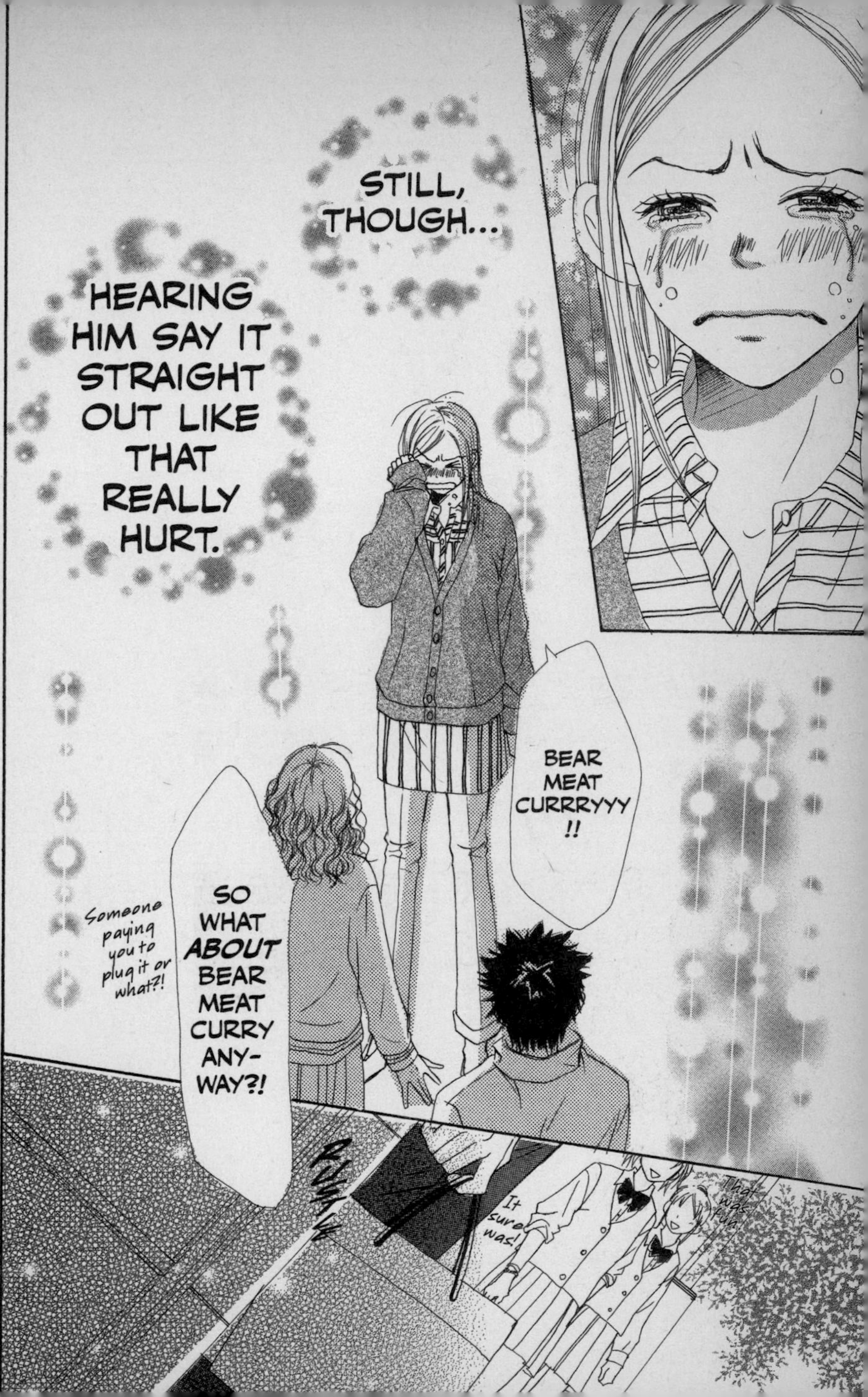
STILL, THOUGH...
HEARING HIM SAY IT STRAIGHT OUT LIKE THAT REALLY HURT.
BEAR MEAT CURRRYYY!!
SO WHAT ABOUT BEAR MEAT CURRY ANY-WAY?!
Someone paying you to plug it or what?!
That was fun.
It sure was!

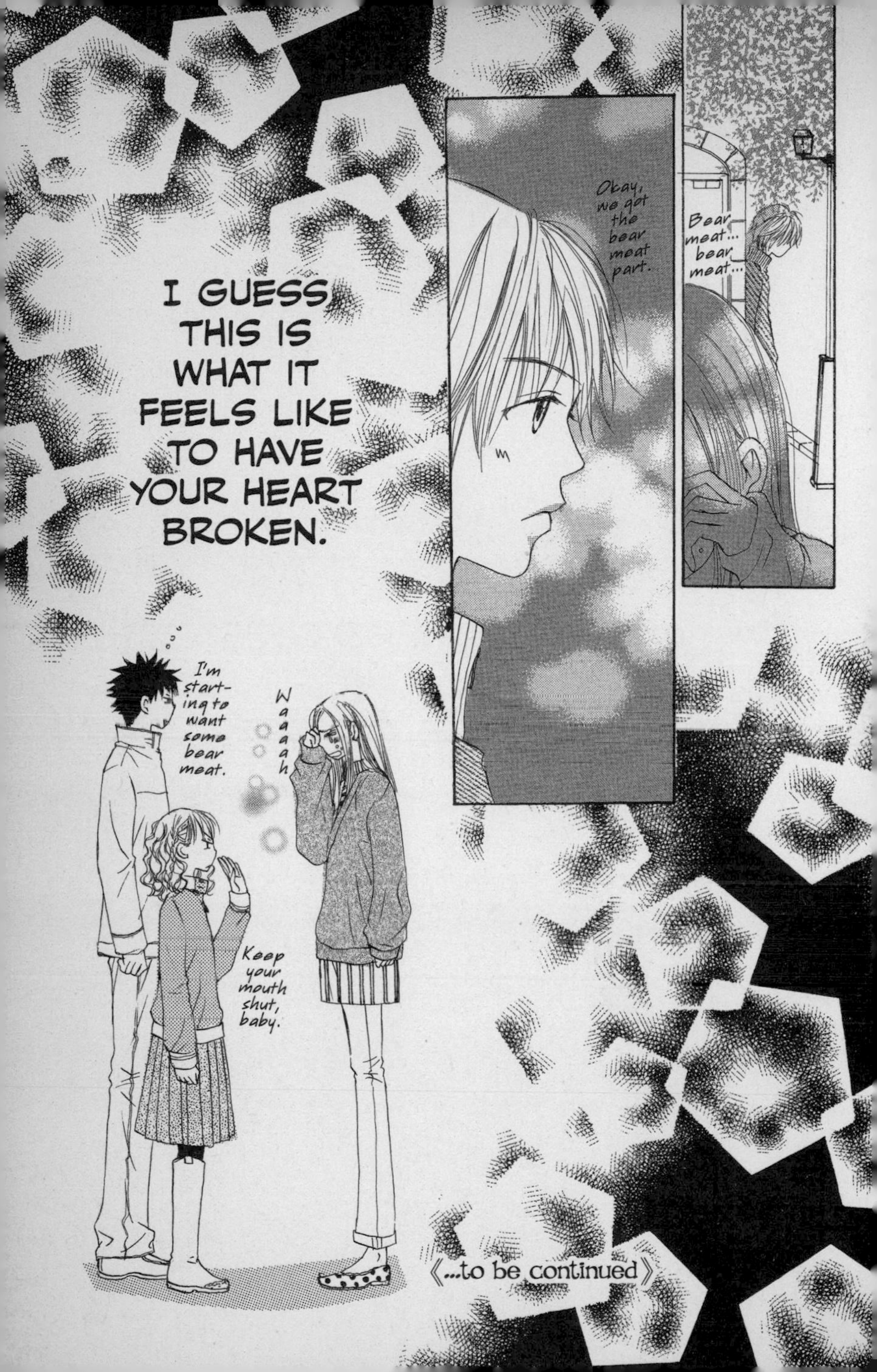
Bear meat... bear meat...
Okay, we got the bear meat part.
I GUESS THIS IS WHAT IT FEELS LIKE TO HAVE YOUR HEART BROKEN.
Waaaah
I'm starting to want some bear meat.
Keep your mouth shut, baby.
《...to be continued》

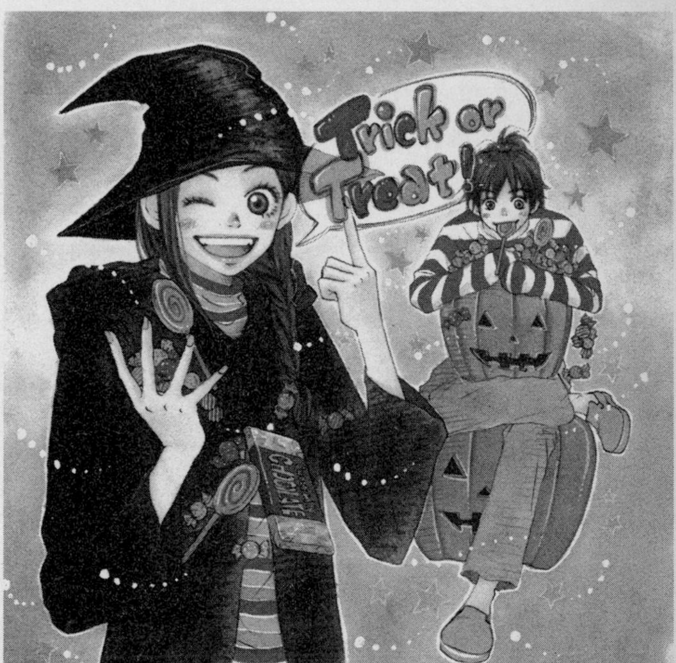
Trick or Treat!

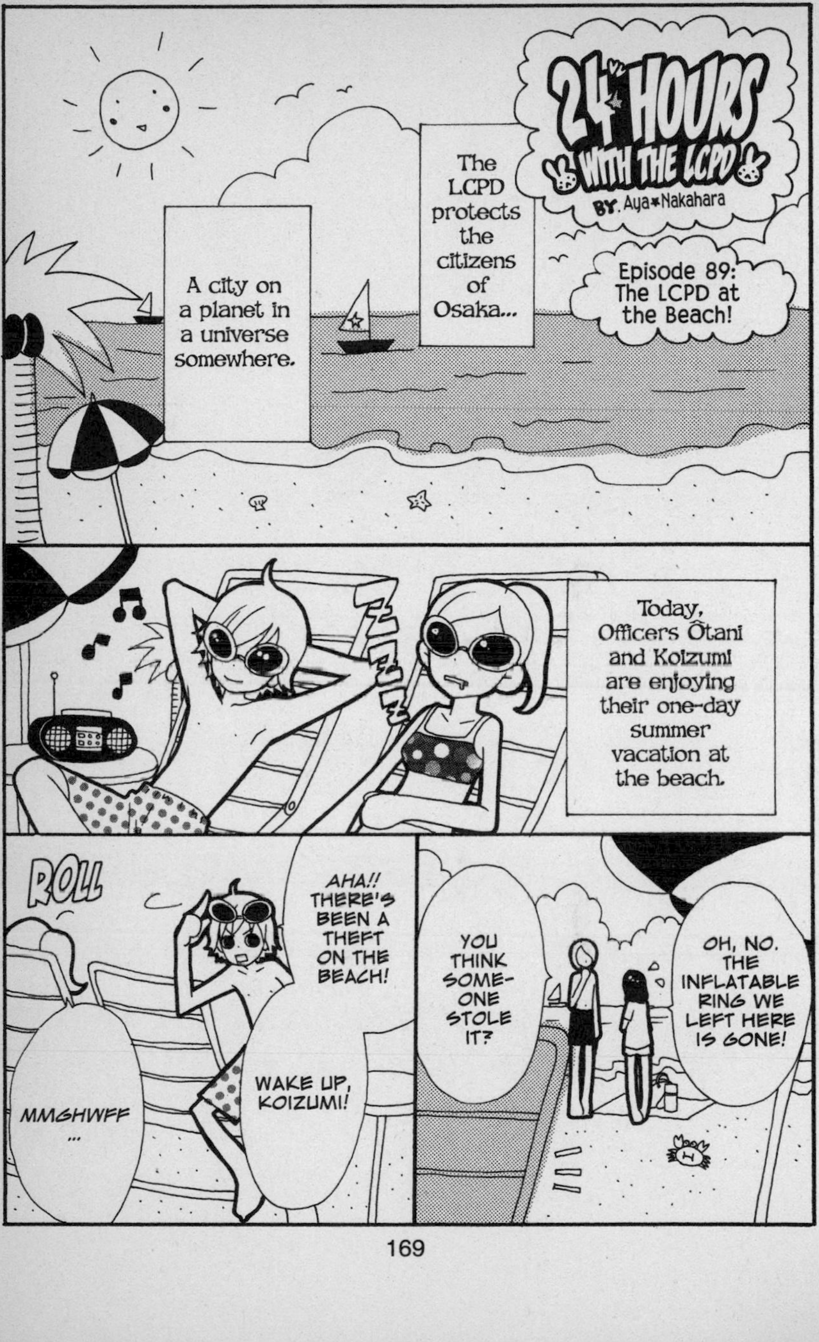
24 HOURS WITH THE LCPD
BY. Aya★Nakahara
The LCPD protects the citizens of Osaka...
Episode 89: The LCPD at the Beach!
A city on a planet in a universe somewhere.
Today, Officers Ōtani and Koizumi are enjoying their one-day summer vacation at the beach.
OH, NO. THE INFLATABLE RING WE LEFT HERE IS GONE!
YOU THINK SOME-ONE STOLE IT?
AHA!! THERE'S BEEN A THEFT ON THE BEACH!
ROLL
WAKE UP, KOIZUMI!
MMGHWFF...

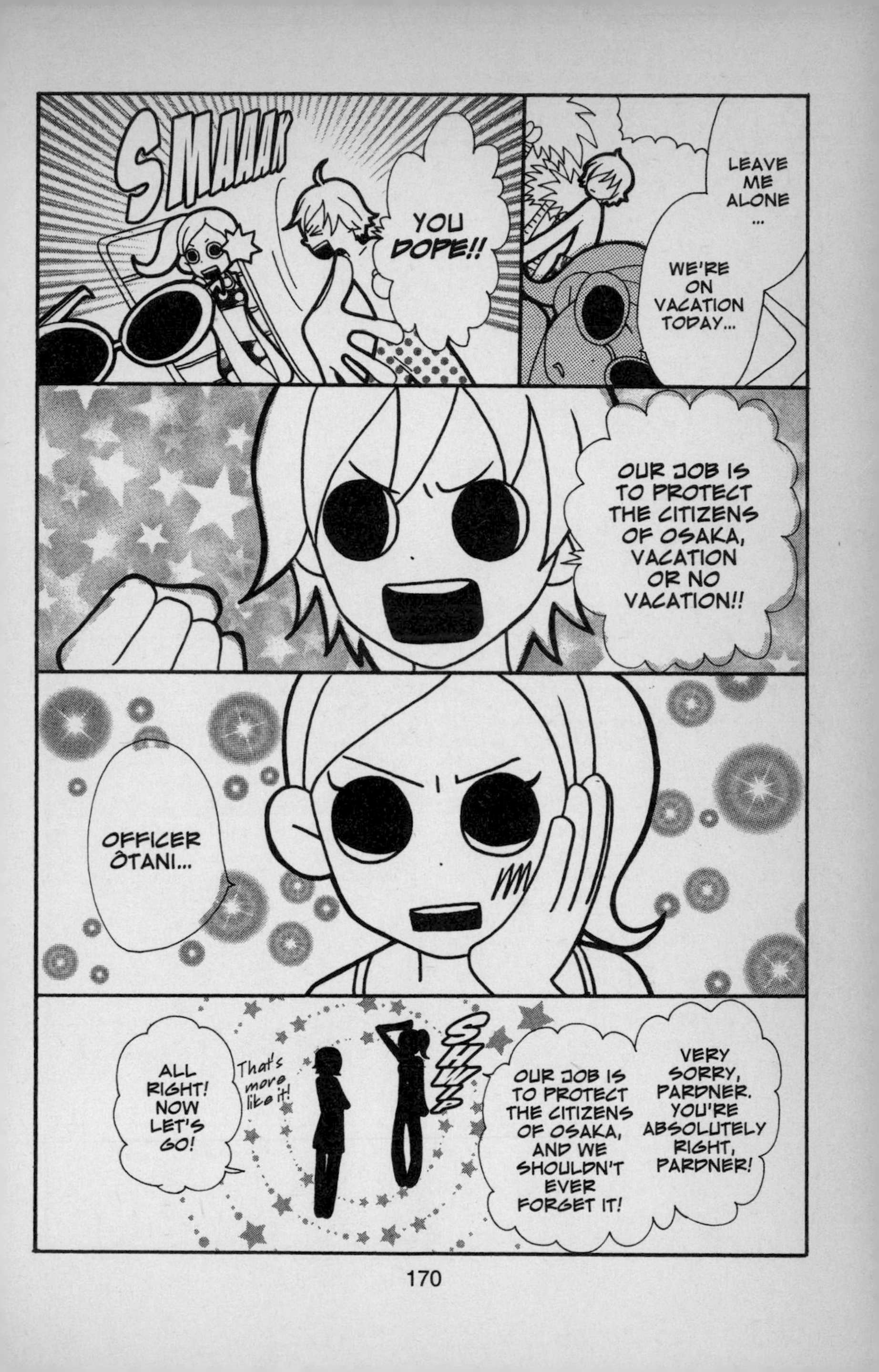
LEAVE ME ALONE ...
WE'RE ON VACATION TODAY...
SMAAAK
YOU DOPE!!
OUR JOB IS TO PROTECT THE CITIZENS OF OSAKA, VACATION OR NO VACATION!!
OFFICER ÔTANI...
VERY SORRY, PARDNER. YOU'RE ABSOLUTELY RIGHT, PARDNER!
OUR JOB IS TO PROTECT THE CITIZENS OF OSAKA, AND WE SHOULDN'T EVER FORGET IT!
SHWIP
That's more like it!
ALL RIGHT! NOW LET'S GO!

OH, HERE IT IS! PHEW.
I GUESS THE WIND BLEW IT AWAY.
WHAT A GREAT DAY TO BE AT THE BEACH!
HEY, WE BOUGHT US ALL LUNCH, YOU GUYS!
BWEEN
IT'S ANOTHER PEACEFUL DAY IN OSAKA CITY.
SENPAI! WE DIDN'T SHOW UP AT ALL IN THIS ONE!
Like we're unwanted!
YOU WON'T GET AWAY WITH THAT AGAIN !!
To be Continued!?

maybe

glossary

Page 5, panel 5: Girl
In the Japanese, Risa calls him "Atsuko," which is a feminized version of his given name, Atsushi. The "ko" means child, and is a common ending for girls' names.

Page 5, panel 5: Miss Ôtani
In the original Japanese, she calls him "Akko-chan," which is even girlier. "Akko" is a nickname for Atsuko, and "chan" is a cute honorific. "Akko-can" also refers to the 60s anime *Himitsu no Akko-chan* (The Secrets of Akko-chan), about a girl with a magic mirror.

Page 6, panel 1: I sure hope I win...
This is another example of *nori-tsukkomi*, A type of comedy delivery when you pretend to go along with the setup, and then turn around and call the other person on it.

Page 12, panel 2: Tokimeki Beach
Tokimeki means "throbbing," "pulsating," or "thrilling."

Page 67, panel 2: Senpai
A term of respect for someone with seniority in an organization, such as clubs, schools and offices.

Page 67, panel 4: Shinsaibashi
Osaka's main shopping district. There's even an American-themed area called Amerika-mura. Check out the official website:
http://www.shinsaibashisuji.com/e/index.html

Page 73, panel 5: Badge
The kanji on the badge reads "umi," which means "sea."

Page 82, panel 4: Yoshimoto
Yoshimoto Kogyo is a theater and entertainment company in Osaka that opened in 1912. When it first opened, Yoshimoto hosted *rakugo*, a form of traditional storytelling. These days, it specializes in *manzai*, or comedy duos.

Page 86, panel 1: triangle on Risa's forehead
This is the Japanese visual symbol for ghosts, and refers to the headwear placed on the deceased at Shinto funerals.

Page 90, panel 2: Rat Man
In Japanese, *Nezumi-otoko*. A character from *Gegege no Kitarô*.

Page 93, author note: Pichipichi Beach
Pichipichi means "juicy" or "bursting."

Page 125, panel 3: Hokkaido
The northernmost and second-largest of the Japanese islands, it is much colder than the rest of the nation.

Page 139, panel 1: Shishi-odoshi
A play on words. Ôtani uses *chorochoro-to*, a word that can mean darting quickly, like a deer. But it can also mean a trickling sound, which is how Risa takes it. She tells Ôtani to stop talking about her like she's a *shishi-odoshi*, the type of bamboo fountain pictured above their heads.

How are you, everybody? Nakahara here. We're up to Vol. 4 and still going strong, so it looks like this is going to be the longest series I've ever done. That doesn't mean its content is any deeper or anything, *ha ha ha*. I figure that whether you go to school or to work, you all have enough to think about every day, so please give your minds a rest while you're reading my manga, at least. If you get a little chuckle out of it here and there, that's enough to make Nakahara-san happy.

Aya Nakahara won the 2003 Shogakukan manga award for her breakthrough hit *Love★Com*, which was made into a major motion picture and a PS2 game in 2006. She debuted with *Haru to Kuuki Nichiyou-bi* in 1995, and her other works include *HANADA* and *Himitsu Kichi*.

LOVE★COM VOL 4
The Shojo Beat Manga Edition

STORY AND ART BY
AYA NAKAHARA

Translation & English Adaptation/Pookie Rolf
Touch-up Art & Lettering/Gia Cam Luc
Cover Design/Amy Martin
Interior Design/Yuki Ameda
Editor/Pancha Diaz

Editor in Chief, Books/Alvin Lu
Editor in Chief, Magazines/Marc Weidenbaum
VP of Publishing Licensing/Rika Inouye
VP of Sales/Gonzalo Ferreyra
Sr. VP of Marketing/Liza Coppola
Publisher/Hyoe Narita

Printed in Canada

Published by VIZ Media, LLC
P.O. Box 77010
San Francisco, CA 94107

Shojo Beat Manga Edition
10 9 8 7 6 5 4 3 2 1
First printing, January 2008

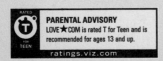

store.viz.com

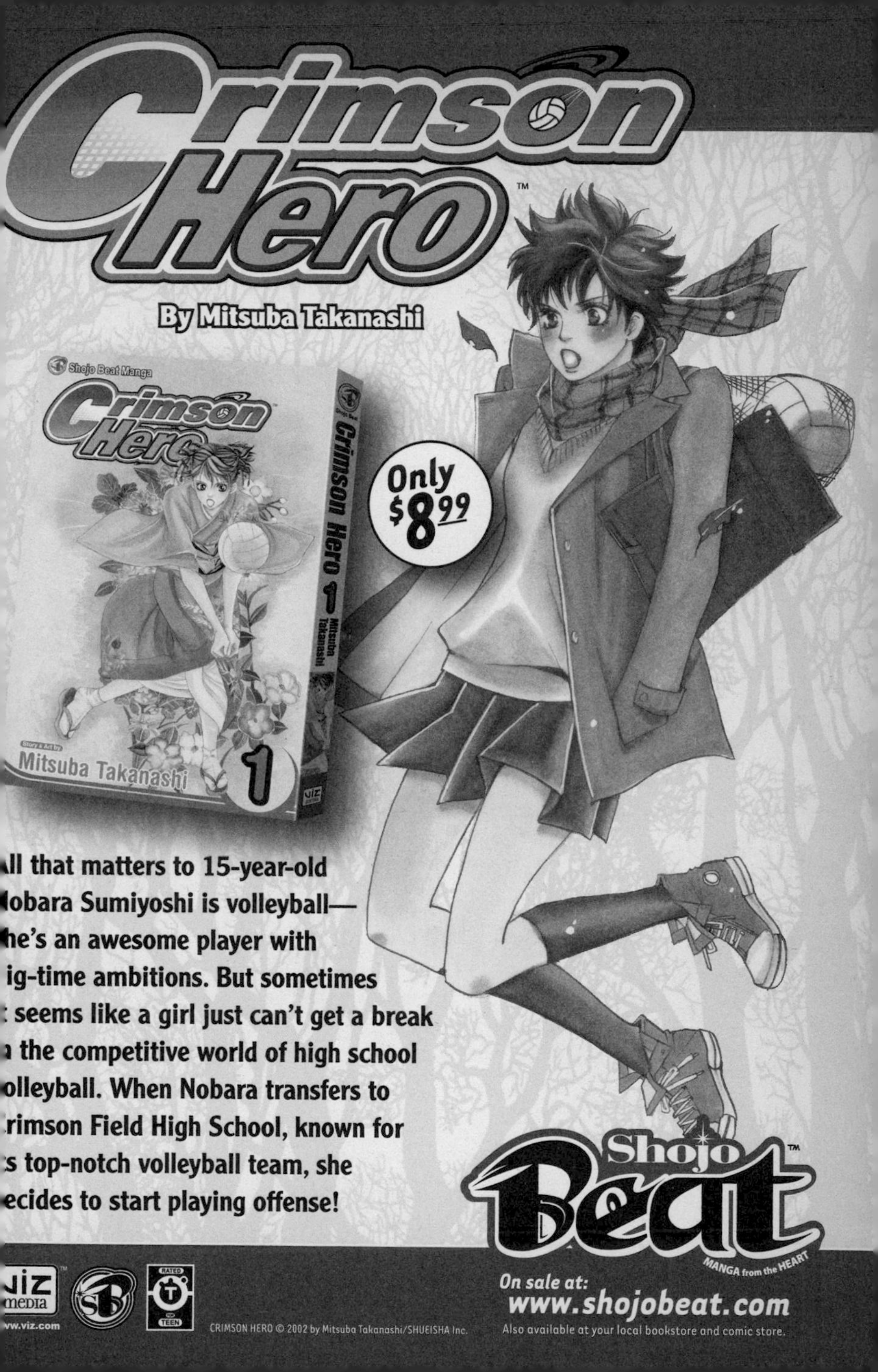
Crimson Hero™
By Mitsuba Takanashi
Shojo Beat Manga
Crimson Hero
Story & Art by
Mitsuba Takanashi
1
Crimson Hero 1 Mitsuba Takanashi
Only $8.99
ll that matters to 15-year-old
obara Sumiyoshi is volleyball—
he's an awesome player with
ig-time ambitions. But sometimes
seems like a girl just can't get a break
the competitive world of high school
olleyball. When Nobara transfers to
rimson Field High School, known for
s top-notch volleyball team, she
ecides to start playing offense!
Shojo Beat™
MANGA from the HEART
On sale at:
www.shojobeat.com
Also available at your local bookstore and comic store.
viz media
ww.viz.com
RATED T TEEN
CRIMSON HERO © 2002 by Mitsuba Takanashi/SHUEISHA Inc.

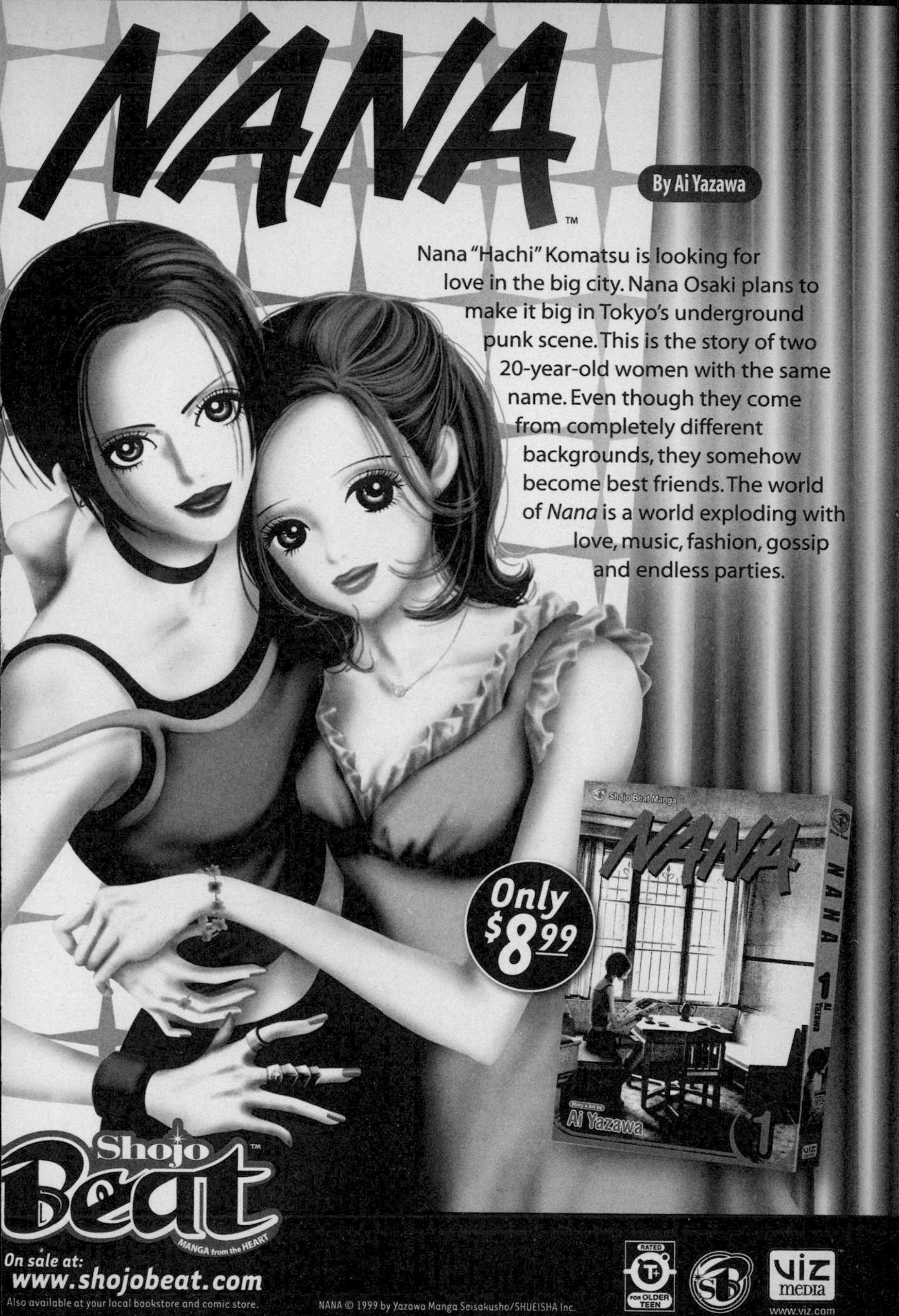
NANA™
By Ai Yazawa
Nana "Hachi" Komatsu is looking for love in the big city. Nana Osaki plans to make it big in Tokyo's underground punk scene. This is the story of two 20-year-old women with the same name. Even though they come from completely different backgrounds, they somehow become best friends. The world of *Nana* is a world exploding with love, music, fashion, gossip and endless parties.
Only $8.99
Shojo Beat Manga
NANA
1
Story & Art by
Ai Yazawa
Shojo Beat™
MANGA from the HEART
On sale at:
www.shojobeat.com
Also available at your local bookstore and comic store.
NANA © 1999 by Yazawa Manga Seisakusho/SHUEISHA Inc.
RATED T+ FOR OLDER TEEN
viz media
www.viz.com

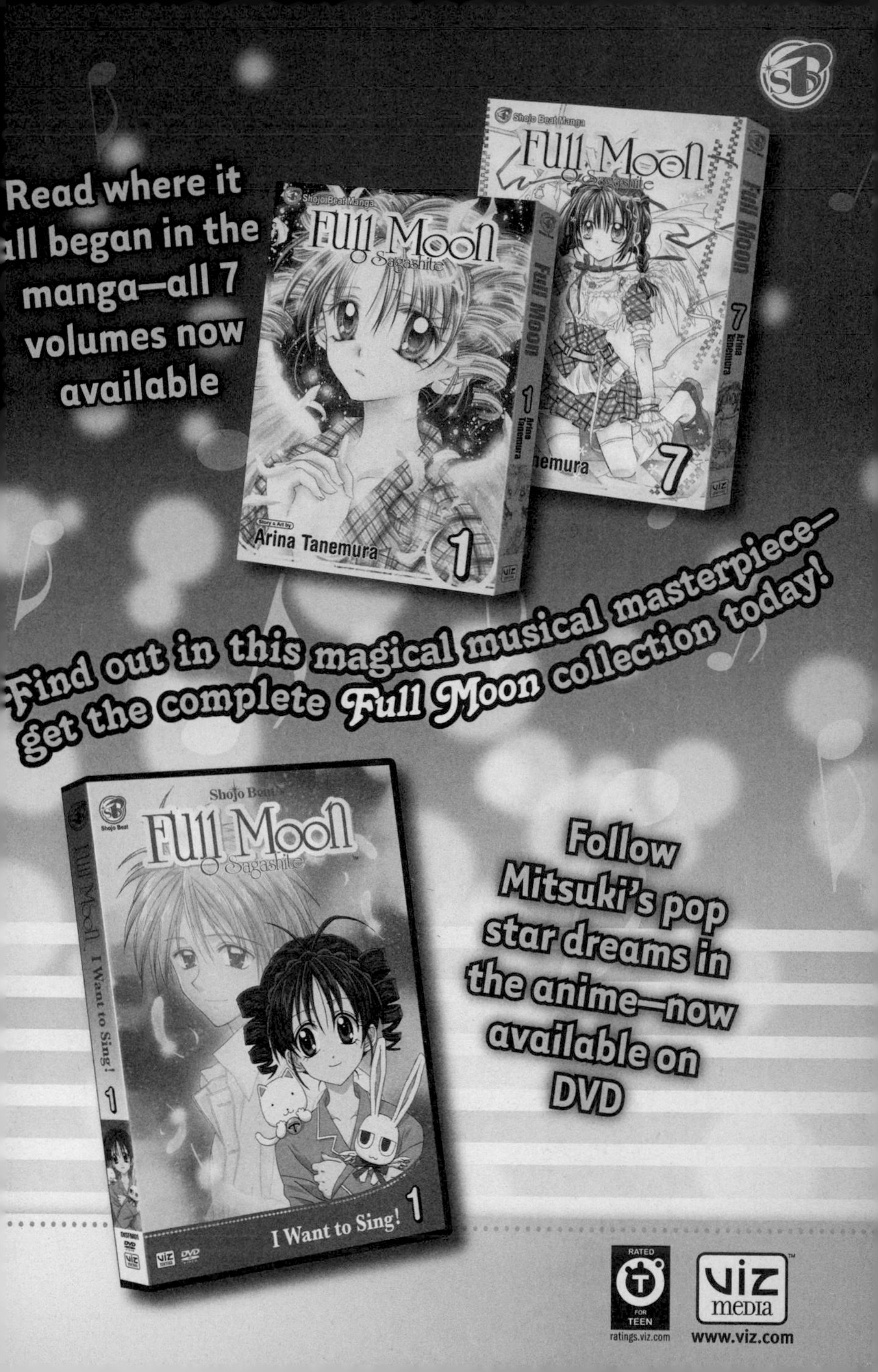
Read where it
all began in the
manga—all 7
volumes now
available
Shojo Beat Manga
Full Moon O Sagashite
Story & Art by
Arina Tanemura
1
7
Find out in this magical musical masterpiece—
get the complete Full Moon collection today!
Shojo Beat
Full Moon O Sagashite
I Want to Sing!
1
Follow
Mitsuki's pop
star dreams in
the anime—now
available on
DVD
RATED T FOR TEEN
ratings.viz.com
VIZ media
www.viz.com

Tell us what you think about Shojo Beat Manga!

Our survey is now available online. Go to:

shojobeat.com/mangasurvey

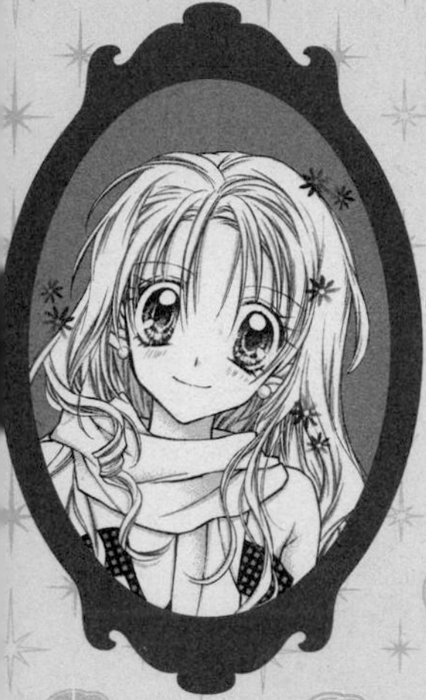

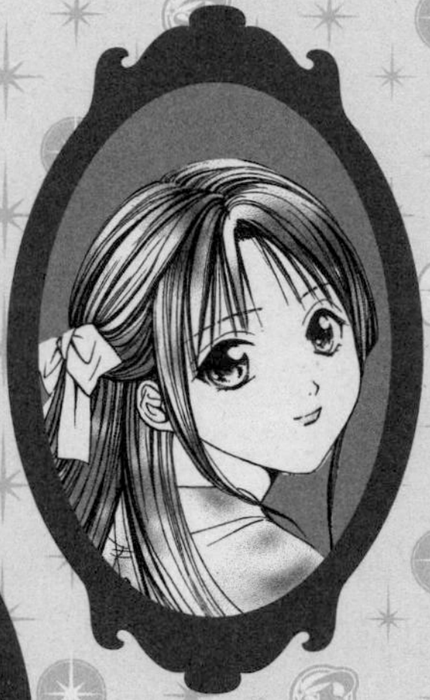

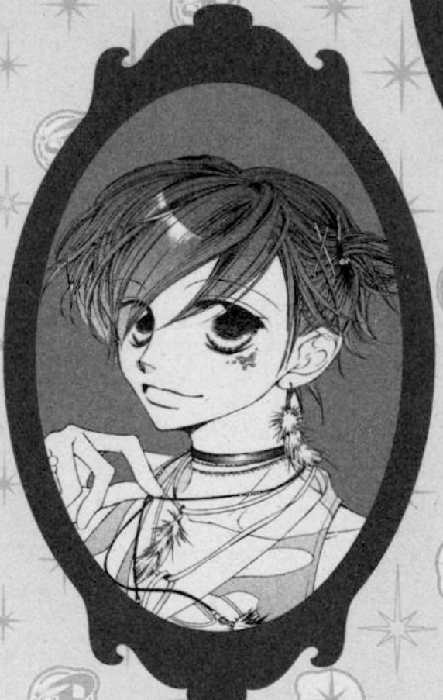

Help us make our product offerings better!

VIZ media

THE REAL DRAMA BEGINS IN...

Shojo Beat

MANGA from the HEART

 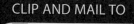